The
Argentine Generation
of 1837

The
Argentine Generation
of 1837

Echeverría, Alberdi,
Sarmiento, Mitre

William H. Katra

Madison • Teaneck
Fairleigh Dickinson University Press
London: Associated University Presses

Associated University Presses
440 Forsgate Drive
Cranbury, NJ 08512

Associated University Presses
25 Sicilian Avenue
London WC1A 2QH, England

Associated University Presses
P.O. Box 338, Port Credit
Mississauga, Ontario
Canada L5G 4L8

The paper used in this publication meets the requirements
of the American National Standard for Permanence of Paper
for Printed Library Materials Z39.48-1984.

Library of Congress Cataloging-in-Publication Data

Katra, William H.
   The Argentine generation of 1837 : Echeverría, Alberdi, Sarmiento, Mitre / William H. Katra.
      p.   cm.
   Includes bibliographical references (p.   ) and index.
   ISBN 0-8386-3599-7 (alk. paper)
      1. Argentina—Intellectual life—19th century.   2. Argentina—History—19th century.   3. Echeverría, Esteban, 1805–1851.
4. Alberdi, Juan Bautista, 1810–1884.   5. Sarmiento, Domingo Faustino, 1811–1888.   6. Mitre, Bartolomé, 1821–1906.   I. Title.
F2846.3.K38   1996
982'.04—dc20   95-17605
                                                                CIP

PRINTED IN THE UNITED STATES OF AMERICA

Contents

Preface

Argentina's Generation of 1837 were the sons of the burghers who led Argentina's 1810 revolution against Spanish rule that erupted after the Napoleonic invasion of the Iberian Peninsula (full independence from Spain was finally achieved in 1816). As children they witnessed and suffered the decades-long civil strife that the independence struggle had ignited. Beginning in the 1830s and continuing for more than five decades, they sought to transform liberal ideals into veritable institutions and practices through their writings and sociopolitical activism. The emergence of new social and political conditions in the 1850s favored their cause, but it was only in 1880 that a ruling bourgeoisie consolidated its power and the status of Argentina as a modern liberal nation. By that time the ideological issues set forth by the 1837 generation in their writings and defended by their actions came to define lasting parameters for Argentine culture and society.

The 1837 Generation was perhaps the most articulate and self-conscious group of Latin American intellectuals in the previous century. They were not only protagonists in the grueling struggles that culminated in the emergence of the liberal state; they were also accomplished writers who recorded well their involvement in those important events. Their written testimonies provide evidence of the changing ideological configurations that each new decade brought about in the century-long clash between traditional and modern or urban and rural groups and their respective world outlooks and political systems.

Although much has been written about the 1837 group and its most prominent members, it is surprising that there does not exist—to my knowledge—any study that treats in comprehensive fashion their multiple contributions throughout the five decades of their public involvement. No previous work critically considers these activists' varied contributions in relation to the complex historical events of the time. My objective here is to elucidate historical and biographical concerns with examples and syntheses of these writers' cultural production.

This work chronologically follows throughout five decades the ideas and public profiles of the 1837 activists in relation to the changing social and political backdrops. I focus primarily on the individuals mentioned in the subtitle: Esteban Echeverría, Juan Bautista Alberdi, Domingo F.

Sarmiento, and Bartolomé Mitre. Other individuals also receive extended treatment: Juan María Gutiérrez, Florencio Varela, Félix Frías, Vicente Fidel López, José Rivera Indarte, José Mármol, and Uruguayans Juan Carlos Gómez and Andrés Lamas.

In composing this work I have attempted to overcome several pronounced deficiencies in much of the existing historical scholarship. First, I realized the imperative of a broad generational focus in order not to exaggerate the importance of a particular member of this group at the expense of the rest and to highlight how the ideas advocated by one of them in a given moment many times corresponded to widespread beliefs of the time. Second, I wished to avoid the distortions resulting from an exclusive treatment of either historical or cultural documents by instead relating cultural data to important political or ideological issues—and vice versa. Related was the third objective of going beyond the political partisanship of some past investigators, or the gross, sweeping generalizations of others, and instead critically analyzing key ideological issues. All of these objectives have led me to highlight the contrasting perspectives of the 1837 activists and even the discontinuities and changes in any one individual's thought over time. Against the background of historical processes or tendencies, I highlight the motivations or objectives of the very individuals who are the objects of my study. With all its potential shortcomings, my "existential" brand of cultural history attempts to restore to the 1837 activists their role as protagonists in and witnesses to the events they lived and suffered.

This work will also be of interest to those literary scholars seeking detailed biographical data for the principal 1837 writers. Of particular emphasis is this study's ideological reading of not only the foundational works of the literary canon produced by them but also of a wide range of secondary texts composed by its other members. A second emphasis is the impact of those books and essays at the time of their appearance and how they—when considered as cultural objects—contributed to the important ongoing debates over the present and future status of society. Yet a third emphasis is how the cultural production of these writer-activists defined and enhanced their participation in social and political affairs.

The application of the term "generation" is justified by the convergence of these individuals' careers at several important junctures. All were all born within a decade of the outbreak of Argentina's independence struggle from Spain on 25 May 1810. For the next twenty years, as children and adolescents, they witnessed the violent struggles between unitarian and federalist partisans or between advocats of urban, liberal, Europeanized ideals and defenders of Hispanic traditionalism. During the 1830s several of these future militants pursued university studies in

Buenos Aires while the government headed by strongman Juan Manuel de Rosas progressively resorted to demagoguery, coercion, and terror in order to maintain its authority.

The year 1837 marks the group's formal association through their meetings in the Literary Salon. Shortly thereafter they commenced clandestine activities under the banner of the Young Argentina, later renamed May Association. When Rosas's disfavor with the outspoken youths assumed threatening dimensions, most sought exile in Uruguay and Chile to continue their insurrectional and propagandistic efforts. Through their pamphlets and newspaper articles in these two countries, they defended a program advocating republicanism in government, free trade, individual freedoms of speech and assembly and, above all, material progress. Understood philosophically their program coupled the utopian Romantic influences of the early century to the more realistic emphasis of the "Eclectic" philosophical school that had ideological links with the "Restoration." As such their particular brand of "liberal," socialista reforms was aimed at containing the turbulence that had resulted from the enfranchisement of the masses during their country's May Revolution. Now these activists anticipated positivism's future thrust. They promoted a government headed by a social and intellectual elite that would protect civil order and property while combatting (what they believed was) a retrograde traditionalism and accelerating the development of the country's social and material potentialities.

With Rosas's fall from power in 1852, the young militants returned to Argentina to become protagonists in the latest chapter of Argentina's civil and political conflict. Events, for the time being, favored the cause of the interior provinces against Buenos Aires's sometimes imperial pretensions. At this time most of the activists shelved literary pursuits in favor of public service. While Mitre and Sarmiento loyally served the autonomous Province of Buenos Aires, Gutiérrez and Alberdi were counted among the most important leaders of the Confederation, uniting all the other provinces under the leadership of President Justo José Urquiza. Eighteen-sixty-two was another watershed year: Buenos Aires, with its progressive institutions, lucrative Atlantic commerce, and large concentration of people, finally defeated the forces of the Confederation and then proceeded to extend its authority over the entire country. Mitre, who served as the first president of the united republic until 1868, was succeeded by Sarmiento. In the next two deacdes—up to 1880 and beyond—Mármol, López, and Frías would also distinguish themselves in Porteño or national legislative bodies while dealing with the country's most trying and transcendent issues.

It was during the early exile period that the 1837 writers produced the literary works that rank among the most important in Argentina's and Hispanic America's entire nineteenth-century repertoire. Heading the list is Sarmiento's *Facundo, o civilización y barbarie* (Facundo, or civilization and barbarism—1845), a work that brilliantly joined sociological, historical, biographical, and political material to a powerful novelized biography of the caudillo Facundo Quiroga and memorable sketches of the character types of the pampas. Mármol's novel, *Amalia* (1851, 1855); Echeverría's long narrative poem, *La cautiva* (The captive—1837); the same writer's powerful story, "El matadero" (The slaughterhouse—written 1837?; published 1871); and lyrical poetry by Mármol, Gutiérrez, and Echeverría complete this short list of literary or fictional works.

The conceptual literature written by these talented activists also is important. Echeverría's *Dogma socialista* (Socialist dogma—1846) provided inspiration and an ideological guide for the entire generation of activists and writers. Sarmiento's fertile pen produced works in a broad spectrum of fields: *De la educación común* (On public education—1849), *Viajes* (Travels—1849–51), and *Recuerdos de provincia* (Provincia memories—1852) treat issues as diverse as public education, constitutional theory, travel impressions, biography or autobiography, and sociology. Alberdi's writings treated similarly important issues: constitutional theory, history, government, war, and the financial organization of the state. Moreover, Alberdi's *Bases y puntos de partida* (Bases and points of departure—1852) provided an indispensable guide for the authors of the Constitution of 1853. Similarly the literary and cultural studies by Gutiérrez; Mitre's *Historia de Belgrano* (History of Belgrano—3d ed., 1876–77) and *Historia de San Martín* (History of San Martín—1887); and López's *Historia de la República argentina* (History of the Argentine Republic—1883–1893), rank among the continent's finest works in their respective genres. These writings only suggest the extent to which this remarkable constellation of talent provided cultural and political leadership for both Argentina and South America during the middle and latter decades of the previous century.

Over the past decade many institutions and agencies have provided funds to assist me in researching and writing this work. Monies from Washington State University facilitated research visits to the Bodleian Library in Oxford, the British Museum in London, and the Biblioteque de l'Arsenal in Paris. In different years travel to Argentina was made possible by grants from the University of Wisconsin-La Crosse, the Fulbright Commission, and the National Endowment for the Humanities. Resources from the University of Wisconsin-Eau Claire assisted in the final stages of manuscript preparation. Countless individuals also merit recognition for their assistance but especially Richard Pinnell, Rioplatense scholar; Jean Bondy, librarian at Wisconsin-La Crosse; Ricardo

Rodríguez and Etilvina Furt de Rodríguez, the generous custodians of the Alberdi Archives at the Jorge Furt Library; Javier Fernández, consummate Sarmiento scholar and bibliophile; and, lastly, Rioplatense scholars Joseph Criscenti and Michael Pratt, who kindly gave of their time to criticize early drafts of the manuscript. Thanks is also due to Sara Katra, whose attention to family matters has made serious research efforts possible. This book is dedicated to my children, Esti and Dan, who have learned to tolerate the quixotic historical and cultural ambitions of their father.

The
Argentine Generation
of 1837

1

The Formative Years

HISTORICAL BACKDROP

The movement for independence from Spain at the beginning of the nineteenth century, the subsequent period of fierce civil wars, and the Rosas dictatorship constitute the historical backdrop for the childhood and adolescence of the 1837 activists. These were highly unsettled times; the colonial society in which their parents and grandparents had enjoyed economic stability and social prestige slowly disintegrated. The optimistic promises of the independence leaders for a free state enjoying peace, prosperity, and democracy were delayed or stymied time and again.

Decades before the outbreak of the independence struggle against Spain, the Río de la Plata region was experiencing rapid transformations and, in some aspects, outright crisis. In 1776 the viceroyalty of the Río de la Plata had been constituted in response to that region's growing population, increasing importance for trade and commerce, and the need for blocking the territorial ambitions of the Portuguese Empire. Globally it was a period of innovation in manufacturing and expansion in commerce while Northern European countries successfully extended their trade networks throughout the world. Spain, still under the cultural yoke of the Counterreformation, took little advantage of these new sources of wealth. French and British trade companies had filled that void; however, by the middle decades of the new century, British interests dominated Rioplatense markets for cereals, textiles, and foodstuffs. The coastal cities celebrated their new modernity, but in the interior the disappearance of uncompetitive cottage industries and agriculture meant massive dislocation for local population groups.

In the provinces of Salta and Tucumán, the site of Argentina's oldest cities and most traditional economy, these changes had a particularly severe impact. The rapid decline of the trade network, historically linking this region with present-day Bolivia and Peru, meant the disappearance of traditional markets for mules, rice, tobacco, and sugar.

Thousands of citizens left, creating a void in the local political leadership. The taxes levied for the war effort further eroded the economic and social influence of urban interests. In *Facundo*, Sarmiento provided a dramatic account of this crisis in the interior; all that was left in previously prosperous regions were "skeletons of cities, decrepit and devastated villages."[1]

As the crisis deepened in the northern provinces, the coastal areas were experiencing an unprecedented prosperity. Since the latter decades of the previous century, demand had grown steadily for this region's exports of hides and jerked beef. Many local businessmen took advantage of the exporting boom by investing in land and involving themselves in the bullish cattle industry. New fortunes and economic prosperity attracted an increasing volume of British trade goods. Buenos Aires, within decades, grew from a dusty outpost into a thriving entrepôt. The nation's wealth accumulated here, where it stimulated a parallel expansion in service activities and cultural institutions. By the mid-1830s the contrast was obvious to all: Buenos Aires continued to attract immigrants and new commercial interests, whereas the cities of the interior progressively lost population and experienced economic decline. Porteño (that of Buenos Aires) trade and cultural ties with Europe, but especially England, were quickly becoming an unalterable way of life. Buenos Aires, the nerve-center of this progress, was emerging as South America's most prosperous urban center. The city's unique location vis-à-vis the region accounts for the "instinctive flavor" of its leaders' centralist political principles and laissez-faire economic doctrines.[2]

Against this backdrop of rapid social, demographic, and economic changes, the region's heroic struggle for independence from the decrepit Spanish empire takes the appearance of erasable black marks on the surface of a magic writing pad; over and beyond the obvious achievement of political independence, few of the innovations promoted by the idealistic independence leaders were to take root and survive into the next decade. Nevertheless, their short-lasting, progressive reforms were to leave an imprint on the collective memory of the people and would inspire new generations of social activists well into the next century.

The struggle for independence dominated the passions of the region's most notable leaders and introduced into the national dialogue a whole new agenda for social and political change. In the first euphoric moments, the support for the goal of political independence clearly transcended class and regional differences. But that spirit of unanimity quickly dissolved before regional rivalries and the threat of a social revolution. When the military campaign emerged victorious, the region's leaders were well aware that an even more challenging task now lay before them: the institutionalization of democratic practices in a population inexperienced in civic participation and accustomed to conflict.

The first generation of revolutionary leaders inevitably failed in their efforts to substitute modern practices for the most offensive aspects of the region's colonial heritage. With a baggage of "doctrinaire" Enlightenment ideas, they alternated between promoting democracy and excluding the masses from political participation. Out of the elites' inherently aristocratic, urban orientation came their distrust and ignorance of rural society. Their nostalgia for the stability of the past explains at least in part their leanings toward monarchical governmental structures as a means of better leading the region along the road of progress. Their attempt to continue with a centralized governing structure, which placed Buenos Aires at the head of all the other provinces, explains the name of their Unitarian Party.

These elitist views were hardly shared by the country's majority population. The poor, largely unschooled people of the interior provinces resented the "dotores"—or university-educated people—of the city; they resisted any political program that would continue the ages-old domination of the centralized, "civilized" city dwellers over the supposed "backward" masses of the countryside. Furthermore the poor distrusted the capital city's pretense of disinterested tutelage because their own experience provided ample evidence that the slow ruin of provincial economies in recent decades had occurred apace with the rapid material enrichment of Buenos Aires. Their trepidation about the Buenos Aires leaders' imposition of disruptive modernizing practices, and their own traditional and inherently conservative cultural values, led them to embrace the theories of federalism.

Meanwhile dramatic changes had taken place in the society of the interior. The *criollo* landowners had resisted the economic crisis better than the urban elites and began to demand through the provincial *cabildos* a role in the region's governance that was proportionate to their economic and military contributions. The authority they came to exercise extended from military to political and social issues. Some despotically sought to expand their spheres of influence. Juan Facundo Quiroga, for example, eliminated his rivals by confiscating their money and cattle; others extended their influence by recruiting lieutenants from among those who willingly demonstrated allegiance to their own leadership. The period of *caudillo* rule had begun.

Early in the century most caudillo leaders came from the principal families of the region, and they enjoyed a relatively high cultural level. However, as the decades progressed, the newer *caudillo* leaders hailed more and more from humble origins and had risen to prominence because of their military exploits in the wars for independence. The division of society based on class interest was not altogether foreign to the type of federalism that came to exist under their authority. But in several instances the figure of the *caudillo* succeeded in leading the entire provincial society through his authoritarian and, at times, his charismatic leadership. It was he who united the entire society of the provinces, from rich to poor, in political and spiritual solidarity in front of their recognized opponents. In this light federalism many times acquired the stamp of a "popular" and "plebeian" movement. The "democratic" nature of *caudillo* leadership derived from their successful defense of local values and traditions and their faithful expression of the will of the interior against the absorbent posture of Buenos Aires.

Liberal historians, partisan to the unitarian outlook of Buenos Aires, have provided a less flattering portrait of *caudillo* rule in the interior provinces. The tragic civil wars following independence saw the replacement of the first generation of federalist *caudillos* with a new provincial leadership obedient to Rosas and dependent upon his corrupting power. Many of these *caudillos* exercised a local autocracy in their despotic authority over servile workers and a small and intimidated middle class. The benevolent paternalism of before disintegrated into arbitrary abuses; local power struggles were frequent.[3] When the local *caudillos* learned that they could not arrest the continuing social and economic decline of their respective regions and could not defeat their enemies in Buenos Aires, they at least could secure their own prominence in the interior.

Through the 1830s the *caudillo* leaders of the interior provinces jealously defended the priorities of their respective provinces against intrusions from without. Yet the majority of these leaders—Artigas, Güemes, Bustos, Facundo Quiroga, E. López, Ibarra, and Heredia—also articulated sincere desires for a national order that would assure provincial authority and protect them from the centralized grasp of Buenos Aires. At least a few of them sought models for a preferred form of national organization in the successful democratic experiments of the United States. They harbored suspicions about many aspects of the liberals' program for national transformation. In particular they questioned whether a national economy based on open international trade caused, in the long run, more benefits than harm; although they welcomed the availability of new consumer products from Europe, they had also witnessed firsthand the ravages that those imports had meant for local productive activity. After 1852 Alberdi and the other principal ideologues of the Urquiza Confederación would again seek in the principles of this type of federalism an estimable model for national unification.

The conflict between unitarians and federalists involved opposing ways of life more than intraclass antagonisms. In 1845 Sarmiento saw this clearly: "There were before 1810 in the Argentine Republic two rival societies that were distinct and incompatible."[4] Without embracing all the sociological ideas of the militant writer, one can accept his basic argument that two separate societies, each with its own class strata, were rivals for power in the region. The urban society, on the one hand, was constituted by a commercial, bureaucratic, and clerical oligarchy; a heterogeneous working class; and a whole range of intermediate occupation groups. Its leaders possessed oligarchic and aristocratic spirit, studied the ideas emanating from European cultural centers, and consumed the products of the trans-Atlantic commerce. On the other hand there was the provincial society organized around the figure of the *caudillo*, whose values and politics tended to reflect faithfully those of the people he led. The federalist *caudillo*, for that matter, often assumed the function of interpreter of the regional will and was friend and protector of the poor. This spontaneous political creation of the American territories was essentially a populist society, even though it had its owners and bosses. From this decisive fact came the great political paradox of the Rioplatense revolution: the oligarchic and aristocratic spirit of the Europeanized and educated forces of the city embraced liberalism as the ideological basis for their struggle, while they were opposed by the radically democratic spirit of the autochthonous, rustic masses of the countryside.[5]

The lofty principles articulated by the inspired leaders of the May Revolution faded rapidly from public consciousness as the entire region sank into a civil war between these two societies. The leaders of each were determined to impose their organizing principles upon the other. The class of urban intellectuals provided the initial leadership for the independence struggle, but their days in power were numbered because the programs they advocated enjoyed less and less support from the interior. Their programs, with a prestigious European pedigree, hardly took into account the deep imprint on institutions and values of three centuries of colonial rule or the country's recent dramatic changes. This lack of correspondence between their programs and the country's realities would explain the rapid disappearance from the public scene of the first group of idealistic revolutionary ideologues and then the inefficacy of the Rivadavia administrations in the early 1820s in effecting substantial and lasting reforms. Rival groups representing newly ascendant cattle interests, for the most part, would henceforth seek a more direct control over the political institutions of the region.

Out of this context arose Juan Manuel de Rosas, the man who dominated the political scene of Buenos Aires and then the whole country from 1822 to 1852. In the first moment Rosas did represent the triumph of rural society over urban prerogatives. But his presence resists such simplification: he was a *criollo* landowner whose electoral supporters included both the propertied class, who saw in him their best option for restoring and maintaining social stability, and the masses, who believed he offered their best guarantee for obtaining greater social justice. Later, with the dictatorial powers granted to him by the legislature, Rosas put his regime at the service of the landowning and cattle-producing class of which he was a member:

> With a very clear awareness of the social reality in which he moved, Rosas utilized the lower classes in order to establish a popular base for a regime that would end up benefiting the landowner class—at that time emerging with a nationalist character—and in particular within that class an oligarchy of the Buenos Aires countryside with Rosas at its center. It was this last group that exercised a monopoly over exports and imports, the jerked meat industry, and the receipts of the nation's customs house.[6]

The new order that came into being under his tutelage was in no manner of speaking a mere "restoration" of the ancien régime of colonial times. But old colonial interests, including the church, did join in backing Rosas because they preferred him to political chaos and the doctrinaire novelties from the period of the revolution. These interests, plus a new class of commercial agents allied to foreign interests, constituted the pillars of support for the Rosas regime.

THE MAY REVOLUTION IDEALIZED

The history of the May Revolution, the civil wars, and the Rosas period has been treated in great detail elsewhere, and there is no need to enter into detailed analysis here. Appropriate here is a discussion of how that period impacted on the early formation and education of the future 1837 activists.

On the positive side the country's struggle for independence existed for all of the 1837 militants as a mystified period of lofty ideals and noble acts. It was, so to speak, the calm before the storm: the brief interlude of idyllic national construction that preceded the country's descent into civil strife. In their thought this period took the mystified form of an irrecoverable past, the lost Arcadia of youth. Here their historical thought was irremediably contaminated with the stuff of idealized memory.

As such the events of the May Revolution would act as a romanticized backdrop for many of their important formative experiences. Sarmiento would write that his infatuation with the legacy of the May revolution came from his beloved father, who had served as a loyal follower of San

Martín. Alberdi, in a similar fashion, would remember the inspiring presence of Manuel Belgrano in his frequent visits to the family's household in Tucumán. Belgrano, second to San Martín, was the most prestigious leader of the region's independence campaign. Vicente Fidel López was to grow up in the shadow of his father, one of the most dedicated servants of the newly constituted democracy, whose disinterested service over decades won near universal respect in progressive circles. Félix Frías's father left a similarly positive memory of the enraptured sacrifices he had made as Belgrano's auditor of war—the civilian supervising finance and logistics—and then as participant in several of the important constitutional assemblies.

Although Esteban Echeverría had no close family relations who attained protagonist status in the May Revolution, his writings still communicated a similarly deep devotion that the generation of his parents imparted to him as a child. He would write in romantically rendered autobiographic notes of his devoted mother's deathbed admonition: "Mankind should aspire to as high as possible. The Homeland places its hope for the future on its children: it is the only mother you have left."[7] Throughout his political and historical writings, he provided positive, even mystified, images of the "Patria" that had emerged as a result of the May Revolution, that "wonderful and magnificent program!" which was the source and inspiration for the principle of democracy throughout the regions of the Plata.[8] In Echeverría the pattern was repeated: the intense optimism of their parents' generation, as a result of their participation in the glorious independence struggle, would become an integral part of their own civic and moral code.

The May Revolution also impacted upon the young 1837 writers through the educational institutions in which they spent long hours of their formative youth. Sarmiento's several years of study in San Juan's recently founded "School of the Fatherland" reinforced the strong, nationalistic sentiments already learned in his home environment. In Buenos Aires, the May Revolution's impetus for education was even more pronounced. In 1823 the progressive national government under the inspired leadership of Bernardino Rivadavia founded the College of Moral Sciences, an institution that was to have an incalculable influence over several of the youths. Echeverría, who studied there only during its first few months of operation, nevertheless would later write with fondness about his experiences. In 1825 Alberdi, at the age of fifteen, won one of the coveted governmental scholarships to study there. (Sarmiento, in contrast, would remember his great disappointment at not having obtained the same.) In those classes the most capable youths from Buenos Aires joined with select individuals from the different provinces of the interior: Miguel Cané, Juan María Gutiérrez, José Rivera

Indarte, Carlos Tejedor, Miguel Irigoyen, José Mármol, Félix Frías, Jacinto Rodríguez Peña, Carlos Eguía, Rufino Varela, and others. Their instructors endeared them to the largely unfulfilled social ideals of the May Revolution that beckoned the beginnings of a new republican age.

The experience of the May Revolution, in spite of its attraction, would also inspire severe criticisms on the part of the 1837 activists. They were eager to learn the negative examples of a previous period of social reform in order to better ensure the success of their own ventures. Alberdi provided a representative judgment—the whole period was characterized by a radical imbalance between proposals and means: "proclaiming, decreeing those economico-political liberties is not the same as creating them. The regime that mandated freedom of labor did not end up creating jobs."[9] However admirable the May reforms might have been, they were destined to fail because they were out of step with the values and expectations of a largely uneducated population. Furthermore Alberdi realized the counterproductive, and in the end destabilizing, influence of the May ideologues, whose revolutionary program did not take into account the priorities of the region's most important economic interests, that is, the network of landowners, salted meat exporters, and commercial agents. His early recommendation for a philosophy that would guide a new age of reforms is, therefore, based on an implicit condemnation of the May experience: that experience featured "the substitution of what was nationalistic by what was exotic; spontaneity by plagiarism; relevance by improvisation; reflection by enthusiasm, and later, the triumph of the majority over the minority."[10]

Echeverría's writings attest to his general agreement with Alberdi. According to Echeverría the May Revolution became derailed because of the mistaken priorities of its leaders; they unintentionally destabilized society in their idealistic attempt to create civil institutions modeled on the dangerous idea that the will of the common people was to reign supreme. He condemned the early Unitarian Party for having failed to unify social and political groups around a moderate program of reforms. Instead they arrogantly attempted to impose an ambitious plan that antagonized the opposition and brought the country to the verge of civil war.

Sarmiento, along with intermittent praise, also called attention to the failures of the May insurrection, whose leaders had been guided more by lofty principles they had blindly copied from Europe than an acute sense of the limits of their own historical situation. Throughout his long and fertile public life, Sarmiento would return time and again to the ideas and ideals of Rivadavia for his own inspiration. But at times, the failures of that early unitarian leader would be the brunt of his most severe, and perhaps exaggerated, criticisms. He rhetorically posed the question: What else should one expect from a program inspired by a political creed that was "plagued by errors, absurd and tricky theories, and faulty principles?"[11]

FORMATIVE EXPERIENCES

The gradual breakdown of the region's social system affected many of the future 1837 activists directly in the form of their families' fall from previous positions of prominence. For all of them the advent of the revolutionary period and then its turbulent aftermath was experienced, on a psychological level, as the definitive loss of the protective environment afforded by the stable society of their childhood. This sense of loss was most visible in the experiences of Alberdi and Sarmiento, who hailed from more traditional environments of the northern provinces. However the situations of Echeverría, Frías, Mitre, and others, who grew up in and around Buenos Aires, offered many points of comparison. Most of them would later be able to remember nostalgically the period of their youth when stability was the rule; when a patriarchal order was presided over by society's most learned and respected citizens; and when society still enjoyed the benefits of peace, harmony, and relative prosperity. Although it is impossible to specify with any degree of certainty the extent to which these factors influenced the attitudes or values of the 1837 militants during the period of their youth, certain correlations nevertheless warrant our attention here.

The accentuated bookish or "culturalist" orientation shared by most of the future 1837 militants was linked, at least in part, to these social phenomena. In the new society of their youth, social authority was less and less a result of one's distinguished family line or its economic power; one remaining claim to prominence was the individual's superior education and versatility in written communication skills. Their bookish knowledge of European pedigree was the factor that set them head and shoulders above—in their terms—the "brutish," "unenlightened" American element. With Sarmiento this culturalist focus combined with a disdain for the lower classes. Also related was his contempt for those social and cultural institutions which had arisen in the country's rural areas as a result of the European settlers' accommodations to the rigors of frontier life. Cultural superiority in Echeverría and Alberdi took a more mild, but hardly less pronounced, form. This is one of several possible explanations for Echeverría's confused advocacy of a "democracy" of the spirit—not of the masses—his defensive moral superiority, in addition to his accentuated sense of righteousness. In V. F. López the positive influence of a stable family life received emphasis both in his life and his literature; in his novel, *La novia del hereje* (The bride of the heretic), he drew a relationship between the psychological balance of those growing up in traditional families and the collective well-being of the stable patriarchal society. The path toward political conservatism in almost all of these young militants was noteworthy. Alberdi, for example, advocated a hierarchical society governed by educated elites, who would actively work against grass-roots social and political participation in the short run.

Information on the childhood and family background of the 1837 militants is hard to come by, and the few existing autobiographical accounts and other sources supply a minimum of data. Many of the young militants experienced the recent decline of the region's traditional ruling class in a direct, anguishing way. In *Recuerdos de provincia* (Memories of provincial life), Sarmiento told of several aristocratic families in the Cuyan region, including both his father's and his mother's, that fell into poverty. Félix Frías, as a child, also suffered from declining status and material need as a result of his father's premature death in 1831. No other member of their generation suffered the same degree of fear of economic marginalization during their impressionable childhood years. For these two economic problems were all the more anguishing when, as youths, they witnessed the ascending fortunes of individuals from relatively undistinguished family backgrounds who lacked the enviable cultural level that they themselves strived to attain.

Previously the families of the future 1837 militants had dominated social, cultural, and political, if not economic, spheres. Now their own advancement in any one of these depended upon the willing graces and, in instances, whim of society's new leaders. Such was the lesson of the young Echeverría, recently orphaned, whose long stay in Europe between 1826 and 1830 was only made possible through the generosity of certain benefactors. Alberdi's situation was similar. His family was not lacking in material resources, but the death of his parents when he was ten acquainted him with the perilousness of his material well-being. The influence of the Aráoz family on his mother's side played a role in his receipt of the coveted scholarship to study in Buenos Aires in 1824 (the same favor was denied to Sarmiento in San Juan a year later). Then, after 1832, Alberdi was careful to cultivate the support of the governor of Tucumán, Alejandro Heredia. With the latter's recommendation, Juan Facundo Quiroga, the *caudillo* from La Rioja then residing in Buenos Aires, generously offered to facilitate Alberdi's project of studying democratic institutions in the United States, an offer that Alberdi later refused. These early experiences of economic need and dependency would drive home, for many of the young militants, the realization that their own advancement was possible only through their service to social and political power.

The recent arrival of new social groups to positions of authority in society, and the concurrent displacement of their own families and friends, was to have a lasting impact on the sensitivities of the 1837 youths. All change is potentially threatening, but this is especially so when it negatively affects one's own social position. As such, the new prominence of the previously excluded class of *criollo*—and, in the interior, *mestizo*—landowners, or individuals dependent upon rural instead of urban sources of wealth, was met with distrust and even contempt.

Especially alarming for the traditional elites throughout the country was the liberation of the masses from the relations of servitude that had been the rule in colonial times and their increased—often destabilizing—participation in society. After the initial outbreak against Spanish authorities, the lower classes assumed a more active social role than at any time in the past.[12] Against the will of the traditional elites, the early military leaders mobilized the masses as a means of bolstering their own authority and expanding their armies. In the north they liberated the Indians; throughout the country they freed thousands of workers from coercive and exploitative work situations. In the long run these policies hastened the breakdown of an already shaky colonial system. Many common soldiers, after sampling the freedom of movement and the euphoria of the *montonera* campaign in defense of the newly defined homeland, would not be easily enticed to return to the drudgery and servitude of before.

The threat of social revolution had an equally strong impact upon the future 1837 militants. During the long years of military conflict, urban leaders looked with horror on the rising influence of the rural *caudillos* and the promises of social revolution that they promised their lower-class followers. This was especially so in the coastal provinces—the Littoral—where the region's more recent colonization and its relatively egalitarian system contrasted with the rigid inequalities prevailing in the more northerly provinces. José Gervasio Artigas, from the Banda Oriental—today's Uruguay—was particularly successful in uniting a popular following, many of them Blacks and Indians. His lower-class army viewed independence from Spain as but a means for obtaining a broad slate of political and economic liberties. Artigas, true to his word, actually implemented many of the promised reforms in the lulls between his constant battles against the Portuguese, the Spanish, and the monarchy-leaning leaders from Buenos Aires.[13]

Buenos Aires's "enlightened" leaders, rather than support the "inorganic" democratic sentiment of Artigas's early federalist movement, instead offered wholesale resistance. There are complex reasons for this hostility which Sarmiento, Mitre, V. F. López, and Alberdi would later assimilate into their historical writings. Surely one of the major factors for the visceral hatred demonstrated by these thinkers was the federalists' incorporation of the lower classes into their ranks. Out of this fear, which has social as well as political implications, arose the myth of the "barbarian" *montoneros*, with it's celebrated clichés and distortions. This myth was already current during the childhood of the future 1837 writers, so they certainly were not its inventors. But the following passage written years later by V. F. López demonstrates the pervasiveness of that myth upon his young formative mind and also his mature thought. López, in the historical text used by generations of Argentine students, referred to the commotion in Buenos Aires over the news of the battlefield defeat of its defender, Rondeau, in 1820:

> Among those terrified messengers bringing the news was an aide to Rondeau, Sargent-Major Miguel Planes. According to him, all was lost: no one knew anything about Rondeau. Balcarce, Rolón, and other colonels: all were either dead or were now prisoners. The infantry and the artillery were in the hands of the *montoneros*. It was easy to project what awaited the city at any moment: its sacking by five thousand unclad barbarians, starved and infuriated by beastly passions. In these cases when individuals come together in an inorganic mob, the most destructive and insatiable instincts of the human beast are unleashed.[14]

The mere thought of federalism's rabble threatening the elitist, Europeanized society must have inspired the greatest of horror in the minds of Buenos Aires's population. Only a small minority of the educated elite of Buenos Aires ever struggled on behalf of the democratic participation of the popular classes. Instead their principal values and attitudes derived from the social role that their families and class had performed in the hierarchical social order of the Spanish colony. These deeply ingrained values of class and race would survive, in modified form, in the historical perspectives later embraced by the 1837 militants. As youths the social turmoil of the 1820s had inspired in them the most feared images of Revolutionary Thermidor. Their later writings reveal their fear of social instability and the dislocations brought on society by rapid or violent social change. Although they would embrace liberal economic ideas, their program for the country's political future was decidedly conservative, if not reactionary. Several of them would return to the advocacies of San Martín and other revolutionary leaders in advocating the creation of a constitutional monarchy that would impose its control over the increasing social disorder.

Also impacting upon the developing consciousness of these young militants was the country's descent into violence and anarchy. Peace did not follow independence. The rebellious lower class posed increasing difficulties for the liberal leadership of the country with progressive yet intractable ideas. In 1820 this leadership called upon the *gaucho* militia of Juan Manuel de Rosas—already a recognized leader among the large landowners in the South—to reestablish social order in the face of a plebeian insurrection and discontent in the army. Rosas's success in this venture contributed to his later fame as "Restorer of the Law." Given the state of anarchy and social turbulence, the central revolutionary authority under Minister Rivadavia passed a series of laws and decrees between 1821 and 1823 which called for the punishment of apprentices and rural workers who abandoned their work place. That regime, whose program has been considered liberal and progressive by present-day historians, in effect reinstated the system of forced labor that had prevailed during the colony.[15]

In most other areas, however, the Rivadavia administration sought to implement an impressive array of liberal reforms that aimed at setting the country firmly on the road to progress. These reforms met with strident opposition from many leaders in the interior who equated liberalism with Buenos Aires supremacy and opposed any reform inspired by modern European thought that threatened their traditional way of life. The successes of federalist armies in armed skirmishes between 1826 and 1827 led to Rivadavia's fall from power and his subsequent exile. Yet the memory of his most significant programs would survive in the collective memory of unitarian partisans. A few of the future 1837 militants would remember that early leader's ideas and accomplishments in their writings; other 1837 militants, when entrusted with the responsibilities of leadership after 1852, would seek to reinstate some of his farsighted policies.

Their collective image of Rivadavia was that of an enlightened statesman who, with impassioned arrogance, advocated idealistic programs in a social and political context not yet sufficiently developed to benefit from them. A Rivadavian measure that acquired symbolic importance years later was that leader's implementation of universal suffrage for provincial elections in 1821.[16] In their own writings Echeverría, Sarmiento, and others would condemn this measure as one of the main causes of the region's fall into anarchy. A more generous observer, however, would conclude that no political or military leader at the time could have forestalled or quelled the growing disorder in any significant manner.

The social turbulence of the time slowly acquired the outer trappings of a political struggle. Much has been written about the heated dispute between unitarians, who defended a centralized nation headed by Buenos Aires, and the federalists, who defended a loosely united national system based on the relative equality and autonomy of the different provinces. But the issues in dispute at the time defy simple explanation. José María Paz, himself an enemy of federalism but, nevertheless, a fairly objective observer, provided a description of the complex web of social and ideological issues at play:

> It may be useful to note that the large faction within the republic which comprises the Federal Party was not fighting only for a mere form of government, since other interests and other beliefs were united in its victory. First, there was the struggle of the most enlightened part of the population against the most ignorant. Second, the country people opposed the city people. Third, the common people wanted to gain superiority over the upper class. Fourth, the provinces, jealous of the domination of the capital, wanted to bring the city down to their level. Fifth, democratic attitudes were opposed to the aristocratic and even monarchical views that were made apparent by the ruling groups at the time of the unfortunate negotiations concerning the Prince of Lucca. All these passions, all these elements of dissolution and of anarchy, were ignited by terrible violence and prepared the way for the conflagration that soon broke out.[17]

The tumultuous events of 1820–21 dramatically affected the sensitivities of an impressionable youth. Sarmiento was but nine years old; Alberdi, ten; Gutiérrez, eleven; Echeverría just finishing adolescence; and Mitre yet to be born. In Sarmiento's San Juan a barracks rebellion resulted in the overthrow and then exile of the provincial governor, Dr. Roza, a respected follower of General San Martín and founder of San Juan's first school. In the following months, coup followed coup in the ongoing struggle between unitarians and federalists, marking the region's sorry entrance into an era of political instability.

Alberdi witnessed similar events in neighboring Tucumán. The 1820 pronouncement by military leaders Heredia, Paz, and Bustos against Buenos Aires was followed by a rapid series of crimes, felonies, and bloody overthrows of its governors. In the tendentious words of Groussac, Alberdi

> [u]pon opening his eyes for the first time, contemplated the revelry of the emancipated slaves who, in those villages, made a parody of the cult of liberty, and whose acts more and more irresistably resembled a rustic theatrical farce. He belonged to the Aráos family, meaning that he witnessed on a daily basis the somersaults of the rural chieftains, who gathered almost daily for horse trading and scheming. He witnessed the assaults and forced evacuations caused by poncho clad barbarians.[18]

Vicente Fidel López has left a personal testimony of equally unsettling events in Buenos Aires that followed the defeat of Buenos Aires forces by federalist troops in the 1820 battle of Cepeda:

I was at the time a tender child, and I remember entering into the parlor that was filled with friends and family afflicted by an indescribable consternation. . . . Mrs. Trinidad Mantilla de Balcarce [wife of the defeated general] . . . uncontrollably sobbed a torrent of tears; . . . her features betrayed the paroxym of despair exploding against the abysmal fatality of misfortunes, her clothes torn from her breast and her locks shaking as if in a wind storm. . . . This gives an idea of the level of fear and agitation of the passions that the news of this fatal defeat had caused. The anguish of the families, the terror of the men involved in the regime that until then had predominated; the indignation of humiliated local pride; . . . the supreme necessity of defending themselves from the followers of Artigas, those enemies driven by the desire to exterminate the people of the capital and reduce the city to wasteland. These thoughts filled with horror those who already believed themselves to be victims of the regime's collapse.[19]

The future historian, then as a young child, was comforted only by the hand of his venerable father. He witnessed firsthand the terror of the Porteño elite before the advance of rude federalist troops. His own fears would be internalized; henceforth he would associate the image of unruly *montonera* forces with ideas of savagery and the usurpation of his civilizing ideal.

Disorder continued. Following the assassination of Buenos Aires Federalist leader Manuel Dorriego in 1828, a new wave of violence swept the country. Righteous and frustrated unitarians who were eager to usurp power considered the federalists to be their intellectual inferiors and defenders of social and political principles that looked to the past and promised to impede the country's progress. In their turn the Federalist leaders in the interior provinces were intent on punishing the unitarians for their attempts to impose an illegal authority over an unwilling majority population.

Sarmiento would record his own traumatic experience with the civil disorder that year. At sixteen years of age, he stood in front of the shop he tended and viewed the entrance into San Juan of Facundo Quiroga and some six hundred mounted *montonera* horsemen. They constituted an eery, unsettling presence, with their "dust covered faces projecting from entangled hair and rags, and almost without bodies . . . it was as if the human rostrums projected from bodies of animals, of centaurs from hell."[20] That sight, with its overwhelmingly negative associations, left an indelible impression on his budding consciousness. For the impressionable youth Quiroga's ascent to protagonist status in the province's affairs was akin to the rape of civilized society by incarnated evil.

In the following months more civil strife continued. Sarmiento personally witnessed the brutal and unprovoked terror that accompanied the uprising of the local militia, later joined by "the rabble and the *gaucho* people" against the unitarian provincial government in San Juan.

His writings highlighted the social aspects of this conflict. No longer was it a clash over political ideas or organizational principles; instead it was the result of the pent-up hatred of the lower classes, predominantly rural in origin, against the province's liberal leaders and its most wealthy and prestigious families. Sarmiento took weapons in hand to defend the beleaguered regional elite. Childhood fantasies about the glories of military conflict were forgotten after viewing the fall of fellow combatants and when he barely escaped death himself. Rebels assaulted prominent citizens and ransacked their properties. The government finally quelled the uprising but only after a bloody confrontation and the execution of several rebel leaders. From all this Sarmiento drew the conclusion that society's elite needed to recur to "vigorous means of repression" in order to contain the rebellious rural masses.[21] Dating from these tragic events, he would henceforth offer impassioned, and at times violent, opposition to any rural leader who opposed the quest of society's educated elite in its providential struggle to "civilize" the region.

These events give an indication of the general turbulence that typified the youth and adolescence of the 1837 participants. It was a period of intense hatred and sometimes merciless slaughter when armed uprisings could explode at any moment. One historian affirms in metaphorical fashion that, because of the violent backdrop to their youth, the 1837 leaders were by necessity sons of warriors who inherited the strength to live in unsettled times.[22]

RACE AND CLASS

Racial aspects of Argentina's turbulent first decades of independence also impacted upon the future 1837 activists. During the formative period of their childhood and adolescence, they internalized many of the attitudes then prevalent in family and society. Racial hierarchies, surviving from colonial society, favored White European descendants, who held that racial purity constituted a prerequisite for elite status: "There existed restraints, both formal and informal, on upward mobility. Anyone who was not white or of acceptable social origin was excluded from membership in the sociopolitical elites."[23] However the provinces began to witness changes in old attitudes which resulted from the traumatic dislocations of the independence struggle. With increasing frequency individuals of *mestizo*, or mixed racial, heritage assumed positions within the social authority.[24] Even though Sarmiento's own family tree included products of this miscegenation, his words about the newly ascendant figures in the provincial government and militia in *Recuerdos de provincia* carried a hint of racial protest. The new provincial governor,

Benavides, was not a bad man, but "the greater part of the men from these countries have no conception of others' rights or justice. . . . Benavides, in imposing his style of despotism, has left imprinted [on the Province of San Juan] his own materialism, his inertia, his abandonment of anything that might constitute public life."[25] Similarly he complained that Cuyo's new strongmen rarely, if ever, hailed from the prominent families of the region and that several new militia leaders had questionable antecedents and even criminal records. According to Sarmiento the "scoria of society" now endangered the province's legacy of political order and cultural refinement. His fear of social instability throughout his life would reflect this perceived threat of racial and class conflict.

In the province of Buenos Aires, the situation differed slightly. Recent research indicates that the social elite of the viceregal period was constituted primarily by wealthy Spaniards; later they were joined by *criollos* of pure Spanish ancestry, who had experienced commercial success in the region. Unlike the situation existing in the interior provinces, only a small proportion of the propertied elite were *mestizos* (many descending from families in present-day Paraguay) or mulattos. For them racial attitudes fused with their sense of class superiority; both came into play when the White elite of Buenos Aires confronted the region's rebellious lower classes. The 1837 Generation's virulent hatred of Rosas found an explanation in the latter's success in winning the loyalty of *mestizo*— generally of the lower class, *pardos* and Blacks. The latter (whether freed or still slaves) constituted one quarter of the total population of the city at the time.[26] For this reason the struggle against Rosas had a clearly racial dimension with Blacks, *pardos, mulattos,* and *mestizos* pitted against Europeans and *criollos* of European stock. Several of the writings of the 1837 militants—Mármol's *Amalia*, Echeverría's "El matadero" ("The slaughterhouse"), and Sarmiento's politicized biography of Angel "El Chacho" Peñaloza—understandably contain explicit racial overtones when they allude to the struggle waged for decades against the hated Rosas regime.

The above serves to explain in large part the disgust, fear, and even hatred exhibited by all the 1837 activists in front of the interior provinces' majority population of mixed-race *mestizos*, attitudes that hardly differed from those held by the overwhelming majority of their class at the time. A similar set of circumstances accounted for the highly negative perspective that flavored the thought of all of them with regard to Argentina's indigenous populations.

From the time of the first European settlements until late in the nineteenth century, the Indian "menace" constituted the foremost danger to White settlements in almost every area of the Plata region. Only in the extreme northeast, in present-day Paraguay and bordering provinces,

had the European settlers encountered Indians with friendly disposi-
tions and sufficiently evolved social values that made a peaceful domination possible. Different Indian groups had accompanied the armies of
San Martín and Artigas during the independence struggles, and they
also fought along side of the largely *criollo* and *mestizo* armies of Rosas,
Paz, and other military leaders of the decades-long civil wars. A benevolent view also was fostered by the highly successful Jesuit missions in
Paraguay, which had instructed and organized several generations of
the docile, hardworking Guaraní. But these contributions were largely
forgotten by the writers and opinion leaders residing in Buenos Aires,
for whom the word Indian became equated with the savage, ruthless
pampa marauders whose raids upon European settlements in search of
cattle, women, and children inseminated terror in the hearts and minds
of European, *mestizo*, and Black alike. Even José Hernández, who seemingly presented an apology for the violent, renegade *gaucho* of mixed
blood in the first part to his masterful poem, *Martín Fierro*, fiercely
condemned the savage Indian of the pampa. Simply stated there existed
no significant sector of Ríoplatense society during the middle decades
of the past century that would have articulated a defense of Indian
rights and would have taken the country's succession of governments
to task for their policy of Indian containment and extermination.

The Buenos Aires public warmly received Echeverría's *La cautiva* (The
captive), the passionate portrayal of Europeanized Brian and his virginal
companion, María, in their near tragic confrontation with uncivilized
Indian hordes. This favorable reception owed at least as much to the
public's appetite for romantic adventure as to its cathartic identification
with the misadventures of the poem's protagonists. Violent confrontations along Argentina's frontiers between White and red populations
was the stuff of reports in the daily press throughout the poet's youth
and, in fact, well past his premature death in 1851.

Even before independence the defense of the frontiers had given rise
to a permanent military organization in the majority of the provinces.
When veteran soldiers had been withdrawn from frontier regions to
fight against the Spanish royalists, hostile Indian groups were able to
raid with near impunity. Criollo leaders in Buenos Aires learned that
the defense against the Indians could never be relaxed, even at the cost
of losing the war against the Spaniards. Even after independence the
danger from those Indians making a livelihood of raiding White settlements did not disappear; it would wax and wane, but was still the cause
for continual monetary expenditures and vigilance for any population
within three hundred kilometers of the outlying settlements. Rosas, during his long years in power, proved remarkably adept at negotiating
with friendly Indian groups and containing the belligerence of others.

Yet the periodical rebellions against his authority often accompanied a breakdown in those negotiated settlements and initiated a new wave of Indian raids. Central to the region's folklore were accounts of Indian atrocities that would prickle the hairs of even the most valiant of listeners. The "Indian problem" simply would not disappear. Civic minded leaders dreamed of the day when the Indian presence would cease to be an impediment to the country's manifest destiny of transforming the "deserts" with cattle and sheep ranches and agricultural colonies. To this end over more than sixty years the national and provincial governments channeled considerable energy and expense. Rosas's daring expedition of 1833 was among the first of such enterprises; Julio A. Roca's highly praised "Desert Campaign" later would bring this chapter of national history to a bloody close a half-century later.

In short the Indian hardly constituted in the consciousness of the 1837 activists a romanticized exotic personage like James Fenimore Cooper's pathfinder, or the sage, judicious chieftain, Chingachcook. Nor did the Indian constitute for them a benign Rousseaulike natural being who joyously awaited the civilizing caress of European culture. Much has been made of Sarmiento's praise of the Indianlike *rastreador* (pathfinder) in the pages of *Facundo*, but one should not assume on that basis that Sarmiento harbored potentially generous sentiments for the autochthonous cultures of his continent. More correct is to view him as a representative of his generation and his class with his decidedly anti-Indian views. His own race and class prided themselves on their own European linkages. In their eyes any regional leader who could attract a significant following of indigenous people for diverse social, political, or military ends—such as Artigas, "El Chacho" Peñaloza, etc.—was likewise contaminated with the stain of barbarism. Sarmiento shared the view with the other leaders of his generation that Argentina's speedy entrance into the select circle of civilized nations was dependent on the containment or even erasure of Indian and *mestizo* influences and their replacement with white immigrant settlers. In this regard one important legacy of the 1837 generation was the transformation of such beliefs into state policy after the fall of Rosas; the *pampa* Indian populations would be systematically annihilated in order to secure new lands for an expansion of cattle-raising *latifundia* and the development of new commercial interests associated with the wool and grain industries.[27]

Facundo Quiroga Promotes Unification

Toward the middle of the 1830s, federalist forces consolidated their control throughout the country. This had resulted from the capture and incarceration of unitarian General José María Paz and the decisive victory at Ciudadela in 1831 of federalist leader Juan Facundo Quiroga over the unitarian armies commanded by General Gregorio de Lamadrid. Although the surviving militants of the unitarian rebellion of 1829 would continue to smolder in resentment from their vantage point in Montevidean exile, their forces of rebellion were, for the time being, exhausted. Peace had been established. Not a harmonious peace, or a generous one for the vanquished; but it was, nevertheless, peace. Facundo Quiroga dictated the terms of the new era of stability that he had prophetically described in an 1830 letter to his erstwhile rival, General Paz: "It's necessary that one or the other triumph, in order that the victorious party oblige the other to bury its arms forever."[28]

In short peace had been achieved after long years of civil skirmishes. Twenty years earlier the liberation of the country from the retrograde Spanish empire had led to institutional chaos. The decrepit forms of colonial governance had been put asunder. Concurrently the traditional elites and social hierarchies that had already been in crisis since the latter decades of the previous century were gradually displaced by newly hegemonic social and political structures. The emergence of a new society and the reconstruction of its institutions could not have occurred overnight. Even with the unitarian threat all but eliminated, occasional disagreements and territorial disputes erupted between the federalist governors of the different provinces. The outbreak of hostilities between Salta and Tucumún in 1834—for which Facundo Quiroga's generous offer at mediation ended up costing him his life—was one good example. The region's most farsighted citizens sought the creation of a legal mechanism that could intercede to resolve conflicts. Many leaders throughout the provinces realized that the moment was opportune for formalizing the existing de facto structures in a constitutional order.

Against this backdrop the constitutional pursuits of Juan Facundo Quiroga during the last four years of his life—from 1830 to 1834—must be interpreted as a faithful reflection of sentiments widely shared throughout the interior and even in the Province of Buenos Aires. This benevolent side to Facundo's character and public activity has been largely ignored by liberal historians, beginning with Sarmiento and Mitre, whose foundation texts portrayed that man as the incarnation of barbarism and violence.[29] In the interest of historical accuracy, it is therefore necessary to summarize briefly those positive advocacies that contrast with the more primitive and even brutal acts of Facundo Quiroga's early career.

At the beginning of the 1830s, Facundo was the indicated person to lead this movement toward a constitution. Although many had trepidations about his reputation for cruelty and violence, they also were aware of his superior intellectual and moral qualities.[30] They realized that Facundo's past violence had responded to the equally terrible acts committed by enemy unitarians.[31] Because Facundo's cause was the protection and preservation of the northern provinces, the people there recognized him as their leader and defender.

Facundo's concerns at this time were well summarized in the letter he wrote to his arch rival, the unitarian General José María Paz. Salta, Tucumán, Santiago de Estero, and Córdoba, he wrote, had all suffered from the incursions by unitarian troops whose only objective had been to dominate them. The provinces had struggled against those invasions out of self-defense and had been forced to buy their liberty through the sacrifice of personal fortunes and the blood of their children. In the pitted struggles that resulted, both sides had committed abuses. But, as Quiroga reminded Paz, the most recent cycle of conflicts had begun as a result of brutalities unleashed by extremist unitarian elements upon Dorrego, the spokesmen for federalism's moderate course. The result, in the words of Quiroga, was "a savage and unjustifiable war, and an assassination that has unleashed violent passions and unfeeling, vindictive actions previously unknown in our country."[32] He closed the letter on a note of pride and defiance: "The provinces of the interior could be dismembered, but they will never be dominated." He suggested that the Unitarian Party could succeed in implementing its selfish goals only by destroying the society of the interior and reducing its people to servitude.

In Facundo's opinion, the best guarantee of the security of the interior provinces was the institutionalization of the country under the authority of a written constitution. At the age of forty-six, his rheumatism attacks prevented a continued military presence. Civilization's lure accounted for his extended presence in Buenos Aires and the attention he gave to the education of his children. There were many indications that Quiroga was beginning to measure his own stature as national statesman and not merely as regional leader.

The moment was propitious. As early as 1831 the governors of Buenos Aires, Santa Fe, and Entre Ríos signed a pact that expressed their agreement about the need to constitute the nation under the governmental system desired by the people. Felipe Ibarra, governor of Santiago, wrote to Rosas proposing the convocation of a Constituent Assembly in order to organize "a superior authority that could neutralize interprovincial disputes, making known to all the obligations as well as privileges of each federal state."[33] Mariano Fragueiro, interim governor of Córdoba and supporter of unitiarian General Paz, wrote a letter urging Facundo, the most powerful and respected figure of the interior, to rise above narrow sectarian interests and work toward the creation of a regional order that would guarantee peace for all concerned. Similar was the Mendoza legislature's 1834 invitation to San Juan and San Luis to unite into a federation under the protection of Quiroga; in several other provinces of the north the idea of a representative assembly presided over by Quiroga received approving nods.[34]

Quiroga, with independent criteria, sought a middle ground between the country's two warring factions. He exchanged frank opinions with some of the leading Unitarian leaders who still remained in the city: Marcelo de Alvear, Valentín Alsina, General Tomás Guido, and others. In addition his influence almost proved pivotal in securing the safe return to Buenos Aires of exiled unitarian leader Bernardino Rivadavia. He wrote to Rosas in 1832: "You know, because I have said it to you on various occasions, that I am not a federalist, rather a unitarian by conviction; but I differ from other unitarians in the humility of my own beliefs and in my vast respect for the will of the people who have continually opted for a Federal governmental system."[35] All these factors anticipated the compromise politics that would emerge a few years hence in the program of the 1837 Generation.

Facundo Quiroga's recent rise to the status of national statesman was bound to provoke the despotic Rosas, who argued that a national constituent assembly was premature, given the climate of violence and continued threat to domestic tranquility. Critics of Rosas, however, interpreted this response as Rosas's reluctance to give up the unlimited powers that he then exercised. His personalist politics, combined with the defense of Porteño landowners and jerked beef monopolists, took precedence over any vision he might have had for the well-being of the country as a whole.[36] Writers of the liberal opposition have argued passionately that it was indeed Rosas who ordered the assassination of Quiroga in 1834. More credible is the studied opinion of Enrique Barba, Félix Luna, and others, that by 1833 Quiroga was becoming convinced about the desirability of deferring to Rosas's superior authority; he was yielding to the logic of Rosas's arguments about the dangers of entering into talks about creating a national assembly at that time.[37] Equally convincing is the explanation that Quiroga, with primitive tendencies to his genius, was slowing becoming seduced by the attractions and corruptions of Buenos Aires. In actual fact no indisputable evidence links Rosas with the assassination of the mercurial Facundo Quiroga near the postal station of Barranca Yaco in April 1834.

What were the opinions of the 1837 militants about Facundo Quiroga? Sarmiento's opinions, as expressed in *Facundo*, are well known and need not be detailed here: he consistently drew Facundo to be the incarnation of barbarism and irrational violence. Other 1837 militants, with close links to the Unitarian Party, followed with similar views, as has the entire liberal historiographic tradition. For them Facundo and other *caudillo* barbarians were "ransackers" and heads of "terrorist" or authoritarian orders. On the moral level the *caudillos* exhibited severe defects, that is, "unlimited greed" or as victims of "their preferred passions."[38]

This negative assessment of Facundo Quiroga's career was not shared by Alberdi, Gutiérrez, and López. Alberdi's views about the contribution of Quiroga are important here because it was he who provided the impetus to the 1837 generation's early military campaign against Rosas, as well as its collective view about the status of the country at the time. (In the 1830s, Sarmiento was all but unknown to the rest, and Mitre was but an aspiring adolescent.) Throughout the decade of the 1830s, Alberdi maintained continual communication with his brother and close friends in Tucumán; he was well informed about political developments and Facundo's efforts on behalf of regional peace and organization. During the period of the Salón Literario, Alberdi visited Quiroga several times in Buenos Aires: "I visited him repeatedly and on many occasions he delighted in long conversations with me that hardly touched political issues. Regardless, I never tired of studying that extraordinary man."[39] Alberdi was favorably disposed to the famed *caudillo*. This is obvious from his remarks in response to the events at Barranca Yaco: "On the occasion of his tragic end, General Heredia wrote me, lamenting that the highest and most esteemed projects had also perished with him."[40] Alberdi's later writings are ambiguous about this early pro*caudillo* stance. Most prevalent in the "public" texts that he saw fit to publish during his lifetime was his persistent promotion of North-European immigration to Argentina in order to supplant or improve the racial stock of the country's Spanish, Indian, and *mestizo* inhabitants—*caudillos* and *gauchos* alike—races, he believed, that were biologically unfit for modern civilization. However, many other writings that remained unpublished during his lifetime (later to be published in the sixteen volumes of *Escritos póstumos*) record a more positive view of Quiroga, in addition to other *caudillos* of the nation's past—José Artigas, Estanislao López, Martín Güemes, and Angel "El Chacho" Peñalosa. (It is important to note that these private views at no time translated into active, public support for the populist rebellions of Peñalosa and Felipe Varela during the decade of the 1860s.) These *caudillos*, because of their popularity among the masses, were for Alberdi "the product of the people, their most spontaneous and genuine personification." They constituted a veritable "democratic" force in their resistance to Buenos Aires's pretension to become the sole governing force for the entire country.[41]

Gutiérrez and López shared Alberdi's perspective; in a letter written to Pío José Tedín shortly after Quiroga's death, Gutiérrez described the *caudillo* as "a man who represents in word and deed the highest ambitions of the people of the interior."[42] In his widely read histories, López offered a dual perspective. On the one hand, Quiroga was a "Lucifer" in his early role as authoritarian leader of *montoneros* against unitarian armies; on the other, he was a moral icon, model husband and father, caste and incorruptable, who never betrayed an ally.[43] For López, Quiroga's politics after 1830 were equally commendable; the early *montonera* warrior later became a respected national peacemaker. With words and a vision resembling those of Rivadavia, Facundo's overriding ambition in the latter years of his life was the constitutional organization of the country; with his unrivaled prestige and force of character, he might have succeeded were his efforts not cut short by his tragic assassination in 1836.[44] About Sarmiento's libelous portrait of Facundo, both López and Gutiérrez reacted with predictable opposition. López called it "a Bedouin history" on account of Sarmiento's forced comparisons of Argentina with nomadic Africa. Gutiérrez was convinced "that the work will have a bad effect on the Argentine Republic, and any level-headed man will see in it a caricature."[45]

What is the significance of this pro-Quiroga perspective in the thought of these three key members of the 1837 generation? Undoubtedly this "view from the provinces" played a highly important role in the thought and activities of those heading up the anti-Rosas movement in Montevideo that sponsored the Lavalle campaign. Instrumental was their pan-Argentine consciousness that granted legitimacy to the organizing principles embraced by several *caudillo* leaders of the interior. Their receptivity to many of the tenets of the federalist creed, embraced by the majority population of the country's interior provinces, contrasted with the insular Porteño perspective of the exiled unitarian leaders.

ALEJANDRO HEREDIA: EARLY PROMOTER OF THE "FUSION" OF TENDENCIES

The extended focus on the constitutional pursuits of Facundo Quiroga in the latter years of his life runs the risk of magnifying beyond realistic proportions his importance in the national events of the 1830s. Our intention here has been to present his campaign for national unification not only as representative of a widespread sentiment of the time but also as influential in the developing world view of several of the 1837 militants. Alejandro Heredia was a disciple of Quiroga in the attempt to overcome historical rivalries and lay the foundations for a new era of peace and stability.

With the consolidation of federalist victories in 1831, a convocation of citizens in the Province of Tucumán elected Alejandro Heredia as governor. Since distinguishing himself earlier as a hero in the independence movement, Heredia had continually struggled on behalf of progressive causes in the north, while avoiding political entanglements. Like Pascual Echagüe, the governor of Entre Ríos during the same period,[46] he had pursued formal studies at the university level. Perhaps as a direct consequence, both governors surrounded themselves with a high caliber of advisors and attempted to improve social and educational institutions. Political reconciliation was also a high priority of Heredia. Early in his administration he decreed a general amnesty for political prisoners and invited a number of the province's principal families to return from Bolivian and Chilean exile. His foremost ambition was to unite the northern provinces under the authority of a written constitution. On this account one historian has called him the "political step-son" of Facundo Quiroga.[47]

Heredia was highly conscious of the need to involve the province's talented and educated youth in its government. He welcomed the contribution of the "dotores" of university extraction and did not fear the possible association of their Europeanized perspectives with regard to what the traditional federalists associated with the Unitarian Party. Impressed with the talents of the young Alberdi, who spent several weeks in the province during 1834, Heredia authorized him to practice law and offered him a position in the local legislature. (Alberdi, who already was projecting a more important role for himself in the public affairs of the country, gracefully declined both offers.) Heredia, in addition, facilitated Marco Avellaneda, Alberdi's companion of studies and an eminent and capable youth in his own right, to assume the prestigious position of leader in the provincial House of Representatives. In a similar fashion Marcos Paz, who would later become governor and then vice president of the nation, exercised his first important public functions as Heredia's private secretary and right-hand man in the unification politics with other northern provinces. Heredia attempted to go beyond the by then largely superseded rivalry between federalists and unitarians. In this light he was a precursor of the politics of fusion that would become a mainstay of the 1837 generation's program, and up until his death in 1839 he would collaborate with them in creating a power center in the north to rival Rosas's influence in the south.

The treatment of Alejandro Heredia by the nation's historians reveals the same patterns as that of Quiroga: provincial partisans and foes of Porteño domination have painted him as a regional hero, whereas the majority with Buenos Aires bias have granted him disdainful silence or a libelous legacy. A hateful biography of 1838 depicted the famous governor as a drunkard, impassioned gambler, and inept general.[48] Renowned historians Saldías, Zinny, and others have merely perpetuated these distortions. There even exists a 1903 novel that presents his character in a most negative light. Pro-Rosas writers cast an image of him as a destabilizing force due to his support for anarchistic unitarian militants.[49]

Among the writers of the young generation, Rivera Indarte, in Montevideo, disseminated a very negative perspective; V. F. López's exhaustive histories (he was known in some circles as a "unitarian" historian) hardly took Heredia into account except in the context of Heredia's personalistic domination over the northern provinces.[50] Surprising is López's complete silence about Heredia's links to Quiroga's politics on behalf of a constitution.

In contrast to these views, the enthusiasm for Heredia's politics on the part of other 1837 militants was early and contagious. Alberdi, first of all, was deeply indebted to Heredia—"he considered me like one of his family"—because of the general's early lessons in Latin, his generosity in providing for Alberdi's early schooling in Tucumán, and his facilitating the scholarship to study in Buenos Aires's Colegio de Ciencias Morales.[51] In 1832 Alberdi's brother, Felipe, a fervent supporter of Heredia's provincial government, enthused the students in Buenos Aires with information about Heredia's enlightened politics. In their short-lived newspaper of 1833, El amigo del país, (The friend of the country) Angel Navarro, Marco Avellaneda, and Juan María Gutiérrez called Heredia "the highest educated public figure of the period."[52] Months later Miguel Marín, M. Paz, Avellaneda, and Alberdi published a collection of verses, "Corona lírica" (Lirical crown), with a praise-filled dedication to Governor Heredia. Alberdi and those who were becoming his devoted followers—Avellaneda, Paz, Silva, Gutiérrez—never approved of Heredia's authoritarian mode of governing; they were entirely silent in their intimate correspondence about the general's apparently increasing dependence on alcohol. These young militants held great store for Heredia's apt and intelligent politics. Alberdi knew that Heredia, having met with Quiroga shortly before his violent death in 1835, shared many of the latter's hopes for the constitutional organization of the Republic. Alberdi's favorable view was fully echoed in Brígido Silva's letter on the occasion of a September 1836 visit with Heredia to Santiago de Estero in order to celebrate the friendly accord recently reached between that province and Tucumán. Silva expressed genuine enthusiasm for that "warrior of the Independence Movement and of philosophical reason who weighs the actions of men on the scale of justice and truth."[53] Alberdi, three years later, wrote to Heredia—a letter that arrived after the latter's assassination—urging his declaration of independence from the Buenos Aires despot.[54] Gutiérrez compared Heredia's 1839 assassination to Quiroga's a few years earlier: both men, he implied, were eliminated because of their nationalist politics.[55]

In short the 1837 militants emerged into public life under the influence of Heredia's (in addition to Quiroga's) politics of a "fusion" of ideological tendencies as a sine qua non for the country's unification under a federal constitution. After 1838, however, they would leave aside this peaceful pursuit in order to organize a military insurrection against the oppressive Rosas government. At that time their strategy to defeat Rosas militarily would depend upon the success of the insurrection in the North, led by Marco Avellaneda, whose objectives followed from the constitutional pursuits of that region's two recent martyrs, Facundo Quiroga and Alejandro Heredia.[56]

ROSAS'S PATH TO TYRANNY

The violent aftermath of Facundo's assassination brought to a close the period of calm that had been established at such a terrible cost only a few years earlier. Observers today have difficulty realizing the sense of collective trauma throughout the country that that event triggered off. The life and deeds of Facundo Quiroga were already the stuff of legend in his own time. He was one of the most feared, maligned, and respected leaders of his time whose influence stretched from point to point across the republic. Facundo, more than any individual since the independence period some twenty years earlier, had a legitimate claim to a truly national leadership. Few could ignore the draconian political implications of his violent death. Facundo had been the undisputed leader of the Federalist Party in the interior, and on the surface he was the most likely target of all for pent up Unitarian rage. Whether or not his murder was the result of such hatred is immaterial. Far more important was the fear that Juan Manuel Rosas, Buenos Aires strongman, was able to inspire among the frightened citizenry. Controlling the media and the sources of information, he played upon the idea that Quiroga's violent end was merely the prelude to the Unitarian Party's newest wave of terrorism. The unitarians, his followers warned, would overthrow existing authorities and implement their own vengeful plan for reshaping the country's institutions according to European objectives.

Nearly a decade before Rosas had first assumed power in Buenos Aires, following the successful pacification of the urban lower class and the forced restoration of peace and calm to the region. Then, a few years later, his highly successful Desert Campaign against the marauding Indian tribes along Argentina's western frontier secured a relative peace that was to last nearly two decades. As a result of that campaign, Rosas made available thousands of square kilometers of land for new settlements and the expansion of the country's prospering cattle industry. In the minds of the great majority of the population, the man had performed undeniable service to the region and the country, and fully deserved the nickname popularly bestowed upon him: *El Restaurador de las Leyes* (The restorer of the law).

Conditions were also right for Rosas to consolidate his stabilizing, iron-handed influence over the rest of the provinces. The confederation of autonomous provinces had granted him little formal authority other than that of conducting the region's foreign affairs on behalf of their collective interests. Yet because he headed the richest and most populated province and controlled the customs house—which was the primary income source in the region—Rosas had been able to exercise considerable influence over the other provinces. By the middle of the 1830s, Rosas had nearly achieved, through extraofficial channels, what several other governments centered in Buenos Aires during the preceding twenty years had only dreamed could be possible: the near universal recognition of Buenos Aires authority—in well-defined areas, at least—over the rest of the provinces.

Following Facundo's violent death in 1834, Rosas successfully played upon the widespread fears in order to manipulate his return to power, again with full dictatorial powers. His politics prioritized national interests, although European—predominantly British—commercial interests continued to prosper under his firm hand. He dissolved the National Bank which had caused the nation's indebtedness to Great Britain. More important was the passage of protectionist measures, banning key imports and taxing others, that had an immediate effect on fortifying the economy of the interior. The legislature of Salta declared that "no government in Buenos Aires up to the present, whether national or provincial, compares with the present one in providing for the well being of the provinces of the interior."[57] The legislators of Tucumán were in agreement: the Rosas regime "has dismantled the harmful economic system that led the republic to the brink of misery." Even Sarmiento, in *Facundo*, would signal his general agreement: "The dictator we could do without, but the dictatorship has done well for the country."

In the political realm Rosas continued with his repressive tactics, establishing new prohibitions for the press and reactivating the *mazorca*, his secret police. His 1835 proclamation resembled a declaration of war against his enemies:

> *Let us resolve*, then, to combat with courage those wicked men who have sown confusion in our land; LET US PURSUE TO THE DEATH those who are

impious and sacrilegious, the robber and the killer and, above all, the disloyal traitor who has the audacity to mock our good faith.

Let us resolve that none of this race of monsters shall survive among us, and that our persecution of them be tenacious and vigorous, *that it terrify and frighten all the rest who might come along in the future. Let us not fear any class of danger, nor should we hesitate to implement any means that we decide upon for pursuing them.*[58]

Rosas made it clear that political or regional conciliation was no longer the order of the day. The threat to the social order was real; in this light he justified an end to discussions about national organization. This verbal wrath was soon born out in acts: the execution of two soldiers accused of plotting his assassination, the forced retirement of dozens of functionaries and 155 militia officers who were suspected of harboring Unitarian sympathies, the implementation of a loyalty oath for university graduates, and a new wave of demagoguery in the press, for example, "Federation or Death!" "Long live the federalists!" and "Death to the unitarians!"[59]

The political program of interparty harmony and national conciliation that the young militants articulated several months later was, in the first instance, an attempt to build upon the good will that had become manifest throughout the country before the untimely assassination of Facundo Quiroga. But their views of 1837 must also be seen as a condemnation of the country's new descent into repression and Rosas's latest impediments to the nation's definitive organization.

THE YOUNG GENERATION'S CALL TO INVOLVEMENT

In 1833 the country's tempestuous political struggle again touched university life in Buenos Aires.[60] Federalist citizens there protested the attempts by Unitarian governor Juan José Viamonte to reinstitute some of the policies that had been in force during the innovative Rivadavia administrations more than a decade before. Viamonte subsequently was forced to resign and leaders of the Rosas faction returned to power. Several months later Valentín Alsina, respected professor of Natural Law and unitarian activist, resigned under increasing pressure. Other professors who refused to swear allegiance to the Federalist Party soon followed. Pressure was particularly intense on Diego Alcorta, professor of philosophy in the Department of Preparatory Studies, who was known for his liberal ideas and his vote in the legislature against granting Rosas dictatorial powers. Years later his former students would remember with unanimous veneration the preponderant influence of

Alcorta, that "teacher of the spirit" who had exercised so much influence over their developing notions of justice and liberty.[61]

In January 1836 university students were subjected to increased political pressure when the government imposed a loyalty oath for any prospective graduate. This did not cause undue suffering because most unitarian activists years before had fled to Montevidean exile. Nor had cause yet arisen for the younger generation to demonstrate open hostility to the party in power. Several members of the young generation received their degrees: Mariano E. de Sarratea, in 1836; the next year Benito Carrasco, Miguel Estévez Saguí, Enrique de la Fuente, Vicente Fidel López, Manuel José Quiroga Rosas, Jacinto Rodríguez Peña, and Carlos Tejedor, all in law. In 1838 Luis Méndez and Santiago Viola would join that list, as would Miguel Irigoyen in 1839 and Rafael J. Corvalán in 1852. Rounding out the list of this generational grouping were the names of those who had graduated before the federalist clampdown: José Barros Pazos, in 1831; Antonino Aberastain, in 1832; Brígido Silva and Pío José Tedín, in 1832; and Marco Avellaneda, Juan María Gutiérrez, Carlos H. Eguía, Demetrio Rodríguez Peña, and Andrés Somellera, in 1835. The most prominent name missing here was that of Juan Bautista Alberdi who, due to his repugnance for the personality of the dictator, renounced whatever pretensions he had for receiving his law degree at that time.

Educational experiences were not limited to university classrooms. These individuals began to study, with attention, the revolutionary magazines from Paris that contained provocative writings by Fortoul, Cousin, Chateaubriand, Dumas, Quinet, Lerminier, Saint Simon, Guizot, Leroux, Jouffroy, Scott, Staël, Sand, Villemain, Byron, Nisard, Lamennais, Hugo, and Tocqueville. In addition, the new availability of journals such as Revue des Deux Mondes (Magazine of two worlds) and Revue de Paris (Magazine of Paris) was changing the reading habits among the learned class throughout the city. New bookstores were established: from five in 1830 to double that number by 1836. In the words of V. F. López, the young university students developed a truly "intense attraction for the ideas and learned opinions over schools and authors . . . our spirit took wing toward what we believed were the heights."[62]

In addition to the rapid increase in the commerce of books and magazines and the circulation of ideas, there were unmistakable signs that the creative and critical impulses of Buenos Aires's own population were, for the first time, blossoming. Chronologically it was Echeverría who inaugurated this new stage in 1832 with the publication of Elvira o la novia del Plata (Elvira or the bride of the Plata Region). Other young writers, eager to exercise their critical skills, wrote about this work in the first studies of literary criticism to be published in the newspapers of the Plata region. Echeverría then cemented his leadership of this suddenly vitalized cultural environment with the publication of a book of poems, *Los consuelos* (Consolances), toward the end of 1834. This was the first poetry of overtly romantic orientation ever published in the region. Echeverría, appealing to the authority of Byron, Goethe, Chateaubriand, and A. March, provided an accurate characterization of this poetic effort: with "lugubrious tone," the "fleeting melodies" of his poetic lyre consoled the sad or suffered reader. The critical note accompanying the poetic collection contained another first: Echeverría's call for the creation of a national literature based on the country's unique customs, predominant ideas, and social types. His *La cautiva* (The captive), a few years hence, was his first attempt to incarnate these ideas in poetic practice.

At about the same time, other writers did their part to revitalize the cultural environment that had been dormant for years. They represented the gamut of intellectual and ideological tendencies, and their topics were diverse. In 1833 General Tomás de Iriarte published the two-volume Spanish translation to a work on moral education: *Cartas escritas por el muy honorable Felipe Dormer Stanhope, conde de Chesterfield* (Letters written by the very honorable Felipe Dormer Stanhope, count of Chesterfield). Pedro José Agrelo came out with his *Memorial ajustado* (Mediated memorial) which dealt with the rights of property owners in relation to sharecroppers and employees. Father Calixto Hornero published the *Gramática latina* (Latin grammar). Important for its impact upon the deliberations of the 1837 youths at the time was the Spanish translation of Víctor Cousin's *Curso de historia de la filosofía* (Course on history of philosophy). José Rivera Indarte came out with a polemical essay, *El voto de América* (The vote in America), which examined the issue of the relationship between the realist government in Madrid and its former colonies in the Americas. Pedro de Angelis, Spanish émigré and future intellectual mainstay of the Rosas regime, published two important collections of documents relevant to the early history of the region. This sampling from the works published during a three-year span gives an idea of the excitement of the period when, after several tortuous decades of civil turmoil, the nation's creative energies again could focus on estimable cultural pursuits.

During these years of university study, the members of the young generation still had time to involve themselves in the rejuvenated cultural dialogue. In December 1834 Alberdi published a short lyrical essay, *Memoria descriptiva sobre Tucumán* (Descriptive memory of Tucuman), that exemplified the new aesthetic and cultural doctrines that Echeverría was promoting. This short work hardly commands the interest of the contemporary reader except that it demonstrates the evolving consciousness of Alberdi at this early point in his career. Perhaps most important was his thesis about the formative influence of nature and society over the values of a people, an idea that would be further developed in his later writings. The essay was Alberdi's imperfect attempt to heed the romantic call to turn away from the themes of classical antiquity and focus lyrical attention on the beauty of his own surroundings. But Alberdi only half succeeded in this venture; although the object of poetic attention was the new-world environment of Tucumán, the lyrical instruments at his command harkened back to the traditional practices of the neoclassical school. Through his stiff and stylized descriptions, Alberdi pleaded the case for the "tender abandonment" of strict classical norms. In their place Alberdi would substitute the prose of romantic melancholy, as exemplified in the writings of M. de Staël, Chateaubriand, Hugo, and Lamartine.

There were other participants in the movement to promote a national cultural expression. Vicente Fidel López spent several months assisting law professor Dalmacio Vélez Sársfield in the preparation of several scholarly books for publication; later he would be named professor of philosophy following the resignation of his mentor, Diego Alcorta. Alberdi, meanwhile, found an outlet for his developing social and political thought in his publication of a pamphlet refuting several key ideas in Rivera Indarte's *Voto de América* (Vote of America). Gutiérrez's early interest in literary studies found expression in an article published in *El museo americano* (The American museum), a Buenos Aires journal of short duration. Shortly thereafter he became the principal writer for *El recopilador* (The digest). This cultural journal, of impressive quality, gave preference to critical articles by the country's growing ranks of writers who shared the editorial team's objective of "promoting the fine arts of our nascent society, because the arts open the doors to the sciences."[63] Among the most memorable of the articles published here was that written by Juan Thompson with the title, "Poetry and music among us."

Rivaling the importance of these early efforts to construct a critical theory linking cultural pursuits with the material improvement of society were the young generation's contributions in the fields of poetry and literary criticism. Toward the end of September 1837, Echeverría's long awaited work, *Rimas* (Rhymes), was published. The work contained, among other pieces, *La cautiva* (The captive) and several important essays on literary theory. This long narrative poem, perhaps the best that he would write during his short but intense career as poet and before his untimely death in 1851, had an immediate and exuberant impact on the small circle of readers in Buenos Aires. The critical judgment of Gutiérrez was entirely correct: the passionate treatment of the country's natural setting and conflict between European and indigenous races

constituted a foundation pillar for a future national literature.[64] Bartolomé Mitre, at only sixteen, published in Montevideo a critical study in
which he predicted that "the author of *La cautiva* has demonstrated that
he is capable of launching a literary revolution."[65]

EL SALÓN LITERARIO

The important gatherings of many of the members of the young generation in Marcos Sastre's Salón Literario (Literary salon) during the
early months of 1837 were preceded by several other attempts at association.[66] Such was the case of the Asociación de estudios históricos y
sociales (Association of Historical Studies), that López and Cané established in 1832. Each Saturday one of the members would make a presentation on a topic of historical interest—for example, Alexander the Great
or the Spanish playwright Martínez de la Rosa—and the others would
then criticize its content or the mode of presentation. They dissolved
the group in 1835 as a precautionary measure when Rosas began his
second term as governor, this time with absolute powers conferred on
him by the legislature. The times were not propitious for such public
gatherings, even though the topics discussed were hardly of a political
nature.

However the growing uneasiness did not interfere with more informal
encounters. At about this time Alberdi and Gutiérrez began meeting
with Echeverría—their senior by several years—in order to study the
ideas that the latter had learned during his five-year sojourn in Paris.
This deepening friendship paralleled a growing ideological bond; over
the next two decades, when weighty issues would divide the young
militants, these three individuals would, as a rule, stand together.

The government's brief relaxation of repressive measures a year later
provided a new opportunity for intellectual dialogue. At this time Marcos Sastre, having recently enlarged his bookstore and increased its
holdings, invited the reading community to form the Salón Literario as
a forum for discussing new ideas and orienting the budding intelligence
of Buenos Aires's most promising youth.

Sastre, born in 1808, was one of several Uruguayans (Andrés Lamas,
Wenceslao Paunero, and Juan Carlos Gómez were three others) who
was to play a protagonist role along side of the Argentine militants
under study. Information is sketchy about his life. Sastre had been a
precursor in Montevideo's campaign for popular education and the instruction of women. An early publication evidenced the man's fervent
religious orientation and his dedication to the study of classical lan-
guages and culture.[67] Discontented over the political instability in Mon-

tevideo, Sastre moved to Buenos Aires in 1833. There his highly successful bookstore led to the establishment of a Gabinete de Lectura (Salon of reading) to propagate what Sastre advertised as "the best works that one could desire for forming a library of good taste, with up to three thousand volumes."[68] His activities attracted numerous participants from the university community, among them Alberdi, López, and Gutiérrez. The success of his ventures motivated Sastre to relocate the Librería Argentina to an even more spacious facility on Victoria Street in June 1836 and to found the Salón Literario. By that year Sastre, a largely self-educated man, had become one of the city's principal suppliers of books and a leading authority on the writings and ideas then in vogue in European intellectual circles.

The initial plans for the Salón Literario emerged from informal conversations between Sastre and the two most spirited members of the student group: Alberdi and Gutiérrez. These three projected a primarily moral and pedagogical function for the new organization. As Sastre stated in his inaugural address, his sponsorship was done out of "the love of wisdom, out of the desire for perfecting its instruction, or for contributing to the learning of Argentina's youth."[69]

All three of the inaugural speeches by Sastre, Alberdi, and Gutiérrez stressed similar points. First, they emphasized their country's inevitable progress because of its participation in a universal historical process. Second, they highlighted the need for the educated members of their community to study the most prestigious thinkers of Europe's intellectual tradition as a means for better inserting their country into that providential system of progress; the writers they singled out for special attention were Herder, Vico, Jouffroy, Condillac, and Cousin. Third, all three speakers mentioned the special role of philosophical or literary pursuits in the improvement of morality, which was, in its turn, a key factor in society's advancement. In this regard Sastre and Gutiérrez singled out certain authors of the Romantic canon: Byron, Lamartine, and Chateaubriand.

A fourth issue of generational agreement was the very negative contribution they accredited to their country's Spanish colonial experience. In particular they emphasized the colonial legacy of weak social institutions and the population's ignorance and inexperience in republican practices. Most surprising were Gutiérrez's strident words that contrast with his discreet, scholarly views on other topics. Echeverría, speaking on this same issue a few months later, more generously conceded that no American community had been better prepared for self-governance than Argentina: "Our society then was homogenious; there were neither classes nor hierarchies; nor were there vices nor deeply rooted prejudices; it exemplified Rousseau's ideal community, with its 'consciousness of an ancient community, but with the docility of a new one.'"[70] Although not denying Spain's legacy of underdevelopment, Echeverría argued that present problems were due more to what had occurred in Argentina since its glorious May Revolution of 1811.

A fifth and last area of convergence was that all three speakers urged their countrymen to channel Europe's scientific, philosophical, and literary ideas toward the larger goal of understanding their own country, its people, and institutions. The study of the characteristic features of the region would help them in improving laws and institutions and in developing human and natural resources to their fullest.

In spite of this common substratum of ideas and orientations, there were a few key differences of perspective in the inaugural addresses presented to the Salón Literario. These differences help to explain the rapid demise of the group within a matter of months and the near total break in communications that would occur between Sastre and the trio of Echeverría, Alberdi, and Gutiérrez. Most important in this regard was Sastre's unmediated praise for Rosas. His call for *realism* was, in fact, a call to celebrate Rosas's success in restoring peace and order to the country. That accomplishment "ought to fill with satisfaction any honorable man and lover of social order; it ought to make all men appreciate our epoch and hold high expectations for the Government; it ought to inspire all to support it and assist it, so that each would contribute in his own way to the common goal of national prosperity."[71] Related to this was his repeated exhortation to the youths present—some of whom already must have been considering a forceful response to Rosas's growing tyranny—to accept the principle of peaceful progress. These adulatory words about Rosas surely rubbed some of the more tempered sensitivities the wrong way. Cané, for example, wrote to Alberdi from Montevideo saying that absolutely nobody there liked the speech by Sastre: "On the basis of his speech, Sastre's thought is not appropriate to the needs of our times; he has such a weak, common spirit; his ideas are cold, frozen. His goals are good, but the means he suggests for achieving them are bad, really bad."[72] In retrospect these views anticipated Sastre's situation in the next decade and a half. After the closure of his bookstore and dissolution of the Salón Literario, he retired to the countryside to raise sheep. After a few years in Santa Fe, he moved to Entre Ríos in 1849 where Justo José Urquiza, then governor, appointed him to the position of general inspector for schools. Back in Buenos Aires after the fall of Rosas, he, along with López and Gutiérrez, would unsuccessfully oppose the movement for succession led by Mitre. Féliz Weinberg's recent condemnation of Sastre on account of a reputed "most extreme xenofobia"[73] does not do justice to his distinguished service on behalf of public education,[74] several important writings on pedagogical issues, and a significant contribution to the literature of the region.[75]

It is also possible that Sastre's ideas did not cause an immediate parting of the ways. His apologetic position in front of the Rosas government was repeated in Alberdi's address to that same body and in his *Fragmento preliminar al estudio del derecho* (Preliminary sketch for the study of law) that would circulate widely within days after the Salón's inauguration. Indeed the pro-Rosas stance of both Alberdi and Sastre was representative of the state of mind of perhaps a majority of the younger generation at the time.

ALBERDI'S *FRAGMENTO*

In this important work Alberdi outlined a general philosophy of society and government that, when applied to his own country, accounted for his surprising affirmation of the Rosas's contributions—surprising because within months the same Alberdi would emerge as the leader of the group of young militants in Montevideo who wanted the forceful removal of Rosas from power. In this 1837 essay he argued that a government's form was normally the result of the majority population's interests and sentiments; it naturally responded to the moral and intellectual situation of that country.[76] As a corollary he argued that only those social or political changes with significant popular support had any chance of succeeding; foreign theories, or changes imposed over an unwilling majority (as the Unitarian Party had attempted) would not survive for the simple reason that they did not respond to widely felt needs. Accordingly Alberdi judged that Rosas's effectiveness as the country's de facto leader was due not only to the harmonious relationship between his political power and the region's predominant economic interests—a factor painfully lacking in the unitarian administrations preceding him—but also to his knack of faithfully interpreting the will of the masses.

Alberdi's *Fragmento* had much in common with another important work written by fellow university student, Manuel José Quiroga Rosas, titled *Tesis sobre la naturaleza filosófica del derecho* (Thesis on the philosophical nature of law). Although Alberdi's was by far the more important, the two works shared basic characteristics: both writers, with youthful optimism, turned a deaf ear to the country's recent history of civil strife and the growing disorder in Buenos Aires's social and political spheres; both traced their intellectual genealogies to the principal European theorists then in vogue, that is, Jouffroy, Condorcet, Leroux, Vico, Herder, and Lerminier; and Alberdi deferred especially to perspectives of Bentham and Montesquieu, while Quiroga Rosas's maximum model was Saint-Simon. Following this latter influence both argued for the central role of philosophical speculation, in that it assisted society's leaders in devising pragmatic means for satisfying material needs and perfecting social and political institutions. Both thinkers called attention to the glaring need of their moment: an independence of the intellect. The key in achieving this was the study and then critical reflection over the new American republics' natural environment and unique cultural attributes. Alberdi's maxim read: "We must first define a philosophy before we can hope to achieve a nationality."[77]

It was, therefore, necessary to leave aside the previous generation's doctrinaire intent to impose governmental structures upon an unreceptive reality. The unitarian constitution of 1820, like others preceding it, was admirable in theory, but it hardly took into account the particularities of the country. It was based—in the words of Alberdi—on "exotic forms" that ignored "the new order" of the new country.[78] Alberdi, in contrast, urged a new constitution that took into account the particular values and cultural orientations of the country's people, the nature of their institutions, and the way they organized society. This was the meaning of his argument for the conquest of "a national consciousness."[79]

Following that line of reasoning, Rosas, with his popularity at its zenith, was far more representative of the country than the exiled leaders of the Unitarian Party. "Rosas, considered philosophically, is not a despot who sleeps under the shadow of foreign bayonets. On the contrary, he is a leader who can rest tranquilly each night knowing that his government responds in good faith to the concerns closest to the people's hearts."[80] Realism spilled into adulation in Alberdi's address to the Salón Literario; Rosas was a "genius" and "an extraordinary man," because of his accurate understanding of the country's condition and possibilities and his ability to create viable political structures on the basis of that knowledge.[81] Alberdi implied that one did not need brilliant theories of government in order to succeed at governing. One needed, first and foremost, to know one's people and their needs. This romantic admonition had potentially conservative implications. It anticipated his views of a decade hence when he again would affirm that leaders such as Rosas, who enjoyed the support of the masses, were the ultimate arbitrators over the choices that had to be made about society's development.

Alberdi's "philosophical" interpretation of *rosismo* had another implication that would not escape the notice of his critics only a few years later, that is, his apparently pacifist orientation. Democratic institutions, he argued, were the product of decades of social interaction; they could hardly be implanted overnight under the authority of the sword. For that reason any recourse to violence against an existing government and abrupt attempts to impose political forms and social structures were counterproductive; there was no substitute for society's slow transition in ideas and customs. Those individuals committed to bringing about social change could not ignore the overriding importance of the "intimate, moral revolution"—the slow change in a people's values and habits—that had to take place before any alteration of institutional and governmental forms could be seriously considered.[82]

Alberdi's views, as expressed in both his inaugural address to the Salón Literario and in *Fragmento,* were destined to spark adverse reactions from several of his compatriots. Avellaneda and Cané, his closest friends, only called attention to the difficulty they and others had in understanding his ideas.[83] Florencio Varela, heading Rosas's unitarian opposition in Montevideo, was more severe in his criticisms. For Varela, Alberdi's attempt at dialogue with the Federalist Party, in addition to his praise of Rosas, was evidence of his very mistaken politics.[84] In the same vein Andrés Lamas reproached Alberdi's mistaken priorities in seeking a philosophical justification for Rosism: "a genius who recurs to fetters and shackles, is not an American genius. . . . We have not broken the chains that tied us to the lion of Castille in order for our necks to receive the yoke of one whose criminal feet stand over the lascerated bossom of the homeland, of one who imposes upon us a tranquility more appropriate for slaves."[85] Months later, after he himself passed to Montevidean exile, Alberdi would affirm, both through writings and acts, his basic agreement with these penetrating words.

ECHEVERRÍA: LEADER OF THE SALÓN LITERARIO

In the inaugural session of the Salón Literario, Echeverría had no public role, but it is evident from Sastre's remarks that he had been consulted about the organization's activities. Yet his absence was striking because he was, beyond dispute, the foremost poet of the city and the country. Similarly no one could rival his familiarity with the most advanced philosophical and literary tendencies of the period which he had acquired during his five years of study in the intellectual capital of Europe.

After his return to Argentina in 1830, Echeverría's circle of personal relations was never extensive. He offered an enigmatic presence. On the one hand, there was the image of the guitarist, skilled in the traditional music of the region and a writer of verses. Although he had extensive European training with the refined *vihuela,* he was more known for his prowess with the guitar. Contemporaries have left a record of his encyclopedic familiarity with folk music and forms. Gutiérrez, furthermore, called attention to Echeverría's penchant for displaying his musical talents in lower-class bars and *pulperías* (country stores) in the outlying neighborhoods of the city. Sarmiento, in 1845, was to add to this image of Echeverría as the guitarist of the masses; when the poet-guitarist resided in the countryside, "the gauchos would gather around him with respect and affection."[86] Members of Buenos Aires's prominent families surely raised their eyebrows over Echeverría's musical activities in such unrefined circumstances; their values relative to class and race led them to disdain any individual, especially one from their own circle, who actively sought out such lowly social contacts.

Contrasting with the image of *cantor para los gauchos* was the rival perspective of Echeverría as refined and melancholic poet with a marked sense of superiority and even snobbery. Contemporaneous observers described him as broody and standoffish. This attitude derived, in part, from his debilitating physical ailments and neurasthenic tendencies.[87] In Gutiérrez's sympathetic description Echeverría projected a self-image of refinement because of his fine Parisian clothing and his repeated gesture of lifting a gold-rimmed monocle to the eye in order to recognize a passerby on the street.[88] In many regards he was the paradigmatic Latin American poet, whose refined tastes and sensitive manner clashed with an underdeveloped surrounding. Echeverría provided a description of this anguish: "The degrading opposition to progress in my country, and my hopes ridiculed, produced in me a profound melancholy."[89]

In 1837 Echeverría's friendship with Alberdi and Gutiérrez provided new opportunities to overcome self-imposed isolation. With his recent poetic triumphs, he now enjoyed respect throughout the university community and the educated sector of the population. The opinion was widespread that without his leadership the enterprises of the newly established Salón Literario would not rise above a mediocre level. This was the sentiment behind Sastre's letter in which he invited Echeverría to assume the leadership of that group:

I believe, Mr. Echeverría, and I would venture to declare publically, that you are the appropriate person to preside and guide the development of intelligent minds in this country. . . . The moment is upon you, with your gift of the word, literary credentials, and young age, to put promptly into action your powerful resources. Don't be immobilized by the criticism or false doctrines of those who, jealous of your talents, are unworthy to grasp the scepter of knowledge. You are the indicated person, don't doubt it: my intervention in this matter has as its sole objective to persuade you to assume the leadership of this Establishment.[90]

Although accounts differ Echeverría apparently accepted this invitation, and he subsequently presented two addresses that impressed many because of his "innovative proposals."[91] In truth Echeverría seized on this occasion to demonstrate a new aspect of his multifaceted character that would earn only the highest praise from his contemporaries: that of a penetrating social analyst who was fully capable of providing solid directions for the country's renovation. Absent here was any trace of the melancholic, subjective effusions that had characterized his lyrical prose. Similarly absent were the flowery, rhetorical abstractions that would abound in his *Dogma socialista* (socialist dogma) a few years hence. No writing by Echeverría up to that moment had given any hint of the weighty political and sociological concerns that he would now address.

The first lecture focused on the topic of the country's weak intellectual tradition.[92] Echeverría believed that the country's descent into instability and civil war in the years after independence was due primarily to its leaders' lack of "talent, ideas." Their vague or erroneous ideas had produced moral anarchy which then led to the release of destructive passions and the reign of anarchy.[93] The miserable living conditions of the masses were rooted in a similar cause; the country's ruling class had not known how to improve their material welfare and raise their level of awareness through education. In order for the country to emerge from the present quagmire, Echeverría prescribed two activities for its educated minorities. First, they needed to assimilate the most worthy ideas of the prestigious European tradition; and second, they had to critically reflect on that learning in relation to the needs and situation of their own society.

Although his first lecture was well in keeping with the moral and pedagogical orientation that Sastre, Alberdi, and Gutiérrez had unanimously urged for the Salón a few months earlier, his second ventured into areas untouched until then: the political economy of the Plata region and the desirable role of government in guiding its development. Realistically he understood that Argentina's primary contribution in the developing world economy was cattle production (Sarmiento, in contrast, would argue for the substitution of the "barbaric" cattle industry with a "civilization"-linked agriculture). However the cattle industry, at the time, enjoyed only a precarious prosperity because existing markets for its jerked beef and hides required only the lowest grade of cattle and hardly offered an incentive for the improvement of breeding and feeding practices. Echeverría argued that the producers, and therefore the country as a whole, would benefit from the application of science and technology. Intelligent governmental action could dramatically improve the region's primary industry; it could also provide legal protections for rural workers and the means for agricultural producers to gain land ownership and credit.

Echeverría contradicted Sastre's adulatory posture by arguing that the country as a whole had not benefited under Rosas and the federalists in government. He suggested that the present regime had continually ignored the long-term welfare of the people in its most important actions. A recent tax passed by the Rosas-dominated legislature had been "monstrously unjust" because its burden fell primarily on those less able to pay. The regime's laws and land policies favored only the rich. It had done "nothing, absolutely nothing" on behalf of the poor, except treat them as inferior beings or servants. In the area of morality, the Rosas regime's abuses were even greater:

> Equality was proclaimed, but the most flagrant inequality has reigned: liberty was shouted, but it has only existed for a certain number of individuals; laws have been passed, and these have only protected the rich and powerful. The poor have no protecting laws, nor do they have justice or individual rights; only violence, an order imposed by the saber, persecutions, injustices.[94]

The intent of Echeverría's words must have been clear to all: by discrediting the Rosas administration, he hoped to incite the youths to civic action. To Echeverría's credit his unambiguous position with regard to the regime in power anticipated the break that was, in the eyes of many, inevitable.

Through these two speeches Echeverría cemented his leadership position over the young group of militants, who were more and more convinced that the situation required them to organize an opposition to Rosas's authority. Alberdi led the way. Although the newspapers he edited would lavish praise on the dictator during the next few months, he was coming to the realization that Rosas had no intention of lifting his repressive measures. Much the same could be said of Gutiérrez, López, and the others. During the previous months they had all learned from Echeverría's inherently romantic view of social and political issues. They accepted his tutelage and imitated his Jacobin rhetoric in defense of the common man. They also internalized Echeverría's romantic thirst for confrontation and shared his idealism in their willingness to challenge any aspect of reality that did not rise up to their high measure. They shared his awareness that they, the country's energetic youth, had the obligation of rebelling against archaic forms. In short Echeverría succeeded in instilling in them the outrage in front of injustices and the commitment to struggle on behalf of social, economic, and political change.

JOVEN ARGENTINA AND THE CREENCIA

The Salón Literario, with its very diverse membership, was not destined to last. One observer stated: "In short, the lack of friendship ties among the participants is one more factor that leads me to predict the dissolution of that society. Gutiérrez could never be a sincere friend of Sastre. . . . Sastre mocks the writings of Gutiérrez, can't stand any mention of Echeverría's poems, and follows the general opinion with regard to Alberdi."[95] In addition to these personality conflicts, several participants had qualms about the pragmatic concerns of its new leader, Echeverría, and protested against the implicit anti-Rosas directions that he signaled for the group's future deliberations. The serious ideological differences separating Sastre from Echeverría, or Alberdi from the pro-Rosas intellectual, Pedro de Angelis, were public knowledge. Sastre, in contrast to the student group, had an inherently conservative and even reactionary orientation. In spite of his bookish interests and his support for the new ideas of the period, he was a man of limited understanding who was guided by strong prejudices.

There were also generational differences; the rebellious student majority had little to learn from the venerated, but conservative Vicente López y Planes. López himself later articulated some of these differences in a letter to his son, Vicente Fidel: "Is it possible that we [of the older generation] still preserve the moral juices from old doctrines learned under the sweet influences [sic] of unperturbed peace, whereas with you [members of the young generation] the voracious workings of revolution have dried them up?"[96] In truth the most ambitious youths were already becoming involved in secret conspiracies aimed at toppling the Rosas regime. Alberdi succinctly wrote: "The Salón Literario was destined to disappear: because it was an open assembly."[97]

Echeverría's challenges and the differences in orientation merely hastened the inevitable. In spite of Alberdi's and Sastre's adulatory words, the dictator increased his pressure. Sastre was forced to close his meeting rooms and auction off his books, and the Salón Literario ceased to meet. According to V. F. López, "Everything else considered, the members of the Salón wrote little, read much, and talked even more."[98]

Meanwhile there were other attempts to activate the stale intellectual environment of Rosas's Buenos Aires. Since the early months of 1837, Alberdi had been searching for ways to instruct the public in the progressive ideas that were then current in Europe. After one failed effort he and Rafael Jorge Corvalán, son of a trusted aide in Rosas's administration, began publishing La moda (Fashion) in November 1837. Alberdi was the main inspiration and driving force, as well as the principal writer. The paper also counted on the collaboration of Gutiérrez, V. F. López, Carlos Tejedor, the brothers Demetrio and Jacinto Rodríguez Peña, Carlos Eguía, Manuel Quiroga Rosas, and José Barros Pazos.

La moda, with its calculated "frivolity," had the larger goal of instructing the reading public in progressive ideas. Its first issue was faithful to the editors' promise of treating issues related to fashion with articles dealing with the latest dress styles in Paris and Buenos Aires, new musical tendencies, and costumbrista essays about daily life. In this issue Alberdi's literary pseudonym, Figarillo, first came to grace the pages of Buenos Aires's cultural life. This name, which paid homage to Spain's great *costumbrista* (custom sketches) writer and critic of customs, Mariano José de Larra, quickly became associated with Alberdi's penetrating powers of observation and fine worldly humor. *La moda*'s second issue featured quotes from Fourtoul, Leroux, and Béranger; Italian patriot Mazzini was presented as "the thirty-year-old collosus, head of Young Europe." Future issues mentioned the names of Larra, Hugo, Saint-Simon, Quinet, Schlegel, Lerminier, Jouffroy, Lamartine, Stäel, Chateaubriand, Scott, Vigney, and others.

This surreptitious attempt at infusing the intellectual environment with progressive ideas was not necessarily motivated by anti-Rosas politics. Indeed it seems evident that the editors of *La moda* made serious attempts, if not to please the Rosas regime, then at least to not provoke further friction. Every issue, without exception, was headed by the slogan, "Long live the Federation." Furthermore praise for Rosas in the different issues was well in line with what Alberdi had expressed months earlier in his *Fragmento* and had stated in his inaugural speech before the Salón Literario. Notable, also, was the total absence of any mention of Echeverría in its pages—an understandable omission in the light of Echeverría's provocative words to the Salón Literario a few months before. After a few weeks of publication, the government ordered the shutdown of the journal; Rosas had not seen fit to impose a similar form of censorship on any other organ of the press. Yet there were no sanctions imposed on the journal's organizers. During the next few months, they were able to continue uninhibited with their activities. But the message was clear: Rosas desired no dialogue whatsoever with the reform-bent militants of the young generation.

Meanwhile Echeverría's inspiring words to the Salón Literario circulated in manuscript form and were having their desired effect. The time was ripe to constitute a new (this time secret) association of those embracing a more activist orientation. This new group would be modeled after those existing across France and in the city-states of what was soon to become Italy. It would have two primary goals: the promotion of progressive ideas and the unification of its membership behind a common program for the country's social and political renewal.

A group of some thirty-five youths clandestinely gathered on the night of June 23, 1838 to constitute La Joven Argentina[99] (Young Argentina) which, some eight years later, Echeverría would rebaptize as the Asociación de Mayo (May Association).[100] There was no indication of a continuing disagreement between Alberdi and Echeverría about collaborating with the Rosas government; on the contrary the two were now of one mind about the need to organize a political opposition. At that meeting the *Creencia* (creed), which highlighted the fifteen "Symbolic Faith Words of the Young Generation," was read and formally adopted as ideological and spiritual inspiration for the group's activities.

The *Creencia* (also referred to as *El código*—the code) was published in *El iniciador* (The initiator) of Montevideo in January 1839 and a month later in an insert of *El nacional* (The national), of that same city. Echeverría was the primary author, with Alberdi writing the brief section that discussed the need for the nation's leaders to follow a program reflecting a fusion of both unitarian and federalist tendencies.[101] In 1846 Echeverría would make minor revisions and then republish the document as an essay of eighty-six pages, renaming it *El dogma socialista* (Socialist dogma) and preceding it with an even longer introduction titled *Ojeada retrospectiva sobre el movimiento intelectual en el Plata desde el año 37* (A brief retrospective consideration of intellectual activity in the region since 1837).

The *Creencia* has elicited a range of reactions from the critics. On the one hand some have minimized its importance by pointing out that it was little more than a rhetorical and philosophical exposition of the "generous and vague" maxims found in Joseph Mazzini's *Young Europe*.[102] Other critics, however, have highlighted the document's "complete originality" in the country's intellectual and political history.[103] Both views are essentially correct but for different reasons.

Contemporary readers have difficulty appreciating the ceremonial function of the document's heavy, dramatic language and quasi-"religious" tone.[104] During his half-decade in Europe, Echeverría had become familiar with the secret societies that were then organizing in youthful revolutionary circles. Similar societies would be promoted by the transcendentalist followers of Ralph Waldo Emerson in the United States and would figure prominently in the Italian independence struggle as well as the European revolutions of 1848. The secret pledges of those groups generally highlighted symbolic or rhetoric flourishes at the expense of conceptual preciseness. Their function was to unite the membership around a coherent set of principles.

Also anachronistic to contemporary consciousness is the *Creencia*'s rarified philosophical idealism. Undoubtedly Echeverría's objective was to provide the young militants with spiritual guidance in their labors to create a democratic society incarnating the most advanced principles of his liberal age. As such moral and pedagogical issues accounted for more than half of the total number of "Words": Association, Progress, Fraternity, Equality, Liberty, Honor and Sacrifice, Compatibility of Principles, etc. In bestowing upon the *Creencia* this "utopian socialist" emphasis, Echeverría borrowed heavily from the lexicon of Mazzini, Lammenais, Fourier, Sainte-Beuve, and Leroux.

The second half of the *Creencia* pointed more directly toward issues relevant to the country's recent history: the need to continue in the glorious tradition of the country's independence movement; to turn away from the retrograde influences of the colonial regime; to cultivate a national, American culture; to promote democratic institutions and progress; and to seek a middle road between divisive political factions. Even in these sections vague generalizations predominated at the expense of specific proposals.

In brief, the document was intended as a celebratory verbal gesture—in addition to its future value as propaganda—to unify the idealistic youth under a common banner. Echeverría, upon presenting it to the group, urged their acceptance by acclamation. It was not yet the moment to enter into discussion over particular issues. Only later Echeverría would urge his fellow militants: "Let us not abandon the practical terrain . . . let's not lose ourselves in abstractions."[105]

Indeed the *Creencia* did not deal at all with several important issues, two of which merit special comment here. First, vague language and even contradictions characterize the document's discussion of the desirable type of political organization for the country and the role of religion in that future government. For example the text rhetorically defended democracy and equality and then justified not granting the vote to the masses because their participation was not guided by "the Goddess Reason." Also contradictory was its condemnation of the unitarians for having allowed the electoral participation of the masses and then for having abandoned the rural masses to their own fate. Underneath its rhetorical flourishes the convoluted argument of the text seemed to be that the young militants would attract the masses to their cause by taking away the power of the vote!

The other area of intentional vagueness was the *Creencia*'s treatment of the religious question. This was a delicate issue; on the one hand the federalists enjoyed mass support on account of their defense of the *Holy Church*.[106] On the other hand the New Christianity that predominated in the thought of many of the young militants, with its antitraditional and anti-Catholic thrusts, resembled the despised atheism of the unitarians. Motivated by political expediency the young generation consequently sought to avoid ideological confrontation. The *Creencia*'s prudent declarations, in this regard, are an example of Echeverría's political finesse in covering bold ideas with harmless words.

The *Creencia*'s vague language with regard to these two important issues demonstrates the reluctance of the young militants to distance themselves publicly from the major principles of the Federalist Party. To do so would have been tantamount to renouncing their intended leadership of the great majority of the country's population. At the same time, however, the group needed to distance itself from both the orientation and the practice of the Rosas regime. This explains, at least in part, the inclusion of several apocalyptic statements in the document such as, "liberty cannot be won without martyrs to its cause," and "Philosophy can only absolve the struggles of liberation, because spilt blood waters the plant of liberty; from the bodies of the fallen new life springs forth; and out of the ruins of the past the community is resurrected."[107] These statements communicated Echeverría's desire to make a clean break with the doctrine of "antirevolutionary progress," and *por ende,* his rejection of the suggestion earlier made by both Sastre and Alberdi about the possibility for a peaceful collaboration with the Buenos Aires dictator.

Contrasting with these areas of conceptual vagueness was the *Creencia*'s presentation of the last "Word" that spoke to the young militants' intention of embracing a political program that borrowed from both federalist and unitarian principles. This section, written by Alberdi, set forth the general lines of a political program that the young militants, well into the future, would attempt to instill in the national dialogue. Their politics of fusion, as defined in this section, has earned the plaudits of historians: it demonstrated the young militants' profound understanding of the conflicts dividing the country's different regions and their desire to rise above political factionalism in their attempt to unite all Argentines around more transcendent issues.[108]

In retrospect Alberdi and Echeverría were probably the most committed of the group to this last idea of a fusion of political principles. Most of the other participants hailed from the privileged sectors of the Porteño society and in all probability had never ventured far from the modernized urban environment of the port city. Historically Porteño society had demonstrated ignorance and even disdain for the traditional beliefs and practices of the country's majority population in the interior. Deeply held prejudices sometimes fueled a sense of racial and ethnic superiority. Growing up in the cradle of unitarianism and being schooled in the ideological tendencies of that movement, the young Porteño militants probably had great difficulty admitting that Facundo Quiroga, Rosas, and other poncho-clad conductors of rural sentiment were, indeed, to be counted among the precursors of the country's future constitutional organization. But it was a period of heightened emotions. The order of the day was the euphoric approval of their common creed. In future years only a nostalgic memory of momentary, intoxicated unity would remain as the different individuals formerly constituting the group would have to decide about their continued commitment to the principle of "social and political fusion."

Perhaps the greatest value of the *Creencia* was its role in uniting the young militants in the common generational task of renovating the country's institutions and providing for its emergence from a period of prolonged social and political strife. Ingenieros was only partially correct in the opinion that Young Argentina "did not pass beyond the project stage, and had at best a minimal influence in Buenos Aires."[109] Correct is the acknowledgment that the time had not arrived for the members of this secret society to pass from theory to action and that their deliberations were not yet justified by the acid test of historical praxis. Also essentially correct is the inference that the *Creencia* was deficient as a program of generational action. But Ingenieros, continuing the passage above, provided its most persuasive refutation: the Young Argentina "had . . . the good fortune of counting among its members some youths who, through the group's activities, learned how to think and emerged with an innovative spirit that they were able to communicate to the *young generation of Argentines.*" In short order, its members would disperse throughout the continent, distributing copies of that document to other restless youths equally committed to bringing about a new and better life for their country.

The *Creencia* was the statement that defined a generation, but it inevitably bore the mark of its principal writer. Echeverría, whose self-education largely excluded political theory, combined an aristocratic sensibility to an enthusiasm for the new liberal ideas learned from his diverse readings. His preeminently moral orientation to politics was influenced by certain political theorists whose respective visions for the future were linked to a idealized vision of the past. Especially important in this regard was the Enlightenment focus for Montesquieu's democratic republicanism, according to which the motor for society's advancement was the constant sacrifice of patriotic citizens on behalf of collective goals. Also influential was the medieval orientation of Saint Simon, who argued that society's advancement was predicated on the prior existence of a common, shared morality. Apropos was the focus of Leroux, which linked virtue with progress by means of a civil religion—the religion of the new century—in which unity, equality, and humanity would coexist harmoniously.

None of these theories took into account the preponderant transformations that, by midcentury, had already brought about definitive changes throughout the developed West with regard to the role of government and the links joining individuals to society. They did not take into account the dramatic effects of commerce and material progress and, consequently, the place of individual striving and the profit motive within a desirable hierarchy of moral values. Specifically Echeverría's work—especially the first part which preached a model of moral rectitude as a foundation for social democracy—was destined to be an anachronism within a decade of its conception. To many people then, and to even more today, its rhetorical flourishes, celebratory images, and vague generalizations seemed remote and out of place in the discourse of government and politics. The work had an undeniable importance in the first moment as a guide for the young activists who were committed to society's renovation. But within a decade its importance would quickly pale before the groundbreaking writings of Tocqueville, Adam Smith, and others, and the writings of both Sarmiento and Alberdi, with their eminently Argentine focus.

INSURRECTION AND CONSPIRACY

In contrast to the academic orientation of the now defunct Salón Literario, the young militants constituting the Young Argentina from the beginning committed themselves to cultural and political activism. But they were divided over what types of activism were appropriate. On the one hand there were the followers of Echeverría who were convinced that before attempting a forceful overthrow of the Rosas tyranny, the country first needed to undergo a "moral revolution." As such the objectives of this subgroup were primary pedagogical and political; they would expend their energies to promote the education of the populace and the foundation of a national political party.

On the other hand there was a subgroup—apparently led by Alberdi—with explicit political objectives: they believed that their most urgent task was the military overthrow of the Rosas government. Alberdi was to write: "The young generation immediately put aside their goals for a cultural revolution and embraced armed revolution: they left behind ideas and committed themselves to action. For them that path seemed preferable because it was shorter. Diplomacy, concessions, parliamentary negotiations, all were put aside as were cultural pursuits: without looking back, they proclaimed open war with tyranny."[110] Even Gutiérrez, abandoning his "passive antipathy" to violent means, endorsed this militant course.[111] Unfortunately none of the participants have provided written testimony about these meetings that would better clarify the division in the ranks of the group and the means they used toward furthering their respective plans of action.

The fragile truce that had existed between rival social and political forces in Buenos Aires was rapidly disintegrating. The country had been at war with the Confederation uniting present-day Bolivia and Peru since May 1837, and tensions had mounted considerably with the ever-rebellious Pampa Indians along the Buenos Aires southern and western frontiers. Added to this problem was the insurrection of Fructuoso Rivera that deposed Uruguay's president Manuel Oribe, who was supported by Rosas. These disruptions culminated in the French blockade of Buenos Aires in March 1838, which aggravated the already beleaguered economy; the cessation of trade caused hundreds of people to be thrown out of work, a dramatic increase in inflation, and an abrupt fall in the country's revenues. Discontent rose throughout the province. In a period of months, the regime multiplied by sixfold its expenditures for defense and internal security. The government, threatened from without and within, clamped down on the activities of the press. It expanded its network of spies and secret police in order to maintain continual surveillance over the activities of political rivals and potentially treasonous youth.

During this period of mounting tensions, the Young Argentina, now under Alberdi's leadership, continued meeting. Alberdi's new orientation must have surprised many observers. The young man, with delicate health and sensitive nature, had acquired, in previous years, the reputation of musician and socialite. In truth, he had dedicated considerable time and energy to the perfection of his musical skills on the piano, and his essays about musical technique and theory were widely praised. Only recently had the new interests of political theory and law begun to dominate his multifaceted spirit; his important publications between 1835 and 1837 offered unquestionable evidence of a fine legal mind. Furthermore, his costumbrista essays, which evidenced gracious style, sagacious observations, and caustic wit, must have surprised all but his most intimate collaborators.

Only those not intimately familiar with Alberdi would have been perplexed over his apparent change in politics. Beneath his outward compliance with the Rosas regime during most of 1837, he must have been experiencing an excruciating tension. Because of his efforts to communicate with the Rosas government, he had been the brunt of ridicule; for decades to come his opponents would criticize his attempts at accommodation. His growing antipathy to Rosas and anything smacking of a loyalty oath explain his difficult decision to forfeit the degree of doctor of law to which he was entitled. Among his classmates he was the only one to make this decision. His friends—Echeverría and Gutiérrez, especially—realized that instead of ambiguity and indecisiveness, Alberdi's apparently contradictory position betrayed a profound understanding of political realities and a keen eye to strategy. Whatever was said by others, his friends knew him to be a person whose actions obeyed only the most strongly held principles. More and more the majority of the young activists now looked to him for leadership in their growing militancy.

Alberdi knew that his activities and publications already marked him as persona non grata in the eyes of the regime.[112] Too shrewd simply to await the repression that surely lay ahead, he crossed to Montevideo and safety in August 1838.

True to Alberdi's prediction the government's surveillance progressively increased, as did its repressive measures directed against the youths. Day by day the Mazorca (literally, "corn husk" or "más ahorca"—"more killing through hanging"), which was the dictator's secret body of hired thugs who were skilled in tactics of terror and intimidation, escalated its attacks on members of the political opposition or those suspected of organizing against the regime in power. The situation went from bad to worse. In late 1839 the landowners in the southern parts of the province rose in rebellion. Support for this "Insurrection in the South" was also forthcoming from militant groups within Buenos Aires itself, which included a subgroup of the Joven Argentina called the "Club of Five," in addition to prominent Federalist leaders whose economic situation had been jeopardized by the French blockade. This subgroup united Jacinto Rodríguez Peña, Rafael Corvalán, Carlos Tejedor, Benito Carrasco, Santiago Albarracín, Enrique Lafuente, and Ramón Maza, the son of the Federalist president of the province's House of Representatives. Their links with the failed uprising were discovered, and the younger Maza was executed by Rosas's firing squads two days after his father's assassination in the Legislature building. Any remaining hope for dialogue with the regime disappeared when several participants from the ranks of the Young Argentina were arrested. Among them was José Mármol, who was detained for a week in the municipal prison. Gutiérrez later would spend four months in the feared prison, Santos Lugares. Other participants of the Young Argentina either went into hiding or sought a hasty exit from the city in order to escape from Rosas's wrath.

The Rosas regime responded ever more harshly to the increasing threat to its control. Military victories led to cruel and bloody reprisals. Rosas, freely exercising the dictatorial powers entrusted to him, personally ordered executions without trial. The Mazorca, obedient to his whim, stepped up their activities of looting, killing, torture, and intimidation.

This was the beginning of more than a decade of exile for the majority of the Joven Argentina activists. Posadas, Tejedor, Peña, Frías, Gutiérrez, and several others crossed the estuary and joined Cané, Alberdi and Lamas in the security of political exile in Montevideo. The few who remained in Buenos Aires kept a low profile in order to not provoke the suspicions of the police. Echeverría, in fragile health, left the dangerous streets of Buenos Aires and sought for the time being the safety of his brother's estancia near Luján in the northern reaches of the Province of Buenos Aires. "Nothing as sad as emigration" were his words to describe the experience of a generation over the next decade.[113] Vicente Fidel López left for Córdoba at the end of February 1840. Mármol, after being released from prison and spending more than a year in hiding, boarded a small vessel bound for Montevideo in November of that same year.

2

Exile: A New Set of Priorities (1838–1852)

FROM THEORY TO PRACTICE

The activities of the Association during the first few years of the young militants' Montevidean exile revolved around the figure of Alberdi, who emerged as the group's undisputed leader. Echeverría had been the indicated person for providing inspired leadership for the young generation in its initial stage; in their few secret meetings in Buenos Aires he had successfully instilled in them a consciousness of their mission. But Echeverría's strength had been his pedagogical orientation and spiritual disposition. Now his introverted personality and nervous tendencies made him an unsuitable choice for leading the group in the militant direction that he himself had urged. Alberdi, in contrast, proved more adept at adjusting to the trials of exile and leaving aside solitary study for group organization and effective practice. Their time and energies were now directed toward the new imperative of organizing an armed resistance to the Rosas regime.

There was no doubt that Alberdi was the head and inspiration of the group of young activists. In a letter Félix Olazabal expressed his adhesion to the goals of the Association and praised Alberdi's leadership.[1] Two enthusiastic letters from Manuel Quiroga Rosas also demonstrated the deep respect held by the rest for Alberdi's judgment and the unquestioning faith they put in his directives.[2] In a similar manner Gutiérrez's letters—written during his brief trip to the northern provinces—revealed his subordination to Alberdi's leadership though that did not preclude his offering frank, critical advice.[3]

Although Alberdi assumed the responsibility for inspiring and overseeing the initiatives of the Association at this time, Gutiérrez was his right-hand assistant. Soft-spoken and with a contemplative disposition, Gutiérrez hardly shined in the public forum, but clear thought and unwavering commitment made him a leader in any group he joined. The task of representing the group through its written correspondence fell primarily to him. According to Alberdi, "Gutiérrez condensed and expressed better than the rest of us our group thought, but upon making it public he ceded to impulses of his character which, although mild mannered, was always disinterested and upright."[4]

Gutiérrez also assumed the important tasks of inspiring in the young militants a sense of group purpose and defusing potentially devisive jealousies. In his opinion, their cause could not prosper without the unity firm, affective bonds would provide. Only through their example of group unity could they win the allegiance of a mass following. As future social leaders they needed to combine intellectual knowledge with common sense: "Our societies . . . need, like any unfortunate person, a soft hand that consoles and caresses. . . . Love, lots of love, seriousness and conviction—good faith and sights always raised—these are the essentials for achieving one's objective."[5] With this in mind Gutiérrez advised Alberdi (as he would later counsel Urquiza and then Mitre) not to let the organizing task blind him to the personal factors that endeared individuals to the group and led to their strong esprit de corps. As leaders they had to search continually for ways to attract new members and engage the energies of those who demonstrated interest in their goals. To this end he urged a special treatment for the young Mitre, who already displayed uncommon aptitudes: Mitre "is learning fast and combines well his intimate sentiments with the ideal of the fatherland."[6] About Alberdi's understandably bruised sensitivities toward the arrogant Florencio Varela, he urged his friend to forget the negative and do whatever was possible to mend fences in the interest of the group's long-term objectives. The affective element, for Gutiérrez, was the key to the organizing mission that they had undertaken for the whole country: "I am persuaded that more than ever before we need to be united and overcome personal grudges. If this generation becomes divided: then say goodbye to the only remaining chain with links intact and strong enough to save the ship! Pardon my use of the classical allusion."[7]

Gutiérrez's role as advisor and critic extended into the fields of literature and culture. The mutual give-and-take of criticism, for him, was an integral part of the process of constructing a united corps of militants. "I have no real desire to lecture our compatriot"—he wrote in 1839 in reference to a published essay by one of the group—"but I hope you will excuse the frank manner we have chosen to communicate to one another, given our objective of enhancing as much as possible the actions taken by the generation to which we belong."[8] With this end in mind, he rendered frank criticism of an erroneous idea articulated several times by Alberdi, that is, their *new* movement united the *youth* of the country against all that was decrepit and old. In contrast to this view, Gutiérrez argued: "I would prefer that you were not so exclusive in your idea of 'the youth' of the country:—many good people might have due cause for alarm if they saw themselves segregated from a more noble group only because they have lived longer than that in which we include ourselves.—It's necessary to extend our circle, not reduce it.— 'Youth' ought to refer to any person penetrated by the new spirit."[9] Gutiérrez clearly understood the need for their group to steer clear of exclusivism or parochialism and to welcome any individual, regardless of age or antecedents, who was willing to embrace their common goals.

The group's foundation document, the *Creencia* (Creed), proved to be highly effective in enticing others to their banner. In their letters to Alberdi, Gutiérrez and Quiroga Rosas urgently requested more copies for distribution to interested individuals in the northern provinces. Gutiérrez praised Alberdi's team of writers in the Montevidean press on account of the "effective force" of their writing and the appeal of their ideas.[10] Accounts of the enthusiastic reception of the document also came from Félix Olazabal and J. Domínguez. In his *Facundo*, Sarmiento would also underline the importance of the *Creencia* for himself and his San Juan circle; with the accompanying library of Quiroga Rosas, it had made possible their emergence into a new world of modern ideas.

The young writer-militants under the leadership of Alberdi did not hesitate to launch themselves into activity. The first order of business was to continue with the Association's plan of disseminating progressive ideas through the press and, in that manner, to prepare the ideological terrain for the struggle against Rosas. In this they paid homage to the admonition of Echeverría that the principal function of their group had to be to "enjoy the protection of public opinion, whether through the press or the tribune, 'and in that way the order of existing things might be changed and revolution might once again raise its head.'"[11] To this end they wrote for newspapers wherever they went. This was not only their preferred means of earning a living, it was also a most effective weapon for carrying on their struggle.

The journalistic activities of the young militants were first manifest in Montevideo. Even before the arrival of Alberdi and the others, Cané and Lamas were already active in directing *El iniciador,* in whose pages the *Creencia* was first published in January 1839. Alberdi later joined these two in publishing *El nacional,* which immediately became the young militants' most important organ of expression. In the pages of this last journal, they would publish the second edition of the *Creencia* (1839); portions of Sarmiento's *Facundo* (1845); and the patriotic poetry of Mitre, Mármol, and Echeverría. They would also translate and publish texts written by the foremost European theorists of "social romanticism," from whom they derived their own theoretical directions: Saint-Simon, Leroux, and Lamennais. Mármol, Domínguez, and Rivera Indarte were the principal names associated with several short-lived news-

papers from among the young generation. Three of these newspapers—
El grito arjentino (The Argentine shout), *¡Muera Rosas!* (Death to Rosas!),
and *El puñal* (The daggar)—had the specific goal of disseminating a
highly politicized, negative image of Rosas. Later *El talismán* (The talis-
man) and *El tiroteo* (Gunshot), directed by Gutiérrez and Rivera Indarte;
La nueva era (The new era), under the direction of Andrés Lamas; and
Alberdi's *El corsario* (The privateer) would join the list of progressive
publications. After the demise of most of these publications, Florencio
Varela's *El comercio del Plata* (Commerce of the River Plate), founded in
1845, would become the region's most praised organ for disseminating
democratic thought.

In the provinces the impact of the young militants' journalistic activities was also substantial. In San Juan, Quiroga Rosas and Sarmiento
published several issues of *El zonda* (Zonda) during 1839. The next year
Juan Thompson, in Corrientes, founded *El pueblo libertador* (The liberating people), and V. F. López, in Córdoba, published eleven issues of *El
estandarte nacional* (The national banner).

The journalistic contributions of the young generation of writers in
Chile were no less distinguished. Early in the decade of the 1840s, Sarmiento and V. F. López launched their famous polemics defending Romanticism and a renovated Hispanic American language against the
followers of Andrés Bello from the pages of *El mercurio* (Mercury) and
La revista de Valparaíso (The magazine of Valparaíso). In 1842 Sarmiento
founded *El progreso* (Progress) in Santiago, which would later print important articles by Mitre, as well as those by Chileans José Victorino
Lastarria and Francisco Bilbao. Later Alberdi, Mitre, and Uruguayan
Juan Carlos Gómez would publish important articles in Santiago's *El
siglo* (The century), as well as in *El comercio* and *El mercurio* of Valparaíso.

A second major concern of the young militants was to spread their
progressive ideas throughout the country in order to unite behind their
banner the pockets of anti-Rosas militancy. Quiroga Rosas described the
missionary-like zeal with which they undertook this task. Their journalistic labor was

> apostolical and progressive. . . . To found associations like our own in Cór-
> doba, in Tucumán, in Salta, in Cuyo, and link their actions and program with
> ours; to establish in all these communities a lasting journalistic press and, if
> I have the time, to found also new schools. At the very least I can inspire
> these same desires in the youth who might listen to me.[12]

In 1838 Quiroga Rosas accompanied Antonio Aberastain back to San
Juan, the city of their origin, after having spent most of the previous
decade in Buenos Aires pursuing the course of studies that would lead
to a law degree. In addition to possessing several copies of the *Creencia*,

Quiroga Rosas was outfitted with an entire library of books written by the European writers then in mode: Villemain and Schlegel, in literature; Joufrroy, Lerminier, Guizot, Cousin, in philosophy and history; Tocqueville, Pedro Leroux, writing about democracy; the *Encyclopedia,* which offered a synthesis of all the doctrines; and a hundred other names.[13] For the next two years, the San Juan group, which united Domingo F. Sarmiento, Aberastain, Dionisio Rodríguez, Indalecio Cortínez, and the brothers Franklin and Guillermo Rawson, met frequently, at times daily, to discuss the new ideas learned from their readings. Other progressive activities also resulted from this nucleus of talent: the foundation of a school for young women, a society dedicated to sponsoring theater events, and a regional newspaper, *El zonda* (Zonda). But, similar to what was occurring in other regions of the country, the steadily deteriorating political situation brought a premature end to all of these activities. Before the end of 1840, most of the young activists were forced to flee the region and relocate in Chilean exile.

The generating ideas of the Association also were carried to Tucumán and Córdoba. In Tucumán, Benjamín Villafañe brought together Marco Avellaneda, Brígido Silva, and other progressive youths. In Córdoba, where Miguel Irigoyen and Vicente F. López arrived in March 1840, there arose a similar association uniting Paulino Paz, Enrique Rodríguez, and Avelino and Ramón Ferreira, under the leadership of Francisco Alvarez. This group became the focal point for the revolution that erupted in October of that same year, which resulted in that group's leader assuming the governorship of the province.

All of these activities attested to the young militants' early success in carrying their doctrines to all parts of the country. They were able to instill in the youth of the country a sense of the unity of their endeavor which would later translate into political action aimed at toppling the Rosas dictatorship and promoting progressive ideas. Perhaps the clearest example of the group's success in disseminating their progressive ideas is the experience of Sarmiento. His writings after 1838 clearly indicated a new stage in his thought that was a direct consequence of his introduction to the ideas of the Association and the lessons learned from the ambulatory library made available to him by Quiroga Rosas at that time.

The Montevidean Theater

Toward the end of 1838, Alberdi crossed the estuary and resided in Montevideo. He encountered a number of Argentine exiles who were hardly united with regard to the means and ends of their struggle.

Among the youth several were attempting to organize an armed opposition to the Rosas government, while others contined to embrace a largely pedagogical mission. The exile community, in general, was highly divided. General Paz, in his memoirs, called attention to the disputes between the young supporters of Lavalle and the militants gathered around José Rivera Indarte. V. F. López, in his autobiographical writings, underlined the rifts existing between the Unitarians and the Liberals of the Federalist Party—the "lomos negros"—who had arrived in Montevideo in 1835 after the revolution of the "restauradores": Generals Enrique Martínez, Tomás Iriarte, Félix Olazabal, the priest Pedro Pablo Vidal, and Dr. Pedro Agrelo.

The now aged leaders of the Unitarian Party had been living in exile since their defeats across the country in the early 1830s: Martín Rodríguez, Dr. Julián Segundo de Agüero, Salvador María del Carril, Valentín Alsina, Juan Cruz Varela, and his younger brother, Florencio. Their party, like their ideas, had been discredited because of its political failures in the early 1820s and its defeats on field of battle a decade later. Now, in the mid and late 1830s, these individuals constituted little more than an embittered, vocal opposition. The great majority of them had grown rigid in their doctrines. The terrible civil war now in its third decade had hardly modified their philosophical and political orientations. Their abstract liberal ideas on constitution, individual rights, anticlericism, free trade, and material progress were admirable. However their sensed class superiority and arrogant belief in the "Goddess of Reason" led them to despise the majority of their compatriots. They continued, dogmatically, to aspire the implementation of inflexible ideas without granting due consideration to the widespread ignorance of the people who were committed to traditional beliefs and customs. In addition to their ideological shortcomings, the Unitarians—with their Rivadavian, Morenist, and Saavedrist factions—were sorely divided by doctrinary squabbles and personal rivalries.

The "young reformists" (soon to be known as "Young Alberdians") were decidedly offended by the unitarians' acute sense of ideological and class superiority. In *Facundo*, Sarmiento captured the opinion shared by the young militants about the liberals of the previous generation. The prototype unitarian, he wrote,

> walks straight ahead, head held high; he does not turn around, even if he were to hear a building collapse behind him; he talks with arrogance; he finishes a sentence with disdainful gestures and haughty glances; he has fixed, invarabable ideas. . . . It is impossible to imagine how a generation so committed to reasoned analysis, so deductive, or so enterprising would nevertheless be so lacking in practical sense.[14]

Particularly offensive to the young militants was the self-infatuation of the unitarians who came to regard themselves as the chosen group whom others needed to follow. In their speeches and proclamations, the unitarians exhibited a profound contempt for the ignorant masses whom they nevertheless attempted to sway to their anti-Rosas program. In spite of their long experience in the politics of the region, they seemed to have learned little from their party's disastrous defeats some years earlier. During 1852 and after the elimination of Rosas, they would still advocate many of the same programs and transformations they had articulated a whole generation before.

The most important militant in unitarian ranks was Florencio Varela. In 1827 Varela, at age twenty, had only recently received the doctorate of law from the University of Buenos Aires, but he was already marked for future leadership in the Unitarian Party, if not the country as a whole. His indirect involvement with the overthrow of Dorrego a year later led to exile in Montevideo, and he became an early participant in the struggle against Rosas. By 1838 the exiled community of Argentines had constituted the Argentine Commission in which Varela was recognized as the principal spokesman and leader. Originally opposed to French collaboration in Lavalle's campaign to oust Rosas, his diplomatic efforts proved pivotal in convincing the representatives of that country to carry out their blockade of Buenos Aires in 1839. Similar efforts on behalf of Varela would lead to the joint French-British blockade in 1845.

His contemporaries, including the Association members, regarded Florencio Varela as perhaps the most distinguished and capable of the entire group of Argentine exiles. Ricardo Rojas (writing decades later) did not exaggerate when he wrote: "There were in Varela the superior qualities of a statesman, which he possessed to a degree far exceeding any other member of his generation, which did not lack talent. He would have been an extraordinary public figure: he was a 'doer,' capable of converting his civilizing ideal into fertile reality."[15] Varela's influence was not limited to unitarian circles; his participation was sought after by Montevidean officials, and his articles treating the status of affairs of the Plata region were eagerly read by the highest officials in France's and England's foreign ministries. In 1845 Varela founded what was to become the journalistic organ of perhaps the most lasting value during the entire decade, the *Comercio del Plata*, which he directed until his assassination by Rosas's henchmen three years later.[16] In Varela's widely read editorials, readers found perhaps the clearest exposition available of the issues then at stake in the ongoing conflict in the Plata region. It is to Varela's credit that several of the key ideas associated with the program of the young generation were first discussed in his columns:

the need to center the anti-Rosas movement in the provinces of the Littoral, the benefits of free navigation along the country's rivers, and the necessity for a strong state program in order to attract Europe's emigrant population to the shores of the Plata.

In contrast to these positive aspects in the advocacy of Varela, there were other, decidedly negative qualities. V. F. López, while recognizing his undeniable intelligence and untiring struggles against Rosas, noted, "The unitarian dogma, and his hatred of Rosas, came to be in him an obsession, which drove him to condemnable abberations, like that of attempting to violate the territorial integrity of his own country if in doing so he could bring about the defeat of Rosas."[17] Echeverría was definitely in agreement with López's asssessment of Varela. But what stands out in the public record are Echeverría's seething complaints about the indifference of Varela and the unwarranted silence of the latter's press with regard to the young generation's most important accomplishments.

In all probability some of the Association's militants never forgave Varela because of his presumptuous and patronizing reaction to their own doctrines. Varela, in contrast to his other diplomatic skills, never exhibited an abundance of tact and discretion in dealing with his generational peers. His comments about Alberdi's speech to the Salón Literario and the *Fragmento prelimilar* were blunt and negative; in those early years his image of Alberdi never rose above that of a presumptuous young upstart with uncertain, if not dangerous, profederalist tendencies. Undoubtedly these insults in turn affected Alberdi's perception of Varela. Nevertheless the clear difference in their points of view on several important issues is reason enough to account for Alberdi's meditated attacks on Varela's ideas in several of his publications.[18] In the few years before his assassination, Varela would also provoke the anger of Sarmiento for similar reasons, mainly, his indifference to the latter's literary achievements. In brief, the friction between Varela and the other young militants unfortunately was very real and must have contributed to weakening the anti-Rosas campaign as a whole. In spite of undeniable talent and his total commitment to the anti-Rosas struggle, Varela's limited vision of the issues at stake, added to his testy and arrogant personality, impeded collaboration with the other young exiles.

Varela provoked the irritation of Alberdi and his followers for another reason: he lent a deaf ear to the ideas of association and utopian social reform that had inspired and animated the young militants' own discussions. They could collaborate with Varela and the commission that he headed with regard to the military and propagandistic struggle against Rosas, and they agreed in theory with many, if not all, of the programs he advocated. But they realized that Varela did not share their commitment to studying the reality of the country and its people as a basis for achieving a truly independent and national culture. Furthermore Varela's vision for the country's future was decidedly limited; he demonstrated little, if any, awareness of the need for promoting agriculture or new industries in the region, and he seemed blind to the problem of Buenos Aires's stifling domination over the other provinces via its monopoly of the nation's customs revenues. On the political level Varela's sectarian views also went against one of the principal advocations of Echeverría and Alberdi: the need for a fusion of doctrines and parties as a means of overcoming the decades-long rivalry that had torn the country asunder.[19] In the opinion of these two, Varela's "aristocratic vision" and partisan Unitarian views were bound to provoke continued animosity among many who did not share his somewhat rigid (and perhaps self-serving) opinions about the need to return the direction of the country to the hands of Buenos Aires's educated elites.[20]

Yet Varela was not without his supporters in the Association; Miguel Cané was his brother-in-law, and his regular correspondence with Gutiérrez over the years demonstrates a mutual respect on the basis of many shared interests. In addition to their relatively similar political orientations, both were literary critics, and both exhibited a passion for collecting and analyzing the historical documents of the region. Furthermore it was to Varela's house, that "intimate lecture-room and literary salon," where Mitre turned for criticisms of his drama, "Policarpia Salavarrieta."[21] Mármol's most outstanding journalistic contributions during this period were also in collaboration with Varela, who, in turn, was one of the poet's most penetrating and supportive critics.[22]

After years had passed, when the revolutionary romanticism of the former militants of the Association would be supplanted by the consciousness of society's overriding need for order and progress, their general opinion about Varela would be more generous. Only after they themselves suffered two decades of defeat and exile would they come to understand the early hesitancy of Varela and the other unitarian leaders to commit themselves to one more campaign that was long on idealism and short on realism. Toward the end of the 1850s, Félix Frías would provide testimony of Varela's exemplary figure and solid ideological criteria. In his devoutness and conservative doctrines, Varela would have provided "a necessary order before the revolutionary spirit, after having defended the principle of liberty before the absolute power of Rosas."[23] Similarly Alberdi, writing about Varela years later, would hardly mention the personal grudges felt by Echeverría and himself at the time; those would bear little weight before Varela's undeniable talent and otherwise indisputable contributions. Throughout Alberdi's notes and writings, Florencio Varela would continually be grouped with the hemisphere's most outstanding leaders.[24] Indeed it was to Varela's credit that during the last few years of his life he came to embrace many of the Association's early ideas as his own.

Another figure associated with the Unitarian Party, whose presence inspired both the condemnation and praise of the young militants, was José Rivera Indarte. Similar to Varela his youth and early educational experiences in Buenos Aires placed him squarely within the ranks of the 1837 generation. But also similar to Varela, his aloof manner, intellectual arrogance, and dogmatic politics distanced him from the young militants who followed the early lead of Echeverría, Alberdi, and Gutiérrez. V. F. López, in his historical writings, would passionately denounce Rivera Indarte's early support for Rosas while not giving due credit to Indarte's inspired opposition at a later moment. For López, Rivera Indarte was "a misanthropic neurotic . . . he was a sick man." The historian Adolfo Saldías, writing at the turn of the century, called attention to Rivera Indarte's "very violent, hateful and impressionable character."[25] Rivera Indarte was a perplexing figure whose hate-filled politics, shifting moral principles, and possibly sexual politics, in all likelihood offended more traditional sensitivities.[26] The damning portraits offered by Echeverría and Sarmiento indicate that Rivera Indarte's excessive zeal in his personal vendetta against Rosas transferred into irresponsible yellow journalism. Yet he was author of several important publications and was universally recognized as one of the leading writers and intellectuals residing in Montevideo at the time.[27] His book-length diatribe, *Rosas y sus opositores* (Rosas and his opponents—1843), which became a best-seller and a classic in its own day, was characterized by the same belligerent tone. This work suggested a very controversial option in their war against Rosas: the idea that "It is a holy action that of killing Rosas." Several historical accounts accredit Rivera Indarte for having carried through with that verbal threat by orquestrating the means whereby the *infernal machine*—a small box wired to discharge a bullet at he who opened it—almost found its target in the figure of Rosas's daughter, Manuelita.[28] The 1837 militants' immediate reactions to that stunt are not recorded in the existing correspondence. But for Alberdi, writing in 1872, the idea of justified political assassination was "a puerile slap in the face typical of an immature student"; had the assassination succeeded, it could have initiated an uncontrollable wave of destructive civic passions.[29] Even Sarmiento, who at a later moment (the 1863 events surrounding the death of "El Chacho" Peñalosa) would order or approve of a similar act of political homicide carried out by his subordinates, registered his disapproval of Rivera Indarte's idea.[30]

The written record indicates that the other 1837 activists were more generous with Rivera Indarte than he was with them. He had been offended by Alberdi's article treating the "Poetic Competition" of 1842 because the latter did not pay sufficient attention to his own role in that event. His smoldering grudge against Alberdi and Gutiérrez then reached the proportion of a "war to death," in the words of Rivera Indarte,[31] after the early departure of these two from besieged Montevideo in 1842. Gutiérrez's 1845 letter to Alberdi from Valparaíso, however, would express his strong attachment to "Echeverría, Indarte, Domínguez, and Mármol" and would recount his warm memories of their collaboration in Montevideo some years before. Alberdi's later writings also would return pat for slap; he would praise Rivera Indarte's poem celebrating the victory at Caa-Guazú: "Regardless of its defects, it is the most perfect of its genre that has appeared yet among us, superior even to those appearing during the period of the independence struggle against Spain."[32] After Rivera Indarte's untimely death in 1845, Alberdi bestowed upon him the ultimate honor by grouping his name with the others who had paid with their lives in their country's most important struggles.[33] Mitre would publish a praise-filled biography in Montevideo and Valparaíso that highlighted Rivera Indarte's journalistic and literary contributions in the struggle against Rosas.[34] In Mitre's "Profession of Faith" of 1852, Rivera Indarte's name would be grouped with a short list of public writers who had given their lives in the service of the homeland.[35] In the eyes of the young generation, Rivera Indarte's role as martyr was obviously preferable to that of active collaborator.

In addition to the activists of the exiled Unitarian Party, several individuals whose doctrinaire Federalist ideas had earned the wrath of the Buenos Aires dictator and who now joined in the movement to overthrow him were also to be found in the environs of Montevideo. Many of these Federalist leaders had fled the country after the aborted 1839 plot led by Colonel Ramón Maza, son of the president of the legislature. Central to these Federalists was their fidelity to many traditions surviving from the region's colonial past, their defense of provincial autonomy before Rosas's increasingly heavy-handed control from Buenos Aires, and their stubborn resistance to a central organization that would undermine their dedication to provincial institutions. To many members of the Association, the federalist credos that looked to the past presented an obstacle to the country's future development. They were repelled by the federalists' oftentimes parochial outlook, their fear of innovation, and their abhorrence of any ideas of reputed foreign origin. Compared to the federalists' *criollo* sentiments of *patria chica*, the members of the Association dreamed of transforming the most innovative ideas from Europe into workable guidelines for the country's material and institutional transformation.

THE LAVALLE CAMPAIGN

While Alberdi and the others daily dedicated a few morning hours to their journalistic labors, the greater part of their time was spent organizing the military struggle against Rosas. Any previous idea about collaboration with Buenos Aires's maximum leader in the hopes of infusing his popular, nationalist government with progressive ideas was now definitely shelved. The time was eminently favorable for an armed revolt against the Buenos Aires despot. The economic effects of the French blockade of 1838, combined with the popular backlash to Rosas's increased oppression, had triggered discontent everywhere. Numerous signs indicated that rebellion would explode on all sides. While the Argentine Commission, under Florencio Varela's initiatives, organized the main focus of opposition in Montevideo, Alberdi attempted to coordinate other points of rebellion in different parts of the country. The "Club of Five"—a spin-off group of the Young Argentina—promised to support a Buenos Aires uprising led by Ramón Maza, a disgruntled Federalist and Rosas bureaucrat. Domingo Cullen in Santa Fe, Berón de Astrada in Corrientes, Marco Avellaneda in Tucumán, and Pedro Castelli in the southern reaches of the Province of Buenos Aires, all indicated a willingness to rise up in arms. The only factor lacking was a catalyzing agent in the form of a leader with sufficient prestige to unite all rebellious factions.

A letter written by Gutiérrez to Alberdi in early 1839 revealed their preoccupation over the leadership void that had to be filled. Gutiérrez suggested the unlikely figure of Fructuoso Rivera, the crude, popular caudillo from the Banda Oriental, who was until then a committed Rosas foe: "Rivera will be, then, The Predestined One.'"[36] The foremost need was to select a military leader who would accept their advice and who could inspire the devotion of the uncultured masses. In spite of their obvious dislike of many of Rivera's qualities, they recognized his popularity among the common soldiers. Yet Rivera proved to be unreliable and not exactly pliable to their influence. This was patently demonstrated when, months later, he callously abandoned his erstwhile allies and temporarily aligned himself with the Buenos Aires tyrant.

Alberdi and others then settled their sights on General Juan Lavalle, veteran of the War of Independence, as the most promising candidate for the leadership of their movement, in spite of significant reservations. Although few doubted Lavalle's competence on the field of battle, there were grave questions about his political judgment. It was, after all, Lavalle who had ordered the execution of Manuel Dorrego in 1828—an act that had reignited the bloody war between the country's rival factions. Perhaps of even greater concern was the perception that Lavalle was not the type of general who could inspire a high degree of loyalty in a fighting force of uneducated peasants. Similarly Lavalle, with his cultured manner and Unitarian past, was hardly the person to incite a popular uprising in Buenos Aires against the tyranny of Rosas. It also occurred to the young militants that perhaps these were obstacles that could be overcome if the general were receptive to their tutelage and if they were able to organize effective publicity in his support through the local press.

The task of theorizing over the new role of a leader such as Lavalle in relation to the objectives of their movement fell on Alberdi. Transparent in these words is the "utopian" dimension of their thought. Lavalle, Alberdi reasoned,

> will be most popular . . . always where art, ideas, and civilization have acquired the greatest progress. . . . Favor for [Lavalle] will not be widespread among the ignorant masses, but rather with the educated masses; and in order that the educated masses of the country be stronger than the ignorant masses, it is necessary to seek connections with educated elements of foreign lands. Only in this way—by allying themselves with representations of foreign civilization—can the educated minority of the country succeed in subordinating the semi-barbarous majority.[37]

Alberdi correctly perceived that even with Lavalle's prestigous leadership and the devotion he inspired in his soldiers, their movement would still have to reckon with Rosas's immense popularity in and among the creoles, *gauchos*, and Blacks of Buenos Aires. It would be nearly futile, he reasoned, for his group of young writers to expend their energies in attempting to win the sympathies of the uncultured and largely illiterate masses. A better strategy would be to win the support of the "the educated masses," who could then successfully oppose the "the ignorant masses" that supported the tyrant. Did there exist such a group, and was this a realistic assessment of the forces that could be organized in opposition to Rosas? In actual fact the educated sector of Rioplatense society constituted, at the time, only a small but growing minority. Clearly the young militants hoped to lead this group through their journalistic and educational efforts; this was precisely the "moral" revolution envisioned by Echeverría. But was it not wishful thinking to suggest that that social sector, inspired by Lavalle (who, in turn, had been armed by the French and was advised by a small cadre of enlightened intellectuals), had a large enough following in order to constitute a veritable challenge to the Rosas regime? As events would later reveal, the region would have to wait another twenty years—for the Mitre revolution after Pavón—for such a coalition of forces to launch a credible opposition to the *caudillos* of the interior.

Meanwhile, the young militants went ahead with their plans. Although almost every other reputable historical source ignores his contribution, Alberdi, in his own writings, granted himself protagonist status—alongside of Florencio Varela—in convincing the reluctant general of his "destined" role to lead the liberation struggle against Rosas. In recognition of Alberdi's extraordinary organizing abilities and clear articulation of the issues at stake, Lavalle designated him as his personal secretary for the campaign—a distinction Alberdi would later yield to Félix Frías. Eventually the movement would also call upon the leadership of Generals Gregorio de La Madrid, with support primarily in the provinces of the north, and José María Paz, with a power base in Corrientes.

Alberdi's initiative of enlisting Lavalle as leader of the anti-Rosas movement was enthusiastially taken up by the members of the Argentine Commission in Montevideo, headed by Florencio Varela and assisted by Uruguayan Andrés Lamas. A second initiative, that of enlisting French support for that effort, met with initial resistance. In his memoirs Alberdi recounted the extreme anger of Juan Cruz Varela—famed poet, Unitarian politician, and elder brother of Florencio—over the "French question," which was indicative of the animosity existing between the erstwhile allies in the struggle against Rosas. Later, when Alberdi supplied sworn statements from the French disclaiming any territorial ambitions, some progressive voices from unitarian ranks, led by Florencio Varela, would join in the coalition of forces. In the next few months, Alberdi, in conjunction with Andrés Lamas and F. Varela, succeeded in uniting most of the exiled population in what became a joint military adventure.

Central to the strategy of Association members was the construction of a social coalition that would respond to their reasoned leadership and oppose Rosas in the name of "civilization" and progress. Repeated throughout their early writings was the expressed need for a leader who accepted as his own the ambitions and objectives of the movement and who would, in turn, inspire his loyal following with charisma and by personal example. Alberdi would make reference to a world dominated by *great men*, and Sarmiento would talk about a struggle between "titans." For both it was a struggle between representative figures, each champions of their respective causes. This Manichean struggle was central to their interpretations for the social conflict of their time. At times—especially in Sarmiento's writings—the ensuing struggle was depicted as occurring between rival ideas with the successful leader emerging as the one whose objectives best reflected the predominant intellectual currents of his time.

In 1839, when Lavalle finally embarked on his long-awaited expedition, it was Félix Frías who now accompanied him as private secretary. The rivalries among the allied leaders had considerably weakened the movement. At this time Alberdi decided to stay in Montevideo, perhaps because of his growing dislike for direct action, or perhaps because of his premonitions about their campaign's future demise.

Enthusiasms plummeted when the French government suddenly announced withdrawal of its support. Until then French assistance had been indispensable in blockading the port of Buenos Aires, seizing the Island of Martín García, and transporting the troops across the Río Uruguay to southern Entre Ríos. Upon learning of the impending French withdrawal, Lavalle and the Unitarian leadership in Montevideo appealed to French authorities for a reconsideration of the decision, but to no avail. There were two other major setbacks at this time: General Fructuoso Rivera, probably resenting Lavalle's sudden prominence, withdrew his forces from the invading force and even used his authority in Montevideo to obstruct its organization; later, Pedro Ferré, governor of Corrientes, obstinately prohibited the militia from his province from joining the larger movement against Rosas. Lavalle, taking stock of his weakened military position and predicting the paltry support that a *unitarian* and French-backed invasion would garner among the traditionally federalist and nationalist masses in and around Buenos Aires, renounced any plans to march upon the capital city itself. In doing so he in effect abandoned to Rosas's fury the brave conspirators in the regions of Tandil and Azul—towns to the south of Buenos Aires—whose rebellion would have coincided with the arrival of Lavalle's troops. Instead caution supplanted audacity when Lavalle announced his intention to lead his invading troops northward toward the Province of Entre Ríos.[38]

Led by Alberdi and Florencio Varela, critics denounced Lavalle's decision to avoid confrontation in the Province of Buenos Aires. They had spent a lot of time and their reputations were on the line in coordinating a series of uprisings across the country that would have coincided with Lavalle's march upon Buenos Aires. Varela wrote a letter seething with accusations to the general.[39] Over the next few months, passions ran high in Montevideo as news trickled in about the brutal defeat of the "Insurrection of the South" and Rosas's heavy-handed reprisals against conspirators in Buenos Aires itself. Echeverría, who was residing on his humble estancia near Luján, feared for his personal safety after signing anti-Rosas petitions circulating in his region. His desperate flight to Montevideo early in 1841 saved him from sure reprisals and perhaps even execution. Echeverría would later express the general disillusionment of his generation by characterizing Lavalle as "a sword without a brain."[40] In contrast to Varela's and Echeverría's very negative views about Lavalle, Félix Frías (after serving as Lavalle's private secretary throughout the tragic campaign) would provide a positive testimony of the controversial general's personal and professional qualities in *La gloria del tirano Rosas* (The glory of the tyrant Rosas—1847).

Between 1839 and 1841 rebellion against the Buenos Aires tyrant broke out in several areas across the country. Rosas, however, was able to take advantage of the divisions in the movement's leadership, and his armies won victory after victory. In mid-1839, the "Insurrection of the South," uniting liberals in Buenos Aires to disgruntled Federalist landowners in southern Buenos Aires, was mercilessly crushed. Within months Lavalle's army was defeated, and the general, with a small protective escort, was chased toward the Bolivian border. After Lavalle was killed in a surprise attack, his few remaining followers fled with his bodily remains into Bolivian exile. Similarly tragic was the defeat experienced by the Northern Coalition, which ended with the brutal execution of its leader Marco Avellaneda.

The circumstances surrounding Avellaneda's death are particularly noteworthy. Earlier I mentioned the probable participation of Avellaneda in the events surrounding the assassination of Tucuman governor, Alejandro Heredia, in 1838. At that time Avellaneda, the head of the Provincial Legislature, orchestrated the appointment of a loyal follower to the post of acting governor, and he himself assumed the leadership role in the Coalition of Northern Provinces that united the armies of Tucumán, Salta, La Rioja, Catamarca, and Jujuy under the direction of General Gregorio de la Madrid. Avellaneda, a close friend of Alberdi, shared the anti-Rosas outlook of the Association members in Montevidean exile. Responding to Alberdi's call to revolt, Avellaneda, on behalf of the province, wrote the 1840 declaration, declaring open rebellion against the "Buenos Aires monster."[41] Their plans indicated a surplus of audacity, but a deficit of realism; they aimed to convert their poor region, recently recovering from a taxing war with Bolivia, into the center of the national struggle against Rosas. Avellaneda wrote in a letter to Alberdi: "I have my misanthropic tendencies and my remnants of romanticism." It was a romantic struggle in which good was dramatically pitted against evil. Avellaneda's highly rhetorical prose communicates the sense of predestined mission that he must have felt: "In this moment the destiny of the Argentine Republic will finally be determined, and we will need great courage in order to save it."[42] Was Avellaneda aware of his scant chances of success in leading this ill-armed provincial insurrection against the seasoned troops of the tyrant? His doctoral thesis of a few years earlier had communicated a favorable disposition toward martyrdom.

In the inevitable military confrontation, Avellaneda's forces were thoroughly beaten; high-sounding political goals failed to transfer into battlefield prowess. The victorious federalist forces under the command of Gregorio Sandoval executed the prisoners, Avellaneda among them, by throat-slitting—the *degüello*. Avellaneda's severed head was then paraded throughout the region as a deterrent to future uprisings against the country's federalist leaders. The brutal circumstances of this death enraged Rosas foes everywhere and even became the pretext for an outstanding poetic gesture by Echeverría some years later, that is, the narrative poem, *Avellaneda* (1849).[43]

The events of 1839–41 constituted a great disappointment to the members of the young generation who witnessed the defeat of the different focal points of their rebellion against Rosas. Powerless they followed the news of Rosas's new measures which were aimed at consolidating civil authority and persecuting political foes. Within months, when the dictator ordered the land siege of Montevideo, they would personally witness the extent of Rosas's determination to neutralize the perennial military threat that emanated from that city. A whole decade would pass before another credible challenge to the dictator's authority would arise.

For the members of the Association in their Montevideo base, defeat ushered in a whole new set of priorities. Echeverría, in his timely poem, "A la juventud argentina en mayo de 1841" (To Argentina's Youth in May 1841)," expressed the anger and sadness of so many victims in their unsuccessful revolt against the dictator. After such devastating defeats it would have been counterproductive to continue organizing military opposition. Echeverría counseled his fellow militants to sheathe the sword and turn to other, more constructive pursuits. "With your faith never waning, prepare your mind / For the huge task of renovation."[44] Alberdi, who had unerringly predicted the fiasco that would result from the individualistic motivations and in-fighting among the Montevideo-based Unitarian leadership, shared Echeverría's sentiments about returning to point zero in forming a totally new resistance to Rosas. Needed, this time, was a core of leaders united around a commonly embraced set of objectives: "The country's youth will continue meeting and will finally get down to work . . . I have not lost the hope of seeing the revolution reorganized around a better set of principles than those operative until now."[45]

At this time Alberdi composed the pamphlet, *Memoria sobre la nueva situación del Plata*, (Memory about the new situation of the Plata region), in which he provided a clear interpretation of recent events and reaffirmed his revolutionary commitment.[46] He pointed the finger at the faction-ridden leadership of the Unitarian Party for having undermined the movement and having brought about the disaster that all of them now faced. Unitarian leaders, with "pedestrian ideas," had squandered a valuable opportunity. Their anti-French propaganda had caused a serious "disturbance in public opinion" that contributed to the tragedy.[47] For example, it was reputed that Juan Cruz Varela's poem expressing his opposition to the French blockade had been read by members of the French government and had contributed significantly to their decision to terminate their support for the anti-Rosas insurgents.

Yet Alberdi's anger was misplaced. In all probability there was nothing that the Unitarian leadership in Montevideo could have done to alter the French government's decision to withdraw its fleet from the Rioplatense theater, because that country then confronted far more serious problems elsewhere. Alberdi's romantically inspired reflections about the campaign as a whole had a false bravado. In his words the campaign had failed because of the defective leadership of the Unitarian Party—"old, behind the times, without courage." Had Alberdi's group of young militants been in charge, with their plan of "bold strategies, with bold surprise tactics, with couragous and unpredicable blows," then the results would have been distinctive.[48] Using this mythified dichotomy between incompetent elders and the "newer element, a bolder one," it was easy to place blame and award excuses. Alberdi's words of 1840 prefigured the self-apologetic attitude of his group, even after the tragic denouement to the events they had helped put into motion: "Seen in this way, the youths of the country have done no wrong, and the unitarian faction, no right. The thought of the Young Generation created the revolution; unitarian thought, in contrast, lost it."[49] These words constituted an ideological balm for placating the author's inner torment, but they hardly constituted a viable ideological base that would serve to prepare for the next, inevitable battle.

Total defeat brought with it every sort of recrimination among the exiles. Collaboration was now impossible between the young militants and the aging unitarian leadership. In Montevideo the scarcity of food and materials due to Rosas's land and sea siege added to the conflictive political environment. Echeverría, after delaying some months, would finally leave Colonia del Sacramento for Montevideo. Failing health and a perennial shortage of funds merely aggravated his already pronounced melancholy and aloofness. The young Mitre—by now accepted as a junior member of the Association—enthusiastically published poems in the city's press while continuing to serve under Uruguayan General Fructuoso Rivera as lieutenant of an artillery company. Alberdi and Gutiérrez, unenthusiastic about participating in the military defense of the city, turned their aptitudes toward cultural and educational pursuits. Gutiérrez advanced with his life-long investigations into the culture, literature, and history of ideas of the Río de la Plata region. Alberdi finally completed the requirements for the law degree and, consequently, was able to supplement his meager resources with monies earned through legal activities. The greater part of his energies, however, continued to be spent reading and writing. The next chapter of 1837 activism would feature literary and cultural renewal. The successful military campaign against their generational foe, Rosas, was still a decade into the future.

THE CHILEAN THEATER

Due to its proximity to Buenos Aires, Montevideo was destined to be the center of the anti-Rosas activities. But, during the same time period, a number of young militants established themselves between Valparaíso and Santiago, Chile, and organized a second front for the propagandistic campaign against Rosas. Heading the list of the young militants in Chile was Domingo F. Sarmiento, a native of the Andean province of San Juan, whose passionate hatred for Rosas was matched by an exuberant intelligence and inspired writing style. Over the next few years, the community of young exiles would grow to include Benjamín Villafañe, Carlos Tejedor, Guillermo Rawson, Manuel G. Quiroga Rosas, Demetrio Rodríguez Peña, Juan G. Godoy, Jacinto Rodríguez Peña, Julián Navarro, Leopoldo Zuloaga, Caupolicán de la Plaza, Gregorio Gómez, Antonino Aberastain, and Vicente F. López. At a later moment both Alberdi and Mitre would reside in Chile and would contribute substantially to the anti-Rosas campaign there.

The Chilean-based members of the young Argentine generation did not have a feuding unitarian leadership to contend with, meaning that their collective energies were more concentrated on the struggle against Rosas. They organized an Argentine Commission similar to that in Montevideo, but unlike the latter this commission was headed by some of the most respected civic leaders from the interior provinces, many of whom had impeccable Federalist credentials: Gregorio de Las Heras, a general in the Independence struggle; Gregorio Gómez, San Martín's intimate friend and advisor; Gabriel Ocampo, ex-governor of La Rioja; Martín Zapata, a prominent member of the Mendozan community; and Domingo de Oro, relative of Sarmiento and former Rosas intimate whose recent disenchantment with the dictator and with the federalist movement accounted for his exile and opposition. The commission members quickly integrated the young militants into their ranks when the militants' impressive talents had been demonstrated.

Between Valparaíso and Santiago the young Argentine militants were able to combine energies with the older generation of Rosas foes for a united effort against the Buenos Aires dictator. The geographical distance from Buenos Aires, however, meant that their efforts were restricted almost entirely to propagandistic objectives. In late 1841 Sarmiento attempted to steer the group toward a more belligerent stance, but the defeat of General Gregorio de Lamadrid's army in northern Argentina meant that his efforts went entirely toward the rescue of that fighting force's straggling survivors. For the next nine years, the primary anti-Rosas activity of the young militants in Santiago was the publication of provocative articles in the political press of the region.

There were other issues affecting these Chilean-based militants that assumed importance in the context of the competing ideologies and political movements of the time. Heading this list was Sarmiento's early decision to lend his writing energies and allegiance to the Chilean Conservative Party, whereas several of the other young Argentine exiles, differing stridently with Sarmiento, closed ranks behind the liberal opposition. Several years earlier the primary architect of the conservative regime had been Diego Portales; his name henceforth would be used in relation to the period in Chilean political history that would last until 1861. A few years prior to Sarmiento's arrival, Portales had been assassinated, and Manuel Bulnes had been elected president. One of the primary figures in Bulnes's cabinet was Sarmiento's future intimate and supporter, Manuel Montt, who would be elected Chile's president a decade later. Within months after his arrival in Valparaiso, Sarmiento's budding talents as a writer and thinker were obvious to all, and he received invitations from both the liberals and the conservatives to serve in their ranks. What were Sarmiento's motivations for turning his back on the Liberal Party when he shared its objectives to no small degree? In contrast to some mistaken commentary, the conservative Portales regime offered positive avenues for progress.[50] Indeed the conservative governments of Portales, Bulnes, and Montt successfully encouraged an active press, created an intellectual climate conducive to progress, founded the national university and a training school for teachers, and laid the foundations for a public education system that would become a model for the continent. All of this occurred in a period when Rosas, across the frontier, was driving the members of the educated elite into exile, restricting funds destined for educational endeavors, and discriminating against innovative ideas emanating from foreign sources. Under Portales and his successors, Chile definitely was not reverting back to stagnant colonial practices. More correct was the judgment of José Victorino Lastarria, Chilean liberal and lifelong friend of Sarmiento— although the two disagreed about the merits of life in Chile under the conservatives. Lastarria, in 1868, was to characterize Chile's government of the past thirty-six years as "a small, intimate oligarchy with all-powerful, repressive powers, that is to say, a small number of men and wealthy families who have controlled access to the regime and have sustained it."[51]

Sarmiento's position was representative; he, like Alberdi, Frías, V. F. López, and several other young Argentine militants in Chile, would find in that country's government an admirable model of constitutional authoritarianism. That governmental system, with the support of the existing socioeconomic elites, sincerely worked on behalf of civil reforms, the moral improvement of the masses, and material progress.[52] His acceptance of the government's invitation to direct its official newspaper probably surprised few of his intimate friends. Not untypical was the precedent he gave to order and authority over his liberal agenda promoting liberty and democratic participation. Alberdi, Frías, López, and others demonstrated a similar contradictory ideological baggage: with eminently conservative social values they, paradoxically, were to become the leaders in Argentina's liberal transformation after the fall of Rosas. Their diverse ideas anticipated the conservative brand of liberalism that was to predominate in Argentina after the fall of Rosas and would remain in place well into the next century. It was a liberalism that would promote new productive practices, free trade, immigration, and education; it would fortify a political regime dominated by the region's powerful economic interests which ·would prioritize order and stability over mass participation.

LITERARY AND CULTURAL PURSUITS

After 1841, the focus of the young militants' activities took a decidedly cultural shift. The disastrous denouement of the Lavalle invasion and the series of regional uprisings against Rosas during the previous two years were to leave them with deep scars in their sensibilities. Their campaign against Rosas had suffered a major setback, and several of the young militants had perished. Defeat was truly a bitter pill to swallow. As was expected the responses of the survivors differed, although few if any would abandon the principles that earlier had inspired their struggle. The majority realized that in spite of their ignominious defeat, they must now continue their struggle against the Rosas dictatorship and on behalf of liberal progress in other channels. They had to abide their time in exile, channeling their energies in new and constructive directions. They knew that it was only a matter of time before a new opposition to Rosas's strong-armed rule would call upon their now-seasoned leadership.

A half-decade earlier Echeverría had defined the directions that their energies would now follow. They had to encourage a "regeneration" of

American "intelligence" and lead society's institutions in a process of development to overcome the retrograde feudal and medieval institutions inherited from the Spanish colonial system. Through their writings, they would continue to argue the relevancy of contemporary European thought as the key to creating an ideological and cultural terrain conducive to progress. Transformations in the country's cultural and social institutions would then cause pressure for similar changes in government. This plan of "moral regeneration" was the route they now chose for combatting Rosas; it would be slow, but its end result was certain.

The young militants, regardless of their different places of exile and their varied cultural or educational experiences, were in basic agreement about the philosophical underpinnings of this cultural mission. They shared a common intellectual formation in their readings of Tenneman, Leroux, Cousin, Montesquieu, and Mazzini in philosophy (to only name a few of their principal influences); Guizot and Michelet in history (through whom they also assimilated the ideas of Vico and Herder); Chateaubriand, Hugo, and Larra in romanticism and literature; and Tocqueville—the "the book occupying the seat of honor" for their generation—in democratic thought. At the time their critics in Buenos Aires disrespectfully referred to them as romantics, but they preferred the label of *eclécticos* (the eclectics) or *socialistas*, names that they took from writings of Claude-Henri de Rouvroy or the Count of Saint-Simon.

Beginning with their recognition of the need for a moral or cultural revolution, the young militants defined the four general areas of cultural activism: the study of progressive ideas, the dissemination of those ideas through educational action, journalistic writing in order to disseminate those progressive ideas and carry on their ideological struggle against Rosas, and the creation of a national culture and literature. All these areas of activity pointed to one primary goal: the preparation of their society for institutional change. The infusion of progressive ideas would have to occur simultaneously on all levels of the region's culture: politics, philosophy, religion, science, art, and industry. This total revolution in cultural practices, ideas, and institutions was what they meant by their goal of the "emancipation of the American spirit."[53]

The members of this talented generation came together in embracing this plan for cultural and institutional renovation. Their common doctrine can be summarized as follows:[54]

(1) Occidental societies participated in a historical process, guided by Providence, that evidenced continual improvement in technology, material well-being, and social, political, and cultural institutions.

(2) The development of a given society was seen as integral, which is to say that the condition of any one institution generally reflected the stage or level of development of the society in its totality. With this understanding a cause of concern for the young militants was the discrepancy between the political and social status of their young country: it had won political emancipation from Spain a generation before but had yet to achieve independence in the realm of the "intelligence." According to Alberdi, "[I]f cultural emancipation is the primary goal of our nation, then the first step toward achieving it is to energetically break with the stagnant Spanish intellectual tradition."[55]

(3) The youths of 1837 viewed favorably the Romantic literary movement in that it participated in the task of breaking down the vestiges of Spanish culture. Romanticism's rebellion before Classicism parallelled their own struggle to overcome the region's decrepit colonial tradition. "Literature will not be for us Virgil and Cicero," wrote Alberdi.[56] Sarmiento, in his turn, argued, "Anxious to shake the existing political and literary chains, we eagerly put ourselves at the head of any group that even remotely resembled a movement."[57]

(4) This rebellious attitude before Spanish colonial or feudal traditions accounted, at least in part, for their attraction to European ideas. They recognized the need for "importing from Europe's intellectual and literary traditions"—in the words of Gutiérrez—and especially those from France, England, and Prussia (present-day Germany). But the value of those new ideas or cultural products would be assessed only in relation to their effect in "giving us an analogous education that would harmonize with our own people and our own culture."[58]

(5) This anticlassical position also manifested itself in the field of language. Their country, newly independent and developing its own resources, required a language similarly independent from its European origins that would evolve in accordance with the lived reality of the Argentine people. According to Gutiérrez, "We shouldn't aspire to a frozen norm of elegance and purity [in the language inherited from Spain], for reasons related to the state of society resulting from our political emancipation from the the former metropolis."[59] Sarmiento utilized this same line of reasoning in the early 1840s in vociferously promoting reforms in the Spanish alphabet and spelling system.[60]

(6) In the first instance, Romanticism in thought and literature had contributed in the glorious movements for emancipation in the West: the French Revolution and the successful struggles for in-

dependence of the United States and the Hispanic American republics. However too large a dose of a good thing was bound to have negative consequences. Such was the destiny of Rousseau's *The Social Contract*, the romantic work par excellence of the previous generation, whose extreme doctrines about democracy were responsible, at least in part, for having ushered in a period of libertarianism and disorder that was now necessary to bring to a close.

(7) Some of the 1837 activists confusedly repeated the saying popularized by Victor Hugo, that for all intents and purposes Romanticism was liberalism incarnated in literature. As self-proclaimed liberals, they therefore rushed to proclaim their nominal adherence to literary Romanticism. But they took offense when others called them "Romantics," a term associating them with the promoters of unruly, reckless rebellion. With more confidence they embraced the label of "socialistas"—at least up until the revolutionary outbreaks of Europe in 1848. A safer term for self-identification was "liberal"; they embraced the theories of classical liberalism in its defense of free trade and exchange of ideas, but the "liberalism" of their social and political advocations was tinged with a strong dose of elitism that would have offended Rousseau, the radical educator from Geneva.[61]

(8) On the political level—which in Alberdi's writings was generally referred to as the "philosophical" level—they embraced many of the doctrines of the "Eclectic" School and thus identified with the conservative "restoration" movement in Europe that sought to undo many of the excesses of the French Revolution and return society back to order and progress under the leadership of the propertied and intellectual elites. This explains their somewhat confusing combination of liberal and conservative advocacies. Although they sought a renovation of culture and a regeneration of values and ideas, they generally favored stable social and political systems in which the educated elites exercised a paternalistic influence over the unschooled masses.

(9) In defining their literary and cultural program, the 1837 writers recognized the diversity of their formative influences. According to Sarmiento, "Romanticism, eclecticism, socialism, all those diverse systems of ideas had enthusiastic followers, and the study of such social theories was carried out in the shadow of a despotic system that was hostile to any form intellectual questioning."[62] "Socialism," the precursor movement of positivism, combined ideas learned from the writings of Saint-Simon, Fourier, Leroux, Lamennais, and others. Uniting all of these

thinkers was their promotion of mankind's development in all dimensions of social existence. Understood as such their "socialism" bore little resemblance to the revolutionary and collectivist advocations that, toward the end of the 1840s, were popularized throughout Europe by Marx and Engels under the same name.

(10) *Socialismo* was the term that the young militants generally used (until the late 1840s) in reference to their diverse baggage of ideas and advocations. According to their understanding of *socialism*, art, literature, and other social and cultural discourses contributed to the overall objective of promoting the development of the human spirit. Alberdi wrote, "We are profoundly convinced that art, in its essence, ought to enjoy a tight, harmonious intimacy with social objectives."[63] According to Sarmiento, "Socialism, pardon our use of the word; socialism, that is to say, the need for science, art, and politics to join together with the sole goal of improving the plight of a people, favoring liberal tendencies, combatting retrograde concerns, and rehabilitating the common people, the mulatto, and all those who suffer."[64] Because of the importance they granted to literature and art in the advancement of society, contemporary critics have labeled their ideas "utopian" and "idealist."

(11) With the exception of Larra, no contemporary presence on the Spanish intellectual scene offered a worthy example for the young Argentine intellectuals in their own quest for South America's literary and cultural emancipation. For most of them the source of progressive ideas was, in the first instance, France, and, to a lesser extent, England. Later Alberdi and Sarmiento would add as worthy models the creative work emanating from the United States of North America.

(12) The literary mission of this generation of writers and future statesmen was to lay the foundations for a bona fide *national* literature. Echeverría was the first to glean from romantic theory this national quest; the most authentic *modern poetry* was that by the writers who eschewed imitation and fueled their creativity of characters, thoughts, and forms from influences in the world immediately surrounding them.[65] Sarmiento, in a letter of 1846 (later published as part of *Viajes*— Travels), prophetically called attention to some of the earliest contributions of this guise by members of his own generation:

Ascasubi utilizes at times with admirable facility that popular [gauchi-political] genre that translates the concerns of the masses into measured accents. . . . Echeverría describing the scenes of the pampas, Maldonado imitating the singer's affable language, full of countryside images—what the heck!—why shouldn't I also include myself here, my efforts to describe in *Quiroga* the life and instincts of the Argentine cattlehand; and Ruguendas, painting with exactness the customs of South America; we have here the beginnings of that fantastic, homeric literature that captured the barbaric life of the gaucho. . . .[66]

The above twelve points constituted the philosophical foundation for the literary mission embraced by the principal members of the 1837 Generation. In tracing the path of dissemination of these ideas, there is little doubt that it was Echeverría who served as teacher and mentor for the youths during the crucial stage of ideological definition and initiation of group praxis. In identifying the pages that contain the most precise and detailed exposition of the above points, the assiduous reader could point to some early essays of Echeverría, Alberdi, and Sarmiento—especially in the latter's articles for the literary polemics in the early 1840s.

THE POLEMICS ON LANGUAGE AND LITERATURE IN SANTIAGO

In chronological order, the first of several polemics on literature and culture that involved members of the young generation took place between Santiago and Valparaíso, Chile. The setting was ripe for some type of confrontation; the social and political contradictions affecting several of the young Argentine exiles were bound to find strident release in one form or another. Perhaps most exasperating was the frustration felt by the enterprising Argentine youths whose superior intellectual talents could hardly find an outlet amid the more humble cultural practices of the host country. Then there was the inevitable backlash of local resentment on the part of some of the local writers. Further friction was forthcoming on the political level; Sarmiento and a few of his associates found ready acceptance in the folds of the ruling conservatives after declining to offer their intellectual and journalistic talents to the Liberal Party, which on paper seemed to be most compatible with their own social and political agenda.

The Chilean environment was, therefore, ripe for confrontation. When it did occur, few people were caught by surprise. The precipitating issue was a polemic over the role of language and literature in society that pitted the militant perspectives of Sarmiento, V. F. López, and other Argentine exiles against the more conservative tendencies of Santiago's cultural elite. It would be a mistake to believe that this elite was a bastion of reactionary, feudal thought. Andrés Bello, native of present-day Venezuela and the continent's most distinguished legal expert, literary scholar, and philosopher, headed the list of polemical foes. Bello's revolutionary credentials could hardly have been in question; several years before he had distinguished himself as teacher and tutor of republican ideals for Simón Bolívar. After years of European exile, Bello, with a truly pan-Spanish American consciousness, had chosen Chile as the site of his future endeavors; that country's social and political stability provided the appropriate atmosphere for the important philosophical and intellectual endeavors that he would undertake. In his Chilean residence from 1829 until his death in 1865, Bello was to produce the finest chapters of an intellectual *oeuvre* of breadth and rigor which had no comparison in the Hispanic American republics of his century. Among his accomplishments are seminal works in the philosophy of aesthetic appreciation, perception, and intelligence; detailed examinations of Roman and Spanish jurisprudence to provide the new Latin American republics with a legal system worthy of the ideals of their independence; the finest poems and essays in the region's neoclassical canon; and a grammar of Spanish-American language usage to serve the new republics in the construction of a truly national culture.

Given the progressive orientations of both Sarmiento and Bello, the polemics that erupted between them and their cohorts could hardly have been over transcendental issues. Instead these polemics can be compared to the ripples on the surface of a flowing stream. In truth, both sides were in essential agreement over the most substantive issues: the commitment to Chile's material progress, technical and productive innovation, and invigorated cultural life. Regardless of this agreement, neither Sarmiento nor Bello hesitated to air publicly their differences over more formalistic concerns.

The different camps for these publicly aired debates over language and literature quickly rallied around the banners of neoclassicism and Romanticism. In frank contrast to Bello's ideas of a decorous language and literature that would follow established norms and respected models, Sarmiento defended a writing practice based on spontaneity, emotion, and love for one's national culture. To their credit several young Chilean intellectuals—Manuel Antonio Tocornal, Salvador Sanfuentes, José Victorino Lastarria, and others—ended up embracing the principles of the Romantic ideology that Sarmiento defended. The spirit of the time favored cultural renovation. Sarmiento, quoting from the Spanish liberal, Mariano José de Larra, won adherents by arguing that a critical writing practice anticipated and promoted cultural progress. This aspect of the Romantic ethos coincided with the primary advocacy of Saint-Simonian *socialismo:* the imperative of directing all linguistic, literary, and intellectual activity toward the primary objectives of material and institutional progress.

POETIC COMPETITIONS IN MONTEVIDEO

After their disappointments in war, many of the Montevideo-based Argentine exiles returned to their first callings: journalism, cultural history, and literature. For some a militant brand of journalism was a natural and timely extension to their previously impassioned efforts to organize military opposition to the Rosas tyranny. But how should one account for the turn to poetry of several, if not the majority, of the principal figures of this young generation? Several of them who already possessed a strong poetic inclination sincerely embraced the objective of promoting a national literary and cultural tradition. All were attracted to the life of the spirit and the intellect; all repeatedly demonstrated their appreciation for the artistic and literary efforts of their countrymen. Poetic creation, in part, also served to sublimate the frustrations deriving from the military defeats they had suffered.

The need for the country's writers to give birth to a truly national literature had been a guiding idea since their initiation to public life. Echeverría's introductory notes to *Los consuelos* (Consolations) in 1834 contained perhaps the first announcement in the Plata region of the romantic imperative of clothing one's poetry with "its own original character [in order that it be] at the same time a live sketch of our customs, and the highest expression of our prevailing ideas, of those sentiments and passions that result from the clash of rival social interests. . . ."[67] This idea of an "organic" literature, in its basic form, would be repeated by Alberdi in his *Fragmento* (1837) and would acquire the status of generational mandate by its inclusion in the young generation's *Creencia* that same year. The youthful Bartolomé Mitre, in one of his first undertakings as commentator of the region's cultural and intellectual activity, demonstrated at that time the widespread acceptance of this concept among the region's youth when he declared the "genius" of Echeverría's *La cautiva* as "American Literature" because it communicated "the heart that Americans speak."[68]

By 1841 the young militants in Montevidean exile fully embraced the objective of promoting an emancipated "intelligence" and a national art. Even those of neoclassical persuasion were in agreement. Unitarian poet Juan Cruz Varela, and even more so his brother Florencio, embraced the *Creencia*'s call for an art and a poetry that would sing of "heroism and liberty, and would solemnly celebrate all the great acts, private as well as public, in the life of nations."[69] What better way to soothe the wounds of defeat and promote new harmony among Montevideo's otherwise feuding factions than to celebrate the anniversary of the region's independence from Spain? What better way to harness the considerable artistic talents of the city's residents than through a friendly "poetic competition"? That was what the city's leaders intended.

The enthusiasm engendered by the poetic competition would be hard to understand today. Competition was intense, with the best poetic minds in the city submitting some of the finest compositions written to that date on patriotic themes. The jury, headed by Florencio Varela, awarded the top prize to Juan María Gutiérrez for his composition, "Canto a Mayo." The other poets who were recognized constituted the cream of the literary society of the city: Luis Domínguez, José Mármol, and José Rivera Indarte, from the ranks of the militant youth; and the venerable Uruguayan poet and civic leader, Francisco Acuña de Figueroa. Varela, in the newspaper article treating the poetic competition, revealed—to no one's surprise—his adherence to prestigious classical tendencies and his general intolerance for the romantic ideas and modes of expression then in vogue in Europe as well as the Hispanic American capitals. The jury he headed bestowed top honors upon the members of the young generation—more because of their thematic treatment than their poetic style. Alberdi then decided to add his own perspective to the polemic in an article printed in the local press.[70] He could hardly complain about the jury's winning selections, but he criticized the criteria that were based on "old ideas" which hardly took into account "the new tendencies" with "all their faults and beauties." He contradicted Varela's opinion that their national poetry had emerged at the time of the Revolution of 1810; instead, he asserted that no truly independent mode of versification predated the poems written by Echeverría and his disciples that appeared only in the past decade.

If the poetic competition of 1841 served to unite the young militants in defense of a new artistic sensitivity, a similar event in 1844 precipitated a split in their ranks. The dispute resulting from the latter event did little to spread new ideas; it merely blemished the reputations of those participating. At the 1844 event, different readers recited the poems submitted to a packed audience in the city's theater. Those poems by Domínguez and Echeverría were applauded enthusiastically, while the uninspired delivery of an otherwise fine poem by Rivera Indarte was less warmly received. Rivera Indarte apparently took offense by this. In his published review of the competition, he chose to ignore entirely the participation of Echeverría, which set off a series of public exchanges between the two that featured petty invective and pathetic rationalizations. In the following weeks both Domínguez and Echeverría poured

out their feelings about the entire matter in letters to Juan María Gutiérrez, then residing in Santiago, Chile. But Gutiérrez, the generational
peacemaker, was only able to intercede with belated advice after the
harm had been done. Gutiérrez counseled Echeverría, whose physical
and intellectual decline must have been of concern to all:

> But I must confess to you that I learned of the affair with great sorrow, because
> those who find themselves on the same side shouldn't draw each other into
> bloody battle. . . . Your conduct in that affair—as always—was to all appear-
> ances discrete and noble. . . . I do request that you put all that has happened
> behind you, that henceforth you not speak or write against Indarte. . . . Con-
> tinue advancing on your own writing projects, my dear Esteban, and put
> totally out of your mind the possibility that a thorn here or there could pene-
> trate to prick your foot.[71]

Echeverría's creative talents were on the decline even though his reputation as a poet remained intact. The romantic movement in the Plata that
he had initiated nearly a decade earlier had won enthusiastic recruits
from among the young generation. Within the next decade Echeverría's
disciples would produce their finest works, which today constitute the
foundation of the nation's literary tradition.

The Anti-Rosas Campaign in Writing: Rivera Indarte

The first of the great propagandistic works written against Rosas was
José Rivera Indarte's *Rosas y sus opositores* (Rosas and his detractors—
1843). Published initially as series of newspaper articles, the widely
read work had an indisputable impact on several influential European
readers. The work enumerates hundreds of crimes allegedly committed
by the Porteño dictator in the first fourteen years of his government and
placed the number of his victims at over twenty-thousand. Perhaps of
even greater resonance at the time was the work's seventy-five-page appendix entitled, "It is a holy war that with the objective of killing Rosas,"
an essay that united philosophy and classical erudition in presenting an
apology of tyrannicide.[72]

In spite of the work's remarkable effectiveness as anti-Rosas propaganda—and perhaps even because of it—Rivera Indarte's reception
among the young exiles was strikingly mixed. On the one hand his
apologists—Mitre, Sarmiento, and others—lavished praise on the work,
finding nothing reprehensible about its endorsement of political assassination and nothing delirious in the author's invitation for Rosas's own
daughter to attempt to kill her father.[73] On the other hand Echeverría,
Domínguez, Alberdi, and others, although admiring the fresh, dar-

ing language of the work, were repelled at the savagery of its content. Largely in response to the writings of Rivera Indarte, Echeverría would curse, until the time of his death, the harmful legacy of the Montevidean-based propagandists in their irresponsible ideological campaign against *rosismo*. Undoubtedly Echeverría's hatred of Rivera Indarte had other, more personal causes. But, if one is to believe the words of Domínguez, an Echeverría partisan in this affair, the disrespect for Rivera Indarte in Montevideo was fairly widespread: "Indarte, in general, is quite detested by those constituting the literary community."[74] Alberdi's severest criticism of Rivera Indarte's ideas would anticipate his general reaction to the national state that would emerge in the 1860s under Mitre's and Sarmiento's leadership: "Liberty is too beautiful to have ever been born from crime."[75]

Sarmiento's *Facundo*

The 1837 activists had theorized about a national literature in the form of poetry, drama, and the novel, but they hardly knew how to respond when they first confronted what posterity has unanimously recognized as the "foundation book" for not only Argentina's literary and cultural tradition but also Latin America's Romantic canon. This is probably because they, as well as the contemporary reader, found in this singular work a confusing mixture of discourses: the imaginative or creative, the historical, the sociological, and the essayistic. In an earlier letter written to Alberdi, Sarmiento had prophetically provided a worthy definition of the writerly impulse within himself that later became manifest in its pages; a sort of "literary libertarianism" was manifest in both his own character and that work.[76]

In Sarmiento's words the work was composed, in a "rapture of liricism" during a few intense weeks; it was originally published by installments in *El progreso* of Santiago, but within months it was circulating throughout Argentina and the Plata region in book form. It is impossible to do justice here to its many complexities, ambiguities, and contradictions, which have been thoroughly analyzed by a century and a half of criticism. Briefly the work unites three highly contrasting sections. The first, which was inspired by sociological or ethnographic theory, in addition to the idiosyncratic beliefs of the author, attempted to account for the present state of the Argentine society as it existed after twenty years of devastating civil skirmishes. As such four successive chapters focus respectively on the region's landscape of endless pampas; the psychology of rural inhabitants that resulted from their residence in that primitive environment; the social institutions arising in that physical setting and in accordance with the particular values and orientations of its inhabitants; and the historical events of recent years that were the product of this totality of geographic, psychological, and social factors. Within these chapters Sarmiento did not fail to include memorable *costumbrista* (custom sketches) passages that romantically portrayed certain character types of the Argentine pampas: the *pathfinder*, the *cattle hand*, the *bad gaucho*, and the gaucho *singer*.

The work's second section, which was Sarmiento's subjective incursion into biography and romantically rendered history, lambasted the life and exploits of the Promethean caudillo from La Rioja, Juan Facundo Quiroga, whose assassination had sent the whole country into turmoil eleven years earlier. Sarmiento's own origins in the neighboring province of San Juan gave him access to firsthand data that provided a semblance of authenticity to his historical and literary portrait. However his skewed selection and presentation of that data largely followed from his political objective of attacking Quiroga and, by extension, Rosas.[77]

The third section, which Sarmiento saw fit to exclude entirely from the 1851 edition, denounced Rosas's tyrannical practices. In the first two chapters, Sarmiento demonstrated how the assassination of Quiroga and its repressive aftermath served Rosas well in his overall plan of bringing the entire country under his own draconian authority. His bold thesis was that in spite of a nominal allegiance to federalist principles, Rosas in fact succeeded in imposing over the entire country a "absolutist unitarian government" whose authority was centered in himself. In the second chapter, "Present and future," Sarmiento optimistically argued that the "new generation" of "studious youth" to which he belonged, with its origins in the Association that first met in Buenos Aires in 1838, promised a "new government" that would lead the country back into the orbit of progress and morality once the dictator fell. This was the young generation's most ambitious statement to date of their mandate to assume the future direction of the country. In these pages Sarmiento did not hesitate to embrace two controversial positions already assumed by Alberdi and the Montevidean-based militants. First he defended the correctness of their alliance with France in order to "save European civilization, its institutions, customs, and ideas that have taken root on the shores of the Plata."[78] And second, in the interest of a "educated government" that would promote a Europeanized *civilization* in the Plata region, he attacked the "*American* principle" of the Rosas regime, as well as the federalists' defense of a "nationality" that was at odds with the interests of the European powers.

Although his generational cohorts found in this work an eloquent and passionate defense of their own beliefs, they were almost unanimous in their private correspondence in denouncing Sarmiento's distortions and exaggerations.[79] Was this negative reaction a result of the disdain that the sons of the Porteño cultural elite might have directed at any provincial upstart? For Carlos Tejedor the book was little more than a "political libel," and in V.F. López's opinion, it was a type of "Bedouin history."[80] Echeverría, however, was more generous. In the *Ojeada retrospectiva* (Retrospective glance) of 1846, he praised Sarmiento, calling him "the most complete and original [writer] to have emerged from the ranks of the young Argentine exiles." But in spite of Sarmiento's historiographical accomplishments in selecting and interpreting data and arriving at convincing conclusions, Echeverría called attention to a notable lack: Sarmiento was "deficiently dogmatic," meaning that the impetuous writer sacrificed system and perspective in favor of dramatic exposition.[81] Four years later, after reading Sarmiento's hardly complimentary comments about himself that were published in *Viajes*, Echeverría expanded upon this negative assessment in a letter full of complaints to Alberdi; he now called attention to the predominance in Sarmiento's writing of "fantastic lucubrations, descriptions with a torrent of sterile prattle." "Sarmiento's going mad," he wrote, due to his obsession with the Buenos Aires dictator: "The ghost of Rosas pursues him, haunts him, rattles him, and leads him to make a most pitiful fool of himself."[82]

Then there was Gutiérrez, whose criticisms were never taken lightly. On most occasions his opinions rose above petty invective, but Sarmiento's *Facundo* hardly caused a favorable impact with him. In an indignant letter to Alberdi, he accused Sarmiento of slighting the cultural and institutional accomplishments of Buenos Aires (a criticism that Alberdi in a later moment would indirectly refute). Nor could he agree with Sarmiento's tragic interpretation of the country's past and future: "The Argentine Republic is hardly a pool of blood: our progress cannot be reduced to the progress of public schooling in San Juan." Gutiérrez, a shade less than infuriated, charged that the serious reader could hardly accept the work as a serious historical study: "Any level-headed man will see it for what it is, a caricature . . . it will have a negative effect on the Republic."[83]

Initially Alberdi probably did not share the indignation of Gutiérrez. In spite of the impassioned polemic between him and Sarmiento after 1853, Alberdi's comments in *Cartas quillotanas* (Letters from Quillota— 1853) were remarkably evenhanded. These were the first of many paragraphs that he would write about Sarmiento's ideas in the course of a long career. Although he praised the "infinite talent" of the author whose considerations had "much truth," he criticized the author's tendency to exaggerate, romanticize, and dramatize the events treated.[84] Sarmiento mistakenly identified the city as the center of civilization and the countryside as the source of barbarism. Indeed Alberdi pointed out a fundamental paradox that the work demonstrated things that contradicted the conscious design of its author: "*Facundo* is not only the history of barbarism and the process of the Argentine caudillos, but also the history and process of the errors of Argentine civilization, as represented by the Unitarian Party."[85] Regardless of this conceptual confusion, Alberdi approved of Sarmiento's implicit endorsement of their generation hallmark in his attempt to distance himself from the destructive policies of unitarians and federalists alike. In this regard Alberdi believed that the work contributed to the struggle against Rosas and was in favor of the country's modernization.

In spite of this point of agreement, Alberdi's critique contained a seed of discontent that would grow to large proportions in the coming years: his complaint that Sarmiento's acts and publications subsequent to *Facundo* increasingly betrayed a neounitarian stance in support of Buenos Aires localists. This emerging position signified Sarmiento's abandonment of the evenhanded position presented in *Creencia* and his increasing distance from the 1837 generation's conciliatory position that had sought a "fusion of the political tendencies."

Only Mitre among Sarmiento's generational brethren registered a totally favorable reaction to the work. This is perhaps because the two men, in this early moment of their involvement in the affairs of state, already shared a common ideological and political perspective which would become more and more pronounced as the years progressed. Both would become protagonists in the historical project of bringing the interior provinces under the authority of Buenos Aires; as historians both would be leaders in the revisionist project of erasing from the collective national memory any positive influence of the *caudillos* hailing from the country's interior regions.

The other young militants reacted much more favorably to Sarmiento's employment of the civilization-barbarism dichotomy than have critics in our own century.[86] Indeed Sarmiento's application of the dichotomy was hardly original; similar slogans were to be found in the writings of some of the most prestigious historians or European observers of Rioplatense events at the time. For example there is the strong possibility that Sarmiento found a prestigious model for his description of Argentina's "barbarian" gaucho society invading the "civilized" cities in French historian François Pierre Guillaume Guizot's portrayal of Europe's "barbaric" Middle Ages that followed the glories of Roman civilization.[87] Most probably Sarmiento was also influenced by articles published in the important *Revue des deux mondes* (Magazine of two worlds) and the widely read travel account by Francis B. Head, representative for British mining interests, all of which also utilized civilization-barbarism dichotomies in describing life and society in the Rioplatense region.[88] Among his generation of militant writers, Sarmiento was not alone in assimilating this opposition into his own analytical discourse; appearing within weeks of *Facundo* were the articles written by Andrés Lamas for Montevideo's *El nacional*. Like Sarmiento, Lamas described Rosas's Argentina in terms of a rural population, similar to Asiatic nomadic tribes, invading the civilized city and supporting the dictator in his quest of reviving the retrograde customs and institutions of the Spanish colony.

Another key perspective that Sarmiento shared with several of the other young militant writer-activists was what Gutiérrez had criticized as a fatalistic interpretation of the nation's experience. In Santiago, Sarmiento, together with V. F. López, Chilean José Victorino Lastarria, and others, had come under the spell of the "philosophy of history." This was the "historicist" practice of Chateaubriand, Cousin, and Guizot that turned away from the Enlightenment's pursuit of impartiality and instead attempted to define the "soul" or "spirit" that lay behind historical events. In assimilating these orientations, the young writers projected an "artistic" role for the writer of history who "idealized" his data and grouped his facts in a harmonious fashion.[89] According to this reasoning, if Sarmiento interpreted the land, climate, and psychology of the Argentine people to be inherently violent, then that violence would necessarily be reflected in historical events and in the acts of the country's leaders. Following this logic, he argued that the rise of Quiroga, the tyranny of Rosas, and Dorrego's assassination were all logical and even necessary occurrences. From *Facundo* we read:

> An evil exists because that's the way things are, and if you search for it in them you will find it; if a man represents it, and we then do away with that personification, then it will exist again in isolated form. . . . Lavalle didn't know at the time that by killing the body [of Dorrego] the soul would not disappear; nor did he realize that the character and existence of political figures are merely a reflection of the ideas, interests, and objectives of the party they represent.[90]

This is one example of Sarmiento exercising his interpretative powers as "philosopher" of his country's history. More rigorous and systematic (or "dogmatic") thinkers such as Gutiérrez, Alberdi, and Echeverría believed this practice to border on the irresponsible, even though they largely shared the opinion registered by Sarmiento about the negative contributions of Rosas in forcibly imposing his "caudillo" regime over the country.

At this time, Sarmiento and Alberdi largely came together in their judgments about the country's recent historical past, but, as mentioned above, there was one issue about which they demonstrated a significant discrepancy: the desirable role of Buenos Aires in the country's necessary transformation. In this regard Gutiérrez's early criticism about Sarmiento's supposedly harsh treatment of Buenos Aires in the pages of *Facundo* quickly faded in importance. In retrospect it was Alberdi who rendered the more accurate reading when he called attention to Sarmiento's almost dogmatic insistence that Buenos Aires, in its role as the country's dynamic metropolitan center and receptacle for Europe's progressive influences, was the country's best, if not only, hope for a rapid assimilation to civilized norms. In subsequent writings Alberdi would express again and again his profound disagreement with Sarmiento's localization of the cities as incarnating the impulses of civilization and the countryside as constituting the essence of barbarism. He would point out that Sarmiento's arguments in favor of Buenos Aires, the city, liberal ideals, and European influences—and the latter's corresponding condemnation of the *gaucho,* the *caudillo,* and many aspects of rural life—anticipated Sarmiento's emerging political agenda that largely favored Buenos Aires at the expense of the country's interior provinces. Within a few years the friendship between Sarmiento and Alberdi would totally dissolve when they followed opposing political options. Sarmiento (at least up until about 1880) would defend the central role of the metropolitan center in the country's drive toward progress. Alberdi, in contrast, would argue steadfastly that the accumulation of the country's financial and economic resources in Buenos Aires constituted the origin of backwardness and barbarism and was the primary factor accounting for the absence of a truly national capital.

Ironically the recent interpretation by Noël Salomon, although on the surface contradicting Alberdi's position, actually enriches our understanding of Sarmiento's own complex and contradictory orientations. Salomon authoritatively argues that Sarmiento's seminal work functioned as a harmonious "hymn to the Andean piedmont." His important thesis is that the worldview of the young Sarmiento was largely formed as a result of his identification with the progressive elite, which, during his youth, had led the province of San Juan into a golden epoch of economic prosperity, political republicanism, and high cultural attainments. As such the baggage of liberal ideas that found expression in *Facundo* spoke as much to Sarmiento's idealized conception of the unrecoverable provincial environment of his childhood as it did to an ideal plan of reforms inspired by his recent readings or his own limited firsthand knowledge of the country.[91]

MORE ANTI-ROSAS LITERATURE: LAMAS AND FRÍAS

The third great anti-Rosas diatribe was Andrés Lamas's *Apuntes sobre las agresiones del Dictador arjentino D. Juan Manuel de Rosas* (Notes about the aggressions of the Argentine dictator, D. Juan Manuel de Rosas), which united newspaper articles first published in 1845 in Montevideo's *El nacional*. For his extreme youth at the time, Lamas's list of accomplishments was already impressive. Born of a family dedicated to public service, he was still in his teens when he took charge of Montevideo's *El nacional*. His criticisms of Blanco (white party) president Manuel Oribe for having granted generous concessions to Rosas led to his first Brazilian exile in 1836, during which time he made friends with the young emperor, Dom Pedro II. From that time on, his dedication to the anti-Rosas struggle was total. During most of the years of the blockade (1841–52), he served as "political chief" of the city and at times doubled as chief of police, advisor, and cabinet member under the Colorado (Red) Party's General Rivera. Given his energy, broad education, and pro-Brazilian orientation, he was the logical person for the Argentine Commission to send to the Brazilian court in 1848 in search of support. In 1852, with a similar objective, Lamas returned to Brazil and succeeded in securing that country's participation in what would be the successful military incursion against Rosas under the leadership of Urquiza.

Many contradictory accounts have been written about Lamas's role in seeking Brazilian support for the Argentine exiles' cause against Rosas. Suffice to say here that, at the time, the members of the young generation—perhaps excepting Echeverría—saw in Brazil a possible ally because that country's young emperor was as intent as they were upon implementing a liberal plan of reforms in their backward and rebellious lands. A decade and a half later—on the occasion of the War of the Triple Alliance against Paraguay—Alberdi would fiercely criticize Mitre's policies of collaboration with an expansionist Brazilian state that desired annexation of Rioplatense territories. But with regard to the Brazil of 1845–52, the young militants demonstrated sincere gratitude for its assistance in their struggle against the Buenos Aires tyrant and granted Lamas major credit for gaining that support. The words of Frías to this effect were representative: the presence of the Brazilian army would help to "recover our liberty" and reestablish "a firm authority."[92]

In *Apuntes*, Lamas excerpted from Rosas's speeches and proclamations to document some of the accusations made by Rivera Indarte in *Rosas y sus opositores*. As such, the major value of the work was its documentary nature; the two-hundred-fifty pages of text were followed by an equal number dedicated to notes. Similar to the other two anti-Rosas works, his criticisms were largely on the political level: Rosas's abuses revolved around his conversion of the Argentine State into a war machine; his employment of "extraordinary" administrative powers led to gross violations of the public trust; and his armed insurgents destabilized the legitimately constituted authorities in Uruguay. There were also offenses of

a moral nature: Rosas encouraged religious fanaticism and biased reporting in the highly censored newspapers of the country—he was
"fully aware of the implications for this sad enterprise."[93] With the exception of frequent references to Uruguay, Lamas's arguments hardly
differed from those of Rivera Indarte and Sarmiento. Indeed, the "philosophical" reasons given for Argentina's endemic social problems were
remarkably similar to those offered by Sarmiento. According to Lamas
"in a material sense, [Rosas] obstructed civilization's defense as the
countryside progressively struck it down, and in doing so he facilitated
barbarism's reaction, which was its invasion of the cities through the
imposition of the customs of its nomadic tribes or those surviving from
the uncultured colonial epoch."[94] Similar to Sarmiento, Lamas depicted
an epic struggle that placed the civilization of the cities at the mercy of
the resurgent barbarism of the countryside; like Sarmiento he depicted
the latter as surviving in the region's retrograde colonial culture and
through the gaucho masses that resembled uncultured nomadic herds-
men. Sarmiento must have noticed the ideological and political affinities
linking Lamas to himself; in his April 1852 letter to Mitre, he praised
the latter: "What an admirable degree of prudence and practical ability
. . . [Lamas is] a treasure for our countries."[95] Mitre hardly needed this
recommendation, however. At least five years earlier he and Lamas had
already committed themselves to promoting each other's ideas and careers.[96] However, the same could not be said about Alberdi, who increasingly believed that views such as those propagated by Lamas were
dangerous, if not irresponsible. Alberdi, after mid-decade, increasingly
sought the means for dialoguing with Rosas. Yet the neounitarian tone
of Lamas's call for a "holy war" against Rosas[97] invited a return to the
destructive civil strife of a decade earlier. Alberdi could not totally agree
with the call by Lamas, Mitre, and Sarmiento for a centralized, urban,
and European mode for the country's future progress.

Féliz Frías's *La gloria del tirano Rosas* (The glory of the tyrant Rosas—
1847) also featured the abuses of the Rosas regime. After dedicated service as Lavalle's personal secretary during the tragic campaign of 1839–41,
Frías resided first in Bolivia, then in Chile, constantly battling poverty
and seeking responsibilities worthy of his estimable talents. In 1847,
shortly after publishing *La gloria*, Frías set off for Paris, where he would
serve as foreign correspondent for a Chilean newspaper until 1862. After
that date, he would reside in Buenos Aires, serving with distinction in
the legislature and continuing with his journalistic activities.

Frías prefaced *La gloria del tirano Rosas* with a letter written in praise
of Alberdi and Lavalle: the first for having motivated him to join in the
struggle against Rosas and the second whose "magnanimous action"
remained unblemished even in defeat. In the work Frías weaved a his-

tory of the region, lavishing praise on Rivadavia and eulogizing the Argentine martyrs (among them Rivera Indarte) whose struggles still remained unfinished.

Three ideas treated in this work invite further elaboration. First Frías was solidly behind Alberdi and Sarmiento in calling for an influx of North European immigrants whose orientations and culture offered a definite improvement over the country's majority population of Spanish descendants, *gaucho* half-breeds, and Indians. Second his conservative orientation led him to criticize time and again the dangerous rhetoric of revolutionary change that threatened the social stability needed for progress. In particular, he attacked the "socialist tendency of the revolutionary spirit" that, as recent events in France had demonstrated, endangered the principles of justice and morality.[98] The third idea, which came to assume the status of a crusade as the years advanced, was the indispensable role of religious instruction in educating citizens for a responsible role in democratic societies. The last two ideas will be treated in greater detail below.

ECHEVERRÍA AND *DOGMA SOCIALISTA*

Out of the whole generation of young militants, Echeverría suffered the greatest hardships and challenges in exile. After 1837, with the increase in Rosas's oppression, he had been extremely reluctant to absent himself from his homeland in spite of obvious dangers. After others from the recently formed Young Argentina were incarcerated or had fled to Montevideo, he sought the relative safety of his brother's humble *estancia* some twenty kilometers from Luján. There his meager means provided the bare essentials for material comforts. In this relative solitude he occupied his time by writing several ambitious poetic and didactic works. Any objectives he might have had some months earlier of organizing a resistance to the regime in power had been temporary shelved. His often quoted words, "To emigrate is to end your utility for the country," had obviously been coined during a moment when cultural and educational praxis on behalf of progressive causes was still possible.[99] A few years into his countryside sojourn, when Lavalle's march on Buenos Aires became a real possibility, Echeverría did not hesitate to join the local residents in signing his name to a petition demanding the tyrant's withdrawal. The failure of that campaign left no other option; in January 1841 Echeverría was forced to flee to Colonia del Sacramento in Uruguay. After several months there he finally moved to Montevideo.

Echeverría, whether in financial resources, occupational skills, or disposition, was hardly equipped for the trials of exile. In addition he suffered from an accumulation of physical ailments that merely accentuated his neurasthenic tendencies. His forced relocation in a society that placed little value on his superior intellectual and moral qualities contributed to his depression. His closest friends among the young generation, Alberdi and Gutiérrez, urged him to no avail to become active in their plans. After Lavalle's final defeat the three of them made plans to escape the besieged Montevideo and travel to Europe. However his fragile health and precarious economic condition forced him to stay behind.

After the departure of Alberdi and Gutiérrez, much of Echeverría's time was spent alone. Luis Domínguez wrote in a letter to Félix Frías: "Ever since he came to Montevideo, [Echeverría] has relegated himself to total inactivity. In vain we all have attempted to motivate him to do something: but he has not written even a line of prose or verse. I don't know what has become of his old aspirations."[100] Echeverría did demonstrate his willingness to participate in the military defense of the city, but his health impeded him from assuming an active role. When invited to apply his writing talents to the poetic and journalistic campaigns against Rosas, he refused. To do so, he reasoned in an 1844 letter, would be to contaminate the writing craft that he esteemed so much; in addition he argued that "the press has no effect, it's useless in the war against Rosas."[101] That year, when he finally became inspired to enter the poetic competition celebrating the May Revolution, the result was an increase in tension. Even though his composition received one of the top honors and warm applause from the crowd, what mattered most to him was the demonstration of petty jealousy and slander on the part of Rivera Indarte and others with regard to his contribution.

Echeverría's withdrawal from the active struggle confirmed his compatriots' fears that he lived in a totally different mental world. With every passing day he became more resigned to his approaching rendezvous with death. With "meek resignation" he accepted his humble task of reworking several long poems that he had been elaborating for years now. These poems, he believed, would be appreciated only in "the future, [they are] poems that my friends characterize as inopportune." Yet—as he explained in that same letter of 1844—the lonely task of enriching the literature of his homeland was to his way of thinking a noble form of patriotism. Latter day critics argue that nothing he wrote during his long exile compare in poetic force with his earlier works, that is, the melancholy and lyrical *Consuelos* and the colorful narrative epic of the pampas, *La cautiva* (The captive). In October 1842 he published the long autobiographical narrative poem, *La guitarra* (The guitar). Off and on for the next two years he worked on *El angel caído* (The fallen angel), which he would consider as his most important poetic effort.

His *Manual de enseñanza moral* (Manual of moral instruction—1846) clearly placed him in the ranks of Sastre and Sarmiento as one of his generation's leading advocates of public education. At the same time he teamed up with Lamas in founding the Historical and Geographical Institute of Uruguay. His poetic output continued. Before his death in 1851 he would complete two other long narrative poems treating the early events in the struggle against Rosas: *Insurrección del Sud de la Provincia de Buenos Aires* (Insurrection of the South of the Province of Buenos Aires) and *Avellaneda*.

Undoubtedly his growing disillusionment with the leaders of the rival anti-Rosas factions in Montevideo contributed to his lessened desire for direct involvement and his growing commitment to develop and disseminate the ideas that would benefit society in a less conflictive moment of the future. "I have decided to dedicate myself to promoting the ideas that our group inaugurated in Buenos Aires," he wrote to Alberdi in 1844, in reference to his plans to revise and republish the *Creencia* that had reached only a few hands some six years earlier. "This work is indispensable for the future. . . . it's a symbol, a banner, and it's necessary that all of us take it into account if we want to avoid divisions in our ranks. In the absence of any better document of its type, we ought to eulogize it."[102] Foremost on his agenda was the promotion of the young militants who had taken a protagonist role in the anti-Rosas movement over the past half-decade.[103] True to his word the revised work, coupled with the long essay "Ojeada retrospectiva sobre el movimiento intelectual en el Plata desde el año 1837" (Retrospective glance at intellectual movements in the Plata Region since the year 1837), was published in 1846 under the new and definitive name of *Dogma socialista* (Socialist dogma). At the same time he proposed the reestablishment of the society of young militants that had been formed previously in Buenos Aires under the new name of the Asociación de Mayo (May Association).

Important for understanding the ideological content of this seminal publication are four important letters written by Echeverría during this same period. First there were the two long letters published in response to Pedro De Angelis's review that appeared in the pro-Rosas journal, *Archivo americano* (American archive).[104] Here Echeverría's prose rose to a new height of clarity and concreteness as he refuted several criticisms and offered additional rationale for a number of his most important ideological positions. Also important were the letters, accompanied by copies of the freshly published *Dogma*, that Echeverría sent to Joaquín Madariaga and Justo José Urquiza, governors respectively of Corrientes and Entre Ríos. From his vantage point at the mouth of the Río de la Plata, Echeverría prophetically predicted that the most likely center of

future resistance to the Rosas tyranny would be the prosperous provinces of the Littoral, whose governments Madariaga and Urquiza
headed. In these letters he explained the objectives embraced by the
1837 movement and invited each to consider assuming leadership of the
future struggle.

José Ingenieros has provided an exhaustive study of all these writings
and articulates well the changes in Echeverría's perspectives since the
publication of the *Creencia* a half-decade before.[105] There were seven
points of contrast:

(1) *Dogma* (considered here as including "Ojeada retrospectiva") was
antirrosista, whereas the *Creencia* was not;
(2) Echeverría, in 1846, was passionately anti-unitarian in contrast to
the mild opposition expressed before;
(3) now he expressed a Christian–anticlerical perspective, in contrast
to what was formerly a Christian-liberal orientation;
(4) his writings now had a nationalist orientation rather than a humanitarian one;
(5) there was now an attempt to relate ideas to an Argentine context,
whereas before what predominated was the gloss of doctrinaire
European texts;
(6) the work now reflected the "socialist" influence of Leroux, in contrast to the mystical, democratic-social influence of Lamennais of
before; and
(7) finally, Echeverría's new objective was to put forth the program
for an Argentine political party, in contrast to the earlier objective
of founding the Plata region's equivalent to Young Europe.

A few of the above points require longer explanations.

How can one account for Echeverría's recent antiunitarian sentiments?
Ingenieros mentions his wounded vanity as a result of the unitarian
leaders' continued silence over or scorn for his ideas and writings. More
important was his recent memory of how the unitarians' inner-party
rivalries had brought about the terrible defeats inflicted by pro-Rosas
forces. In the pages of *Dogma socialista*, Echeverría called the unitarians
egotists, power hungry, and unprincipled; little good would result were
they ever to assume the leadership of the country. This negative view
was echoed by Sarmiento in *Facundo*, published only a year earlier. One
of Sarmiento's most memorable passages depicted the typical *unitario* as
arrogant, ideologically dogmatic, snobbish, pompous, and totally lacking in practical sense.[106] But Echeverría's reasons for hating the unitarians also had to do with the antidemocratic and antinational focus to

their struggle: "Because [the Unitarian Party] turned its back on the democratic tradition of the [May] revolution and its program took little or no account of our history or our social state."[107] This last passage contains some perplexing words. Wasn't it true that Echeverría and the other exiles had allied themselves with the French in organizing an invasion against the nationalistic Rosas? And wasn't it also true that Rosas, at the time, represented better than any other individual the crude "democratic" sentiment of Argentina's majority population? Some passages of these uneven writings suggest that Echeverría was well aware, at least in a few lucid moments, of these paradoxes in his advocacies. The words quoted above reveal Echeverría's rarified idealism: he spoke of a utopian form of democracy and national society that would be based on the intelligent deliberations among men of equal station. It was this rarified dream of future possibilities that led him to condemn the crude practices of his own day.

Understandably the other young militants did not register enthusiasm in public for Echeverría's ideas. Echeverría expressed his anger in a letter to Gutiérrez that none of Montevideo's newspapers, and not even Florencio Varela's El comerico de la Plata (Commerce in the River Plate), gave Dogma the attention he thought it deserved: "The press of Montevideo, represented today exclusively by V. [Florencio Varela], has been totally silent: it has not wanted to, or better yet, it has feared to get involved in this issue."[108] Gutiérrez wrote back from Valparaíso, stating that the press there would not touch the subject either.[109] José Mármol's response was perhaps representative: while demonstrating his respect for Echeverría's work, he stated that he could not embrace in full the ideas it expressed.[110] Sarmiento must have had similar reservations about the lasting value of Dogma socialista, given that he mentions the work only twice in passing in his voluminous writings. In typical fashion he seriously misread some of Echeverría's most important thrusts: "Nobody has pointed out the objections to democracy more vigorously that you," he wrote.[111] In spite of these negative responses, Echeverría continued to emphasize the importance of this work: "[It], meanwhile, has been received with universal applause by Argentines and Uruguayans. Very soon it will circulate in Entre Ríos, Corrientes, and Buenos Aires, and I hope that it will solicit deep sympathies there."[112] In retrospect this prediction was entirely correct; even though the poet's idea of founding a new political force, or a May Association, was never actualized, Dogma was favorably received by Urquiza. The latter, within months after his victorious campaign against Rosas in 1852, invited Gutiérrez to incorporate many of Echeverría's ideas into his early speeches and, later, into the governing program that would prevail during the life of the Confederation.

PROPAGANDISTIC WRITING AND THE EUROPEAN CONNECTION

The young militants had learned that European support for their struggle against Rosas was a mixed blessing. With it they dramatically increased their possibilities for military success. There were, however, two major risks in recurring to foreign assistance: they ran the risk of losing whatever support that might be gained from the nationalistic masses, who disliked foreign influences; and they might have to meet unpalatable demands in exchange for that assistance. There was an additional danger—as the young militants had learned in 1841—foreign support bred dependency, and its sudden denial endangered their whole campaign. Yet the benefits still outweighed the costs. With no Argentine leader powerful enough to challenge Rosas, the young militants continued seeking the means for convincing the French government to renew its activist role in the River Plate region and persuading the British government to terminate its conciliatory relationship with Rosas. As they saw it their activity as writers and propagandists was essential for achieving these ideological objectives.

However the exiled militants found few individuals in Great Britain's power circles willing to embrace their cause. Since the latter decades of the previous century, Great Britain had incessantly pursued commercial and naval interests in the region of the Plata. In 1832 the British navy had ignored the protests of Argentina, the United States, and France when it took possession of the Malvinas Islands, renaming them the Falklands, in order to establish a naval base and outfitting station for any future trade in regions bathed by Southern Atlantic and Pacific waters. By the 1840s European interests, primarily British, had assumed direct control over at least half of the commercial establishments and stores in Buenos Aires. With this advantageous position the British government defended a conservative, basically noninterventionalist position vis-à-vis Rosas.[113] The exasperated exiles continually petitioned the agents of the British government for a change in this policy, arguing that the articulated objectives of the British state coincided more with their own liberal orientations than with the retrograde program of the Rosas government. But they frustratingly came to realize that British policy was not liable to change. In spite of the differing opinions within both the British government and the British community residing in the Río de la Plata, that country's official policy of "neutrality" in effect bolstered the position of those engaging in a highly lucrative trade. Indeed those British citizens were not about to risk their long-standing relationship of "reciprocal predilection" with the regime in power in spite of its authoritarian nature.[114]

More hope lay in the direction of the French. In the latter decades of the previous century, Spanish officials had allowed Anglo and French interests to compete for trade with the southern colony. In the intervening decades since Argentine independence, British firms had gradually established their predominance. French commercial agents, supported by an activist Foreign Ministry, were now making new attempts to penetrate the near monopoly enjoyed by British interests there. The intervention of 1838–41 had the precise goal of terminating those unfavorable conditions. But—as discussed above—a change in governmental leaders and more pressing imperatives in other parts of the globe had led to France's decision to shelve temporarily its ambitious plans for economic expansion in the Plata region.

With these realities in mind, the exiled Argentine propagandists launched a campaign to win the French back to their cause. Noteworthy were articles or pamphlets written by Alberdi, V. F. López, Sarmiento, and F. Varela, which circulated widely, several in translated form.[115] They launched strong attacks against Great Britain on account of that country's tacit, and, at times, direct support for Rosas during the entire period. In contrast they generally spared undue criticism of the French, perhaps because they knew that a renewal of that country's support could well furnish the guarantee for a victory over Rosas in a future moment. Varela expressed the collective sentiment that the European powers should assist their cause given that they, and not Rosas, defended the liberal principles at the heart of Western Europe's democratic movement. This factor, in their eyes, far outweighed the pronationalist and, therefore, prorosist stand of Argentina's uneducated majority. According to Varela's way of thinking, the sine qua non of a successful campaign against Rosas was French or British support. Following military victory continued European assistance would guarantee their plans to impose an enlightened, centralized governing structure over the country's sometimes rebellious population. As he wrote in an English-language pamphlet, "Europe has a right to demand these conditions from the American Governments, but it is also her duty to protect amongst these new States, by the weight of her civilizing influence, the Governments which shew themselves to be interested in promoting the civilization and improvement of these countries."[116]

CONTRASTING VIEWS ON NATIONALISM

In spite of the many areas of apparent agreement, the exiled militants were increasingly divided over the feasibility or desirability of implementing democratic political reforms in the society that would come into existence after the fall of Rosas. Alberdi's and Echeverría's writings, in particular, manifested the beginnings of a deep contradiction; whereas their hatred for the dictator's authoritarian and violent measures knew no limits, they, nevertheless, viewed him as incarnating the democratic sentiment of the nation—a factor they could not easily ignore. Therefore they began to warn their colleagues against an over-reliance on foreign, primarily European, support in their efforts to topple Rosas. Instead, their emphasis was placed on winning the support of groups within Argentina itself. Echeverría wrote to Gutiérrez and Alberdi in October 1846: "Enlist people over there; our plan is to open our association to any Argentine patriot, regardless of social class or condition: he who does not serve with ideas can always contribute with his hands. It is necessary to form a wholly new party, a unique and national party that has as its standard the democratic banner of the May Revolution, the one that we have carried."[117] A month later he wrote to Gutiérrez: "Let's not harbor any illusions: we cannot not count on any foreign element in our struggle to overthrow Rosas. The revolution must come from our own country, it should have at its head the caudillos who have risen in Rosas's shadow. If it be otherwise, we will not have *patria* (fatherland)."[118] Alberdi was more or less in agreement with the new nationalist thrust to their program: "The force of our struggle resides in the quality of our ideas, in our systems, and not in the number of our soldiers. . . . Liberty has only one legitimate incarnation in the world: The People [El Pueblo]. There is only one force that can successfully oppose a tyrant: the people."[119] Yet within a few years Alberdi would replace the idealism evident here with a more realistic emphasis on economic forces. He would also define more precisely what he meant by a desirable *Pueblo:* he would foresee the need for the country to populate its vast expanses with a white North-European immigrant population.

Echeverría's growing opposition to foreign involvement obviously obeyed strategic considerations, given the fickle support in the past from the British and the French for the cause of the liberal exiles. But there also was evident a growing conviction on his part that Argentina's future culture needed to be based solidly upon the national elements that then constituted its social and demographic reality. Whereas other Association members advocated a transformation following the principal inspiration of European and North American models, Echeverría remained constant in supporting a new society that would selectively borrow from European modernity in order to enrich the profoundly *criollo* and inherently *mestizo* national experience. A sociopolitical reading of *El matadero* (The slaughterhouse, ca. 1839)—apparently written at this time, although published for the first time only in 1871—highlights Echeverría's affective pact with the cultured, Europeanized elite of the region. However, this view, and his accompanying disdain for the brutish, uncouth masses obedient to the Rosas regime, constituted perhaps only a minority voice within his complex web of impressions and values. In most other writings, Echeverría was far more generous with the mixed-race common people of his country whom he pitied because of their suffering at the hands of a highly deceitful *caudillo* leader. This latter perspective predominated in his address to the Literary Salon in which he declared his distrust for economic theories constructed in relation to European realities and his call for a science that was based on the lived experiences of his own countrymen. This voice also predominated in his poetry, which still constitutes one of the highest tributes to Argentina's creole nationality. In the latter years of his life, he came to fear the preponderant European influence that future modernizers like Sarmiento and Mitre—and from a different variant, Alberdi—were beginning to defend so stridently. The emerging faction of the Association led by Echeverría, Alberdi, and Gutiérrez was already projecting ahead toward the post–Rosas period, when it would attempt to infuse the spirit of progress among those individuals actually exercising authority over the country's masses: the *caudillos*.

Sarmiento, in all probability, had heard an anticipation from the mouth of Echeverría of some of these ideas during his brief visit to Montevideo in 1846. Although Sarmiento himself registered a generally favorable reaction to the person of Echeverría, his comments in *Viajes* communicate serious reservations about some of Echeverría's ideas. In certain passages Sarmiento's comments suggest that regardless of the high merit of Echeverría's lyrical production, his projections for Argentina's future were contaminated by a harmful dose of barbarism:[120] "Echeverría is the poet of desperation, the shout of culture trampled on by the horses of the pampa. He is the moan of one who is alone and unmounted, when he finds himself surrounded by infuriated cattle who bellow and scrape the ground around them, positioning their bodies to charge. Poor Echeverría!"[121]

In contrast to Echeverría, Sarmiento, along with Rivera Indarte, Mitre, and others, would travel at least halfway with Varela, Lamas, and the more radicalized elements of the Unitarian Party, who now sought European aid at any cost. Rosas's widespread popularity among the *gaucho* and *criollo* masses was, for them, evidence of his brutish, petty nationalism. In *Facundo*, Sarmiento denigrated Rosas's *americanismo* because of his association with the most despicable aspects of rural barbarism and authoritarian government.[122] In contrast Sarmiento sought the means to promote "universal values," which he equated with European "civilization." Sarmiento's firm conviction was that the country's Spanish colonial heritage and racial stock of Mediterranean, *mestizo,* and indigenous peoples acted as an impediment to its material and social development. This belief provided one more rationale for his support for North European initatives in the region. In his 1846 visit to North Africa, Sarmiento offered a new defense of Europe's privileges when it came to infusing progressive industrial and commercal practices in that undeveloped region: "Oh, no! Let's put aside all that prattle about national differences and pray to God that He finance European domination in this land of devout bandits."[123] At that time Sarmiento and his cohorts placed the struggle against Rosas on an equal plane. Their overriding mission was to wage total war against the inferior Spanish-American tradition headed by Rosas. They would promote the civilizing influences of Northern Europe as a means of saving their land from total marginalization in the world order that was then emerging.

Perspectives on Imperialism

In 1846 the armed intervention of Britain and France once again provoked an outbreak of nationalistic reaction on the part of the Rosas regime. Changes in the foreign ministries of both countries accompanied a resurgence of gunboat diplomacy. The two powers banded together to force the Argentine government to terminate its long-standing prohibition against European ships penetrating the interior rivers of the country in pursuit of potentially lucrative commercial ventures. Several vessels laden with goods, accompanied by twenty frigates of war, powered their way up the Paraná River to Rosario, but only after meeting heavy resistance at a point in the river recorded by historians as the Vuelta de Obligado—named for the turn in the river bordering lands owned by the Obligado family. The expected trade bonanza never materialized for Britain and France, and the Rosas government capitalized on the entire affair to score a propaganda victory. Although the young exiles supported this new foreign venture indirectly, their subsequent writings hardly mention it. But their propagandistic statements in support of European adventurism marked them for a share of the dishonor that inevitably accompanied defeat.

The Vuelta de Obligado incident stirred up a high degree of local furor and resulted in little, if any, financial gain for the commercial interests involved. Policy makers in Britain and France therefore sought a negotiated peace with Rosas which was signed in 1850. Those two countries had to bide their time for only two years. After the dictator's defeat they would pact with the victors and gain through peace what they had not been able to win in war: free access along Argentina's interior rivers for the commercial interests that flew their respective banners.

Of all the 1837 militants, only Sarmiento demonstrated a critical comprehension of the newly evolving relationship between the European powers and countries like Argentina. In a series of lucid articles written between 1841 and 1842, he described the qualitative difference between the old-style imperialism of European powers that had predominated in the past and what he now called "modern colonialism."[124] Under this new system direct European intervention and administrative control over productive activities were no longer necessary. Instead local elites accomplished that task far more effectively. Meanwhile British and French private interests would limit their activities to finance and commerce more and more, while their governments would provide naval and military protection for these operations. Sarmiento observed that by the early decades of the nineteenth century, this commercial system, supported by the world's most powerful navies, had extended itself throughout the whole world: "Like a cruiser anchored in front of Europe, the British Isles serve in that part of the ocean as a centric point that joins the threads enveloping the whole earth as might a spider web. Their merchant marine and navy cover all the seas and their system of naval stations is now complete."[125]

The success of this new type of system depended upon the effectiveness of Britain or any of the other European powers in winning the compliance of local elites. Sarmiento traced a typical chain of events: the corrupt official, lacking local support and nationalist scruples, seeks out financial assistance and support from equally corrupt agents of the European government. The price for their assistance was that official's willingness to enter into a commercial agreement with the European companies or individuals, regardless of his own country's long-range interests: "Here is the pact that they make: I will hand over to you the the principal economic resources—says the government—and you must help me to suffocate any political resistance. With this agreement agreed upon and signed, it is easy to predict the harmful consequences that fall upon the American republics and the organization of their governments."[126] Sarmiento penetratingly observed that the self-styled "universal philanthrophy" of British foreign policy in Argentina was, in practice, little more than a mask for their pursuit of selfish material interests.[127]

Interestingly enough Sarmiento was never again to return to this topic of "modern colonialism"—ideas that fully anticipated the fruitful studies of imperialism by Hobson, Lenin, and other observers writing a full half-century later. Indeed the second half of Sarmiento's same article largely contradicted the insights of the first when he reduced the whole dynamic of neocolonial domination to a moral issue. He argued that a few misguided or corrupt functionaries had led Britain in blind pursuit of commercial interests at the detriment of liberal and democratic principles.

Sarmiento never explained his reasons for abandoning the neo-imperialism critique expressed in the articles of 1842–43. By mid-decade his ideas hardly differed from those expressed by the other activists of his generation, who continued to seek European assistance for their own goals. In *Facundo* he proudly associated his name with the pro-French policies of the other young activists in their campaign against Rosas. Near the end of the decade he once again publicly demonstrated his support for the European, especially British, presence in the Plata Region. In a published letter to the British representative, Harry Southern, he attempted to win British support for the exiles' cause by arguing that the British, by continuing to support Rosas, violated their own liberal values and worked against their own commercial advantage.[128]

Sarmiento's schematic dualism of civilization-barbarism explicitly expressed the fundamental axis of his generation's thought on this matter. For the entire group of young militants, the most vital issue of the time was their struggle against Rosas's retrograde *americanismo*, which could only be overcome through the transformation of Argentine institutions and values according to the criteria of European civilization. For that reason, French support for the exiles' cause in the events of 1839–41 had the primary objective of (in Sarmiento's words) saving European civilization in the region of the Plata. Sarmiento's idea, which was shared by most of the young militants, was that the European population, customs, and trade were the key to the region's future. As a group the young militants were convinced that mutual benefits were to be derived for both European interests and the South American republics alike when they engaged in trade. They concurred with regard to Latin America's necessary apprenticeship in the Europe-dominated world economy as a means of developing its own financial and industrial potential.

Into the 1850s and beyond (after Echeverria's influence would wane), these individuals would remain united around the belief of the fundamentally positive role that European influences played in the civilizing project of the country. Alberdi, in almost identical words to those used by Sarmiento, argued in 1845 that "civilized America" was the equivalent of "Europe established in America."[129] This essential message would hardly change by 1867: "I have always believed that South

America's civilization can only be Europe's civilization when it is acclimatized to that part of the New World."[130]

DOGMA SOCIALISTA AND PERSPECTIVES ON DEMOCRACY

Echeverría's diverse written comments about the ideal role of the masses in the country's government have given rise to several different readings. For some *Dogma socialista* revealed the author to be a "fanatic" of equality;[131] for others (particularly Sarmiento) those same passages contained his generation's most convincing arguments *against* democracy. To understand this disparity in meanings is to understand the deep contradictions at the base of Echeverría's own values.

In truth, Echeverría held ambiguous ideas about the value of democracy. Along with the other principal members of his generation, he totally condemned Rivadavia and the other early leaders of the Unitarian Party for having unleashed destructive social forces in the early 1820s, when they enfranchised a voting public that was unschooled in the practices of civic participation. When social anarchy resulted, Rosas, at the command of a rural militia, was called upon to restore order. The social and political system that Rosas then proceeded to construct provided a second example of democracy gone astray; the broad support of the uneducated masses led not to the implementation of long-needed reforms but rather to the restoration of authoritarian practices that harkened back to the region's colonial period. Clearly Echeverría and the other young militants were in a quandary. These unacceptable examples of democracy in their country's recent history contradicted their most respected intellectual influences, who argued that the supreme cause of their age was the struggle on behalf of freedom and democracy. In writing *Dogma*, Echeverría had to directly confront his dilemma: while criticizing the unitarians' realization of universal suffrage and calling attention to the defects of Rosas's grass-roots democracy, he simultaneously wished to persuade the reader of his support for the democratic ideas then in vogue.[132]

If one takes into account this argumentative contradiction, *Dogma* and his other writings of the period reveal a fairly consistent position; in spite of Echeverría's forthright defense of the abstract principles of liberty and democracy, he argued only for their gradual implementation in the distant future. Apropos the epigraph of his *Manual de enseñanza moral* (Manual of moral instruction—1846)—a quotation from Benjamín Constant—addressed the need for society's very gradual progress toward democratic practices:

For a people recently emerging from slavery and dependency, Liberty can only be consolidated after an entire generation has been educated through an instructional program that is entirely adequate to their new needs, that corrects the habits and opinions fostered by despotism, and consecrates liberal customs and beliefs.[133]

A similar idea is found in his 1847 letter to de Angelis. "[T]he most absolute equality" achieved under Rosas had made a sham of the name of democracy; instead it was necessary for the region's elites to educate the masses "gradually" over a period of twenty-five or fifty years, in order for the *pueblo* to exercise wisely the promises of self-government.[134]

These perspectives, as articulated by Echeverría, were well in accord with the evolving positions of the other thinkers of his generation. In the writings of Sarmiento, Alberdi, and Frías, one continuously encounters rhetorical endorsements of democratic ideals or a "democracy" of the spirit. However, in contrast to the language *Creencia* of 1837, this utopian rhetorical element was more and more overshadowed by a praise for conservative political systems such as the Portales regime in Chile, whose stability conducive to progress was achieved through a sometimes despotic control over the lower classes.

Although nearly all of the young militants came to accept the general idea of controlled or elitist democracy, Echeverría's writings perhaps demonstrate the strongest commitment to "populist" ideals. With greater insistence than any of the other young militants, he argued that the domination of the masses by a landed or wealthy class was wrong not only in principle but also in practice. Instead the system he promoted would be characterized by

the equality of classes, [it would] proceed decisively to expand to the fullest the reign of liberty, individual, civil and political liberty. . . . In order to emancipate the ignorant masses and open for them the road to sovereignty it is necessary to educate them. The masses have only instincts: they are more sensitive than rational; they want the good but know not where it is found; they want to be free, and don't know which road leads to liberty.[135]

The educated elite would only provide a "caretaker" government which would disappear once it performed its function of guiding the masses in the development of their reasoning faculties. When their instincts finally yielded to reason, they would be ready to assume full and equal participation in all social institutions. Such was the idealism of this apostle of democracy whose ideas were as radical for his own society as they are for the Argentina of today.

This idealistic faith in the masses and its accompanying ideology of benevolent paternalism was not fully shared by his contemporaries—at least in the period from 1845 on. For example, during the years of his exile, Sarmiento believed that Echeverría's "beautiful ideas about liberty and justice" were the product of "serious lucubrations" by a poet who, day by day, was losing all contact with reality.[136] In the 1847 speech, upon being admitted as a member of the French Historical Institute, Sarmiento, in all probability, was reacting to the Jacobin nuances of thinkers like Echeverría, who advocated a decentralized democracy with broad grass-roots involvement: "Our first obligation, and we will fulfill it with courage, firmness and prudence, is to destroy those vague ideas that our country's first government has imposed upon the spirit of the generation now exercising power. . . . [E]very people ought to be free, but it is necessary that the forms of liberty exercised by a people correspond to their particular civilization."[137] Sarmiento was anticipating the civil disorder that would shortly erupt in the streets of Europe as a result of what he would call the licentious exercise of democratic rights. Undoubtedly the linkage in his mind was that the promotion of a more democratic system for Argentina would result in the consolidation of barbarism, not its eradication. These views are important because, even taking into account the distance between his own views and those of Echeverría, Sarmiento was the thinker of this generation who, in the post-1852 period, would be most known for his defense—hardly constant, but nevertheless significant—of a political system based on grass-roots democracy for the country's future.[138]

ALBERDI'S CONSERVATIVE TURN

After their short visit to European capitals, Alberdi and Gutiérrez separately made their way back to the South American continent. There was no returning to Montevideo, which continued to be sieged by the land forces loyal to Rosas and Oribe. They also associated negative memories of the querulous, faction-ridden group of exiled Argentines with that city, as well as the irritating rivalries they had experienced with Florencio Varela, Rivera Indarte, and others. Montevideo, with its small population of exiles, uncultured *criollos*, and ragamuffin immigrants, also elicited memories of political and cultural claustrophobia and hardly offered opportunities for the professional growth that the two now ambitioned.

With money scarce Gutiérrez spent several weeks in Río where he visited his former companion of books and arms, José Mármol, and the venerated unitarian leader Bernardino Rivadavia. Then he was off to Valparaíso before moving on to Lima, La Paz, and other cultural outposts in the Andean region. His life work was well underway: the collection of historical and cultural documents of his continent and the promotion and study of its most important literary creators. It was not until Rosas's defeat in 1852 that he would once again enter into the political foray.

Alberdi had different dreams. On arriving in Chile in April 1844, his family connections facilitated a series of official appointments, the most attractive being that of the Santiago correspondent for *El mercurio* (Mercury) of Valparaíso. After completing the necessary requirements for his certification as a lawyer, the government offered him the important post of secretary of the Intendencia of Concepción, which made him, in effect, the head of the governmental bureaucracy for one third of the national territory. However the extreme isolation of that small coastal city and its impoverished cultural setting were hardly conducive to Alberdi's ambitions. After a year he moved back to Valparaíso, the commercial center of the region, where he established what was to become a very successful law practice. Foremost among his clientele was the American entrepreneur, William Wheelwright, whose business deals would shortly expand from Chilean steamships to railroad and transportation enterprises across southern South America. One biographer has argued that Alberdi's close dealings with Wheelwright resulted in his own rapid enrichment, as well as what would become his lifelong interest in the promotion of foreign commercial ventures in Chile and Argentina, as opposed to enterprises by private nationals or state intervention in finance and banking.[139] In addition to legal activities, Alberdi maintained a high profile in the local press with his writings on the organization of a pan–South American congress, Chile's national finances, and penal law and legislation. His occasional writings that treated the state of government and society in Argentina ascended him to a prominent position in the Argentine exiled community of the Valparaíso area.

During this period Alberdi, along with nearly all the Argentine exiles residing in Chile, held a very favorable impression of that country's government, which had succeeded in maintaining order and authority while implementing progressive reforms. In the postindependence period Chile had been more fortunate than almost all the neighboring South American states in having avoided debilitating civil wars and violent unrest. This was largely due to the uninterrupted rule of the Conservative Party since 1829 (its predominance would continue until 1861) under the successive leadership of General Joaquín Prieto, assisted by the able minister Diego Portales, and General Manuel Bulnes, with his equally competent lieutenant (and future president), Manuel Montt. In spite of their outright liberal credentials, several of the young Argentine militants, on arriving in Chile, turned their backs on the local Liberal Party and lent their support to the Bulnes government. They recognized that that regime's method of structuring authoritarian practices within a constitutional mode had guaranteed the slow and steady progress of the Chilean society in almost all aspects of life. They said or wrote little about the repressive measures against all dissidence—in Portales's words, "under the weight of the night"—believing this to be the necessary price for saving the fragile social order that had emerged after the crisis of independence.[140] For Sarmiento, Frías, and Alberdi, the years spent in the service of this regime were to leave a lasting mark on their own ideas for Argentina's future society and, more abstractly, for the authoritarian brand of liberalism that they came to advocate. Yet their support for the Chilean Conservative Party was not unambiguous. Most telling in this regard was Sarmiento, who, in spite of his faithful service to Montt and the Chilean government in several capacities over more than a decade, never relented in his journalistic campaign to "shake" up society, educate newly franchised citizens into social and political participation, and jar the masses out of the complacency and passivity that the Portales regime otherwise encouraged.

Alberdi, perhaps unique among his generational associates, had never fallen under the sway of the romantic rhetoric that advocated popular democracy. He had remained constant in his support for strong leaders who guaranteed order and stability within the framework of a constitutional order. Earlier—before 1837—he had demonstrated his willingness to participate halfway with the Rosas regime in spite of, or perhaps because of, its authoritarianism, but this gesture had dissolved before the dictator's recourse to terror against enemies and stubborn opposition to free trade policies. Over and above his later opposition to Rosas, Alberdi's perspective on the desirability of a strong government did not change. His brand of liberalism granted priority to liberty in the economic sphere, while it implicitly restricted access to society's political life.[141] His conservative conception of natural law meant that the role of constitutional government was not to change society but rather to preserve it. The Bulnes government in Chile, for that reason, set a high example for other countries. The positive role of that government, Alberdi wrote in 1846,

> consists in conserving, strengthening, and financing consecrated institutions; maintaining peace and the stability of the social order as basic principles of Chile's national life; promoting progress, but without precipitating it; avoiding abrupt advances and violent solutions in favor of a gradual progress; abstaining from action when information is limited or options are not clear; protecting the public good, but without ignoring individual needs . . . ; government must also preserve by making changes, adjusting to new conditions, correcting . . . ."[142]

Although these words had been commissioned by the Chilean Conservative Party for promoting its reelection, Alberdi, nevertheless, revealed in them his sincere ideological convictions. Like several of the other Argentine exiles, he could only admire the luminous accomplishments of the first Bulnes administration: the founding of the Normal School, the Academy of Sacred Sciences, the Military Academy, the Nautical School, the University of Chile; the construction of bridges and roads; the promotion of banking services for nascent industries; its support for commerce and the merchant marine; the improvement of national finances and the economy; its termination of the war with Bolivia; and the general strengthening of the country so as to earn Spain's recognition of Chile's independence.[143] His words constructed an implicit comparison with Argentina, where ruled a tyranny that delighted in slitting the throats of its adversaries and seizing their properties. Given that state of affairs, Alberdi slowly gravitated toward a position that he would advocate for the rest of his life: the desirability of placing the fate of a strife-torn country such as his own in the hands of "the free, enlightened monarchs of the civilized world."[144]

At this particular moment in his career, a notable change in emphasis was evident in Alberdi's social and political thought. Mill, Spencer, Cormenin, Chevalier, and Tocqueville were now the influences most frequently cited, not Chateaubriand, Hugo, Lerminier, and Leroux of before. Gone was the idealistic notion predominating in *Fragmento* of nearly a decade earlier, according to which ideas were perceived as the motor of history. Replacing that was an emphasis on "political economy," which presumed that if a society were able to achieve material progress, then other aspects of modernization would follow accordingly. In 1847 he wrote the following words in the prospectus of a newly established newspaper:

> Politics, although a dignified activity that is worthy of one's full attention, shall not be its preferred focus . . . the only type of politics that our paper will occupy itself with will be political economy that, according to our perspective, is the true politics of these countries. They have to be governed in such a way that their wealth, population, and social welfare increase, that their ports be populated with ships, that our coasts be full of movement, that its markets be richly supplied, and its population be well housed and clothed, and all its necessities be provided for. . . . This, then, is the complete prescription for good government; these are the most important objectives for the domestic politics of the South American countries.[145]

These words were an indirect slap at Sarmiento, whose writings on matters related to public education were then beginning to appear. Sarmiento and his followers continued to place the onus of development upon society's educated elites, who, through their activities in the press and the school, acted to elevate the cultural level of the continent's masses and transform them into agents for progress. Contrasting with this was Alberdi's view: "Primary schools, roads, banks, are in themselves only insignificant means to a greater end."[146] Alberdi, with an increasingly acrid tone, lashed out against the shortsighted South American leaders who continued to favor an education for their elites emphasizing "political rights" and "moral sciences" over more pragmatic considerations (in this he even criticized the College of Moral Science, founded by Rivadavia, which had guided his own intellectual development during several crucial years). Such training, in his opinion, had little relevance for the needs of the underdeveloped American republics. Comparable was the act of buying firearms when it was prohibited to use them. Small wonder that the majority of his generational brethren had turned to newspaper journalism whose social contribution was questionable. "Rousseau said that doctors cause diseases; who knows to what degree it might be true that journalists cause social commotions."[147] These words, and the sentiment behind them, began to ruffle the feathers of Sarmiento and Mitre, both of whom continued to exhibit decidedly literary orientations and who thirsted for the public applause won through their public writing.

Alberdi's materialist conception of progress contrasted the more moral and institutional focus of at least a few of the other exiled militants. Sarmiento and others argued that peace and harmony in the social order would be achieved through education, and that these, in their turn, would attract immigration and wealth. Alberdi argued the reverse in his 1845 essay, "Acerca de la acción de la Europa en América" (On the action of Europe in America): "Only with difficulty can one grow from seed the plant of civilization. . . . Natural reproduction is a slow, imperfect process. Do we want to form great States in only a short time? Then let's import only elements from Europe that are in an advanced stage of development and are ready for transplanting."[148] Alberdi argued that the more cultural or institutional aspects of progress would naturally derive from technological change and the improvement of productive practices. Europe's role in all this was crucial. Investment capital and know-how would be forthcoming from Great Britain and other European countries for the construction of Argentina's productive and transportation infrastructure. This was not the same pro-Europe position that Alberdi had defended a half-decade earlier. At that time he had favored the military intervention in the Río de la Plata. Now, in contrast, he argued on behalf of those countries' peaceful participation: "The peaceful influence of the foreigner is the redemption of the American people, but his armed intervention will always be sterile, impotent, and harmful."[149]

When Alberdi wrote about the necessity of importing European civilization as the sine qua non of South America's own progress, he meant not only customs, institutions, machines, and fruit seedlings, but also whole population groups. His bias favored North European people and culture over what was autochthonous to South America:

I know of no gentleman who would pride himself for having descended from Indians. . . . All the good that we possess we owe to Europe, including our race, which is much better and more noble than that of indigenous people, even though poets, who fuel their imagination by reading fables, will tell you otherwise. . . . Civilized America is that part of Europe that has been established on American soil.[150]

With radical pessimism about transforming the Indians and mestizos of the continent into bonafide citizens for the future, he advocated their substitution with a totally new immigrant population: "Social order or broad-based cultural pursuits will prevail only after the masses have internalized the habits that accompany order and civility."[151] This theory of the "vital transplant" from Europe to America satisfied not only his obsession for progress but also his conservative fears about the disorder and tyranny that characterized any barbarian society.[152]

Alberdi's ideas on progress suggest a curious, even paradoxical series of affirmations. The homeland, he argued, did not consist of a piece of real estate labeled national territory; instead it was the mesh of customs and institutions that had grown up under the guidance of civilization: "The *patria* is liberty, order, wealth, and civilization on one's native soil, all organized under the name and standard of that same land."[153] For Alberdi what was "national" in South America was not autochthonous but rather what was of foreign origin. What was national were the racial elements and intellectual currents that came from that region's Mother civilization. A century before that civilizing font had been Spain, which subsequently had been replaced by France and England. Nevertheless Alberdi argued, "Europe will always rule in America; whatever of value that might exist in America is European in origin."[154]

DIFFERENCES IN PERSPECTIVE

Alberdi was hardly alone in identifying Europe as the force that would civilize the American continents, nor was he alone in embracing the ethnocentric and racist implications of these ideas. The assiduous reader will find similar opinions in the writings of Félix Frías, Florencio Varela, and Sarmiento; the other major figures of the 1837 generation—with the possible exception of Echeverría—were of a similar mind.

This is definitely the case with Félix Frías, an intimate friend and Alberdi loyalist. During the exile years Frías consistently sought ways to further progressive causes with his exceptional abilities, in spite of a perennial shortage of economic resources. His father had been auditor for the armies of Belgrano and then member of several important assemblies during the early independence period.[155] The father had died in 1831, leaving his children impoverished but enamored with the ideal of sacrifice on behalf of the homeland. Félix, inspired by the call to action issued by Alberdi, crossed to Montevidean exile in 1839. He served loyally as General Lavalle's principal aide for two and one half years. Within months of his devoted commander's death near the Bolivian border in 1842, his exceptional talents came to the attention of that country's president, General José Ballivian. After occupying several minor charges in Bolivia, Ballivian named him Bolivian representative in Santiago, Chile. There he joined other exiled Argentines—Alberdi, Sarmiento, Demetrio Peña, Miguel Piñero, and V. F. López—in journalistic labors. In 1848 he accepted an advance of capital from Alberdi, in addition to an appointment as European correspondent for *El mercurio*. Frías was party to most of Alberdi's ideas. His 1848 essay with the ironic title, *La gloria del tirano Rosas* (The glory of the tyrant Rosas), began with an excerpt from the letter he had written to Alberdi the previous year: "Each time that I read a page from your pen or from that of our compatriots, I am filled with pride knowing that I belong to the same political movement, which at the same time authorizes me to call myself your friend."[156]

Alberdi counted Frías, in addition to Domínguez, Gutiérrez, López, and Cané among his most loyal disciples. But what, precisely, was the position of Echeverría with regard to Alberdi's newly materialistic thrust and condemnation of the region's gaucho and Spanish-descendant populations? As pointed out earlier Echeverría was hardly a rigorous thinker with regard to social and critical theory. In a few important moments before the young generation's forced exile, he had attempted to orient their thought in pragmatic and concrete directions. ("Let's concentrate on practical concerns, not lose ourselves in abstractions, and always keep an intelligent eye on the inner-workings of our society," he had written in the 1837 letter to the membership of the Young Argentina.[157]) But over and above those momentary incursions into rigorous thought, there predominated an inherently romantic sensitivity that was ignited by his readings from idealistic European philosophers who had been in vogue at the time of his Parisian sojourn. In contrast to Alberdi and most of the others, Echeverría had not assimilated a new set of readings and influences during the decade of the 1840s. This was for him a period of heightened psychological anguish and disorders. Sarmiento, in 1845, left a written testimony of the Echeverría he had come to know during his brief visit to the besieged city of Montevideo. Echeverría, according to Sarmiento, was "a very elevated spirit on account of his contemplation of . . . beauty;"[158] he was the upstaged poet who had distanced himself from most worldly concerns. But Sarmiento chose to ignore Echeverría's solid essayistic writings of only a few months earlier, that is, the *Ojeada* and the revised *Creencia*, both of which were soon to be printed under the new title, *Dogma socialista*. Nor did Sarmiento do credit to the political savy of Echeverría, who correctly understood how the changing dynamics of power in the region would bring Justo José Urquiza, governor of the Province of Entre Ríos, into opposition with Rosas. To his credit Echeverría acted upon that intuition as early as 1846 when, in a letter, he invited Urquiza to assume leadership of a national movement whose objective was the removal of Rosas from power. In short the figure of Echeverría in this period projects to the contemporary reader a contradictory set of images that alternates between distanced dreamer and informed political strategist.

What, then, was the status of Echeverría's ideas in Alberdi's thought, or vice versa? Ingenieros affirms that if Echeverría was the early mentor of Alberdi, then Alberdi's "political sense" undoubtedly influenced the former in his writing of the *Ojeada* in 1846.[159] That same year, Echeverría—now nearly disabled from an accumulation of physical and mental ailments—specifically designated Alberdi as his ideological heir: "I bequeath my ideas to my friend Alberdi, in the event that I lack the time necessary to realize them."[160] Two years later, after a lapse in the correspondence between the two, Alberdi's words to Echeverría might have been more the product of condescending pity than forthright honesty: "It pleases me to see that you and I, just as before, continue to embrace the same political ideas."[161] Echeverría, a few years later, dedicated his poetic composition, *Avellaneda* (1849), to Alberdi (Echeverría's first idea was to dedicate it to V. F. López). Although Echeverría left no other written evidence, he seemed to lean toward Alberdi, and away from Sarmiento, in the emerging division in the ranks of the young exiled community.

This emerging split in the ranks of the young generation was precipitated in part by a most audacious essay published by Alberdi in 1847 entitled "La República Argentina 37 años después de su Revolución de Mayo" (The Argentine Republic 37 years after its May Revolution). Much of the essay can be read as a continuation of Alberdi's important paragraph in the *Creencia* a decade earlier, which had promoted a new political movement that would be a "fusion" of the two parties that had waged war on one another since the early years of the independent republic. Characteristic was Alberdi's attempt to rise above factionalism and seek a common ground upon which to base a peaceful settlement to the dispute between Rosas and the young Argentine exiles. With "impartiality and good faith," Alberdi stated that the country had progressed little in the nearly two decades of government under Rosas. That leader, instead of working for solid, positive improvements in the country, had satisfied himself with the noisy show of power: "To make noise and concentrate power in oneself out of the sole desire of appearing powerful in the exercise of authority, is frivolous and childlike."[162] Over and above its deficiencies, however, the regime had realized one positive objective: the centralization of national power. In words similar to those used by Sarmiento in 1845, "The unitarians have lost, but unity has triumphed; the federalists have won out, but the federation has died." But although Rosas had succeeded in establishing *order*, what still awaited fulfillment was the long postponed dream of *liberty*. Conciliation of the country's warring factions could only be achieved through peaceful means. A constitution approved by the vote of the population was "the most powerful means possible for pacifying violent social elements and achieving internal order." Up to here few among the militants who had spent the prime years of their youth in exile would find little reason for disagreement.

But Alberdi dropped the bombshell near the conclusion of the essay when he urged the young exiles to set aside hostilities and now collaborate with Rosas in bringing about the country's long deferred regeneration. He did not suggest that the young militants yield or surrender before Rosas's heretofore impregnable position. Instead, he intended the essay as an invitation for Rosas to cease his repressive practices and negotiate an end to all hostilities. Rosas, to no one's great surprise, did not even respond to this proposal. However perhaps Alberdi's gesture of dialogue had his desired effect on the man destined to replace Rosas at the nation's helm. According to one historian, "Rosas failed to understand [this attempt at conciliation], but it did gravitate in the spirit of General Urquiza and other leaders, and posterior events demonstrated that it did make a positive difference."[163]

Perhaps the most acrid of responses to Alberdi's bold invitation to reconciliation with Rosas came from among the ranks of the young generation itself.[164] This is understandable given the terrible suffering inflicted by Rosas upon them and their families and close friends. Alberdi's olive branch hardly compensated for the decade of their youth that had been spent in mortal opposition to the ruthless despot. Carlos Lamarca was furious; Enrique Lafuente angrily demonstrated his complete disagreement with such "extravagant ideas." Carlos Tejedor, from the pages of *El copiapino* (The Copiapió—a Chilean city), indignantly characterized the essay as a "confused mixture of hypocrisies." Even Echeverría was taken aback: "You have provided motives for others to make strong accusations against you—their diverse interpretations of your

words can only harm your reputation. For my own part, I won't participate in those attacks, but I disapprove of your essay because I find
absolutely nothing useful or fruitful in it." Only Alberdi's faithful friend,
Frías, had somewhat positive words to say about the controversial
position:

> You have chosen to position yourself above the two disputing parties and it
> is to be expected that neither one will totally approve of your ideas. . . As for
> me, I confess to you that I consider myself unable to appraise the current
> situation of my country except through unitarian eyes, on account of all that
> they have seen—especially the brutal way that we have been treated outside
> of Argentina."

This was only the first of Alberdi's many essays that would be the object
of opprobrium and condemnation on the part of even those members
of his generation who had shared with him the rigors and sufferings of
a long exile.

1848: New Perspectives on Democracy

In response to the social turbulence across Europe that culminated in
1848, Echeverría was the only one of the 1837 militants to register a
decidedly favorable stance. In the period of months since writing the
Ojeada retrospectiva and its printing in *Dogma socialista*, his thoughts took
a distinctively revolutionary turn. Before, his ideas on grass-roots democracy had always been tempered by the conviction of the need for
an educated elite to guide the masses during the first moment of their
social participation. Now, in the light of new readings and confronted
by the rapidly evolving situation across Europe, he reaffirmed his faith
in the will of the masses and seemingly dispensed with the accompanying idea of their necessary tutelage. The revolutionary thinkers of
the day depicted the French Revolution in positive terms, over and above
the violence and social dislocations that had resulted. Echeverría, attuned to this literature, incorporated their ideas into his own discourse.
The myth of the masses as idealistic, progressive citizens now dominated his thought. He endowed the masses with legitimacy because of
their role at the vanguard of human progress. In his article published
in the *El conservador* (The conservative) of Montevideo, he depicted them
as a community with "a mind and a heart; with the intelligence for
imagining and the practical sense for realizing in practice the highest
ideals that mankind has conceived."[165] He described the recent three-
day uprising in Paris with intoxicating hyperboles; it was "a revolution
without precedent whose future impact is impossible to estimate." This

was because in one blow it had done away with the vestiges of the monarchical feudal regime whose leaders had been guillotined a half-century before. This apocalyptical event foretold the coming of a new era that would necessarily affect the newly independent South American republics. He suggested that studious American leaders, upon learning about France's "murmors of emancipation," would attempt to "move the heart of the masses and convulse American society." The revolution of the masses on the South American continent was eventual and necessary; its outbreak would occur forthright.

In a follow-up article Echeverría interpreted in philosophical terms the importance of the 1848 uprisings in Paris. Without hard data about those events, his comments took the form of armchair speculation. His enthusiasm was such that he could see no evil, even when it came to discussing the tumultuous consequences of social revolution. Within his weave of revolutionary myths, Echeverría did not fail to call attention to the solidarity and communion of an idealized "proletariat" (a word he introduced to the political discourse of the region), the high level of "congeniality and morality" in the measures they had chosen to further their ends, and the Christian value of charity that would motivate others to join in solidarity with their struggles.[166] All of this would culminate in a world that sounded too good to be true: "the Epoch of man's complete emancipation."

Weeks later, when Echeverría was confronted with the disturbing evidence of dehumanizing violence and wanton destruction that resulted from this social militancy, his reaction was predictable. He would not abandon the attractive idea of a spontaneous mass uprising but would qualify its occurrence. The result of those meditations was the narrative poem *Insurección del Sud de la Provincia de Buenos Aires* (Insurrection of the South of the Province of Buenos Aires, 1849), which commemorated the fallen martyrs of the October-November 1839 uprising against Rosas that had been centered in the communities of Dolores, Chascomús, and Tandil. In a letter to the editor of the *El comercio del Plata*, he explained that his forthcoming poetic effort was aimed at consecrating "the most noble and glorious event of Argentine history, with the exception of the May Revolution."[167] These hyperboles praised what for him were the positive attributes of that uprising: the absence of intraparty rivalry and the masses' spontaneous, but controlled (and therefore not anarchistic) response. In short this uprising was special because of its "*caracter* of justice and legitimacy" which had been absent in all the previous revolutionary outbreaks of his country's short history.

As to be expected these lofty, idealized visions met with stony silence from Echeverría's fellow exiles. A decade before the prophet had fulfilled his mission of initiating a movement; now his impetus was too anachronistic or too rarified to be even a hindrance. His words were ignored, and they didn't even have to be "violently forgotten." This is because the more pragmatic of his former disciples now dominated the anti-Rosas stage. In spite of Echeverría's unshackled idealism, the European events of 1848 served to confirm their deep doubts about the value of grass-roots democratic participation.

The opinions that Félix Frías set forth in a letter to Uruguayan liberal, Juan Carlos Gómez were representative. Frías's livelihood for the past several years had been as Parisian correspondent for Valparaíso's *El mercurio*. He personally witnessed those historic events in the streets of Paris, which he described as "grave symptoms of decadence."[168] In complete contrast to the rosy philosophical treatment by Echeverría, he registered disgust for the lumpen and working-class militants participating in a "destructive revolution." Far preferable would be a moderate program of political action aimed at ameliorating the material conditions of workers' lives while not endangering social order, morality, and justice. Two years later he would write to Juan Thompson saying that the republic resulting from the licentious exercise of democratic rights in France was the mother of serious social abuses: the new republic "has ended up crowning all the egotisms and aspirations, and proscribing the virtues of the national conscience."[169] His vehement message to Alberdi at about that same time would make the young Argentine militants shelve forever the word that they had previously used to define their movement: "Socialism . . . is no more than the plebian philosophy of sensual pride, it is no more than the science of envy, . . . the natural fruit of an immoral civilization . . . of a corrupt civilization . . . the blueprint for crime."[170] Frías's suggested cure for these massive social ills was a strong government with unrivaled force and moral authority. In all these letters he returned again and again to the issue that would dominate in his writings and public advocacy from that moment on: the need for society's leaders, utilizing both public and private organs of expression, to inculcate a strong religious orientation among the population. For him, "El principio civilizador . . . no es literario ni filósofico; es moral, es religioso."[171]

Alberdi's reaction to the same European events was even more severe. Gone was his vague, ambivalent promotion of the popular classes. Instead, he now demonstrated a radical pessimism about the inability of the masses to contribute constructively to a democratic state. He singled out the ideas of French socialism for having encouraged the irresponsible revolutionary activities of Francisco Bilbao and Mitre in the Chilean uprisings of April 1851, which were only brought under control eight months later. Alberdi, at that time, was retreating more and more into a conservative shell: "Governing is becoming difficult everywhere. . . .

Humanity is sick; a wise political leadership ought to realize this and carry on as well as it can with infinite care."[172]

In summary the 1837 participants—again, with the possible exception of Echeverría—learned a common lesson from the European insurrections of 1848 that superseded the vague, idealistic projections of their earlier writings. The lesson was that a spontaneous revolutionary movement of oppressed popular forces, though not altogether impossible, was entirely undesirable.[173] This was the belief that would guide them in the period of their own exercise of public authority, which began after the fall of Rosas in 1852.

ON THE EVE OF CASEROS

The years of exile left their mark on all of the young militants. At first they had expected that their objective of overthrowing Rosas would be realized in a matter of months. But the dramatic defeat of Lavalle, the federalist victories of 1840–41, and the successive failures of 1845 and 1847 in igniting an effective resistance convinced them of the relative invincibility of their foe—at least for the time being. Until now objective conditions had not supported their desire to terminate the dictatorship; now the militants had to bide their time in exile and plan their strategies accordingly. But how long would they have to wait?

As months turned into years, they realized that their long years of opposition to Rosas would absorb the totality of their youthful years. Hardly a day passed without them remembering their less fortunate companions: Quiroga Rosas, Avellaneda, Rivera Indarte, Florencio Varela, Piñero, and others—some falling in struggle, others dying from natural causes during the exile years. The name of Echeverría would be added to this list of martyrs before the defeat of Rosas would allow the rest of them to return to their homeland. Exile, most of them sullenly came to realize, was at best the signpost of their youth; at worst it was the gravestone that marked a career and a worldly presence cut tragically short.

Geographic displacement was the most obvious cause of suffering; in several cases there were even more severe forms of alienation. Undoubtedly the most anguished victim was Echeverría, whose psychological disorders and physical ailments were aggravated beyond any hope of remedy by the solitude, poverty, and general inconvenience associated with his carpetbagger status. Mármol also manifested severe symptoms in his "migratory" character, that is, his desire for movement and the inability to commit himself for long to any one course of action or professional undertaking. Gutiérrez, in spite of his wanderlust traits, was able to channel discomfort into a scholarly commitment to reconstruct the cultural history of his continent. Sarmiento, Alberdi, and a few others adapted well to new environments and even prospered on account of their superior talents. Others such as V. F. López and Frías were perpetually struggling to find gainful employment worthy of their advanced cultural level; one form of mediation for sometimes disguised anguish was their dedication from time to time to cultural tasks which they increasingly performed with heightened subjectivity. Only a few of the young militants—Florencio Varela, Cané, and Mitre—found solace in the company provided by marriage and family. But the positive features of marriage oftentimes accompanied an additional psychological burden when their dependents were subjected to the dangers of the struggle or when forced absence made it necessary to leave those dependents in another's care for extended periods of time.

Nevertheless the long period of waiting and frustrated opposition to the Rosas regime was approaching its end. All waited for the governor of Entre Ríos, Justo José Urquiza, to make his long awaited pronouncement against Rosas and lead the forces that would topple the Buenos Aires *caudillo*. Echeverría, after his burst of combative writings in 1846, knew that his days on earth were numbered, and he dedicated his remaining energies to finishing several long narrative poems. Sarmiento, Mitre, and Alberdi continued to bide their time in Chile; Sarmiento and Mitre were ready at a moment's notice to board a ship that would carry them to the war theater once the active struggle commenced. Alberdi, meanwhile, was already projecting his imagination ahead to the moment when his advanced ideas would be useful for guiding the newly constituted government into a more promising era. Gutiérrez, after leaving Chile for Peru in 1848, continued his scholarly and erudite activities of documenting the literature and intellectual presence of the Hispanic American republics; he eagerly awaited the day when such projects would be complemented by activity that would yield more immediate benefits for his countrymen.

At this point, it is useful to focus more closely on the four key members of this talented generation—Echeverría, Alberdi, Sarmiento, and Mitre—in order to summarize their individual tendencies and strengths in the months before Rosas's fall. It is necessary to summarize how their individual perspectives had developed since they emerged as protagonists in their country's intellectual and public life more than a decade earlier.

Echeverría

First there was Echeverría, increasingly isolated with deteriorating health, whose thoughts alternated between rarified dreams for Argentina's democratic future and contempt for many of his erstwhile allies in the struggle against Rosas. After the disheartening military defeats, Echeverría had become more convinced than ever that his countrymen needed to experience a regeneration in consciousness before any lasting and beneficial change in institutions or living standards could occur. Of all the members of his generation, he was perhaps the most traditional in his orientation; among his generational brethren only he would launch a radical critique of modernism such as it was beginning to manifest itself in the region. One can understand his refusal to participate in the propagandistic attacks against Rosas that other writers were waging through the Montevidean press; the written word for him was a mark of cultivated excellence that must not be squandered or demeaned through yellow journalism or demagogic slander. In this light his repeated criticisms of the "moral anarchy" and "egotism" of Argentina's leaders acquire significance.[174] This moral corruption had accompanied the rapid social and material advancement of many social groups. What other explanation was there for Rosas's wide appeal than the general decadence of the times which had resulted from a whole country shelving more noble sentiments in favor of the "saintly idol [that] is worldly pleasure"? Some of his written passages seemed to condemn in a similar fashion the moral values of his followers among the young generation; the "sensualist" philosophy of Condillac and Tracy, along with the utilitarian principles of Bentham, he argued, were largely to blame for the spread of materialist values and atheism among the educated elites whose examples were emulated throughout society. (Gutiérrez, in compiling the poet's complete works, had the good sense to criticize this perspective.) Echeverría's *Manual de enseñanza moral* (Manual of moral instruction, 1846) was written primarily to combat these negative influences, for only among a morally purified youth could the principles of liberty and democracy thrive. He believed that those new ideas and practices would best prosper among citizens who had already acquired through their religious teachings a respect for authority and a sense of civic obligation. The moral regeneration that he prescribed had the objective of directing citizens back to traditional values; he believed it imperative to recapture a spirit of the past, when family, home, and religion had provided a worthy orientation for all.

Among the entire group of young militants, this strain of Echeverría's thought characterized him as the most utopian, if one understands the term as the projection of an ideology with anachronistic and perhaps impossible goals. As with many similar individuals, his rarified idealism was accompanied by defensiveness, if not a well-mediated aversion. The title of his largely autobiographical poem typified him well; he was an "Angel caído"—fallen angel—whose severe moral code was impossibly out of step with his own fallen reality and the bitter struggles of his contemporaries on behalf of the country's modernization. He was, as Sarmiento metaphorically characterized him, an "voracious angel from a different century."[175]

And yet Echeverría's "lucubrations"—again in the words of Sarmiento—added a popular dimension that otherwise was glaringly absent in the advocations of the majority of his 1837 associates. It was Echeverría who most persistently promoted an Argentina for the Argentine people. He was almost alone in arguing that in order for the struggle against Rosas to be victorious as well as meritorious, it would have to be won by the citizens of the country itself and not by foreign forces.

It follows from this that out of all his generational fellows, Echeverría's faith in the masses was greatest. He consistently demonstrated his confidence that the popular classes would rise up to bring an end to the Rosas tyranny. Only he, among his young colleagues, indicated a receptivity to the creative destructiveness that an uprising of the masses might cause. In many moments he demonstrated eagerness for the collective wisdom that would result from a grass-roots insurrection. He was hardly consistent in this view, however. These same popular classes, to his way of thinking, would constitute the mainstay of Argentina's democracy of the future. In this light he argued most consistently of all the militants of his generation for a decentralized political system in which the communal power of the villages, departments, and provinces would be sovereign. The "radical and regenerative revolution" that he envisioned had to be centered in the will of the multitudes and had to have the interest of the people as its foremost concern.[176] Many of his words in *Dogma* sound strongly utopian in their defense of social equality, the sovereignty of the people, and the righteousness of "the collective will." True to form Echeverría's response to the European revolutions of 1848 was similarly favorable—a position that contrasted with the more sober and negative reactions of his colleagues of the association. Few of them shared his populist orientation; few, if any, would have taken Echeverría's advocation of democracy—as expressed in the pages of *Dogma*—at face value or as a sincere expression of immediate or short-term aims.

Perhaps it was his early contact with the urban lower class, or his great love for the music and lore of the common people, or perhaps his communion with the ranch hands living on or near his humble estancia some eighty kilometers west of Buenos Aires that instilled in him a respect for the autochthonous population of his country. He was the only major figure of his generation who sincerely believed that Argentina's glorious future did not have to depend on the successful transplant of a new set of cultural norms and the substitution of the country's largely native and *criollo* people by a future nation of immigrants. Only he, among his generation of militants, could say with entire sincerity, "A great politics is not achieving the heights of civilization, but rather achieving the heights of the country's needs."[177]

An additional facet of the May Revolution—or its mythology—that inspired Echeverría (but elicited less and less enthusiasm among his colleagues as the years in exile advanced) was the perceived need of a movement that sought a united front of Rosas opponents and a fusion of all progressive doctrines. One side of this issue was his continual insistence that their movement be based on undisputed principles and not personal ties. This explains his choice of the new title, *Dogma socialista*, which supplanted any previous labels for this important generational manifesto. It was more than chest-thumping when Echeverría plaintively argued that he was the only one of his generation of writers and militants who was sufficiently "dogmatic"—in the sense of having a well-defined mission and philosophy underlying his militancy. Another side to the same issue was Echeverría's almost quixotic striving for unity among his associates. He went to great lengths to harmonize potentially conflicting perspectives and rise above sectarian or self-promotional politics. Yet his fate—like that of George Washington during the second presidency—was to be upstaged by active elements who were more attuned to the evolving conflicts that increasingly divided them. Approaching the end of the 1840s, his gentlemanly hymn of "abnegation," "fraternity," and "fusion"—or ideological unity—ignited the imagination of only his most idealistic followers. In the wake of the publication of *Dogma socialista* in 1846, he had to accept stoically the relative indifference of his compatriots in Montevideo, Valparaíso, and Santiago. For many of them he was merely a poet and a dreamer. His messages of grass-roots democracy, equality among social classes, and harmony among dissident positions had to be silenced. Or, better yet, he himself unerringly understood that his mission of creating a literature and a communal dogma would only be appreciated by future generations.[178] His untimely death from natural causes surely saved him from greater disappointments later. Like other dangerous visionaries he and his message had to be exiled from the Republic that would soon be constructed in his name.

One aspect of Echeverría's multifaceted predication that has often been ignored in the light of his other roles as poet, literary writer, and political activist is that of educator. Posterity has recognized the significant contributions in the field of education of one such as Sarmiento, whose lifelong promotion of public schooling was integrally related to a modernizing zeal for society as a whole. But out of the entire cast of eminent personalities in his 1837 generation, Echeverría best incarnated, in both ideas and acts, the identity of educator. His pacifist inclinations, dislike of the public forum, and refusal to compromise ideals on behalf of political expediency elevated him above his peers. Sarmiento was uncannily correct: Echeverría—he lamented—"is neither a soldier nor a journalist." The sensitivities of these two individuals could not have been more distinct.

Undoubtedly Sarmiento was correct in judging that the struggles confronting the country at midcentury demanded a more activist temperament than what Echeverría had to offer. But it could be argued that if Sarmiento's pragmatic imagination best served the country in the next turbulent period of consolidating the nation, then Echeverría's vision would best speak to future generations. At the core of Echeverría's system of beliefs was the conviction that his country's institutional emancipation was first and foremost an issue of individual improvement. Of all the members of his generation, Echeverría spoke less to the objectives of material progress and technological improvement. Not that they lacked importance in his mind. Instead he believed that injustices rooted in social inequality and exploitation would only multiply without a prior revolution in the values and the consciousness of men. In retrospect Echeverría's fine spirit was decidedly out of place in his tension-ridden context: he was a moralist in a field studded with positivists and an educator in an age favoring warriors and statesmen. Yet he spoke to the future. Even today contemporary readers can find inspiration in his memorable pages in their own struggles on behalf of Echeverría's still unfulfilled dreams.

ALBERDI

Then there was Alberdi, who consistently demonstrated greater tolerance than the rest for collaboration with the federalist *caudillos* dominating the country. As a young man he had revered General Heredia from his native province of Tucumán, over and above that leader's distasteful authoritarian practices. Only the young Alberdi, out of all his generational colleagues, had had positive dealings with the already legendary Juan Facundo Quiroga. Furthermore it was only Alberdi who even considered collaboration with Rosas; up through 1837, and in spite of a growing antipathy to that leader's spiraling abuses of power, he had tried in every possible way to construct a meaningful dialogue between the young generation and the despot. In 1847 he again offered to lay aside hostilities and collaborate with Rosas, provided that certain conditions were fulfilled. Let there be no doubt: Alberdi, with profederalist and proprovincial orientations, occupied an extreme position in the collective ideological spectrum of the young generation.

In spite, or perhaps because, of Alberdi's close ties to several federalist leaders and his proud origin in the provinces, it was he who first suggested and then untiringly promoted the generational idea of a "fusion of the parties." This was the conciliatory orientation that he initially shared with Echeverría and was then able to inculcate in the receptive minds of Gutiérrez, Frías, Domínguez, Cané, and V. F. López. But a few of the others whose family allegiance to the unitarian cause had been nourished by blood probably did not embrace this idea so sincerely.

Somewhat surprisingly (given these antecedents), it was Alberdi who provided the impetus for forging the alliance in Montevideo between the members of his young generation and the unitarian-dominated Argentine Commission. The rigid intellectual views of several of the old unitarians, their ignorance and even disdain for the interior provinces of the country, and their strident Porteño perspectives must have deeply offended him. His writings reveal a profound disillusionment with those haughty leaders whose egotism and petty rivalries were, according to his analysis, the prime cause for the disasters that befell the anti-Rosas campaign between 1839 and 1841. His bitter experience with the unitarians, in addition to an entangled relationship with the young woman who bore his illegitimate son,[179] provided important motivations for Alberdi to violate travel restrictions and hastily exit from Montevideo in 1843.

His contempt for those leaders was evidently reciprocated as Echeverría's comments of 1846 suggest: "There have circulated . . . warnings in the River Plate region about Mr. Alberdi. He has committed—it is said—errors."[180] Criticisms about him also came from the ranks of young militants. For example Domínguez and other association members who chose to remain in the besieged city of Montevideo condemned as cowardly and unprincipled the flight by the person who had had the audacity to call himself "Head of the Young Generation."[181] Within a few years other young militants in the Chilean theater would have related reasons to question the ethics of the talented young writer who at times seemed to place self-advancement above all other objectives (this was the meaning of Sarmiento's accusation of 1853 that Alberdi was a "lawyer-journalist"). Was the accumulation of others' distrust a cause for the increasing rigidity of some of his positions? The hallmark of Alberdi's advocacies after 1852 was the inflexible belief that Buenos Aires's geo-political ambitions about reimposing a centralized system similar to the one existing during the colonial period was the main cause of the disastrous civil wars before 1835, the rise and consolidation of power of the Porteño Rosas, and continuing difficulties with approving and then implementing a constitution for the entire country.

Alberdi's exit from the Montevidean arena undoubtedly was related to another major facet of his actions and thought: a deepening disillusionment, if not cynicism, about the potentialities of the region's Hispanic population for assimilating the standards of European progress. This accompanied his growing condemnation of institutions and governmental structures inherited from the Spanish past. Sarmiento and he must have been of similar mind (although there is little in the written record to document it) about the worthless *criollo* and *mestizo* generals leading the struggle against Rosas in the Montevidean theater and the *gauchos* in *chiripá* (diaperlike pants) who constituted the supposed forces of "liberation" from *caudillo* tyranny. These essentially negative ethnographic and racial views about the fitness of the great majority of his countrymen for the task of constructing the republic of the future help to explain his deepening conservatism, his pact with British imperialist interests, and his increasingly radical views about the need to supplant the country's existing population with immigrant groups better suited for civilization. These would be the fundamental orientations of *Bases*, his work that would serve as model for a conservative yet progressive Argentina of the future.

Herein lay the fundamental contradiction of Alberdi's advocacies, which his detractors did not hesitate to emphasize: his commitment not only to social order but also to progress. On the one hand his *Fragmento* had underlined his essentially conservative view that only a *legitimate* government could provide order and stability. Legitimacy derived from a government's success in winning the support of society's propertied classes, in basing its programs on the traditions and history of the society, and in inspiring the allegiance of the people. According to this criterion the Rosas regime was entirely legitimate: "Mr. Rosas, considered philosophically, is not a despot supported by foreign bayonets. Instead, he is a representative supported in good faith and out of sincere sentiments by the people of the country."[182] This positive appraisal of the Rosas regime's political foundations accounted in large measure for Alberdi's attempts at dialogue with the dictator before 1838 and again after 1847. But, between these two years, Rosas's oppressive security measures and resistance to innovation outweighed other factors. In Alberdi's eyes the Rosas regime was deficient because it impeded access to European ideas, immigration, and trade.

Toward the mid-1840s Alberdi's extreme disillusionment with the "revolutionary" program of the unitarians and the continued popularity of the Rosas regime within Argentina must have appealed to his conservative sentiments. Alberdi was later to write, "the worst form of social order is preferable to any incomplete revolution, because that form of order will always allow—at a minimum—for the spontaneous and fatal development of civilization. People absorb themselves in work and study, as they await the emergence of a more favorable order."[183] A most desirable situation would result if Rosas, already the champion of stability and legitimacy, were to respond to the advice of a progress-minded intelligentsia. This prospect was tempting. The younger generation, if granted an influential role in the existing government, would be able to achieve a great deal. While Rosas maintained order and stability, they would be able to create the mechanisms for attracting an educated immigrant population and reforming the country's decrepit institutional structures. In 1847 Alberdi once again viewed the situation as ripe for such a collaboration. However none of his colleagues agreed with that assessment; nor was the dictator—as it turned out—receptive to such a dramatic change in governmental priorities.

All the young exiles experienced changes in their political and ideological positions during the long exile years, but Alberdi's were perhaps the most dramatic. Witness the abrupt transition in 1837 from seeker of dialogue with the Rosas regime to stalwart leader of the militant opposition; witness the passage from instigator of alliances with the imperial powers between 1839 and 1842 to disillusioned nationalist afterward; and witness his about-face in philosophical orientation from idealist promoter of a revolution in ideas to sober realist—even with taints of cynicism—about the preponderant role of economic forces in social and individual development. In contrast to the others, Alberdi did not hesitate to stake out a new position once he was convinced of its necessity; nor did he feel the need to mask programmatic changes under the cover of ambiguous verbiage or feign respect for the dubious principle of ideological consistency. He had probably learned this facet of his intellectual endeavor from the writings of Montaigne, whose commitment to truth openly allowed for honest contradictions. Alberdi, unlike many of his fellow exiles, held a negative view of the journalist's or "propagandist's" task, undoubtedly because his lonely commitment to truth meant disdain for those who by necessity compromised or shaped their ideas according to readers' tastes. In contrast, Alberdi, with perhaps the finest mind of his generation, hardly needed to defer to the opinions of others. Herein lay his strength as a thinker but also his weakness as a leader.

In spite of those changes in orientation, the majority of the young generation continued to recognize Alberdi's leadership. Those with stronger unitarian orientations and hatred for Rosas might not have accepted his 1847 suggestion of collaboration with the dictator even if the opportunity had arisen. But others, even though initially taken aback by the audacity of Alberdi's overture, nevertheless might have been persuaded to follow along. At this time Alberdi's intellectual honesty was never in question. Even Sarmiento, as late as 1852, sincerely sought out Alberdi's approval and collaboration in dealing with the new political realities following Rosas's defeat at Monte Caseros. For this reason weighty judgments by historians Julio Irazusta, Juan Pablo Oliver, and Tulio Halperín Donghi, which question the soundness or inner coherence of Alberdi's ideas and advocacies or the sincerity of his philosophical enterprise at this time, seem largely misplaced.[184]

Alberdi was now at a threshold in his career. The above reasons, in addition to his ever-fragile health,[185] led Alberdi to alter dramatically his type of involvement. Before, he had demonstrated bountiful energy in personally directing all aspects of the struggle against Rosas. Henceforth, however, he would eschew group action and would attempt to influence events in his country through his writings only. For the time being, his now lucrative law practice occupied the greater part of his time. After 1852 he would turn down invitations to help organize the Paraná government, preferring instead to represent its interests in Europe and to advise from afar. Over the next decades his defense of sometimes hard and potentially unpopular truths would be unencumbered by the entanglements of personal loyalties and day-to-day passions.

SARMIENTO

Sarmiento, the third of the four most dominant personalities of the 1837 generation, succeeded best in overcoming the potentially adverse circumstances of exile. In Chile his buoyant, energetic spirit led him continually to seek worthy projects for his substantial intellectual and leadership capacities and earned him increasing prestige and respect among allies and adversaries alike. In contrast to the physical and moral afflictions of Echeverría and the inconsistent commitment of Alberdi, Sarmiento seemed to move from one success to another: his uncanny abilities as writer for the daily and weekly press; the instantaneous trust he inspired in Chile's conservative circles; his inspired leadership of Santiago's first normal school; the publication of *Facundo*, which was immediately recognized as a political and literary tour de force; his fruitful travels to Europe and the United States in search of worthy models for South America's educational institutions; his highly regarded writings on any number of progressive issues; and his emergence as political and ideological leader in the struggle against Rosas. The talented Sarmiento rarely hesitated to act, at times more out of impulse and intuition than reasoned strategy. His tendency to offend was unsurpassed, but he never failed to impress a principled following.

Sarmiento's *Facundo* is a most faithful barometer of the state of flux in his ideas at the time. Like Alberdi there was an evident transition from a Romantic and utopian view of national reality to a more realistic and conservative perspective. The French critic, Noël Salomon, has seen the first part of that work as an elegy to the progressive Andean society that existed in Sarmiento's youth, while other readers have called attention to how several aspects of its last section anticipated the ideological con-figurations of the dependent-liberal society that would predominate after the fall of Rosas.[186] It is, therefore, a work riddled with anguishing contradictions, a work anticipating what for Halperín Donghi was Sar-miento's permanent confusion between freedom and authoritarianism, between democratic faith and oligarchical solidarity, between his contra-dictory advocacies of nationalism and universalism, and what would become his double allegiance as Porteño in the provinces and provincial among citizens of the nation's first city.[187]

Although Sarmiento was the object of selective praise, there were those among his generation who harbored doubts about his value for Argentina's future. Echeverría, offended by Sarmiento's published words about him, in turn criticized the latter's writings: Sarmiento's obsession with Rosas, according to Echeverría, hardly justified his twisting or dis-torting of facts.[188] Similar opinions would be registered by others after 1852 in reaction to Sarmiento's belligerent opposition to Urquiza, the violence he would direct against Angel "El Chacho" Peñaloza, and his savage hatred of anything related to *caudillos* or *gauchos*. With unchecked passions he spoke and wrote in exclamations. Every gesture revealed the brusqueness of his headstrong character. However all of this was combined with a sharp intelligence and a surplus of talent. In time of war or struggle, he was the kind of man one wanted as an ally and feared as an adversary. Yet, in time of peace, the dionysian furies of the man had trouble finding expression through constructive channels.

Another potentially troublesome aspect of Sarmiento's character and actions was the blind energy he sometimes expended to achieve hastily formulated objectives. Action took precedent over deliberation. This, in part, was what Echeverría meant in his criticism of *Facundo*—that it demonstrated a glaring lack of "dogmatic" thought. Echeverría inquired, "Where in his works can one find reasoned arguments and profound conceptions?"[189] The present-day reader would at least grant Sarmiento credit for some of the most profound observations about the country's historical, sociological, and sociopsychological realities that were to be penned by any writer his century. But Echeverría was entirely correct with regard to his other point: not only in his writings, but also in political action, Sarmiento sometimes tended toward politically expediency and did not shrink from demagogic propagandistic practices.

Throughout this period Alberdi and Sarmiento embraced remarkably similar political, social, and, in general, ideological perspectives. For example, throughout the 1840s, both found models worthy of imitation in the prevalent institutions and practices of the United States. They admired the regime then in power in Chile whose moderately repressive tactics in the political sphere guaranteed the conservation of a traditional social system which nevertheless promoted material progress. In addition, they wrote and spoke almost as one with regard to the means for achieving a desirable future for Argentina: an aggressive immigration policy which would attract a northern European population, the free and open commerce along Argentina's interior rivers, and the accelerated push to develop a transportation and communication infrastructure as the sine qua non of Argentina's economic development. In the short run both of them came to share a distaste for the *criollo* element of their native land; this, they believed, perpetuated a retrograde *americanismo* in values and orientations that was an impediment to the region's moral and material progress.

Regardless of these essential similarities in ideological perspective, there were differences that would assume importance within only a few months. It was Alberdi who best articulated the unease felt by several young militants before Sarmiento and his inspired book: the evidence of Sarmiento's inclination toward the "party politics of liberal hot-heads."[190] Although most of the other principal figures of the 1837 generation had sought a middle road between federalism and unitarianism, many passages in *Facundo* revealed Sarmiento's deep sympathies with the latter. This would mark Sarmiento's growing opposition to the moderation of Echeverría, Alberdi, López, and Gutiérrez. These four, in contrast to Sarmiento, believed that any successful revolt against Rosas and any positive transformation of the country had to spring from the estimable traditions and values of the country's past and present and had to have support that went beyond the confines of Buenos Aires.

The obstinate Sarmiento must have been aware of the ever-widening gap between his own body of ideas and those uniting the early leaders of the association. Witness his provocative—and largely mistaken—response to the 1847 publication of *Dogma socialista*, when he argued that nobody had pointed out better than Echeverría the dangers of democracy for the countries of the Río de la Plata;[191] and witness the calculated insult in dedicating to Alberdi his *Campaña en el Ejército Grande del Sur* (Campaign in the Grand Army of the South) of 1852. Sarmiento, whose views in themselves were a bundle of contradictions, surely had learned to grant little priority to the reservations expressed by others concerning his own actions. Nevertheless, his undisputable talent, sense of historic mission, impetuous character, and Promethean will to act made him a figure who had to be contended with by friends and foes alike. Added to this was the prophetic quality of his ideas. In truth subsequent generations of readers would generally agree that many of the orientations expressed in *Facundo* faithfully anticipated the directions that the country would follow subsequent to 1852.

MITRE

The fourth main figure of the 1837 Generation was Bartolomé Mitre, who was several years younger than the rest of the association militants. He was born in 1821 of a father who had been a loyal supporter of the liberal reforms set forth by Rivadavia. The family moved to Montevideo in 1833 to escape the the increasingly hostile environment in Rosas's Buenos Aires. Labeled "a hardened, incorrigible lad" by his father, Mitre spent several months on the *estancia* of Rosas's brother before fleeing to Montevideo and surfacing as an aide to Uruguayan General Fructuoso Rivera. In 1837 he studied the science of artillery warfare in the Military Academy of Montevideo. Writing articles and poems for publication in the press of the city, he came into contact with the other young Argentine exiles. He gained valuable field experience serving in Rivera's unsuccessful military ventures between 1842 and 1845. During this period he met the young Italian patriot, Guisseppe Garibaldi, and he then impressed Sarmiento during the two months that the latter spent in Montevideo at the beginning of 1846. In April of that year, Mitre left his young family in Montevideo and for the next five years continued his exile between Bolivia, Peru, and Chile.

In Bolivia and Chile, Mitre joined other Argentine exiles in defending local liberal leaders through journalistic activities. In 1847 he distinguished himself as head of the Colegio Militar, chief of staff, and artillery commander under Bolivia's liberal president, General José Ballivián. In Chile, his quick intelligence earned him responsibilities in the journalistic medium first as editor for *El comercio* in Valparaíso and then as a writer for Santiago's *El progreso*, the newspaper founded by Sarmiento a few years before. The young and impetuous Mitre could not desist from active political involvement in spite of his status as exile. Incarcerated for his participation in the armed conspiracy against the newly elected conservative president, Manuel Montt, Mitre gained a safe passage to Peruvian exile only after Sarmiento's plea for clemency. Alberdi, who, along with Sarmiento, continued to be a staunch conservative supporter, wrote at this time, "Mitre is leaving on this steam ship, exiled to

Peru on account of the socialist ideas that he has propagated here. He's but an unfortunate young child."[192] This would not be the last time that Mitre's headstrong, romantic inclinations would earn him that label.[193] However, a few months later, he triumphantly returned to Chile and experienced for the first time the enraptured applause of an impassioned liberal street following. This time he only stayed a few weeks before joining Sarmiento and future general Wenceslao Paunero in passage to Montevideo. A new resistance to Rosas was taking form there under the leadership of the Entre Ríos governor, Justo José Urquiza.

At this juncture of his career, the activists of the young generation hardly viewed Mitre as an ideological or strategic leader. His extreme youth meant that he naturally deferred to the others for political and ideological orientation. His writings up to that time were mostly in a literary vein: *Soledad,* a novel written in 1847 and published shortly thereafter in Ayacucho and Valparaíso, and a continuing flow of poems primarily treating patriotic themes. He had already demonstrated his talents as a writer with *Instrucción práctica de artillería* (Practical instruction for artillery—1844), *Biografía de José Rivera Indarte* (Biography of José Rivera Indarte—1845), and a manual for military practitioners. Revealing of his embryonic thought during this period was his conception of military discipline as a training ground for democracy. In an article of 1846 in *La nueva era* (The new era) of Montevideo, he argued that the army was a school for democracy because its "conscious and reasoned" discipline inculcated in the future citizen a spirit of "generous sacrifice, modest abnegation, defense of the homeland, preservation of its laws, love of glory . . . in a word, militancy at the service of ideas."[194]

Sarmiento's 1846 description of the young militant captured the most salient features of his personality during this early period of his involvement: "I have frequently enjoyed the company of Mitre, poet by vocation, gaucho of the pampa as a form of punishment imposed on his intellectual instincts; artillery specialist, without a doubt seeking the shortest road for returning to his homeland; easy-going disposition, always moderate personality, and excellent friend."[195] At the time few would have predicted the important role in the affairs of the country that Mitre would play within months of Rosas's overthrow.

3

Buenos Aires versus the Confederation (1852–1860)

THE ROSAS DICTATORSHIP IN RETROSPECT

The emergence of the 1837 youths into public life coincided with their break with, and then struggle against, the government of the Buenos Aires strongman, Juan Manuel de Rosas. Rosas, in that sense, was their nemesis; their passionate opposition to his authoritarian and increasingly violent practices motivated their greatest contributions in literature, political theory, and social activism.

Echeverría, Alberdi, Sarmiento, and the others correctly pointed out in their respective writings that the Rosas dictatorship arose as a consequence of the turmoil that followed the independence struggle from Spain in the initial decades of the century: it was the period of restoration that had followed a decade of revolutionary change, just as the dictatorship of Napoleon had succeeded the revolutionary convulsions in France after 1789.

According to this view the Rosas period was a conservative reaction to the flurry of reforms set into motion by the idealistic leaders of the May Revolution. In part the historical function of Rosas—they argued—was to "restore" aspects of the vanquished colonial order. Rosas, for example, had seized upon some forms and symbols of the decrepit colonial culture as a means for consolidating his own power such as his pact with the church, his slogans of xenophobic nationalism, and the exalted status of rural culture. Similarly many actions taken by his succeeding administrations had the effect of rolling back reforms or undoing the promising innovations enacted by the progressive governments that had preceded him. He dismantled the national bank, closed institutions of learning, opposed the spread of agriculture, revived the slave trade, resisted new forms of technology and production, and restricted the circulation of ideas. Undoubtedly these were the measures that motivated Alberdi to write in 1847: "Rosas has done absolutely nothing useful for the country."[1]

In spite of these retrograde measures, the country had nevertheless advanced during the Rosas years—a fact that many of the young militants could only admit begrudgingly. Even with the dictatorship's restrictions on European trade companies, economic activity in and around Buenos Aires had grown considerably. In the 1820s Buenos Aires had been little more than a dusty urban outpost with less than fifty thousand people; thirty years later it had become a thriving entrepôt of commerce and industry with a population of one hundred thousand or half of the population of the province.[2] The economic growth of the region was similarly impressive. At the beginning of the Rosas period, there had been a yearly slaughter of sixty thousand cattle for international sales of salted meat, a figure that was to be surpassed ten times over by the end of his governmental tenure.[3] These figures suggest the very lucrative position enjoyed by the cattlemen and commercial agents of Rosas's small circle who, over the two decades of his despotic rule, gained a near monopoly over the most bullish sectors of the economy. This new prosperity was especially evident in the coastal areas, where exports had grown constantly—100 percent over a fifty-year period— and imports of textiles, beverages, and metal articles had increased apace.[4] In addition the region had continued to attract an industrious immigration population, in spite of the exiles' declamations to the contrary. At the beginning of the 1820s, the foreign presence in and around Buenos Aires had been scant; but by the fall of Rosas, foreigners constituted the majority of the economically active population in the city, and their industrious work habits were triggering profound transformations in the countryside.[5] This progress was not limited to Buenos Aires and the Littoral. Many interior provinces, in particular Córdoba, Santiago del Estero, and Mendoza, also boasted of boom economies with rapidly rising standards of living.

Another accomplishment of the Rosas period that the dictator's detractors could only begrudgingly concede was the definitive consolidation of the nation under Buenos Aires leadership. This had been the guiding objective of the early Unitarian Party. But that party's arrogant push toward centralization of social and political institutions met strong resistance in the interior, where resentment continually flared into armed civil conflict. Rosas had come to power waving the banner of federalism and defending the widespread demand in the interior for provincial autonomy. But a most important force in the Plata region opposed the federalist principle, as Sarmiento had so clearly perceived: the wealth of the nation was destined to concentrate in the nation's coastal regions, which enjoyed dramatic population growth and favorable location for oceanic trade. Rosas, in Buenos Aires, had been able to take advantage of the substantial receipts from duties paid to the national customshouse for all the region's imports. These monies, when added to the lucrative profits from the jerked beef trade, provided his government and the province with the means for dominating over all the other provinces. They also financed his interminable military campaigns and the generous subsidies he provided for those leaders in the interior who proved pliable to his policies. By playing regional interests against one other, he created an economic and political system that was entirely obedient to his bidding. Alberdi concisely articulated the irony: "The unitarians have lost, but unity has triumphed; the federalists have won out, but the federation has died."[6] Ironically it was Rosas, a self-proclaimed federalist, who had been able to accomplish the most cherished dream of the Unitarian Rivadavia: the unification of the country under the authority of Buenos Aires.

Significant changes had also occurred with regard to the internal organization of society. Foremost in the minds of many people hailing from the dominant classes was Rosas's success in reestablishing peace after a decade of revolutionary struggle and civil war. Early in his administration he had been universally acclaimed as "Restorer of the Law," for having clamped down on civil disorders, dissolved a destabilizing revolutionary army, and vanquished a rebellious urban sector. In the countryside his forceful measures had achieved a significant reduction in vagrancy and the return of the rural proletariat to the tasks of cattle production on the estancias. His successful "Expedition to the Desert" at the beginning of the 1820s had the effect of neutralizing the Indian menace for an entire generation. His tactics for imposing order were often heavy-handed, and in the later years of his tenure they involved increasing doses of terrorist tactics. Notwithstanding all this he was remarkably successful in attracting and maintaining the support of the masses. At the fall of Rosas, Alberdi proposed that the permanent contribution of his regime was the domestication of the masses and, as such, the inauguration of a new relationship between power and society that placed Argentina in a most favorable situation compared to all the other countries of South America.[7] The challenge of the new generation of national leaders would be to build upon Rosas's not insignificant contribution: they would add liberty to Rosas's order and substitute a regulated and institutionalized authoritarian power for his arbitrary rule.[8]

In spite of Rosas's undeniable contributions, the latter years of his administration witnessed growing problems that inevitably contributed to his fall. The jerked-meat industry centered in the Buenos Aires Province—the economic mainstay of his regime—had caused grave distortions to the economy and society as a whole. Although providing huge profits for the small monopoly of land owners with connections to the

Rosas circle, its low technological impact and the feudal labor relations and society it engendered in Argentina and elsewhere (its principal markets were the slave plantations of Brazil and the Caribbean) retarded the progress of the region as a whole. That regime rewarded its loyalists with access to those markets and opportunity to acquire huge landholdings. Corruption from above had penetrated all levels, causing widespread demoralization and immorality.[9] While dispensing vast sums to maintain a military force in perpetual state of alert, Rosas dismantled the previous regime's incipient programs for immigration, agriculture, schooling, technological innovations, and land divisions. In short his government's actions significantly fortified the position of a new provincial oligarchy, which was primarily interested in its own enrichment, often at the expense of the development and progress of the region as a whole. By the mid-1840s Rosas's positive contributions to the country had already run their course. Yet he was enamored with power, and the groups that continued to benefit from this system were reluctant to lose their control. In their name he recurred more and more to force in order to impede the processes of change that threatened their predominance.

Political economist Ricardo M. Ortiz has called attention to the challenge of the *saladera*—or jerked-beef industry—hegemony by the more progressive interests in Entre Ríos and the Littoral. In the preceding years these regions had experienced significant progress because of the rapid increase in wool exports that were in high demand throughout Europe. In those regions qualitative changes were evident in productive practices: sheep production required the importation of superior animal breeds, the application of new technology (fences, etc.), and the assimilation of Europe's most up-to-date know-how with regard to animal insemination, feeding, and care.[10] In a series of articles of 1851, Sarmiento called attention to how these changes in Entre Ríos had led to indisputable improvements with regard to free speech and newspaper distribution; public education for males and females alike; and the training of teachers, immigration, and commerce.[11]

But the case for Entre Ríos's progress should not be overstated, because land tenure and social power were still concentrated in few hands. Similar to Rosas, Urquiza represented his province's latifundia cattle owners, jerked-beef monopolists, and commercial elite. A new configuration was evident in the power elite of the region: the newly ascendant landed interests of Entre Ríos now rivaled the corresponding groups in the Province of Buenos Aires for national prominence.

The rapid development of resources in the Province of Entre Ríos and the other provinces of the Littoral coincided with Buenos Aires's slow slide into recession. In short Rosas's defeat at the Battle of Caseros by forces commanded by the Entre Ríos governor represented in part a realignment of regional interests; change could no longer be constrained by an anachronistic, reactionary despot. Now, the foremost questions of the day were, What would become of Buenos Aires's previous monopoly over the country's customs revenues? In what ways would previously excluded social groups and geographical areas be allowed to participate in the management of the country?[12]

THE TURBULENT AFTERMATH OF CASEROS

The young militants succeeded in their persistent calls for unity among Rosas's opponents: disgruntled Federalists from the provinces of the Littoral joined in coalition with exiled Unitarian leaders from Buenos Aires and the other provinces. They all understood the military challenge to Rosas that could be launched by the Littoral, with its new economic prosperity and with plentiful horses and a highly trained militia. Sensing Urquiza's growing dissatisfaction with the constrained politics of Buenos Aires, the exiled militants invited his assumption of leadership over their movement. This was the purpose of Echeverría's ground-breaking letter to Urquiza in 1846, which accompanied a copy of the recently published *Dogma socialista*.

The groups constituting this new coalition were united on only one essential issue: the need to remove Rosas from his position of regional and national leadership. Whatever unresolved disputes that still existed between them were temporarily shelved under Urquiza's guiding hand. But perhaps neither he nor anyone could have succeeded in resolving through peaceful means the aggravated hostilities that still divided the country.

In Santiago, Sarmiento, Mitre, and others were anxiously anticipating Urquiza's declaration of war against Rosas. Within weeks after receiving the news, accompanied by Wenceslao Paunero and Pedro León de Aquino—military leaders who were to play an important role in subsequent events—they were on their way to Montevideo to offer their services. In December 1851 their "Ejército Grande" began its march toward Buenos Aires. Mitre occupied the position of lieutenant of an artillery division. Sarmiento, whose inflated ego had led him to expect an appointment to the army's general staff, nursed his resentments in the relatively modest position of *boletinero* or editor for the army's newsletter. Victory was a foregone conclusion. The only setback was occasioned by the revolt of several hundred federalist soldiers who had been impressed into the army after their surrender at Montevideo; during that mutiny General Aquino and several members of his staff were brutally assassinated, and Mitre barely escaped the same fate. On February 3, 1852

Urquiza's forces routed Rosas's Loyalists in the Battle of Caseros and marched upon Buenos Aires, stopping just short of occupying the city.

Immediately following the events at Caseros, the Porteños lived under a cloud of uncertainty, fearing that the victorious troops from the interior would sack the city and that Urquiza would follow the council of his Unitarian advisors and seal his victory with the mass execution of Rosas collaborators. But this was not Urquiza's intention. To the consternation of his more militant followers, he announced that "there would be neither victors nor vainquished" when he freed the seven thousand soldiers who had been captured during the battle. But the execution of the two hundred soldiers who had taken part in the Aquino mutiny and the severe punishments meted out to those caught looting during the chaotic aftermath of the battle caused an "impression of horror" to any visitor to Palermo (Rosas's official residence east of the city center), and contributed to the reign of fear in Buenos Aires about the intentions of the victorious general.[13] This merely exasperated the historical disdain and even hatred of the Porteño population for any national leader who did not come from their own ranks. Convinced of their own superiority in wealth, education, and cultural refinement, they would resist turning over the leadership of their province or the nation to an individual from any other province.

Some informed observers have remarked that whatever Urquiza might or might not have done short of handing the provinces over to Buenos Aires, he was bound to fail in winning the adherence of that province to his initiatives for organizing the country.[14] Added to the Porteño population's resistance was the growing hostility of the intransigent Unitarians, in addition to Sarmiento and other members of the young generation who had participated in the victorious movement against Rosas. Their anger grew as Urquiza slowly unfolded his plan to base his regime not upon the prestige of the small group of intellectuals and writers who had waged war upon Rosas from exile but rather on the influence of the Federalist *caudillos* who continued to exercise authority across the interior regions of the country. To be sure there were isolated cases where a new leadership arose to supplant those individuals who had come to power under the protection of Rosas. But, by and large, the provincial leadership proclaiming loyalty to the new provisional president was almost exactly the same as that existing under Rosas. Unitarian anger was provoked when Urquiza ordered a military intervention in order to overturn the popular liberal uprising in the Province of San Juan and to restore forcibly authority to Nazario Benavides, the Federalist governor and former Rosas supporter. Similar events occurred in Tucumán and Corrientes.[15] One historian hostile to the Urquiza legacy states:

> The complices and collaboraters of the Rosas dictatorship, then, continued dominating the provinces, supported by Urquiza and collaborating with him. Therefore, the consecrated system was neither federalist nor democratic, but rather fedual and dictatorial, and the provinces continued vegetating in the same form as before the Battle of Caseros.[16]

As a result of Urquiza's pro-Federalist stance, several personages of note, foremost among them Sarmiento, publicly broke with the new government. Sarmiento had been nursing his rising discontent with Urquiza ever since joining the liberating army and seeing firsthand the general's autocratic mode of leadership. His diary written during the campaign constituted a veritable libel against Urquiza and would later be published in book form as *Campaña en el Ejército Grande Aliado de Sud América* (Campaign of the Allied Grand Army of South America—1852). But, within days after Caseros, his patience ran out, and he began predicting Urquiza's demise. The general's order for his loyalists to don the red sash—a practice that held for many a bitter association with the detested Rosas regime—was the pretext that Sarmiento sought. He angrily announced his opposition to the measure, and shortly thereafter returned to Chilean exile to initiate a journalistic campaign against the Entrerrian leader. His parting letter to Urquiza could not have had "the value of being moderate in tone and simple in message," as he described it to Mitre, because it produced in the general no small degree of irritation.[17] His violent opposition to Urquiza skewed the "neutrality" that he now proclaimed before the widening split between Buenos Aires and the provinces and contributed to the hostility that the Porteño population would henceforth express toward the Entrerrian leader.

Regardless of these signs of incipient rebellion, Urquiza took the first steps for constituting the country under a legitimate authority. Most important was his call for the nation's governors to meet in the town of San Nicolás, in the Province of Buenos Aires, in order to establish the procedures that would then guide a future constitutional convention. Meanwhile General Urquiza accepted the responsibilities of provisional director of the Confederation, with the additional charge of overseeing the country's foreign relations during the months before formal elections could be held.

Given the mutual suspicion and hostility existing between the Porteño elite and the Federalist leaders of the interior provinces, heated disagreement was inevitable. Buenos Aires representatives boycotted the convention at San Nicolás, and the deliberations of the provincial leaders present took a predictable anti-Porteño direction. One article of the resulting accord had the positive intention of establishing Buenos Aires as the independent capital of the country, but the means for bringing this about was bound to provoke the wrath of the Porteño population, that is, the proposed political and administrative independence of the city of Buenos Aires, and therefore its separation from the provincial hinterland, was interpreted as the interior's attempt to reduce the size and power of that province. Another article called for the nationalization of the country's customshouse, whose revenues until then had been at the exclusive disposition of Buenos Aires. Also provocative was the article that would have established equal representation for each province in the country's future government, instead of assigning representation based on percentage of population; the latter option would have granted greater congressional influence to the heavily urbanized areas in and around Buenos Aires.

In Buenos Aires the news of the San Nicolás Accord caused panic among those who now feared the loss of privileges they previously had enjoyed. A heated discussion in the provincial legislature led to the violent rejection of the Accord and that body's resolve to oppose the new national government. Given the new grounds for dispute, Mitre, Dalmacio Vélez Sársfield, and Valentín Alsina emerged as leaders of the coalition of forces uniting many of the young liberals with the previously antagonistic unitarians and *saladera* monopolists. The latter groups now came together in the defense of the prerogatives of Buenos Aires before the rest of the country. They attacked Urquiza and the Confederation that was under his leadership. Urquiza, however, had three key supporters from the ranks of the young generation: Alberdi, in Chile, along with Vicente Fidel López and Juan María Gutiérrez. Although Porteños by birth the last two followed the inspiration of Alberdi (in addition to venerated Buenos Aires leaders Francisco Pico and Vicente López y Planes), who did not hesitate to place his trust in Urquiza's initiatives to constitute the nation.

Mitre: Leader of the Buenos Aires Rebellion

In the rapidly unfolding events of 1852, Mitre established his protagonist status in Buenos Aires public affairs. He quickly emerged as the most prominent voice in the provincial legislature. At the same time his legislative labors were seconded by his influential writings in *Los debates* (Debates), from April to June 1852, then in *El nacional* from October to November. Later, when the province came under attack by groups armed or encouraged by Urquiza loyalists, the Porteño government called upon Mitre to lead the provincial defenses.

From the vantage point of editor of *Los debates*, Mitre exercised considerable influence over public opinion in Buenos Aires. His "Profesión de fe" (Profession of faith), published in the first issue of *Los debates* at the end of March, affirmed with moderate tone Urquiza's protagonist role in "the great revolution" and "the great principle that triumphed in the battlefield of Monte Caseros." However Mitre was also careful to point out the inconsistencies in Urquiza's position that could possibly work against Porteño interests. In theory both he and Urquiza were in agreement over the desirability of establishing a new constitutional order based on federalist principles: "Federalism is the natural basis for reorganizing the country. . . . The Argentine Republic, saved from federalism, ought to reconstitute itself along federalist lines."[18] But Mitre's arguments here had the intention of reminding Urquiza and the upcoming meeting of provincial governors at San Nicolás that if they were to act sincerely upon their Federalist principles, then they would respect Buenos Aires's demand for continued control over matters within that province's jurisdiction.

The first issues of this newspaper carried the banner, "Long Live the Argentine Confederation," which demonstrated Mitre's initial support for Urquiza's efforts to constitute the country—in contrast to Sarmiento's immediate and strident opposition. Indeed one editorial surprisingly treated an idea that had already been defended by Alberdi: Mitre argued that in the interest of achieving the long desired national unification, Buenos Aires had to overcome "narrow and petty provincialism" in its own ranks and subordinate its interests to national objectives.[19] However these trepidations about myopic localism would fade in the next few months before an even more important principle in his hierarchy of values: the need to follow local sentiment, as expressed through the deliberations of the provincial legislature.

When the provisions of the San Nicolás Accord became known to the Porteño public toward the middle of June, the post-Caseros euphoria in Buenos Aires suddenly disappeared. Mitre's editorial in *Los debates* established the basis for the future dispute, such as he saw it: "The Argentine Confederation is sick in spirit. . . . If we wish to establish liberty, then lets begin by sanctioning it by law."[20] Previous moderation was thrown to the wind. Bowing to his demagogic impulses, Mitre now linked the cause of Buenos Aires with the cause of "liberty." Anticipating the arguments of Porteño spokesmen over the next decade, he argued that if the nation truly desired a representative and republican form of government, then it should not betray the very principle that it wanted to save by establishing in the first moment an "irresponsible" dictatorship. His speech several days later to the legislature passionately interpreted the anger and fear that had been unleashed throughout the city. He denounced the "dictatorial," "irresponsible," and "despotic" powers that the Accord granted to Urquiza as the country's temporary head of state. Meanwhile he remained totally silent about what were perhaps the major issues at stake: the economic interests motivating certain Porteño sectors to maintain their province's autonomy and the financial loss that the province would incur if it were suddenly to lose the revenues from the national customshouses and defer to a political majority centered in the internal provinces.

Perhaps more important than the content of Mitre's speeches was his impassioned tone. His oratory revealed a carefully calibrated style that would excite the enthusiasm of his fellow representatives and inflame the passions of unruly street followers. In truth recent months had witnessed an increasing number of disruptions by interested citizens, who exerted an increasing influence over legislative deliberations. Mitre's flair for impassioned rhetoric was not entirely without precedent: months before he had been exiled from Chile on account of his participation in the revolutionary activities of the liberal extremists! Mitre, who understood better than most the opportunities presented to the charismatic leader in Buenos Aires's fluid pubic life, ended up carrying the day. The growing body of impassioned newspaper readers, added to a legislative following inspired by his fiery speeches, accounted for his sudden emergence as Buenos Aires' newest *caudillo* with nearly undisputed authority.

Detractors, taken aback by Mitre's sudden prominence in the revitalized political life of a country long conditioned to despotic authority, reacted with predictable scorn. They accused him of demagoguery in his appeal to the passions of the unruly majority of provincial delegates and that the "false position" of his arguments hardly took into account the economic factors at the root of Buenos Aires's opposition.[21] Gutiérrez, in a personal letter to a confidant in Chile, denounced Mitre's conversion of weighty issues into a politics based on the inconstant winds of "popularity"; also offensive was the latter's demagogic attack on power and authority in the name of the vague concept of "liberty."[22]

Although Porteño opponents justifiably criticized Mitre because of his demagoguery, they failed to take into account his success in interpreting the bruised sensitivities and real fears of a Buenos Aires elite unaccustomed to deferring to the dictates of provincial authority. Similarly they chose to ignore the fears of liberal intellectuals, in addition to unitarian extremists and moderates, about the rigidity of Urquiza's character and his doubtful commitment to the goals they held for national reunification.[23] Mitre, interpreting these fears in his speeches before the legislature, "carried the day." The losers were V. F. López and Gutiérrez, whose reasoned arguments favoring the Accord and vesting Urquiza with temporary powers were insulted and jeered. These two individuals were even threatened with physical violence. In short, spokesmen for Porteño self-interest ended up winning over those advocating interprovincial collaboration.

Mitre was hardly alone in his defensive anger: several of the city's most prominent journalists shared his initiative in printing inflammatory newspaper articles attacking Urquiza and the Accord. This, in turn, led to Urquiza's ill-advised decree of 1 July that imposed a partial censorship of the press and proscribed Mitre and several other Porteño leaders to Montevidean exile. The participation of Gutiérrez, V. F. López, and Marcos Sastre in these strong-handed measures against Porteño free speech and assembly accounts at least in part for the hostility the three would experience before the Buenos Aires public for decades hence. That attempt at censorship proved to be entirely counterproductive, for they merely confirmed in the minds of Porteño detractors what they had feared most until then, that is, Urquiza's *caudillo* mode of governing and his dictatorial intentions.

Mitre's response was decisive. From Montevidean exile he helped plan the insurrection that broke out on 11 September. When news of its success reached him on the other shore of the the estuary, he promptly returned to Buenos Aires to assume leadership over the rebellious Porteño masses and prepare the provincial militia for a possible confrontation with Confederate forces. The Revolution of 11 September brought about a unique convergence of previously antagonistic political forces who were now united against the challenge emanating from the internal provinces. The unlikely alliance between the province's veteran Rosas Federalists and obstinate Unitarians was symbolized by the public embrace of Lorenzo Torres, the former spokesman for the dictator, and Valentín Alsina, the Unitarians' spokesman, whose views had hardened after nearly two decades of exile.

Between October and November, Mitre exhibited a significant change in political orientation. The demagoguery that had carried him to regional prominence now yielded before a more responsible and moderate vision. His legislative speeches, in addition to his articles published almost daily in *El nacional*, now pointed the way for the farsighted leadership that he would exercise a decade hence. Except for Sarmiento in distant Chile, he, almost alone among the city's leaders, defended a "national" role for the Buenos Aires revolution. Opposing this perspective were Alsina, Carlos Tejedor, and Nicolás Anchorena, who continued to defend Buenos Aires's autonomy from the other provinces. Mitre's 7 October speech to the legislature, in which he outlined the basic points of his "nationalist" perspective, is still regarded as one of the most memorable in the nation's tradition. He argued that Argentina, although disorganized, existed chronologically before any of its separate provinces. He called attention to the "profound sentiment of nationality" in the heart of all Argentines, who, in spite of short-term political differences, considered the country as a single, large family. He predicted that because this sentiment took precedence over regional loyalty, no individual or interest would be able to impede the eventual reunification of the entire nation.[24] In this and other utterances, Mitre's constant theme was the necessity of uniting the country in order to overcome the harmful legacy of the now-deposed Rosas regime and to realize the long-postponed promises of the Argentine Revolution of 1810 that spoke to a future of liberty, freedom, and economic development. He firmly believed that, given the lack of support for liberal principles among the provinces of the interior, it now befell Buenos Aires to continue struggling on behalf of those revolutionary promises, even if this meant opposing the Paraná government headed by Urquiza.

POLEMIC: MITRE VERSUS MÁRMOL

An important voice to rise from the Porteño ranks in search of a moderate path between the bellicose positions of both the nationalist Mitre and the autonomist Alsina was that of José Mármol. He had spent the greater part of his exile years in Montevideo, where he had earned the distinction of being the most versatile writer of his generation. His patriotic poem, "Al 25 de mayo," had won second place in the public competitions of 1841; his dramas *El poeta* and *El cruzado* (The crusader— 1842) were among the most outstanding of their kind that appeared in the besieged city; a primitive version of his novel, *Amalia*, was first published as a pamphlet in 1844, and half of the novel even came out in serial form in Montevideo's *La semana* in 1851; his highly regarded lyrical poem, *Cantos del peregrino* (Songs of the pilgrim), was published in 1847; the political essay, "Asesinato del S. Dr. D. Florencio Varela, Redactor del *Comercio del Plata*," came out in 1849 and "Manuela Rosas" a year later; and finally, his articles regularly appeared in the most reputable organs of the Montevidean press: *El nacional, Muera Rosas, El conservador,* and especially *El comercio del Plata.*

At the first sounds of victory announcing the fall of the hated Rosas, Mármol made his way back to Buenos Aires and quickly assumed an active position in public affairs. His profound admiration for Florencio Varela, victim of an assassin's attack some six years earlier, and his intimate links with his "most intimate friend," Alberdi, determined, to a great extent, his style of intervention in the post-Rosas period.[25] He himself had described Varela as "a fertile spirit, active, an intelligence capable of rapid conceptualizations, a frank and passionate heart," a man who longed for a time when "peace, liberty and social order" would replace the oppression and conflict of the present.[26] That spirit of serenity before youthful passions, of order before revolutionary chaos, was perhaps what he admired most in both Varela and Alberdi. This, perhaps, explains the unlikely title of *El conservador* for the newspaper he founded shortly before the fall of Rosas and on the eve of what promised to be a social and political revolution. Like his description of Varela, he believed himself to be "suspended between two generations of entirely different tendencies." His own role in the post-Rosas period would be to continue with his mentor's role of mediator or "contemporizer" between antagonistic factions.

Despite the estimable value of his objectives and perspectives, his brand of obstinate independence was destined to provoke the wrath of many committed participants. Like Mitre, he was elected to the first provincial legislature of 1852, and he supported the uprising of September that established Buenos Aires's autonomy before the rest of the provinces. Some accounts mistakenly group him with some of the more extremist defenders of the Buenos Aires revolt; in actual fact, Mármol's writings and legislative speeches reveal only a tepid—and not altogether consistent—support for the directions assumed by the new Buenos Aires political establishment led by Mitre, V. Alsina, and Pastor Obligado. After 1855 Mármol's voice would merge with those of Miguel Estévez Saguí and Nicolás Calvo, and sometimes Félix Frías and Luis Domínguez, in rejecting the militant stance of both the autonomists and the nationalists, and in searching for a peaceful means whereby Buenos Aires would be reunited to the other provinces in a national federation. Then, after 1861 his voice would be counted among the supporters of Adolfo Alsina (son of the venerated Valentín), in their pursuit of a continued independent course for Buenos Aires's development.

In his debut as "contemporizador" in the Porteño political scene, Mármol met with strident opposition. Toward the end of October 1852, he launched an attack on the provincial leadership of Mitre, Alsina, and Obligado from the editorial columns of his recently founded newspaper, *El Paraná*. Defiance was evident in the choice of his title, which happened to be the name of the city that the Confederation's government was intent upon claiming as the nation's new capital. His accusation that "the September revolution has gone astray" accompanied a proposal that was meant to establish a middle position between those Porteños seeking a national role for Buenos Aires and those urging provincial autonomy. Mármol, in effect, argued that given the state of exasperated tensions between the Porteño elite and Urquiza, and in the interest of avoiding new bloodshed, Buenos Aires should seek the advantages of autonomy for a short period of years in order to foster its material advancement and strengthen its nascent democratic institutions:

> And it is a truth as clear as light and as undeniable as the existence of matter, that Buenos Aires needs to draw back and concentrate its energies on itself

for a period of time in order to solidify its own order and give itself a provincial constitution. Then, at a later moment, it will be able present itself before a national government as an example for other people, with its internal structures developed and its multiple forces enjoying prestige.[27]

After a period of concentrated growth in population and material wealth, Buenos Aires would enjoy the undisputed admiration of the other provinces; only then could she lead them toward the realization of "a positive nationality."[28]

Mitre, meanwhile, found in this polemic an outlet for the impassioned journalistic prose that he had previously revealed in Bolivia and Chile. He argued that Mármol's pacifist orientation was inappropriate, given that the large majority of Porteño leaders rejected such a stance. His verbal belligerence captured the rebellious mood of the Porteño representatives in the provincial government, who were now egged on by noisy street demonstrators. In his speeches he urged immediate preparations for armed conflict with the forces of the Confederation. At the same time he realized—in apparent agreement with Mármol—that at present Buenos Aires was in no position to offer more than a heroic defense against any military initiatives which Urquiza might launch.

In this polemic Mitre carried the day, and the reputation of Mármol was partially discredited. However subsequent events bore out the soundness of Mármol's views that Buenos Aires's temporary separation from the rest of the provinces would provide the necessary time for it to grow and strengthen its powers and thus prepare for its eventual victory over the rest of the Confederation. This early polemic revealed to close observers aspects of Mitre's leadership skills that would acquire even greater importance later on: his ability to position himself at the vanguard of public sentiment and his tendency to feign adherence to the uninformed majority view, while struggling patiently behind the scenes to win others over to his higher vision.

Engaging Mármol in public debate offered Mitre a means for further enhancing his standing among the more radicalized elements of the Porteño population. The series of editorials he wrote in response was a polemical ploy: in accordance with the journalistic conventions of the time, he partially distorted Mármol's position, thereby creating a straw enemy appropriate as a target for his own arsenal of verbal darts.[29] Surely the majority of Mitre's informed readers recognized the fundamental similarities in the views of the two and that their hollow dispute was more over tactics than ends. Both Mitre and Mármol were, in the end, Porteños to the core, and both argued for the supremacy of Buenos Aires over a united Argentina.

Undoubtedly Mitre had found in the figure of Mármol a convenient means—and an expendable ally—for attacking the position of a more troubling political foe: the group that was emerging as the province's Autonomist Party. Even still, this emerging division between Mitre's nationalist principles and Alsina's—autonomist,—or localist projections, was primarily over long-term objectives. In spite of the verbal antagonism between them, the two groups came together in their defense of Buenos Aires before the new military threat from Paraná. Indeed, at the beginning of October 1852, it was Mitre whom Alsina, then acting governor, called upon to organize the defense of the province. Later Mitre would be formally recognized as the province's minister of war and the navy. Henceforth—until the defeat of Confederate forces in 1862—Mitre's role in the legislature and in the province's journalistic medium would take a distant second place to his functions as leader of the Buenos Aires military forces.[30]

ALBERDI: A NEW CONSTITUTION

Regardless of his personal shortcomings and the tense political environment, the greater part of Urquiza's actions throughout 1852 and into the early months of 1853 demonstrated restraint and moderation. Following the Porteño rebellion of September, he judiciously refused to lead an army into Buenos Aires. Instead he sent a commission that negotiated the temporary autonomy of that province from the provisional government. His thinking was that once the constitution were sanctioned, the Buenos Aires legislature would ratify it, and the basis for that province's lack of confidence in the national government would disappear once and for all. This optimism proved to be unfounded. The Buenos Aires legislature, rather than joining in the attempt to reconstitute the country, contradicted the orders of the acting president by refusing to disband. Later it sent its armies to prohibit the convening of the Constitutional Congress. That plan frustrated it withdrew its own delegates and turned its back on the delegates from the other provinces who were involved with the task of drawing up the new constitution.

These provocations emanating from Buenos Aires contributed to the slow erosion of Urquiza's power base. Among the younger generation Sarmiento was not alone in the offense he felt at the brunt of the general's actions. Vicente Fidel López's recent legislative defeat in Buenos Aires over the San Nicolás Accord was followed in short order by utterly disheartening experiences with Urquiza; that leader was, for López, "vain, ignorant, vacillating, he has no other quality to compensate for these defects than a very noble heart with regard to his political intentions. . . . [H]e continually offended individuals by interrupting conversations with his outbreaks of passion and anger."[31] Also withdrawing support was Luis José de la Peña, a respected educator who had taught philosophy to many of the young generation during their years at the College of Moral Sciences. While serving briefly as minister under Urquiza, his alienation grew with that leader's crescendo of rhetoric about a "war of extermination" against Buenos Aires.[32] Friends and detractors were in agreement: in spite of the isolated words of praise in response to the general's actions at this time,[33] a widening group of opinion makers were becoming more and more convinced of Urquiza's deficiencies as a national leader. He lacked what was needed to attract a solid core of advisors to compensate for his own shortcomings. Impartial observers have called attention to his acute practical sense in understanding the seriousness of the region's economic problems and the urgency for resolving them. But many times his cloak of statesman could not entirely cover the defects of his intellectual formation as a *caudillo* of the plains.

Meanwhile Alberdi, in Chile, decided to ignore the mounting criticisms emanating from his former collaborators and did everything possible short of joining Urquiza's cabinet in order to counter the slow hemorrhage of Confederation support. Involvement from a distance had its disadvantages, the most obvious being the long delay of news and correspondence. But there was also an advantage: Alberdi's removal from the petty passions of the political forum meant that he could focus his attention on the larger, underlying issues. In this he was entirely true to his introverted character; his dislike of political infighting grew at pace with his preference for philosophical analysis and contemplation. His idea was on target: after the removal of Rosas and the restoration of calm, the provincial representatives would need to formulate a constitution for the future governance of the country. Who was more qualified than he to guide them in this monumental task?

Such was the origin of Alberdi's most famous work, *Bases y puntos de partida para la organización política de la República Argentina* (Bases and points of departure for the political organization of the Argentine Republic), more simply known as *Bases*. The first edition was dated Valparaíso, May 1, 1852—the anniversary of Urquiza's pronouncement against Rosas. Copies were quickly dispatched to Urquiza, Cané, Gutiérrez, Frías, Chilean liberal Santiago Arcos, Mitre, and to other friends in Paris, New York, Mendoza, and Buenos Aires.[34] The importance of this 183-page work was immediately recognized. Sections were reprinted in *El constitucional de los Andes* (The constitutionalist of the Andes) of Mendoza and in *El nacional* and *El progreso* of Buenos Aires. Urquiza immediately ordered a new printing at the expense of the provisional government, which gave Alberdi the opportunity to add ten chapters to the original twenty-eight and to include, among other materials, a prospectus for a national constitution.[35] Two other editions of this expanded and corrected version appeared before the end of the year, and even more revisions were added for the printing of 1856. Sarmiento's *Argirópolis* (1850) and works by other individuals also impacted on the individuals charged with writing the nation's new constitution. But it was Alberdi's work, universally praised from the moment of its appearance, that served as the cornerstone for the deliberations that would result in the Constitution of 1853.

Praise rained in from all quarters. There is little debate about the central role of Alberdi's ideas in the Congress at Santa Fe. Delegate Mariano A. Pelliza wrote:

> The reading of that practical, erudite, and philosophical manual established the direction for our ideas . . . the assembly wholeheartedly approved the suggestion of representative Gutiérrez, that we promptly request of Dr. Alberdi his proposal for a Constitution moulded from the ideas expressed in *Bases.* Dr. Alberdi did not delay in sending us a second edition of his book, which included a proposal to serve as a guide for the labors of the commission encharged with that task. From that moment on, [the Congress] resolutely began to elaborate the Constitution, and its deliberations toward this end consumed more than a few months of its time.[36]

Anticipating the utility of Alberdi's work, Sarmiento demonstrated his enthusiasm as well:

> Your constitution is a monument. You know that I have become an apostle for the realization of good ideas. You, in contrast, are the legislator of good sense who is guided by scientific forms. You and I, then, are inextricably linked in our efforts, not on behalf of the petty events taking place in the Argentine Republic, but rather on behalf of the great South American campaign, which we will initiate—or, better yet, will conclude—in short order.[37]

These were prophetic words. In spite of the noisy dispute that would soon explode between Sarmiento and Alberdi, their most basic orientations and the vision held by each for the future of their country were remarkably similar.

As was to be expected, the ideas of Alberdi met with strident criticism from Buenos Aires. But Mitre, years later, would rectify the unfavorable opinions that he himself had emitted during those heated times. In an article published in *La tribuna nacional* in 1883, he would even rise above the invective caused by decades of Alberdi's caustic criticisms. Mitre, at that time, would praise *Bases:*

> few books throw more live light upon the events of Argentine politics and no other contains clearer ideas or points of departure more secure for the study of our constitutional law. . . . Alberdi represents true creative intelligence, he is a politician of mature ideas and vision in the midst of a group of men of

action. Among all them, he was the most indicated for constructing and founding an institutional regime, that was adjusted to the needs of the present and the future.[38]

BASES

Much has been written about Alberdi's "foundation book," and it is our intention here to comment only on certain aspects pertaining to Alberdi's ideological position. The work hardly offered a new perspective; indeed, many of its key sections had been copied from Alberdi's previous writings: chapter 15 of *Dogma socialista* (on the fusion of political tendencies) and key paragraphs from *Memoria sobre el Congreso americano* (Memory about the American Congress), "Acerca de la acción de la Europa en América" (On the action of Europe in America), and "La República 37 años después de su revolución" (The Republic 37 years after its revolution), which have already been treated above.

Significantly the work's emphasis was the need for an *original* constitution that addressed the lived reality of the inhabitants: the customs, beliefs, and past history that were specific to the country itself. More important, however, was the need for the framers of the constitution to look toward the future. A consensus existed about the need for the nation's modernization but not about the constitutional means for realizing that objective. With this type of pragmatism, Alberdi left behind the vague, utopian projections that had dominated his earlier writings and those of his generational brethren a decade before. His language, as well as his message, was strikingly clear about the priority that had to occupy the attention of his countrymen in the next period of the nation's history: "Today we ought to constitute ourselves, if you will permit this language, in order to attract new populations, in order to have railroads, in order to see our rivers navegated, in order to see our States opulent and rich."[39]

With "materialist" criteria Alberdi believed that the radical task awaiting his generation was the development of the country's material and productive resources, from which all other attributes of moral, institutional, cultural, and intellectual progress would henceforth derive. Such was the "essentially economic mission" of the new constitution.[40] But this was not to deny the importance of moral and religious forces and the necessity of reconciling these with desirable economic progress: "I don't intend for moral considerations to be forgotten. I know that without them industry is impossible."[41] Here Alberdi argued two different issues: first, that a people's most important moral orientations were learned not through pious lessons, but in their daily contact with the work-place; and second, that the proper environment for inculcating a religious orientation was in the home. He therefore defended the family's and the church's prerogatives of providing an *education* of religious values or orientations, but he argued against the *instruction* of those same topics in the state-sponsored school. While affirming the central role of "our Christian religion" in the development of South American culture, he argued against the constitutional sanction of one specific religious practice, knowing that the formal tolerance for all beliefs would best attract the immigrant masses to the country's shores.

The evidence was already overwhelming for him as well as for his receptive readers that the nation as a whole had to take Buenos Aires, Valparaíso, and Montevideo as models for the future development of the region as a whole. Key to the rapid progress of these three cities in recent years were several related factors: proximity to the sea; accessibility of foreign trade; receptivity to new ideas, technology, and customs from the developed countries of the Northern Hemisphere; and, most of all, open immigration policies to attract the industrious North European races that would transform the country's vast expanses into fertile cropland. In Canal Feijóo's words, the constitutional objective of Alberdi, which was synonymous with his civilizing project, was to "transform Mediterranean and internal America into Littoral and maritime regions."[42]

Given the continuing economic stagnation in the land-locked provinces of the interior—in contrast to the relative prosperity of those with access to the sea—the great majority of constitutional delegates at this time would not have had serious reservations about this liberal prescription for the country's progress. Out of necessity they were prepared to consider new solutions to their predicaments. They were ready to do away with the trade barriers between the provinces that had arisen in response to the retrograde mercantilistic policies of the Rosas regime; they were also eager for opening the interior rivers of the country to Europe's commercial vessels. Most of them, with federalist convictions, undoubtedly understood that the economic policies of the Rosas regime had accomplished until then the necessary political function of maintaining the integrity of the country in the face of imperialist threat. But they also understood the economic costs of Rosas's relative successes in that area. Change in the Rosas policy was needed, and Alberdi's document provided viable solutions. *Bases* did its part in convincing the few remaining skeptics among the leaders of the interior that liberal policies in the economic sphere would only work to the benefit of their respective provinces.

Power brokers of the Littoral were similarly receptive. The practices associated with economic liberalism already had been successfully implemented in the Province of Buenos Aires, over and above Rosas's ambiguous rhetoric which sometimes cast the role of Europe's commercial representatives in a negative light. Similarly the dramatic strides that had occurred in Entre Ríos in recent decades with regard to productive wealth, commerce, immigration, and public education were due precisely to that province having opened its borders to beneficial trade and fertile influences from abroad. With these examples of liberalism's successes, Alberdi's *Bases* tied the knot in persuading federalist leaders. The time was ripe for innovation and change; federalist leaders now accepted as their own the liberal economic ideas that, until then, had been primarily associated with unitarianism, and hence, Buenos Aires.

Alberdi's *Bases* received praise for another—this time not so laudable—reason: the author's strong anti-Hispanic (and implicitly anti-Amerindian) prejudices underlying his ideas on immigration. Indeed the phrase most often associated with Alberdi's thought, "To govern is to populate," must be understood partly in relation to his very strong ethnographic and racial inclinations. In brief his conviction about the biological inferiority of the region's Hispanic descendants led him to insist on the necessity of attracting a large North-European immigrant population to the Plata region. He believed that the North Europeans possessed a superior biological potential on account of their values and customs that oriented them toward progress. Alberdi's radical conviction was that "if we don't modify profoundly the dough or clay that forms our Hispanoamerican people," then any change in the law or government of the region would be to little or no avail.[43] In Alberdi's words, "It is utopian, illusory, totally illogical to believe that our Hispanoamerican race, such as it emerged from the hands of its horrid colonial past, can bring into existence a representative democracy. . . ." It was therefore necessary to "gradually end the predominance of the Spanish racial type in America." This would be done through an aggressive immigration policy aimed at populating the shores of the Plata with the sons and daughters of a North European, even preferentially Anglo Saxon, population.

It is rather improbable that the many *criollo* or *mestizo* Hispanic leaders of the interior provinces warmed entirely to Alberdi's profound skepticism about the biological fitness of their own race. His words attempted to neutralize such doubts: "We need to exchange our people who are unfit for liberty with other people able in its practice, but without abdicating our original racial type, and much less the dominion of the country."[44] The provincial leaders did not have to share fully the long-term "objectives" laid forth by the recluse thinker in order to accept fully the short-term "means" that he so brilliantly set before them. More than likely Alberdi's pragmatic manner of dealing with the thorny issues of his day, and not his polemical racist ideas about the country's past and future, found the greatest merit. In this light how should one accept Canal Feijóo's endorsement of Alberdi's racist ideas—that "strange radicalism"—which contributed to making *Bases* "the most original, strange, and fertile book in American political literature"?[45] In partial response to this question, any endorsement today of Alberdi's harmful racist orientations (which were fully shared by Sarmiento and others of that otherwise inspired generation of thinkers) cynically reaffirms the unfortunate ideological tendencies that predominated in a past historical moment.

What probably impressed the constitutional delegates most was not the "radicalism" of Alberdi's project but rather its "conservatism." Herein lies one of the deep contradictions of his corpus of ideas: although Alberdi's ideas on a desirable constitution had as their main thrust the promotion of material progress, he wanted to assure a type of progress that would not endanger the social order and habits of obedience that had been constructed during the Rosas decades at such a terrible cost. Unlike Sarmiento and Mitre, who could only see the barbarous origins for most, if not all, of the federalist leaders of the interior, Alberdi saw in them a source of present and future stability. Those *caciques* (chieftans),

> who before were crude and brutish, have elevated the cultural level of their minds and personalities through the school of governance. . . . On account of these men, a stable and beneficial order in the interior functions today. . . . To exercise authority successfully in a country as sparsely populated as our own, the leader has to act in accordance with its deeply rooted customs. . . . Social hierarchy, the principles of authority and leadership, and a peaceful social order, have survived and still thrive, in spite of their tumultuous origins decades ago.[46]

Reformers, he argued, had to build upon what already existed, rather than destroy all in order to start anew. Herein lay the central paradox of Alberdi's thought: Although he valued the hierarchies and traditions of the past, he also believed that they constituted an impediment to the country's future progress.[47] This was the frame of mind behind his fierce condemnation of the society and customs of the Spanish colony—the "culminating expression of the Middle Ages"—that still predominated in the newly independent Hispanic American states.[48] This also explains his denunciation in *Bases* of universal suffrage, the practice that had brought the Republic to the brink of chaos a generation before. By now he joined Frías (who continued writing from Paris) in totally rejecting "socialism," a body of ideas that was a the sign of "the disequilibrium of things." Socialism, Alberdi prophesized, would soon experience a "violent rejection" by sensible men everywhere. Alberdi's *Bases* therefore marked the rejection of many ideas he had previously embraced; now he urged the creation of a national government with "aristocratic tinge" and "administrative centralization." By impeding the larger part of the country's population from electoral participation, the elites could assure for future generations the region's security and material advancement.[49]

Undoubtedly of equal interest for the delegates entrusted with composing the country's new constitution was Alberdi's realism in seeking a middle ground between unitarianism and federalism, the two political tendencies that had divided the country since the independence movement early in the century. As such he saw fit to copy into the pages of *Bases* the paragraphs he had written in 1838 for one of the fifteen guiding principles or "Symbolic Words", that is, the need for national leaders to respect the historical antecedents of both political groupings in constructing for the future. His point of departure was that because neither pure unitarianism nor pure federalism were possible, the most realistic constitution had to combine aspects of both: "A middle position that represents peace between the province and the nation, between the parts and the whole, between localism and the idea of the Argentine Republic."[50] In a similar manner the new constitution had to take into account the most important doctrinal precedents in the nation's history: the unitarian principles as practiced under the Spanish crown and as set forth in the principles represented by the May Revolution and the federalist principles detailed in the Federal Pact of 1831 and the San Nicolás Accord of 1852. His repeated admonition was to avoid blind imitation of any previously existing model, whether national or foreign. Any new legal structure had to derive from the nation's own traditions and history and in relation to the population groups and political tendencies then prevalent. In synthesis

all the identified factors belong to and form part of the normal, concrete life of the Argentine Republic and they are intimately related to the foundations of its general government. No constitutent congress would have the power to make them disappear instantaneously through their decrees or laws. These factors must be accepted as the point of departure and, as such, discretely taken into account in writing the Constitution.[51]

SARMIENTO VERSUS ALBERDI

The clash between Sarmiento and Alberdi was perhaps inevitable, given the radically different sensitivities of the two men and in spite of the great similarity of their ideas for the future of the country. Both, with unquestionable patriotism and a burning desire for involvement, had chosen continued residence in Chile after 1852. This vantage point enabled them to ply the writing skills by which they continued their influence back home. Perhaps few people were taken by surprise as the two slowly emerged as champions for opposing factions in the dispute between the interior provinces and Buenos Aires: Alberdi would become the trusted advisor for Urquiza, and Sarmiento would emerge as that leader's most committed foe.

By the fall of the dictator in 1852, Sarmiento was regarded by many of his peers to be one of the most capable of men for leading the nation into the promising era of constitutional government. He had certainly done everything possible to encourage that view. In one instance he accounted for that prominence by presenting an impressive list of books, newspaper articles, pamphlets, and several years of experience as journalist in Chile. Indeed, in his case ideas made the man; he was to explain later that his distinguished activity as "public writer" in Chile appropriately qualified him for assuming even the highest responsibilities in Argentina's post-Rosas era. What were these writings that—he believed—merited so much attention on the part of his countrymen?

After his two-year trip around Western Europe and the United States—with brief excursions to North Africa and Canada—Sarmiento had returned to Santiago, Chile, in 1847 and quickly commenced where he had left off as fiery newspaper writer and strident defender of progressive causes. At this time he married a widow with a considerable fortune, and he moved into her comfortable dwelling in the outlying neighborhood of Yungay. Months later he published *Viajes por Europa, Africa y América* (Travels through Europe, Africa and America—1849), which compiled the letters written during those travels. This work featured Sarmiento's penetrating observations of customs and practices, which were flavored by a familiarity with a not insignificant number of written sources. Sarmiento's pragmatic objectives were of great interest here, particularly as revealed in his comparative method. Underlying nearly every commentary was the implicit comparison with similar phenomena in South America and his desire to have his comments serve a useful purpose there.[52] Noteworthy was his light but fascinating style; his buoyant descriptions of progressive and democratic practices in North America make this—along with the next work to be considered— the most "utopian" of his entire written output.

Then there was *De la educación común* (About public education—1849), only the first of many studies he would publish in the next two decades to promote the free and universal schooling for the masses of the continent. His travels to Europe, Africa, and North America two years earlier had been underwritten by the Chilean government with the expressed purpose of observing and studying the systems of public education then existing in those lands. This new study contained the summary of his findings and set forth a practical plan for implementing a worthy system for public education in the South American republics. He was less than optimistic about the receptivity of the continent's Indians and its "barbaric" *gauchos* to the progressive ideas and practices that could be learned through such instruction. However Sarmiento was truly a precursor in the areas of education for women, special training for teachers, and, in general, the promotion and implementation of universal education. His writings on these topics constitute perhaps his finest contribution.

Recuerdos de provincia (Memories of provincial life—1850) demonstrated Sarmiento's considerable talents as historian and describer of customs. Although originally written with the objective of disproving some calumnious statements published about his supposed disreputable past, the work quickly assumed its rightful position among the best of the continent's autobiographical tradition. The writer undoubtedly had other political objectives in composing it, namely, his desire to project a favorable public image that would be advantageous for future political ambitions. The work thus demonstrates a side to Sarmiento rarely, if ever, viewed before by the other militants of his talented generation: a harmonious personality that revealed an attitude of reverence before venerable predecessors, that respected the traditions of his land, and that serenely gave itself over to the tempo lento of refined language. This hymn of veneration for the progressive patriarchal society that existed in San Juan during Sarmiento's youth now gave voice to the provincial core of Sarmiento's increasingly accentuated cosmopolitanism. It provided an explanation for the conservative character and thought of this man who was emerging as protagonist in the region's struggle on behalf of liberal institutions and an open-ended progress.

Argirópolis (1850) revealed, if nothing else, Sarmiento's audacity: with a brilliant but disorderly intelligence, he attempted to influence the future deliberations concerning necessary institutional reforms and a desirable national constitution. This work demonstrated the convergence of Sarmiento's thought with that of Alberdi and the other liberals of the Asociación de Mayo. All of them defended free navigation along the country's rivers, abolition of interprovincial tariff barriers, free and universal education for the country's citizens, the need to attract European loans in order to develop the country's transportation and productive potentialities, and an aggressive governmental policy to attract a progressive immigrant population to Argentina's shores. But in anticipation of the dispute between Buenos Aires and the provinces over the thorny issue of the location for the national capital, Sarmiento rather fancifully proposed the Island of Martín García some 40 kilometers upstream from

Buenos Aires in the Río de la Plata estuary. This idea was countered by Alberdi in the pages of *Bases* (who returned to one of the theses of *Facundo*) that "whether accepted as such or not, [Buenos Aires] has been the de facto capital . . . Buenos Aires, regardless of the regime in power, will be ascendant."[53]

In spite of the favorable comments in his letters to Alberdi regarding *Bases*, Sarmiento must have gleaned in various pages of that work Alberdi's intent to refute several of his own, dearly held ideas. The elitist character of Alberdi's ideas on public education had been evident as early as the 1845 essay, "La acción de la Europa en América," and *Bases* only made these more explicit. Sarmiento's ideas about the role of education within the total dynamic of social progress had seemed flawed to Alberdi because of their "providential" and not "methodological" thrust; indeed the neoromantic, idealistic thesis underlying Sarmiento's *De la educación común* was that the individual, when elevated through book instruction, would be the motor for society's progress. In *Bases*, Alberdi's more pessimistic and even deterministic ideas on this issue were surely intended as a refutation.[54] Rather than book instruction Alberdi defended industry as "the important instrument for spreading moral doctrines." Contrasts continued with regard to the education of women. Sarmiento, it is well known, was one of South America's earliest proponents and practitioner in the elevation of culture for the future mothers of the continent's masses. Alberdi could not have disagreed more. His reaction to these achievements was, "We need housewives, not artists." Women's role was not to shine intellectually in social gatherings but to provide a moral orientation in the home. For that reason women should not be the recipients of public education. Far preferable was the orientation received in the privacy of the home that prepared them best for domestic responsibilities as wives and mothers.[55] It must be said that these ideas of Alberdi were entirely in line with those of Spencer, Stuart Mill, Blunstchli, and other prominent European thinkers of the period. But in contrast to the perspective of Sarmiento, Alberdi's ideas were "incredibly 'reactionary'"—in the words of Alberdian hagiographer, Bernardo Canal Feijóo.

To question Sarmiento's ideas on universal education was equivalent to attacking his *amour propre*. Simmering hostilities would soon erupt into a public confrontation. The transition in Sarmiento's politics vis-à-vis Urquiza within a rather short period of months, from enthusiastic supporter to vehement antagonist, has already been alluded to. Given the deepening support that Alberdi would lend to the victorious general, a falling out between these two influential leaders of the young generation was all but inevitable. Chile was the initial setting for this ideological dispute so integrally related to the political conflict in Argentina. There the disfavor demonstrated by nearly sixty Argentines over Buenos Aires's rejection of the San Nicolás Accord led to the formation of "The Constitutional Club of Valparaíso" in August 1852, a group in which Alberdi was to play a central role. Sarmiento, recently having returned from his participation in the Ejército Grande, was not invited to participate; this was due, most probably, to his flurry of immoderate public statements against Urquiza and in spite of his very positive comments about *Bases* in personal letters to Alberdi. In this period Alberdi described Sarmiento in a letter to Frías, as "agitator over there, reactionary here." Sarmiento, in spite of his defects—mainly his mistaken politics with regard to Buenos Aires and his tendency to antagonize many people—was still "talented, enthusiastic, honorable, good patriot and potentially useful for any good cause."[56]

In response to the pro-Urquiza position assumed by Alberdi and many Argentines in Valparaíso, Sarmiento quickly established a parallel "Club of Expatriots" in Santiago in order to build support for the cause of Buenos Aires. Then, in October, he sent to Urquiza the famed "Letter from Yungay," which reiterated in violent language his disagreement with the general's actions and his support for Buenos Aires autonomy under Mitre, Dalmasio Vélez Sársfield, Valentín Alsina, and others. Meanwhile Alberdi could not remain silent. In a series of articles published between October and November in *El diario de Valparaíso* (Valparaiso daily), he reproached Sarmiento's attacks against Urquiza and urged him to honor his own words of two months earlier, to the effect of placing principles ahead of personal loyalties in their role as public writers. [57]

The differences between the two had finally reached the breaking point, and courteous polemic was no longer in order. Sarmiento found occasion to elevate this growing embroilment to the level of public feud in *Campaña en el Ejército Grande* (Campaign in the Great Allied Army), which was published in December. Its sustained diatribe in chronicling the ineptitudes and excesses of Urquiza's leadership of the Allied Army in its march from the Banda Oriental (Uruguay) to Caseros was predictable. But even more provocative was the book's strange and provocative dedication to Alberdi. Its disproportionate beginning, "My Dear Alberdi," was followed by a criticism of the latter's cowardly desertion from besieged Montevideo in 1843, months following the military defeat of Lavalle and the routing of unitarian defenders throughout the country.

The other more or less direct slap at Alberdi was Sarmiento's account of the events in his native province of San Juan that resulted from the retrograde politics of Urquiza. During the long period of Rosas rule, oppositional forces to the federalist governors had been growing in several of the provinces. Rosas's defeat at Caseros therefore offered liberal and unitarian groups the opportunity to rid themselves of despised federalist leaders. In San Juan neither of the two parties enjoyed a significant advantage in terms of local influence and support—a factor that would weigh heavily in events there throughout the next decade. Ambitious liberals, who were in contact with Sarmiento, responded to Rosas's ouster in distant Buenos Aires by ousting Federalist strongman, Nazario Benavides, from the governorship. Urquiza, however, had as his immediate objective the construction of his own power base over the same provincial leadership as had existed under Rosas. His order to reinstate Benavides as governor, in spite of the latter's widespread unpopularity and the opposition of the provincial legislature, was badly received by liberal militants. In Buenos Aires the presidential decree was immediately interpreted as a flagrant abuse of Urquiza's powers: the acting president of the federation of united provinces, they argued, did not have the authority to intervene in matters relevant to the politics of a separate province. Porteño liberals therefore interpreted Urquiza's actions in San Juan as a dangerous precedent for whatever future authority he might exercise over Buenos Aires. In the next decade Sarmiento would refer time and again to the example of San Juan as evidence of Urquiza's despotism. Writing in 1853 he represented those events as an example of the "practical politics" urged upon the victorious general by Alberdi: the *"practical politics* that justify enormous abuses that would offend any decent person."[58]

Other passages from *Campaña en el Ejército Grande* reveal additional differences in the perspectives of the two men. Years earlier, when both were just emerging as mature thinkers, they had shared a similar love-hate relationship with the nation's past: On the one hand Sarmiento's admiration for the aristocratic society of his San Juan youth and Alberdi's recognition of the need for the nation's future government to base itself on already existing sources of power and authority had led both to prioritize the need to salvage the positive attributes of the past social order in the construction of the new. On the other hand their passionate hatred of the institutions and customs associated with the region's Hispanic colonial heritage had led them to embrace an apocalyptical vision of a necessary destruction of the past out of which the new society would emerge.[59] By 1852, however, they were no longer joined in this terrible ambiguity: a close reading of *Bases* demonstrates that Alberdi had outgrown his early infatuation with this second perspective of apocalyptic revolution and now gave priority only to the first vision of conservative reform. His new advocation was to preserve the power latent in the provinces: "The new governing program ought to preserve instead of destroy it."[60] This idea surely provoked the choleric outburst of Sarmiento, who was now convinced more than ever that his idealized civilization could only emerge following the total eradication of the *caudillo* order.

Perhaps the most salient feature of Sarmineto's thought during the decade after the fall of Rosas was his obstinate belief in the benefits of a "scorched earth" war against the *caudillo* system throughout the interior. Although many passages from his writings of the period communicate an opposition to violent social change, other passages indicate his conviction that nothing less than that could right the wrongs perpetuated by three decades of *caudillo* rule in Argentina. To this effect a passage in *Campaña en el Ejército Grande* provides a favorable portrait of the leaders of the French Revolution:

> after the Thermidor revolution nothing else was needed in order for society to return to the habits of humanity that it had lost, than for the spirits of those same men whose reputations had been stained by their hideous crimes to calm down and resume their usefulness to the country.[61]

Others undoubtedly believed it a dangerous simplification that a people could immediatelly renew habits of peace and conciliation after a bloody outbreak of fraternal war and repression. At this stage Alberdi and several former colleagues in the struggle against Rosas began to shy away from this dangerous man, whose titanic energies and indisputable talents were more and more guided (according to historian Halperín Donghi) by "an unconfessed nostalgia for civil war."[62]

Now permeating Sarmiento's social thought was the tremendous, chiaroscuro opposition between civilization and barbarism which had provided an axis for his romanticized portrait of Argentine society in the pages of *Facundo* a half-decade earlier. In his schematic way of viewing reality, there was no middle ground between the *caudillo* barbarians and the civilized apostles of an educated urban society. He implicitly rejected the idea of a dialectical movement of history, such as that underlying Alberdi's vision of the crude individuals rising to power throughout the interior who had slowly acquired some of the habits and orientations of civilization. In contrast Sarmiento continued to embrace the schematic perspective of two antagonistic societies in a struggle to the death. With this as a given, he was convinced that the next chapter of his country's history would be written by the soldiers of civilization in their epic battle against barbarism. He had been frustrated in his ambition to exercise under Urquiza a leadership position in the military struggle that was now at hand. Months later he was frustrated again on realizing that Urquiza had no intention whatever of following up his victory at Caseros with a military campaign against Rosas's supporters in the interior. Now he was experiencing yet another disappointment on realizing that Alberdi, his former ally in the struggle against Rosas, was advocating peace and conciliation with those very Federalist leaders whom they had formerly opposed.

With the publication of *Campaña*, the gauntlet had been thrown. Alberdi, in turn, began to prepare a counterattack against his emerging ideological foe. Writing to Frías:

> [Sarmiento] has dedicated to me a demeaning, crazy publication . . ., and he has insulted me in such a way that I have decided to not respond in kind to him, but rather study him, with respect and dignity, through his previous works and more recent ones, and also the tendencies he has more recently demonstrated through his acts. Soon I will send you a copy of that work which will be used to destroy the man who is an obstacle to our country achieving any type of order; he is not a useful soldier to that end.[63]

In March of the following year, Alberdi published what was to be his part of one of the most celebrated polemics in South American political life: *Cartas sobre la prensa y la política militante de la República Argentina* (Letters on the press and militant politics in the Argentine Republic) or more widely known as *Cartas quillotanas* (Letters from Quillota). With elevated tone he analyzed the factors that contributed, in his opinion, to the distorted priorities of Sarmiento. His foremost complaint was that Sarmiento, in his long years of combatting tyranny through the press, had come to acquire many of the negative attributes of his former foe:

> Tyranny, or better yet, violence resides in all of us because we are unaccustomed to obeying rules. The South American press has its caudillos, its "bad gauchos," similar to those in other aspects of public life. And just because they don't take the sabre in hand, like the other caudillos, does not negate their status of caudillos of the pen. . . . The caudillo of the pen is a product of the deserted pampas and the small city; he is a natural product of the underpopulated continent of America.[64]

Following from this perspective Alberdi criticized Sarmiento's self-evaluation as future national leader on the basis of his newspaper writings: "Writing for the political press over a long period of time can hardly be considered a worthy training for the statesman; on the contrary, the former is an occupation which detracts from, rather than enhances, one's qualifications for the latter." But there was also possible praise for Sarmiento in Alberdi's assertion that "there is much of your thought in my *Bases*." He defended Urquiza, in contrast to the well-known confrontational attitude of Sarmiento. Alberdi argued that the writings of both of them had inspired the general, who in turn had accepted as his own many of the principles that they together had defended during their long years of exile.[65]

Sarmiento's terse responses to Alberdi's attacks rarely rose above venomous insults, although his partisans have strenuously argued otherwise. In *Las ciento y una* (A hundred and one), his contribution to this stormy exchange, he depicted Alberdi as: "Soul and face of a rabbit," "Ruffian of the journalistic press," "The dog who shows up at every political wedding," "Eunuch with political aspirations," "A notably quarrelsome person," "Traitor to the educated class of South America," and "carpetbagger lawyer . . . who prostituted his intelligence and personal dignity on behalf of practical business deals."[66]

At moments the polemic touched substantive issues, but most analysts believe that what was primarily at issue was the square-off between two distinct temperaments or antagonistic personality types. For Pablo Rojas Paz there was one man too peaceful against the other who was too belligerent.[67] For Canal Feijóo it was a confrontation between the normative orientation of the first, who sought the "depersonalization" or "systemization" of the self into law, and "the will of an exclusivist, personalist heterodoxy" of the second, which tended to thrust the autocratic self above principles and collectivity.[68] Most commentators correctly call attention to the near identical liberal program defended by both Alberdi and Sarmiento and thus their collaboration in the construction of the new national state that was then evolving. But for the next decade, the two men would be embittered enemies, positioned on opposing sides of the most urgent conflict of their time: the struggle between Urquiza's Confederation and the temporarily autonomous Buenos Aires.

The polemic of 1852–53 hardly altered the respective persuasions of its participants, but it did serve to harden each one's offense before the other and, correspondingly, to hasten their flight from political moderation and compromise. Indeed, from this point on, the neutral observer can detect an increased inflexibility in the views of both. For Sarmiento this period of insult and injury, when angered passions ruled over moderate reason, would last at least up until the time of his presidency. Alberdi, on the other hand, would never again rise above passionate offense before Sarmiento or Mitre. In fact the historical record provides evidence of Alberdi's two distinct personalities from this moment on. First those essays that he saw fit to print during his lifetime document a sustained and brilliant analysis of the most urgent social and political issues confronting the Argentina and South America in his time. And second *Escritos póstumos* (Posthumous writings)—those notes and works published only after his death—are the product of a melancholic, brooder intent upon undermining the fame and reputation of his erstwhile political foes.

Constitutional Debates

Within months the polemic between Alberdi and Sarmiento faded from the public eye as both dedicated themselves to more constructive enterprises. At midyear Alberdi published *Elementos de derecho público provincial para la República Argentina* (Elements of public provincial law for the Argentine Republic—1853), which had as its objective to outline a desirable organization for the governments of the different provinces and to delineate the lines of cleavage between provincial and national legal jurisdiction. A few months later Sarmiento answered with *Comentarios de la Constitución* (Commentaries on the Constitution), which again justified the rebellion of Buenos Aires because of Paraná's "onerous and repugnant conditions," while at the same time reaffirmed the need to struggle against the dismemberment of the country. He provided fresh arguments for Buenos Aires's leadership over the other provinces: the "inimitable laws of commerce" made so that that province's wealth would continue to grow at a disproportionate rate relative to the other provinces. The city, on that account, was the logical center of the country's government and commerce. On that basis he argued for its continued administration of the national customshouse.[69] He took issue with two major aspects of the constitution already sanctioned by the provinces: its call for the administrative severance of the city of Buenos Aires from its provincial territories and its legitimization of the provincial authorities that had remained unchanged since the previous regime.[70] Then, a few months later, he would follow this work up with a shorter study, "Examen crítico de un proyecto de Constitución de la Confederación Argentina, por Juan B. Alberdi" (Critical examination of a proposal for the Consititution of the Argentine Confederation, by Juan B. Alberdi), in which Sarmiento criticized Alberdi for having copied almost verbatim many passages from the Constitution of the United States of North America.[71]

In his turn Alberdi responded with another publication, *Estudios sobre la Constitución argentina de 1853* (Studies on the Argentine Constitution of 1853), which countered Sarmiento's criticism about having copied from the constitution of the United States. Alberdi also reiterated his criticisms that Buenos Aires legislators had no legal justification for rejecting the Constitution. A year later, in response to the act of the Buenos Aires legislature of issuing its own constitution, he wrote *Examen de la Constitución provincial de Buenos Aires* (Examination of the provincial Constitution of Buenos Aires—1854). In this work he returned to his now familiar rhetoric that Buenos Aires, "an insurgent province," had no right to legislate issues pertaining to an independent state. In spite of that constitution's rhetoric of liberal reform, it was a "work of reaction and restauration," because it responded to the interests of the *saladera* monopolists who, in spite of their defeat at Monte Caseros, once again ruled supreme in the province.[72]

Sarmiento and Alberdi were not the only members of the now extinct

Asociación de Mayo who were active in ideological disputes over the new constitution. Félix Frías, from Paris, sent a continual stream of letters and articles to newspapers in the Río de la Plata and Chile in defense of his conservative views. Mention was made above of his condemnation of the radical democracy implemented by "socialists" in the European context, because of the street violence that had resulted. The revolutionary scenes he had witnessed in Paris had caused him to reconsider many of his previous views about the implementation of democracy and liberty in the Río de la Plata. His conservative disposition led him to the conclusion that social order had to be guaranteed before any new rights could be enjoyed. Whatever social change had to concur with, rather than oppose, the deeply held values and orientations of the community. One of his articles published in *El mercurio* of Valparaíso stated that "moral and legal principles are superior to the will of any people."[73] In private correspondence, moreover, he outlined in greater detail his thinking with regard to the ills of modernity, such as he saw them. The ideas of socialism hindered rather than helped French society's advancement, because they contributed to the weakening of "the public's conscience, moral sentiments, and good sense." The philosophical and literary ideas then in vogue were similarly responsible for these losses, "since they are the soldiers of error, and they form the vanguard of evil."[74] As part of the debates among Argentines about the desirable contours of its new national Constitution, Frías's thesis was "the civilizing principle . . . comes from neither literature nor philosophy; it's origin is in morality, in religion."

To Frías's way of thinking, the Catholic Church, and not the state, held the primarily responsibility for inculcating a positive moral and social orientation in the individual. In a new article published in Valparaíso's *El mercurio*, he wrote, "The only foundation for democracy . . . is the religious culture of a people, that is, the culture that recognizes a higher authority for its beliefs and practices in religious law, in the supernatural order."[75] In direct contrast to Sarmiento's call for public secular education as the motor of moral and material progress, he argued for the need to "civilize" the country "with religion as the basis for liberty."[76] This contradicted the position of both his close friend Alberdi and Sarmiento, who independently urged the inclusion of constitutional provisions to guarantee tolerance for all religious beliefs within a secular system of public schooling.

Frías's intervention in the constitutional debate with regard to such important points was bound to ruffle some feathers. Tomás Frías—apparently no relation to Félix—complained to Alberdi in a personal letter about a "certain harshness and exclusiveness to his sectarian tone."[77] Félix's intervention was, for Tomás Frías, "inadequate and perhaps

prejudicial, above all when it is employed on behalf of religious sentiment, or in the interest of beliefs, and especially when it pretends to
defend the true faith." Needless to say, the perspectives defended by
Tomás Frías, Alberdi, Sarmiento, and countless others, carried more
weight among the delegates entrusted with the task of drafting the
constitution. Félix Frías, nursing his wounded vanity on account of this
ideological defeat, saw fit to remain in his Parisian exile for yet another
few years.

Urquiza's New Federalism

Alberdi was largely correct in his criticism of Sarmiento and the other
members of the young generation who now opposed Urquiza; he believed that their position represented a betrayal of many of the principles
that they had formerly defended. This was because Urquiza's governmental program for national reconstruction had successfully incorporated to a great extent the bipartisan and nationalist orientations that
Echeverría and the other early leaders of the May Association had urged
from the start. One can only speculate about where Echeverría's sympathies would have lain had he survived to witness the dramatic events
of 1852. Careful study of his later writings reveals a closer affinity to the
position of Alberdi—whom he had declared his ideological "heir"—
than what was emerging as the pro-Porteño position of Sarmiento and
Mitre.[78] This was but one reason for Alberdi's subsequent support for
the victorious general's cause: throughout the entire period he would
serve as trusted advisor and ideological leader, occupying the official
position of the Confederation's official representative in Europe. He was
joined in this preference by Vicente Fidel López, who served Urquiza
briefly as minister of public instruction in the transition government.
In addition Juan María Gutiérrez became the transitional ministro de
gobierno (prime minister); later, in Paraná, he carried the portfolio of
the ministry of justice, culture, and public instruction until 1856. Then,
for four additional years—until the Confederation's demise in 1860—he
would serve as that government's commercial agent in Buenos Aires.

The new federalist banner that was thrust to the fore by Urquiza in
1852 represented in many respects a fusion of tendencies that the young
generation, through their Creencia and the Dogma Socialista, had been
urging since 1837. On the one hand the policies of Urquiza represented
a continuation of traditional federalist sentiment in its advocation of
the relative autonomy of the interior provinces against the hegemonic
designs of Buenos Aires. But times had also changed. By 1852 the idea
of local autonomy was nearly vanquished because of two factors: the

dramatic economic and demographic growth of Buenos Aires in relation to the rest of the provinces and the previous regime's successes in reducing the provincial leaders to obedient followers of Buenos Aires's initiatives. The question now posed by the neo-Federalist observers advising Urquiza was no longer whether the interior provinces could or should remain autonomous of the cultural, political, and economic leadership of Buenos Aires but rather in what way the resources of that wealthy and powerful province could be redirected for the benefit of the country as a whole.

In spite of his Federalist credentials, Urquiza therefore advocated several aspects of a politics traditionally linked with the Unitarian Party— these were programs at the core of the young generation's plan for national reconstruction. One such issue was the opening of the country's interior rivers to foreign commerce, which involved the termination of trade restrictions that had previously required vessels to unload in Buenos Aires and pay customs fees there. Free and unfettered commerce along the country's rivers had been a farsighted dream of the Rivadavia government a few decades earlier but had then met with the stalwart opposition of Federalists in the interior. The latter had feared that British commercial agents' greater access to consumers in the interior would only jeopardize the rather primitive state of artisanship and the textile industry there. As one researcher succinctly wrote about the political climate of the 1820s, "protectionism is synonymous with federalism."[79]

But again changing circumstances had led the farsighted Federalist leaders of the interior to leave behind this now retrograde opposition to foreign trade. By 1852 the cottage industries and domestic cloth production of the interior provinces had all but disappeared. The depressed economic conditions that still largely prevailed in those provinces meant that the spokesmen for economic interests hardly wielded the influence their predecessors had enjoyed. As such, the provinces supporting neo-federalist principles with greatest enthusiasm were the prosperous ones of the Littoral. Urquiza's conversion to the liberal program of free commerce along the country's interior rivers was hardly born out of altruistic liberal conviction. On the contrary it was a policy that coincided precisely with the interests of his provincial class of *latifundia* cattle producers, jerked-meat producers, and commercial agents, all of whom struggled against the Buenos Aires–centered monopolistic forces to expand their economic dealings in the region.

Alberdi was not nearly as perturbed as Sarmiento about the survival of retrograde *precapitalist* labor relations in the cattle industry of the Littoral, in spite of the industry's new commercial ties with the *procapitalist* international market economy.[80] Although not in favor of that state of affairs, Alberdi nevertheless believed that significant immigration and the development of agriculture and industry would lead the region and the nation slowly to shed off their institutional trappings of the past and somehow assume the contours of modernity. Again Sarmiento opposed this opinion, believing that the bullish economic conditions of Entre Ríos and the other provinces of the Littoral would not bring about a dramatic alteration of the *latifundia* patterns of land tenure and social organization. He continued advocating perhaps the most radical position among the members of his talented generation; he believed that the desirable society of the future could not emerge without the prior liquidation of the *latifundia*.

Regardless of Sarmiento's opposition, Urquiza continued to demonstrate receptivity to the program defined by the young generation in their foundation documents. Indeed his speeches and acts in the months after Caseros demonstrate a seemingly sincere desire to win their adherence to his cause. He invited Gutiérrez to write his speech, which opened the meeting at San Nicolás, as well the inaugural address at the Congress in Santa Fe. Totally in accordance with the young generation's program, Urquiza supported the San Nicolás measures of immediately opening the interior rivers of the country to foreign navigation, abolishing interior tariff barriers, and nationalizing the customshouses located in Buenos Aires. Similarly the initiative of Urquiza was certainly one contributing factor in the Santa Fe convention's endorsement of a constitution that largely followed the ideas outlined by Alberdi.

In the next few years, the Confederation under Urquiza's direction followed in this positive direction. After the ratification of the Constitution by all the provinces minus Buenos Aires in 1853, elections were held, a legislature was formed, and the following year Urquiza formally assumed the post of president. Positive results continued. The government in Paraná provided for the stimulation of industry and the exploitation of farming and cattle-raising resources; contracts for colonizing extensive areas of Santa Fe, Entre Ríos, and Corrientes; immigration of farmers from Italy, Spain, Switzerland, and Germany, especially; agricultural colonies; nationalization of the University of Córdoba; establishment of secondary schools in Mendoza, Salta, Tucumán, and Catamarca; reorganization of the mail service; formalization of national ministries and a system of federal justice throughout the country; construction of roads and schools; establishment of an office of statistics; hiring of engineers for the construction of railroad lines; and, finally, a diplomatic plan to win the official recognition of Brazil, Uruguay, Paraguay, and the European nations.[81]

But this intense labor, although well inspired and executed, was continually thwarted by the Paraná government's scarcity of financial resources. Another problem was the increasingly bellicose resistance of Buenos Aires to be integrated into the Confederation, which meant that the Paraná government was forced to use fully half of its budget in preparation for a possible military solution. Buenos Aires, in contrast, had at its disposal bountiful resources for its internal development and the maintenance of its army and squadron. This pronounced difference in financial resources would remain until the end of the decade as a destabilizing force and a cause for interprovincial conflict.

New Political Alignments in Buenos Aires

Following the Revolution of September, Buenos Aires set itself to its own task of institutional reorganization. Its legislature was converted into the province's constituent convention which wrote and then sanctioned a new constitution. By mid-1854 this had been done, and Pastor Obligado (whom his opponents linked with Rosas's secret police, the *Mazorca*[82]) was subsequently elected president. In December a treaty was celebrated with the government of the Confederation that provided for a temporary truce to armed hostilities and postponed into the undeterminate future any resolution to the political differences between the two.

Two political tendencies had now emerged in the Porteño political scene. First there were the *autonomists* or the *localists*, led by former Unitarian leader Valentín Alsina, rich landowners and former Rosas supporters Tomás and Nicolás Anchorena, and former May Association activist Carlos Tejedor. This group defended the sovereignty of the Province of Buenos Aires as a separate political entity. Second there were the *nationalists*, under the influence of Mitre and other liberals, who sought Buenos Aires's predominance, yet within the nation at large. In a letter to Urquiza, Francisco Pico, the Confederation's representative in Montevideo, defined the differences in the two group's respective politics:

> [N]either group knows what it wants: the nationalists want independent national status for Buenos Aires, but without the Directory, a Congress, or the Constitution, and without having to submit themselves to what the majority decides; they want unity but not its consequences. The other group wants isolation, but without ceasing to belong to the Nation.[83]

Pico emphasized the differences but made it clear that both tendencies aspired the hegemony of Buenos Aires and its leadership over the nation's social and economic development. Alberdi's repeated argument, which has been embraced by several influential historians of our own day, was that whatever differences might have divided these two political tendencies in Buenos Aires, they came together in favoring continued Porteño predominance, and in doing so tacitly joined with those interests that had been the mainstay of the Rosas Regime.[84]

This strident call for continued Porteño predominance whether from unitarian or exrosista latifundists—was hardly "simplistic."[85] "Egotistical" or "shortsighted" are perhaps more accurate qualifiers. Thirty years earlier, when there had existed a greater balance between the power and population of Buenos Aires and other areas, the haughty advocacy of a Buenos Aires–centered regime might have been legitimately assessed as the result of "simplistic" or utopian thinking. However, by 1852, that same political position now corresponded to Buenos Aires's nearly unrivaled predominance throughout the region. That province's leaders from either tendency, egged on by its proud and haughty population, stubbornly refused to compromise with the interests and views of the people of the interior.

Most perplexing for Alberdi, Gutiérrez, Cané, V. F. López, and other liberals siding with the cause of the Confederation was the willingness of Mitre, Mármol, Tejedor, and a few others of May Association past to collaborate with old unitarians and Rosas federalists under the new banner of Buenos Aires hegemony. One explanation for this tolerance or even conversion of interests in Buenos Aires politics had to do with the shared urban roots and orientation of both the formerly exiled Porteño intellectuals and the propertied and commercial elites of the region. The *terrateniente* oligarchy supporting Rosas, in spite of the fact that its power derived from the land, nevertheless hailed, in the great majority of cases, from urban families. Only in the previous three to four decades had these powerful families begun the massive transfer of resources from commercial or bureaucratic enterprises to cattle production. The latter offered not only economic opportunity but also security in an economy dislocated by the effects of free trade and ruinous wars.[86] The returned intellectuals (Mitre, Mármol, Tejedor, and others) joined with the cattle oligarchy and other leading commerical interests in Buenos Aires in defending the province's central position within the association of provinces. While the monied interests in Buenos Aires struggled to maintain their commercial monopoly over the rest of the country, the liberal intellectuals sought the means whereby the interior provinces' recalcitrant barbarism would conform to their new ideas on trade, government, and association.

Another reason for the liberals' willingness to join with federalists who, only months before, had been staunch supporters of the Rosas regime was their particular worldview that derived overwhelmingly from moral and idealist theories of historical change. In almost all their cases, a refined cultural orientation contributed to their belief that the port-city's mission was to inseminate the more backward provinces of the interior with their own ideas of progress and modernity. Their early writings reveal the scant attention granted to issues related to political economy; the ignorance of rural society in the majority of their cases was notorious. This went hand-in-hand with a general underestimation of the role and impact of economic and material forces in the formulation of governmental policy and a parallel overdetermination of the effects that their journalist and educative activities would have over the body politic. According to their "organic" conception of historical change, most of them sincerely believed that a government's decisive actions for improving social services and opening the possibilities for unencumbered trade would automatically yield improvements in all aspects of social life. Conversely they projected that an increase in production and trade, under whatever circumstances, would stimulate naturally parallel improvements in other areas. In general a healthy skepticism about the intentions of the rural landowners in the new governing equation for the province was outweighed by a somewhat unrealistic assessment of their own power to override those prerogatives.

Very much related to this underestimation of the power of economic forces was the lack of attention given to differences in origins and class interests. Sarmiento would not immediately join Buenos Aires in its struggle against the Confederation, but the pro-Porteño aspects to his worldview were obvious in his writings at least as far back as 1845. His thinking on this issue was representative. A general blindness to class differences flavored his assessment of the power elite in Buenos Aires after the fall of Rosas. Although he had correctly assessed the positive accomplishments of the largely agricultural oligarchy in his native province of San Juan in achieving a "prebourgeois transformation" of the region,[87] he erred in projecting a similarly positive role for the cattle oligarchy of Buenos Aires. Out of this came his mistaken equivalence that Buenos Aires's "clase culta" was the same as the "clase propietaria y moral" that wore the "traje del mundo civilizado."[88] This erroneous comparison therefore led him and others to gloss over the vastly divergent priorities and worldviews that separated his own group of liberals and the class of *saladera* monopolists that had been the mainstay of the Rosas regime. In the streets of Buenos Aires, where all wore the *frac* (topcoat), he saw a "fusion" of races, traditions, and ideological tendencies, which was the realization of his dreamed civilization: "[I]t is a consummated fact that the descendants of the old colonists have intimately amalgamated with newer arrivals, thus sealing through blood their community of interests and their commonly embraced tradition."[89] Writing these words in 1853, Sarmiento passed over any class distinctions with regard to socioeconomic function and entirely failed to mention that only a year earlier he and his band of liberal exiles had been waging a war to death against the *saladera* oligarchy of the province that had perpetuated a "barbarous" way of life and had propelled to a position of leadership the hated Rosas. In Sarmiento's schematic vision of Argentine society, those who now wore the topcoat belonged to society's privileged elite and those who dressed in *chiripá* were uncivilized beings who would either have to conform or be eliminated by the emerging modern state.

BUENOS AIRES VERSUS THE CONFEDERATION, 1854–1860

Given the continued state of tension between Buenos Aires and the Confederation, the voices of moderation on both sides progressively lost ground to those colleagues advocating less conciliatory measures. It was a vicious cycle with many historical precedents: When one government initially assumed a belligerent stand, it alienated those individuals within it who were most committed to peace, and the latters' withdrawal from the ruling circle served to fortify all the more the position of the more hardened militants. This state of affairs generally led to the exclusion of those leaders inspired by philosophical or moral points of view and left ruling channels open to the masters of unmeditated action. Each side became inextricably locked into a pattern of action and response, where principles were shelved in favor of expediency and where long range objectives took second place to opportunism and demagoguery. But for one side not to have followed this course of increased rigidity would have made it vulnerable to the opponents' increased hostility. Each new act by one side was read by the other as a provocation. The grounds for moderation and restraint became increasingly reduced in this spiraling descent toward all-out war.

The fragile truce negotiated in 1854 could not endure, primarily because each side was committed, whether explicitly or implicitly, to counteracting the prerogatives of the other. The geopolitical conflict between the two regions was too aggravated to be resolved through negotiation— as such armed hostilities were perhaps inevitable. Nevertheless the intractable leaders of either side made early gestures toward peace: each hoped to buy time in order that a more favorable arrangement might emerge. It was the hope of Urquiza and his most trusted advisors that the Confederation's strong legal case would successfully transfer into commercial and financial advantages vis-à-vis the European powers; it would then be in a stronger position to dictate the terms for Buenos Aires's reunification with the Confederation. The Buenos Aires leadership, in contrast, bet that Paraná's short-term successes in the diplomatic theater would wither before Buenos Aires's advantagous position with regard to population, commerce, and financial resources. Porteño leaders were convinced that the city of Paraná, the sleepy urban outpost of thirty thousand inhabitants that served as the Confederation's capital, would eventually have to yield to the dynamic initiatives of Buenos Aires.

The ideological positions of the respective sides would change little over the next decade. Indeed the words and slogans originally chosen to justify actions taken were repeated time and again with little alteration. It was a sort of "dialogue among the deaf," because neither party was willing to cede on the key issue of who would predominate in guiding the country's reorganization.

MITRE IN BUENOS AIRES

By the time of the provincial debates of March 1854 over Buenos Aires's new constitution, Mitre had secured his leadership position within the provincial legislature. The friction between the country's two regions had become so exasperated that Porteño leaders now argued the benefits of taking into their own hands the exercise of the province's foreign affairs. Mitre, at this time, reluctantly agreed to this new step toward autonomy. Yet in the face of vocal opposition from Tejedor, Anchorena, and others who projected Buenos Aires's future as a wholly independent state, Mitre continued to argue that the province's rightful place was alongside the other "federal states" in a national order that would emerge only after the exit of Urquiza from the national scene.[90]

When the Constitutional Assembly of Buenos Aires approved a constitution that provided for its autonomy, Urquiza was provoked to ire. His speech to the First Federal Legislative Congress was reproduced in the Buenos Aires press at the beginning of November 1854.[91] The Buenos Aires constitution, in his opinion, was a "firebrand of discord"; its calculated purpose was to divide further the Argentine people. The events of September two years earlier had already demonstrated the hatred and shame of Buenos Aires's small clique of leaders, with their "shameful calculations of self-interest." The legislative approval of Buenos Aires's constitution, he believed, meant that war was inevitable; it would be a bloody, implacable struggle.

The publication of those severe words understandably provoked an impassioned reaction on the part of Porteño leaders. Mármol's published reaction was a more reasoned expression of ire. But Mitre, in an unsigned editorial, could not refrain from personal insult and libelous association: "That Message is the last rattle in the throats of the caudillos, whose system is destined to succumb with the fall of general Urquiza, he will be the last monkey to be drowned, because Urquiza, the constitutionally-elected head of government, is nothing more than an imbecile presenting a badly learned, ridiculous farce."[92] Insults continued. Urquiza, with "foolish shortsightedness," had placed himself in the same category as such barbaric *caudillos* as Artigas, López, Ramírez, and Quiroga. Worse yet the Entrrrian leader was the latest in a line of pampa menaces that included Indian leaders Calfucurá and Pichún, because of his actions in arming and inspiring frontier revolts by the "starving hordes of vandals who rob and then slit the throats of their victims."[93] Echoing the intractable opinions articulated by Sarmiento since 1852, Mitre wrote: "[A]s long as Urquiza stands between us and the Provinces, any definitive agreement is impossible."

Within hours after writing these lines, Mitre left the editorship of *El nacional* in the hands of Sarmiento, donned the uniform of a soldier, and assumed the direction of the province's defenses before the growing threat offered by Confederate forces. From this moment on—until after assuming the presidency of the United Provinces after the Battle of Pavón in 1861—Mitre's energies would be dedicated almost entirely to directing the military defense of the province. Only sporadically would he participate in parliamentary debates, and his intervention in the Buenos Aires press ceased almost entirely.

One exception was his essay, "La República del Río de la Plata" (The Plata Republic), that appeared in *El nacional* in December 1856. In this article Mitre assumed once again the mantle of statesman in appealing to all sides for a spirit of compromise and conciliation before the protracted tensions and mutual provocations. Following the customary pattern his remarks focused on political concerns, while almost entirely avoiding the issues relevant to Buenos Aires's geopolitics and the selfish material interests of its elites. Noteworthy was his demagogic appeal for a mystical "liberty" that would allow commercial interests near complete freedom in their activities and an almost unrestricted authority for the Porteño legislature in matters relevant to the province. Rhetoric predominated over analysis: the Confederation united communities that were "enervated by corruption; having lost any notion of good and evil, they are incapable of generous passions and bury any remaining trace of decency in their political whoring."[94] Contrasting with the conduct of the Confederation were the "noble and moderate actions" of Buenos Aires. The national conflict, in short, became reduced in his view to a struggle between a people and a *caudillo*. In spite of this analysis featuring rhetorical oversimplification over reason, the article had the redeeming value of repeating the invitation for a peaceful resolution to the conflict. Mitre reiterated his call of 1852 for the nationalization of the Province of Buenos Aires and the new denomination of the country as *The Río de la Plata Republic*. Given the state of mutual provocation and heightened distrust existing on both sides, this proposal was summarily rejected by the Porteño political leadership. Although Mitre's essay had little, if any, immediate impact in Porteño circles,[95] it did help to pave the way for the conciliatory meetings that would occur between Mitre, Urquiza, and Derqui before the end of the decade.

MÁRMOL: PORTEÑO MODERATE

After his verbal skirmishes in 1852 with Mitre, Mármol continued to exercise important responsibilities in the Buenos Aires Legislature and to maintain a high profile in the city's political life. In November 1853 he once again assumed the role of "contemporizer," this time by publishing as both a newspaper editorial and a pamphlet a letter he had directed to the officials representing Urquiza in Paraná.[96] The letter was written in response to an earlier communication sent to the governors of the different provinces, in which Salvador María del Carril, in his capacity as vice president of the Confederation, celebrated the supposed end to *mazhorqueros* (secret police butchers) and *caudillos*, and the provinces' *unanimous* support for the new Constitution. Mármol's purpose was to call public attention to the false stand of the Carril letter, which neglected any mention of Buenos Aires's negative reaction to the San Nicolás Accord as well as its refusal to endorse the new Constitution.

Mármol also assumed the mantle of Buenos Aires defender, but in this letter he presented himself as an "Argentine Citizen" in order to distance his views from those of the more radicalized Porteño leadership. He began with the rhetorical gesture of reaffirming his confidence in the good faith of General Urquiza. At the same time, however, he called attention to the widespread feeling in Porteño circles that the general's good *intentions* were contradicted by less respectable aspects of his character. He also found fault with that leader's representatives during the San Nicolás debates who, with haughty attitude, had come to Buenos Aires neither to speak nor to listen but only to impose their own views. Mármol argued that the conflict between Buenos Aires and the Confederation that resulted from those debates was not due to the acts committed by the Porteño leadership but rather to the very flawed principles of the Accord itself.

Mármol took issue with the publicists of the Confederation who had denounced Mitre as having exhibited highly irresponsible behavior during this period. Surprisingly—in light of his views published in *El Paraná*

(The Paraná) two years earlier—he now argued that Mitre had acted with respectful moderation in the provincial legislature. Interpreting the good sense of the people of Buenos Aires, Mitre had voted to reject the Accord because he believed Urquiza to be unworthy of the position of provisional president and the near dictatorial powers conferred upon him.[97] Mármol pointed out that subsequent events had borne out the intuition of Mitre and the Buenos Aires *pueblo:* Urquiza had usurped power in establishing a broad dictatorship that went beyond the authority granted to him by the Accord. Also at fault was the Paraná Congress for having demonstrated its total disregard for Buenos Aires's sovereign rights as a province and its decree authorizing Urquiza to use forceful measures against Buenos Aires. Here Mármol anticipated an argument that Sarmiento, in his own writings, would return to again and again in future years: the acts taken by Buenos Aires to segregate itself from the rest of the provinces were taken not only in defense of that province's *rights* (*derecho*), but also in response to the social, political, and geographical *fact* (*hecho*) of Buenos Aires's special status. It was not only that province's right to self-determination but also the fact of its special role in the region that had to be considered as fundamental in any plan for national reorganization.[98]

Over the next several years, Mármol would continue to serve in the provincial legislature, and later, the senate. According to one biographer, while Mármol enjoyed the friendship and respect of many colleagues, his arrogant and tempestuous personality often impeded him from attaining a clear understanding of important issues.[99] Inconsistency was his trademark: one day he would be capable of profound reasonings, the next his arguments would be marred by reversals or inconsistencies. With "hot-headed imagination," with an infatuation for hearing his own speeches delivered "with greater poetic sense than technical rigor," with an occasional inability to distinguish between what was petty or profound, his participation was tolerated, if not loathed, by his more talented colleagues. Blasi recounts, for example, that during the entire year of 1856, he became engaged in verbal disputes almost daily on the floor of the Senate with Sarmiento, who continually attempted to call Mármol back to reality. These negative tendencies in his character and advocacies often led to controversy. On one occasion he was reprehended by the editors of *El orden* for his "irresponsible" and "irreflexive" language in his public writings and his tendency to associate any opponent of the Porteño position with the hated *más horqueros* at the service of Rosas.[100] On another occasion Mármol was criticized for practicing a politics of negativity; he "continually opposed all measures, all laws proposed by the government."[101]

Indeed, by mid-1857 Mármol came to head the list of scapegoats continually criticized by Sarmiento through his daily editorials and articles published in *El nacional*. According to Sarmiento, Mármol had joined Nicolás Calvo and Lorenzo Torres in attempting to obstruct the progress of the Porteño government in every way possible. Since the publication of *Amalia*, Mármol "has disgraced himself by teaming up with any possible movement opposing the government."[102] Later Sarmiento accused Mármol of total incompetence and irresponsibility in his functions as provincial senator. For example, without having even read the "Commerical Code," Mármol, with malicious pride, voted against it in the Senate chamber. According to Sarmiento this sort of action qualified Mármol as *l'enfant terrible* of the Senate, "a malicious delinquent who throws little stones at the magnificent crystal vase that others were admiring."[103]

In spite of his continued conflicts with generational colleagues, Mármol's legislative colleagues demonstrated their respect by appointing him to important commissions[104] and even electing him vice president of the Senate. This continued esteem was due, at least in part, to his growing renown for the 1855 publication of the novel *Amalia*, probably the finest work of narrative fiction by any writer of his generation, rivaled only by Sarmiento's *Facundo* in its sociological, historical, and ideological value in interpreting Argentine politics and society.[105]

Here are highlights of a few key issues of this novelistic tour de force. The first aspect of the novel worthy of emphasis is its tremendous attack against Rosas and the principal figures and practices of his regime. It accomplishes this not only through its passionate depiction of historical figures but also by means of several lengthy essayistic passages pregnant with documentary value. Indeed, in the first few years after the fall of Rosas, Mármol had resisted publishing this novel in Buenos Aires, because he was aware that its powerful political statement could have the power to "wound" or "alienate the good will" of many former Rosas supporters who, by then, had joined with former exiles in supporting the cause of Buenos Aires against the threats emanating from Urquiza's Confederation.[106] But over the next few years this concern waned, especially in the light of another cause vehemently embraced by Mármol: the desire to damn eternally the legacy of Rosas through the legislature's declaration of the former dictator's high treason and the confiscation of his extensive possessions. In effect the republication of *Amalia* in 1855 paralleled his strident legislative speeches and played its role in fueling the growing sentiment against Rosas that culminated precisely in the legislation that Mármol had desired.

A second important feature of the novel is the "unitarian" option that Mármol defended for the nation's future. Alberdi and Echeverría had previously argued for a "fusion" of political tendencies, and Gutiérrez and V. F. López had more recently reconfirmed their faith in achieving a desirable national order through the transformation of the federalist traditions of the interior. In contrast Mármol's novel declared a total war against the federalist creed, that "doctrinal fraud, with deep historical roots, that has provided caudillos of the country with a means for demagogically leading their ignorant followers."[107] In one of the novel's essayistic fragments, Mármol defended "unitarian ideas," as embraced by the country's earliest patriots, Moreno and Belgrano, which were inseparable from "the monarchical principle." Mármol's elitist and racist liberal perspective (which did not differ dramatically from Alberdi's and Sarmiento's ideas) fully embraced in principle the limitation of political participation to the small class of white landowners and intellectuals residing in the country's major cities. According to this view the country's unfortunate mixture of biologically inferior races, its low level of education, the primitive values and customs of its majority population, and its backward traditions demanded the conservation of authoritarian and paternalist, if not monarchical, structures. According to Mármol, "One means for salvaging whatever remained of that principle, was the construction of a unified regime in the Republic."

A third ideological import of this novel helped to explain the otherwise unlikely alliance forged in the latter months of 1852 between the ex-Rosist supporters in Buenos Aires and the newly returned liberal exiles. This was the largely *political* condemnation of Rosas contained in the novel's pages that ignored *sociological* or *sociohistorical* facts. Nowhere did the novel recriminate the sector of Buenos Aires landowners that had supported Rosas, and nowhere did it either discuss or denounce Rosas's alliance with that class. In fact the father of the novel's protagonist, Daniel Bello, is the son of a rich landowner belonging precisely to that sector that had benefited so handily under Rosas. The father was "a true federalist; landowner, partner of the Anchorenas; and enjoying wide prestige in the countryside."[108] The Anchorena family, due to its vast wealth and its close relationship to the Rosas regime, had its enemies in some liberal circles. But in the novel, as well as in the new political life of Buenos Aires, it was now allied to the group led by Mitre and Mármol. The elderly federalist is the devoted father of the liberal protagonist; it is he who almost saves the liberal militants and by extention the anti-Rosas rebellion in the novel's final scenes.

As such it would seem that the large landowners of Buenos Aires constituted precisely the sector to which the 1855 version of the novel was directed; this was the social group that Mármol, through his literary statement, wished to defend and redeem.[109] He joined Mitre and also Sarmiento (in his less lucid moments) in an ideological campaign whose objective was to mystify the origins of Rosasism. Like them his condemnation of Rosas focused on the dictator's moral and political abuses, meaning that whatever wrongdoing was viewed as resulting from the acts of an evil individual with "reactionary principles" or "barbarians" who imposed themselves over a primarily "civilized" and benevolent population. This analysis failed to call attention to the fact that Rosas had his firm and dedicated supporters in Porteño society, who found in the tyrant a defender of their own narrow class and regional interests. In essence this meant that Mármol either chose to ignore or refused to grant due importance to the dictator's intimate ties with the landowning class of Buenos Aires *saladeros* and cattle producers, who had facilitated his rise to power and who then had consolidated themselves as the nation's ruling class under his protection.

The fourth compelling aspect of the novel was the certification it gave to Mármol and his generational cohorts in leading the nation in the post-Rosas period. If the rampant *individualism* of the Buenos Aires citizenry[110] was what had permitted the poisoned "moral phenomenon" of Rosas's government, then a remedy for that situation had to be found in the actions of a close-knit association similar to the group founded by Echeverría which included Mármol within its ranks. This group of intellectuals and publicists, in their long years of exile, had already fulfilled Mármol's first call to disseminate their propaganda against the dictator and encourage a viable opposition. They had also served in his second call—mapping out a strategy and organizing the military campaign against the tyrant. Now, with Rosas defeated and in exile, the survivors of the struggle would continue their progressive actions through "the workings of speeches and writing" in order to teach the youth "that liberty will fail if society does not arise as one in its defense; that all will be at risk—homeland, liberty, laws, religion, public virtue— as long as the spirit of association leaves standing the cancer of individualism, that force which has eroded and continues eroding the spirit of our generation."[111]

By the time of *Amalia*'s dissemination to the Porteño reading public, Mármol was one of the suffered heros who had returned from emigration; he was one of the honored publicists whose writings had contributed nobly to his generational mission. Like Sarmiento, Alberdi, and several others, his claim to prominence in the post-Rosas era was precisely his past accomplishments of the pen and his ability to continue influencing and teaching the population through the press and his oratory. *Amalia* now served a double role in Mármol's struggle for prominence: while its narrative content set forth the criterion for his ascendance, its success as a cultural document certified his compliance with those conditions.

SARMIENTO: PROVINCIAL IN BUENOS AIRES, NATIONALIST ABOVE ALL

In 1855 Sarmiento finally brought to an end his self-imposed exile in Chile and returned to Buenos Aires. In the previous three years he had carried on a copious correspondence with Mitre, through whose letters he had managed to keep abreast of the rapidly evolving situation in the Plata region. Mitre, in turn, had done his best to keep Sarmiento's name in the news and propagate a favorable view of the San Juan native's undeniable talents and commendable accomplishments. Indeed Sarmiento was hardly an unknown to the Buenos Aires public, even though his residence there had amounted to no more than a few weeks after the fall of Rosas. His writings had circulated widely. Although the people on the street might have had initial doubts about Sarmiento's commitment to the Porteño cause, he enjoyed the friendship and total confidence of at least a few individuals who were mainstays of provincial leadership: Valentín Alsina, Pastor Obligado, Juan Cruz Ocampo, Dalmasio Vélez Sarsfield, and Mitre. It was known to them, and would soon become common knowledge—in spite of the image projected by several biographers to the contrary—that Sarmiento, in spite of his origins in the provinces, nevertheless shared most of the urban and liberal biases of these Porteño leaders in Buenos Aires and was particularly receptive to many, if not most, of their concerns.

Sarmiento's views with regard to the conflict between Buenos Aires and the Confederation might have had some ambiguities, but they were unwavering in regard to essentials. None of the intelligentsia ignored the fact that Sarmiento was the first to break with Urquiza following the overthrow of Rosas and that his opposition to the victorious general remained absolute and uncompromising. Similarly it was common knowledge that Sarmiento had organized a group of Argentine nationals in Santiago in support of Buenos Aires's Revolution of September, in opposition to a similar club in Valparaíso that Alberdi had organized on behalf of Urquiza's Confederation. Also of public knowledge was Sarmiento's acrid polemic with Alberdi and his strident opposition to the latter's decision to serve as advisor and European representative of Urquiza's government. In addition to Sarmiento's unquestionable credentials in his political support for Buenos Aires, there were his widely circulating writings that promoted several key aspects of the liberal program which the new leadership in Buenos Aires ambitioned: free trade along the country's interior rivers, public education, and material development; support for freedom of the press and public assembly; and commitment to the parliamentary form of government under leaders regularly elected by the population. In conclusion even those remotely familiar with Sarmiento still accepted him as a powerful ally who was totally committed to the Porteño leadership's campaign against the Confederation.

The aspect of Sarmiento's stance that would have been considered controversial by a significant sector of the Porteño public was his firm and total support for Mitre's nationalist views and, consequently, his opposition to the program of the majority autonomist faction in the provincial legislature. In this Sarmiento was even more intractable than Mitre. In their private correspondence he had continually urged Mitre, "Don't become Porteño, friend. Let's be Argentines always."[112]

Yet Sarmiento also had the ability of disseminating different images of his ideas and actions. At one point, for example, he had advised collaborators and loyalists in the provinces to follow obediently the overtures taken by the Paraná government, at least for the time being.[113] A totally different image was embraced by several of his detractors who saw in his visit to San Juan a year earlier the design of a conspirator who was bent on organizing a violent overthrow of federalist governments through the coordination of liberal insurrections throughout the Andean provinces.[114] Indeed several inflammatory letters he had written to San Juan collaborators had fallen into the hands of Confederate loyalists, who regarded him as "an obstinate and perverse enemy" waging open war against their government.[115]

As a man of recognized talent, energy, and sympathies for the cause of Buenos Aires, Sarmiento became integrated into public life almost immediately. Within weeks after arriving he was named representative in the municipal government; in 1857 he passed to the provincial Senate, in which he would serve until 1861. In the next few years he would serve in several capacities: head of the Department of Schools, member of the Provincial Government Council, professor of law at the university, minister during Mitre's governorship, participant in two constitutional conventions, official of the province's central administration, and, throughout all, a mentor of public opinion.[116]

Between 1855 and 1858 Sarmiento's writing production in *El nacional* was truly substantial.[117] Although his many articles treating national politics consistently took the side of Buenos Aires and were flavored by the schematic worldview that readers both then and now accept as a Sarmiento standard, they nevertheless exhibited an ideological openness not found in the writings by the port city's other defenders. Worthy of note was his consistent objective of educating the reader through the clear and organized presentation of relevant data. Even though his interpretations consistently betrayed strong ideological biases, they still rose above mere propaganda; this is because in nearly every article Sarmiento went out of his way to demonstrate how his own position was the logical result of detailed study. His articles consistently revealed an intimate familiarity with statistics treating the province's or region's economic activities or productive and demographic trends. All these reasons go a long way toward explaining why even today Sarmiento's newspaper articles invite new readings and continue to set a high standard for aspiring journalists.

Almost immediately after arriving in Buenos Aires, his articles began appearing in *El nacional*. Like Mitre his opposition to the objectives of the Porteño localists did not preclude collaboration with them in the struggle against the Confederation. Initially he criticized both Urquiza defenders and the Buenos Aires localists.[118] In one article, for example, Sarmiento went halfway with critics from the Confederation in granting that the independent political course chosen by Buenos Aires was quite probably "harmful, in error, and with problems," but this still did not justify the campaign of lies and falsehoods by certain agents of the Paraná press, nor the acts of terrorism against Buenos Aires, whether sponsored or merely tolerated by the Confederate government.[119]

However this evenhandedness ended after the October 1855 invasion and insurrection led by José María Flores in the northern reaches of the province and a series of terrorist acts by *mashorqueros* sponsored by ex-Rosas loyalist, Oribe, in Uruguay. After those events his views hardened considerably. Over the next decade his fierce verbal attacks against confederate or federalist objectives would resonate periodically across the country.

In his newspaper writing Sarmiento, like Mitre, ascribed a great importance to the high level of public furor in Porteño circles that was directed against Urquiza. While hardly mentioning other, more profound issues, Sarmiento highlighted the widespread reaction in Buenos Aires to the directive requiring all citizens to join in solidarity by donning the federalists' red sash—the same measure used by Juan Manuel de Rosas a decade earlier to instill conformity among a population already intimidated by repressive violence. Here Sarmiento echoed the position of Mitre and Mármol two years earlier in arguing that the illegal nature of Buenos Aires's acts in separating itself from the national government paled in importance before "the sentimental issue,"[120] namely, that the overwhelming majority of Porteños from all walks of life were repulsed by the person of General Urquiza. Given this general animosity any system or procedure favored by the Confederation's leader, regardless of its merits, would be rejected out of hand. In short the name of Urquiza acquired in Buenos Aires the dimensions of a popular myth that inspired hatred among all classes and ages of people. As a way of illustrating this, Sarmiento explained that many youths saw fit to flee from obligatory military service in the war effort against the Indians, but they volunteered in abundance to fight against Urquiza! Similarly street conversations over how to unite the nation or a desirable form of constitution were calm in comparison to the intense reactions elicited by the passionate topic of Urquiza. Sarmiento admitted the largely subjective nature of these observations. But his intuition, which hardly ever erred, firmly convinced him that given such a strong feeling of disapproval on the part of the common people, any attempt at convincing through reasoned arguments would be futile.[121]

Sarmiento also outlined specific reasons for the Porteño public's growing dislike of Urquiza. Most important was Urquiza's haughty style of leadership, obviously learned from his long years as *estanciero* and military general, that worked against the democratic thrust of the institutions he was now charged to organize. Also offensive was his immense economic, social, political, and military power that made the political leadership of the Province of Entre Ríos, in addition to that of the Confederation government in Paraná, pliable to his will and whim. Sarmiento also called attention to Urquiza's reputation for womanizing, a factor that set him apart from the chaste Rosas and contributed to his negative image especially among the female population of the port city. Related was his shameful "provincial" custom of supporting multiple households (Sarmiento put the number at ten different women and sixteen children—counting both his legitimate and illegitimate offspring).[122]

In spite of this generally perceptive analysis, Sarmiento was less than candid about a major factor contributing to Urquiza's very negative image among the Buenos Aires population, namely the campaign of name calling and slander perpetrated by the Porteño press. To a large extent Sarmiento himself had been a precursor in that propaganda effort, with his incendiary writings from Chile. His own schematic view of the nation, divided as it was between the shining powers of civilization and the dark forces of barbarism, now inspired the slogans that predominated in the local press: the port city against the provinces, progress opposed to stagnation, and republicans versus *caudillos*. In propagating this oppositional mind-set, Sarmiento was hardly alone. Many other Porteño leaders and intellectuals articulated a similarly dualistic view of Argentine society. Yet Sarmiento was no mere follower or imitator; his role as public writer alternated between pernicious trend-setter for the public consciousness and interpreter of the vital attitudes of his time.

During his tenure as editor for *El nacional*, Sarmiento never lost sight of the primordial objective underlying all his writings and actions: the creation of a strong nation uniting all the provinces of the Argentine territory. By advocating the creation of "The Río de la Plata Republic"—later "The United Provinces of the Río de la Plata"—he directly opposed those leaders seeking a further dismemberment of the old colonial territory into "republiquetas," (microrepublics) whose small size would prohibit the region from ever fulfilling the role of future world power. In part his mission was to persuade opposing voices about Buenos Aires's constructive motivations in resisting the organizational thrust of the Confederation under Urquiza. In contrast to the "egotism" that Alberdi and his followers accredited to Porteño leaders, Sarmiento argued that "Argentine sentiments" inspired every true Porteño, whose province was "the most Argentine of all the provinces carrying that name."[123]

This view was not merely the expression of a personal bias; it was, in addition, Sarmiento's articulation of a fact of national life such as he viewed it. His analysis followed logically from his profound observation in *Facundo*—and later repeated by Alberdi in *Bases*—that Buenos Aires, due to geographical and historical factors, was destined to occupy the central position in national life. This was even more so in light of the region's recent history: "It is impossible to constitute a nationality without recognizing that the only possible foundation is Buenos Aires."[124] Buenos Aires was not just another province—it was "simultaneously the heart and head" of the country. These words reflected the great changes in recent years with regard to Buenos Aires's demographic, commercial, and economic growth; they expressed fundamental "facts" that no legal or verbal argument could possibly refute.[125]

Several of his articles detailed the ascending economic fortunes of Buenos Aires, in spite of the trade sanctions imposed by the Confederation. He explained that for 1857—five years after Buenos Aires's self-declared autonomy—that province had doubled its production and imports in the space of a year and continued to experience steady gains in revenues from its customs house.[126] In other areas as well, Buenos Aires continued to exercise de facto national leadership: its "free institutions"—its legislature and progress-minded ministries—continued setting the standard for popular, participatory government and had won the admiration of educated observers throughout the country.[127] Over and above any doubts over the legality or correctness of the province's recent politics, these facts alone convinced him of Buenos Aires's growing strength and influence relative to the Confederation; they constituted undisputable evidence of that province's rightful place at the head of the united nation.

As the decade progressed Buenos Aires's advancement on nearly all fronts accelerated. Sarmiento's treatment of the national question now changed tone. No longer did he *argue* his position, now he presented it with a sense of finality and prophecy. Buenos Aires's incorporation and leadership within the united provinces, "Far from being impossible, [. . .] it is inevitable."[128] With the approaching end to Urquiza's term as Confederation president, Sarmiento realized the necessity of demonstrating that any attempt at reelection ran the risk of permanently destabilizing the country as a whole. Sarmiento now attempted to appeal to that leader's sense of dignity, that he should place the welfare of the nation above any personal interest. The fact that Alberdi, Sarmiento's most stalwart ideological foe, would come to advise Urquiza in very similar terms, is an indication of Sarmiento's unerring analysis and the persuasive power of his writings. It is also possible that such an analysis inspired Urquiza's own acquiescence to Mitre's prerogatives on the battlefield of Pavón and in the months subsequent to that crucial encounter. In any event, there is no doubt that these writings by Sarmiento helped to pave the way for the reconciliation between Buenos Aires and Confederate leaders that began to occur toward the middle of 1859—events that will be discussed in a subsequent section.

Even more noteworthy for the contemporary reader than the reasoned and generally moderate political role of Sarmiento's journalistic writings are his impressive articles written in support of causes most dear to his heart: the need for public education, the promotion of railroads, agriculture, and immigration, and the imperative of formulating provincial and national procedures for the distribution of public lands. This last topic especially deserves special treatment here, because of the ideological implications of Sarmiento's authoritative views. Indeed it was he, almost alone among the national leaders of his time, who realized the weighty implications of this issue for the nation's future.

Sarmiento and the Public Lands Policy

In 1856 the provincial legislature of Buenos Aires initiated discussions on the policies and procedures of the state with regard to public lands, when its more militant members expressed a desire to overturn an earlier decree that had prohibited the confiscation of Rosas's properties. Only a few of the legislators realized that the larger question at stake concerned the state's ability to shape the nation's future social and economic realities through the implementation of a coherent and farsighted land policy. The issue certainly was not new. The lands secured through Rosas's Indian campaigns in the 1830s, in addition to the holdings his government confiscated from numerous unitarian leaders, had brought considerable territory under the jurisdiction of provincial authorities. As of 1856 the greater part of that land, although still unexploited, was owned by a few powerful individuals who had benefited from their close connections with the dictator. Other land extensions that still remained under provincial control were inappropriate for settlement because of their location in regions prone to Indian raids, and other properties still under state jurisdiction were occupied by settlers or immigrant colonizers who hoped to transform their rental agreements with the state (enfiteusis) into outright personal ownership.[129]

The management of public lands struck at the heart of Sarmiento's great vision for the future of the nation. In his view a public authority empowered to distribute new territories rationally could effectively combat the country's feudal legacy of cattle-ranching *latifundia* and would help to bring into existence new agricultural zones serviced by modern urban settlements. How would this occur? First land distribution policies would attract new and desirable population groups that were trained in agricultural and industrial activities. In this Sarmiento untiringly argued for an imitation of the North American model of frontier settlement that granted property rights outright to those colonizers committed to transforming the prairie into productive farmland. In a similar fashion both he and Alberdi urged measures to attract large numbers of Anglo-or North European immigrants, as opposed to other groups, because of their belief that these populations would, over time, improve the genetic pool of the entire nation and help the country overcome its "barbaric" heritage. "The land laws," he recognized, were "the laws governing the process of populating the new world."[130]

A second way to promote the region's progress would be to utilize the available public lands to attract foreign investment capital. Recent experience in North America had demonstrated that the construction of new railway lines brought about speedy settlement, the initiation of productive activities, and, consequently, the rapid growth of national wealth. Sarmiento and others knew that one way to attract European financial interests was to cede them extensive property rights along the routes over which lines would be constructed.

An intelligent land distribution policy would yield several other benefits: funds received from the sale of lands could help finance any number of progressive state initiatives well into the future; a planned reservation of lands would assure the availability of inexpensive homesteads for new industrious immigrants well into the next century; and the organized sale of available lands over several decades would guarantee a stability of land prices and would work against speculative activities. All of Sarmiento's contemporaries were in agreement about the necessity of developing the potential of the country, but Sarmiento was nearly alone in perceiving the immense impact that an intelligent lands policy would have over almost all other facets of the country's development. Beginning during this period and continuing throughout his presidency and until his death in 1888, he was almost alone in promoting a type of national development that would occur through the economic, social, and political enfranchisement of new population groups.

Almost alone among the Buenos Aires leadership, Sarmiento realized that if the provincial and national legislatures were to adopt hasty policies leading to a loss of control over the public lands, then a great opportunity would be squandered.[131] Consequently he engaged himself in an all-out campaign through the press to educate the population about his views. With unequaled clarity and vigorous style, he communicated to the provincial readership a wealth of information that he had learned in the previous decade from the careful study of similar issues in the United States and elsewhere. His twenty-odd articles over this issue alone, which he published in *El nacional* during a period of several months, constitute an eternal tribute to the man's vast comprehension and his unyielding commitment to an egalitarian form of democratic participation for his country. His parliamentary activity was similarly inspired. This was the period when he assumed as his own the cause of the Chivilcoy colonists, who wished to buy the rights to the rental lands they had already transformed into model farms and gardens. Sarmiento's speech in January 1857 to the assembled community there, which was reprinted in the Buenos Aires press,[132] has been justifiably recognized as one of the most important in the country's oratory tradition.

Sarmiento understood clearly that his entire dream for a grass-roots, egalitarian society was at stake in these legislative debates. Some foes to his proposed reforms in the legislature, who represented the interests of the large landowners, were clairvoyant with regard to their class interests, and they attacked his ideas continually. Although Sarmiento was learning to break bread in other ways with the province's cattle oligarchy, he was determined to wage against them an all-out ideological war through the press and on the floor of the provincial legislature on the issue of public lands. He intelligently pointed out that for little or no cost the rich landowners had obtained vast extensions of territory through legal loopholes in the *enfiteusis* (or state-rental) programs under both the Rivadavia and Rosas administrations. Furthermore, throughout the past few decades, their fortunes had expanded exponentially because of rising land values. He pointed out that they had benefited more than any other group from the state's defense of the frontier, even though they had been called upon to contribute next to nothing for those services. Sarmiento's anger now grew with recent evidence of this group's search for means to exert its influence over the province's new democratic institutions in defense of its own narrow interests. Instances already existed of the wealthy land owners making or breaking candidates for the legislature, dominating the Senate, the press, and the army.[133] Sarmiento's articles over these topics demonstrate his lucidity about the province's emerging structure of power; they are testimony to his courage to risk denouncing publicly such perversions of democratic governance.

Sarmiento faced not only the opposition of the cattle oligarchy and its paid servants but also the criticism of several of the leading liberals—especially Juan Bautista Peña, Félix Frías, and Carlos Tejedor in the legislature. The opposition of these liberals stemmed from a largely theoretical issue: their opposition to any form of state activism that would impede a "natural" or "free" evolution of society's economic forces. They accepted at face value the benevolent theories defending the play of free market forces and argued against any state interference that would obstruct the proverbial "invisible hand" channeling private initiatives toward the fulfillment of community needs. This perspective reflected their familiarity with the writings of Adam Smith and his brilliant disciple, Jean Baptiste Say, which were then enjoying unrivaled prestige in European intellectual and governmental circles. But the source more close to home for this laissez-faire emphasis was undoubtedly Juan Bautista Alberdi, especially his 1854 essay, *Sistema económico y rentística de la Confederación Argentina* (Economic and revenue system of the Argentine Confederation).

In this work Alberdi gave scant attention to one of the primary concerns underlying Sarmiento's interest in the public lands issue, that is, the desirability of agricultural workers and immigrants to own their own land. He also had little to recommend about the control of a governmental agency over public lands or over any other economic function. In this matter Alberdi's thesis was clear: the government had to yield entirely to private initiatives and totally refrain from intervention in the economic activities of society; it had to *"let happen whatever might happen; leave well enough alone."* This dogmatic affirmation of the laissez-faire principle even led Alberdi to argue against the implementation of regulatory or overseeing functions by the state. Applying the principle of "liberty" in all possible contexts, he argued that to try out new, untested ways of organizing society was to contradict the "admirable sense" of the Constitution and to risk throwing the country into disorder and retard the development of its productive potential.[134] Frías, Tejedor, and other members of Sarmiento's generation uncritically embraced Alberdi's position (as their personal correspondence reveals); they also accepted as "axiomatic" the need for the liberal state to minimize involvement in economic activities.[135]

It is to Sarmiento's credit that he never embraced as dogmatic a position with regard to the ideal role of the liberal state as did nearly all his liberal colleagues.[136] Although the others seemed to have elevated the issue of "liberty" to the exclusion of other social goals, Sarmiento clearly understood the need to compromise that advocacy with a competing, and sometimes more important, social need: equality. Almost alone among this group, Sarmiento realized that laissez-faire state policies, when applied to public lands, ended up favoring the narrow interests of the region's large landowners and therefore served to impede the development of the country. This realization would account, on occasion, for inconsistencies in the liberal program that he advocated.

Although Sarmiento was hardly consistent with regard to the issue of "liberty" in the government's functions, his ideological war against the cattle oligarchy over the issue of public lands was sustained and hard hitting. Yet he must have realized the futility of his stand before their economic, social, and political power. After enjoying a few ephemeral victories in the legislature, his proposal for decisive state control over the sale and administration of public lands was tabled and, in effect, neutralized.[137] Yet his scathing articles continued. In retrospect few times in the country's history have its citizens witnessed such an impassioned and heroic campaign waged against economic privilege. During those early months of inspired journalism, Sarmiento surely incurred the lifelong wrath of many powerful figures, and these would return to oppose his progressive ventures a decade later when he would exercise the authority of the country's president. Yet, after those few months Sarmiento lapsed back into discreet silence, for he knew when to yield to pressure. He realized that he had to survive the present battle in order to be able to rise up and fight another day.[138]

Sarmiento's writings on one other topic demonstrate the gap between his and Alberdi's conception of national priorities and also document a significant change from the ideas he himself had defended a decade before. As mentioned earlier Sarmiento, when in Chilean exile, had embraced the cause of the Montevidean-based militants in their alliances with France against the Rosas regime.[139] He had implicitly accepted the somewhat expedient position defined by Alberdi at the time that the redeemable elements of Argentine "nationality" consisted of those European tendencies and elements which were destined to modernize the deserts of the country and transform its barbarism into civilization. This somewhat esoteric justification for European intervention in the affairs of the Plata went hand-in-hand with the strong arguments he expressed in *Facundo* about a harmful, retrograde *Americanism* in Argentina that was associated with the most despicable aspects of rural barbarianism and authoritarian government under Rosas.[140] Now, in a series of articles published in *El nacional* between November 1855 and March 1856,[141] he reversed that position; he argued in strong terms that residents living and working in Argentina, regardless of their country of origin, were obligated to obey the laws of the land and should enjoy no special privileges over native-born citizens. This was an important rectification of his earlier stance.

He sought ways for incorporating the country's new immigrants as rapidly as possible into national life. Once settled in Argentina they had to comply with certain obligations, even though they were not yet citizens. (Sarmiento and the other members of his generation did not advocate political franchise of new immigrant groups at this time.) This meant that they should be eligible for service on the Indian frontier and that their goods and properties be subject to national laws. If this were not the case, then chaos would reign: "Nothing less than the dissolution of society, and the chaos of disputed jurisdictions and unbridled ambitions."[142] These sentiments contrast with the advocacies of Alberdi, who, at that very time, was stubbornly disobeying the explicit instructions of the Confederation's foreign ministry (headed by Juan María Gutiérrez) in negotiating a treaty that would grant special rights to non-nationalized, Spanish-born residents and dual citizenship to Argentine citizens of Spanish descendancy. (Subsequently the treaty was overwhelmingly rejected by the Confederate legislature.) Sarmiento's opinions about this very issue were categorical: he believed that a country's citizens, as well as its foreign-born residents should "respect the institutions of the country in which they reside."[143] Those foreign-born residents had the right to express their opinions as individuals, but the idea that there existed such a thing as "l'opinion etrangère" about national issues was counter to the concept of nationality. This demonstrated Sarmiento's willingness to rectify the erroneous position previously embraced by himself and the exiled community when they were combatting Rosas. At the same time it demonstrated the nature of his ideas about a desirable type of nationality for the country's future. After 1880 Sarmiento would have occasion to revise once again these opinions about the rights and obligations of the country's immigrant population.

It would be incorrect to end this section without calling attention to a different side to Sarmiento's activism during this stormy decade which, in almost all other respects, wholly justifies the acclaim of his admirers.[144] For example, at different moments Sarmiento demonstrated that he could resort to unscrupulous means in order to achieve what he held to be a greater good. Such was the importance he held for the continuation of his own clique in the provincial government that he himself approved of acts demonstrating "audacity and terror"—his own words—in order to ensure its victory in the elections of 1857 (more on this below).[145] Before Frías's well-founded accusations about his fraudulent tactics in recent elections, Sarmiento responded through the press that he was not alone and that the deficient electoral laws invited illegal measures from all sides. With dubious logic he went on to rationalize the violent means he had employed: "But violence is the remedy for fraud, and one legitimately recurrs to violence in order to combat infractions of fundamental laws."[146]

A different example of contradictory, authoritarian tendencies was his continued support behind the scenes for certain individuals in the interior provinces who rejected peaceful dialogue and instead advocated or recurred to violent means to topple the surviving federalist leadership. Throughout the decade informed observers were in agreement that San Juan's political situation remained perhaps the most explosive of any province. Sarmiento himself had communicated to several friends that he even welcomed in part the outbreak of violence, knowing that in such situations he was precisely the type of individual who would be called upon to exercise leadership.[147] With such views and given the high public profile he enjoyed, it was no surprise that the more moderate members of his generation looked upon him with great trepidation. Months hence his involvement in the events leading up to the battle of Cepeda, and even more so after Pavón, would do away almost entirely with the moderate image disseminated through his journalistic writings. Sarmiento's anger and intolerance would grow in proportion to the violence that would sweep the country.

ALBERDI: SPOKESMAN FOR THE CONFEDERATION

Alberdi, through his writings and diplomatic activities, was by far the most influential defender of the Confederation and, as a consequence, critic of the separatist movement in Buenos Aires. Indeed, during this decade of contention and struggle, neither Gutiérrez, López, Cané, nor any of the other former members of the Association who opted for the cause of the Confederation would produce sustained or substantial publications in its defense. This fact alone goes far in explaining the declining fortunes of the Paraná government as the decade advanced. Initially it proved incapable of attracting many of the country's finest minds, and then—with the notable exception of Alberdi—it failed to retain in its services several talented individuals originally favoring its objectives.

Even a cursory study of Alberdi's writings in defense of the Confederation reveals a significant difference when contrasted with the articles written by Sarmiento and others on behalf of Buenos Aires: it was a literature that highlighted legalistic, philosophical, or even "moralistic" principles and paid little emphasis to the country's recent geographical, demographic, and commercial realities, or the political vicissitudes of the moment. In short his tersely worded and tightly argued pamphlets did not lend themselves as readily to the journalistic medium as did the writings of Sarmiento. Such was Alberdi's style and preference that, after accomplishing his objective of explaining in depth his position, he would not overly concern himself with the popularization of those views through repeated elaborations and wide dissemination through the press. This explains in part why Alberdi's writings on the Confederation were relatively few in number, even though they were held in the highest regard by his devoted followers. Indeed Alberdi's writings stood out against the mediocre intellectual production of other Confederation supporters. Yet, even though genius stands tall and leads decisively, it can leave many followers standing inert under an immense shadow.

Alberdi's attraction to principles instead of circumstances explains in part the nature of his commitment to the Confederation throughout the decade of the 1850s. His fragile health and scholarly disposition were hardly suited to the day-to-day trials of political in-fighting. Similarly, he realized that his singular intellectual talents would be fragmented or even wasted if normal bureaucratic responsibilities detracted from the important intellectual projects he wished to undertake. After turning down Urquiza's invitation to represent the Confederation in Chile (in 1856 and 1860 he would also refuse leadership over the Ministerio de Hacienda—or General Staff), he accepted at the beginning of 1854 the position of plenipotentiary minister before the governments of France, Great Britain, and Spain. In *Bases* he had written about the imperative of the new regime to establish treaties with the European powers: "Our program . . . ought to pay more attention to the foreign affairs of the country than to domestic concerns. . . . Each treaty will be an anchor that will help to stabilize the Constitution."[148] This view was integrally related to the theory first elaborated during his Montevidean exile that the key to the region's regeneration and development was European mediation. The need to attract immigrants to Argentine soils and to accept Europe's and North America's contributions in the form of a "transplant" of technology, progressive ideas, and models of social and institutional organization was seen as the sine qua non of Argentina's own development. Later this view would acquire the simplistic coherence of the statement, "We are an economic appendage of Europe."[149] This explains the importance held by Alberdi for fortifying the country's relationships with the European powers and facilitating as much as possible the flow of European immigrants, capital, and influences into Argentina.

Did these words communicate his doubts about the strength of the Confederation's politics, if he truly placed the issue of foreign assistance before any internal concern?[150] If so, the impression was fully shared by his superiors, Gutiérrez, at that time the minister of foreign relations, and Francisco Pico, former functionary under the respected Rivadavia thirty years before and now the Confederation's representative in Montevideo. Those two agreed with Alberdi that the Confederation could not survive without the formal recognition of the principal European powers. In the words of Alberdi, treaties with those powers would establish the jurisdiction of the Confederation over the province of Buenos Aires; those treaties, signed with the "highest existing authority, [would] support the cause of the integrity of Argentine nationality; they were legitimate weapons to counter the advances of any type or species of filibusterism."[151] That is to say Alberdi viewed the conflict that pitted the Confederation against Buenos Aires as one of right versus might. His legalistic disposition led him to commit his energies and reputation to the side favored by *los derechos* (rights), whereas Sarmiento and Mitre, more pragmatic in their orientations, chose the side favored by *los hechos* (facts).

Throughout the decade Alberdi continued in his role as the Confederation's foremost theorist and ideologue. His most important publication during this period was *Sistema económico y rentístico de la Confederación argentina, según la Constitución de 1853* (Economic and revenue system of the Argentine Confederation according to the Constitution of 1853— 1853), in which he outlined the economic and financial doctrines underlying his constitutional ideas. In it he signaled the reforms that would be necessary for correcting the errors of the region's colonial past and improve its prospects for accelerated growth in the future. Many of the principles expounded by Alberdi here were hardly original, because his objective was to present in organized fashion the ideology of economic liberalism, as expounded by Adam Smith, Jean-Baptiste Say, and other European theorists. He believed that those ideas, if implemented, would hasten the modernization of his own country's institutions and maximize its human and productive resources. This liberal program that emphasized free trade with a minimum of governmental interference or direction was designed to combat the old centralized or monopolistic practices of the Spanish colony and to challenge the new collectivist advocacies of socialism. Alberdi's thesis was that whenever governments engaged in productive or commercial enterprises, they became inefficient managers and even worse businessmen. Instead he argued that when governments expended their limited resources in guaranteeing the optimum conditions for the unrestricted activity of capital and labor, then society's material or productive wealth would increase. Society's goal should not be the enrichment of governments, that which had been the primary objective of the colonial regime, but rather the enrichment of the population. That even his most stalwart opponents heading the government in Buenos Aires would accept the full thrust of this liberal plan for economic progress was evidence of Alberdi's importance as a theorist and the resonance of his timely ideas.

Throughout *Sistema económico*, Alberdi argued consistently, even to the point of dogmatism, the supposed benefits of this laissez-faire doctrine. His critics correctly argue that he defended the universal validity of this ultraliberal program for the state's political economy, even as he pointed out how key aspects of the region's history or land tenure differed conspicuously with similar developments in the Northern European countries. As explained above, he refused to pay homage to the suggestion of Sarmiento that the implementation of laissez-faire land policies at that moment in effect granted monopolistic privileges to the small group of *latifundia* cattle ranchers. He refused to see the contradictions in his own logic that the Argentine state's guarantee of *liberal* economic policies could, in effect, serve to strengthen the power of the region's predominant socioeconomic group, whose livelihood depended in large part upon *feudal* labor practices, a land-tenure system modeling that of colonial times, and the survival of productive activities utilizing antiquated technological practices.

Or perhaps it would be more correct to view this as one of the more ambiguous areas in the thought of the mature Alberdi. There was no doubt that the decidedly conservative orientation to his thought after about 1845 meant that he placed a higher priority on the need for society to preserve order than for its leaders to undertake risky programs in promotion of idealistic goals that at the same time might unleash the destructive anarchistic tendencies of the masses.[152] This helps to explain the faith he held for Urquiza's efforts to organize the nation after Caseros. Indeed who better than Urquiza could reestablish peace and tranquility, given the latter's immense social influence and economic wealth, in addition to his personal command over the nation's most potent military force? Alberdi's writings reveal at times even an explicit apology for the *latifundia* system. Years later he would argue that the greatness of the Argentine Republic was due not so much to its warriors or statesmen, but to those like the large landowner Anchorena who, "in acquiring his personal fortune, made the country wealthy; its government lives from the revenues and contributions received from those individuals who are producers of wealth, not from those with nothing."[153]

This bias for economic power and authority sometimes manifested itself in Alberdi's thought in the form of an "anti–intellectualism" and an implicit disdain for the "doctors" and "philosophers," whose short experiences with political power in the past had caused more harm than good. Related was Alberdi's light-switch support for Rosas. Because the latter exercised the multiple powers that accompanied his role as a large landowner, he succeeded in bestowing upon the country a strong and durable regime.[154] It was only a minority voice in Alberdi's mature writings that approved of the more egalitarian priorities of Sarmiento. For example Alberdi argued at one moment that a constructive policy for land distribution would create a citizenry committed not only to investment and increased production but also to the defense of frontier society against Indian raids.[155]

His "excessive obsession with social stability"[156] and the priority granted to abstract organizing principles worked against any empathy for society's masses that Alberdi might otherwise have felt. Herein lay a significant contrast with his generational opponent, Sarmiento, in spite of the elitist values embraced equally by the two. Throughout Alberdi's copious writings there was a distinct lack of consistent and clear-cut support for governmental action on behalf of the country's dispossessed classes.

However this type of affirmation would be forthcoming from the young José Hernández (future author of the famous poem, *El gaucho Martín Fierro*), who was widely recognized as a faithful ideological disciple of the venerated Alberdi. In an article of 1869, Hernández began by reaffirming the Alberdian position against the state's involvement as land broker but went one important step further by arguing that the long-range interest of the state was to assure the "the division of the land into small lots and their distribution. . . . The subdivision of property, as much as possible."[157] From Hernández came the criticism of the large landowners that their success in increasing land holdings was proportional to the amount of national territory in unimproved or abandoned condition. An intelligent and active worker, he wrote, would not aspire to the greed of possession. The poorest and most backward countries in the world were precisely those where the land was divided up among a few privileged hands.

In *Sistema económico*, Alberdi left in the shadow of ambiguity many of these issues relative to the productive functions of the different social classes and instead focused on economic principles as they affected the alignment of regional power. Yet again there was manifest here an inherent ambiguity or weakness in Alberdi's arguments. He repeatedly urged priority for economic principles—what he called the "the government of things"—and not to idealistic projections or voluntaristic, theoretical persuasions. He continued to harbor optimism that Buenos Aires's hegemony was fast eroding, in spite of much hard evidence to the contrary. Perhaps it was his heated commitment to the Confederation that led him and his disciple Gutiérrez to ignore the fact that free navigation of the rivers did little to resolve the ever-increasing financial woes of the Confederation. In a similar fashion he generally failed to grant importance to the inherent geopolitical weakness of the Confederation's project. He was familiar with the observations of the French government's representative, who acridly pointed out that the poverty of Rosario and Paraná, in implicit contrast to the comforts and relative opulence of Buenos Aires, worked against the Confederation's objective of winning new European commercial contracts. In the words of that French representative, the Confederate pretension of lifting the interior regions up from nothingness to a position of supremacy in the Plata region was based more on "words and poetry" than on "practical sense."[158] Alberdi, however, demonstrated more wishful thinking in arguing that the inferior material situation of the Confederation would change dramatically if its government gained authority over what was rightfully its jurisdiction, that is, the receipts generated by the customshouses in Buenos Aires. Alberdi, in effect, ingenuously insisted that it was Buenos Aires's *obligation* to yield that control over to the national government. He even went so far as to argue that this was in the long-range interest of Buenos Aires, because the enrichment of the provinces inevitably would benefit economic interests there also.

According to Alberdi the future progress of the country demanded the immediate overturning of the retrograde political and commercial monopoly exercised by Buenos Aires over the rest of the provinces. It was precisely that monopoly denounced by Mariano Moreno in 1809, and rudely imposed by Rosas, that the latter's Porteño successors now jealously defended. The irony was that although the enemies of Rosas had succeeded him in power, they nevertheless assumed a defense of the same tyrannical policies that had sustained the dictator for over thirty years.[159] In subsequent years Alberdi would partially absolve Rosas for this same reason. The geopolitics favoring Buenos Aires, and not merely the whims of the dictator, were largely responsible for the most serious abuses that that province continued to commit against the nation. A half-decade later Alberdi would present a similar explanation for the catastrophic defeat of the Confederation in the battle of Pavón: it was due to the ascendancy of Urquiza's pro-Porteño sympathies over that leader's own commitment to the welfare of the country as a whole.[160]

The republication of *Bases* in late 1855 gave Alberdi the opportunity to modify and expand his views in light of Buenos Aires's recent politics. He argued that the constitution promulgated by that province during the previous year duplicated the misdeed of Rivadavia, and its continuation by Rosas, in bestowing upon Buenos Aires certain powers that should only reside in the nation as a whole: "An internal customs house kept by a province as a formal addition to the national customs house— can it ever truly stimulate the growth of commerce?"[161] In its resistance to the Confederation's legitimate attempts to nationalize the port city's customshouses, the Province of Buenos Aires "invades and tramples the dominions of the National Constitution . . . [and] mortally wounds the integrity of the Argentine Republic." Alberdi continued to place the blame for Buenos Aires's illegal and immoral position upon the shoulders of its leaders of the moment, Alsina and Mitre. In indirect reference to the latter, whose exaggerated boasts bordered on the irresponsible, Alberdi warned that as long as there existed public figures who prided themselves on *"knowing how to topple ministers with the discharge of a canon,"* then Hispanic America had no hope of capturing the respect of the rest of the civilized world.[162]

Alberdi was not the only voice speaking and publishing on behalf of the Confederation, but his ideas reverberated with unequaled authority across the interior. Indeed, at this time he was undoubtedly the recognized *maestro* of an entire generation of younger writers and thinkers. One clear example of this was the 1857 pamphlet, "Las dos políticas" (The two politics), which was reprinted several times and enjoyed a broad readership throughout the provinces. The pamphlet bore no signature; although some scholars later accredited it to José Hernández, most authoritative accounts point to Olegario V. Andrade as the true author.[163]

Over and above the issue of its disputed authorship, the ideas contained in the pamphlet were purely Alberdian. It began by recognizing that the dispute between Buenos Aires and the Confederation, although superficially over political issues, was essentially an economic conflict. The provinces of the interior opposed Buenos Aires, because its leaders wished to maintain the monopoly over the region's productive activities and international commerce that the province had enjoyed for over three decades. According to this analysis "the retrograde, localist party" in Buenos Aires gave rise to the tyrannical system of *caudillos* throughout the interior: "The caudillos were the offspring of Buenos Aires's egotism."[164] What Rivadavia had initiated, Rosas completed: Buenos Aires's domination over the other provinces with "strong chains." Even with the change in political leadership, the economic foundations of the Rosas dictatorship remained in force and continued to feed the same politics of Buenos Aires autonomy. "It's the localist party, the party that defeated Rivadavia, that executed Dorrego, that grew strong under Rosas's protection, that today is bleeding the republic."[165] The ideas in this pamphlet gave no quarter to Buenos Aires. That city and the province of the same name were, for its author as well as its widespread readership, the villains in the conflict dividing the nation. According to that view the principles underlying the Confederation were above reproach. As such the pamphlet argued that the only possible resolution to the conflict was for Buenos Aires to give up its pretentions to autonomy and embrace with the rest of the provinces the principles of national organization as set forth in the San Nicolás Accord and the Constitution of 1853.

GUTIÉRREZ: FAITHFUL SERVANT

Juan María Gutiérrez, with unquestionable talent and impeccable honesty, was destined to play an important role in whatever governmental body he chose to serve. Given his spirit of compromise and conciliation and his cherished objective of national unity, the hostility that exploded toward the end of 1852 between Buenos Aires and the interior provinces left him anguished. He wrote at this time to his trusted friend, Vicente Fidel López—for whom Buenos Aires's Revolution of September had also been a traumatic personal defeat—that he suffered "afflictions of the spirit. . . . Hope is abandoning me because past experience darkens what is to come."[166] His faith in humanity had suffered a terrible blow, which also affected his personal health: "I am old and very weakened in health." Yet in contrast to the immobilizing resentment of his intimate friend, who was now intent upon isolating himself from the fickle world of politics and closing himself up "within sweet domestic life,"[167] Gutiérrez realized that the best cure for his own doldrums was to immerse himself in whatever constructive task was at hand and to assume once again the mask of optimism. Far more important than wounded vanity and personal inconvenience was his sensed mission of struggling incessantly on behalf of the future of the country. With characteristic humility, he wrote: "I will fall and others will rise to take my place."[168]

Invitations for his involvement were not long in coming. He was elected representative from the Province of Entre Ríos to be a member of the Commission on Constitutional Affairs, with which he served with distinction along side of Pedro Ferré, Martín Zapata, José Benjamín Gorostiaga, and other notable leaders from the interior. Toward the middle of 1854, when Urquiza was formally elected president of the Confederation, Gutiérrez accepted the position of minister of justice, culture, and public instruction, to which was later added the portfolio of foreign relations.

There was little doubt that Urquiza captured his admiration and respect during this period. In a letter of 1854 to V. F. López, Gutiérrez wrote:

> Do you remember one night when we were leaving Palermo and you said to me, "What sincerity and stature that man possesses," referring to General Urquiza? Well then, many times since I have been motivated to make the same observation . . . he commands my respect and friendship, because his ideas and words possess all the maturity of his age and the energy and novelty typical of the youth of this century.[169]

In spite of his opposition to several important legislative programs of the Confederation and his lack of confidence in several other Paraná leaders, this faith in the integrity and talent of Urquiza generally remained unbroken, at least well into the next decade.

But Gutiérrez had his important differences with the other principal leaders of the Confederation. Alberdi's 1857 treaty with Spain somewhat undermined his confidence in the judgment of his old friend, because the clauses accepting payment for the debt and Spanish citizenship for even nationalized Argentines went totally against the explicit instructions that Gutiérrez had stipulated.[170] In addition his arguments against a vengeful plan of "differential rights"—through which the Paraná legislature attempted to impose economic sanctions on Buenos Aires—fell progressively on deaf ears. Gutiérrez believed that this plan, in addition to being bad economic policy for the nation, was an act of hostility that would only serve to escalate the belligerency between Confederate and Porteño leaders.[171]

His dissatisfaction with these measures, in addition to the intrigues surrounding the government in Paraná, finally led Gutiérrez in late 1856 to renounce his position as head of the Confederation's foreign ministry. Especially disagreeable for him was the plotting of Santiago Derqui, minister of the interior, who would become Urquiza's successor as president of the Confederation three years hence.[172] Also contributing to his disenchantment was Urquiza's decision to support the uprising of General Juan Pablo López, which had as its objective the removal of José María Cullen, a leading member of his wife's family, from the position of governor of Santa Fe. (In 1854 he had married Gerónima Cullen, daughter of the ex-governor, Domingo Cullen, who had been executed in 1838 at the orders of Juan Manuel de Rosas.[173]) The discreet Gutiérrez, who had always urged his friends to remain silent in public about disaffections in their own ranks, hardly needed the advice of Alberdi to keep quiet about the true causes of his resignation from the cabinet. This was because he realized that it was in the national interest for him to remain accessible to Urquiza, who continued to hold him in the highest regard.[174] At that time Gutiérrez left Paraná for Buenos Aires (1856–58). In 1858 he would return to Paraná in the capacity of congressional representative from the Province of Santiago de Estero. After two distinguished terms he would again return to Buenos Aires in 1861 to serve as commercial representative until the Confederation's demise five years later.

In Buenos Aires after 1856, Gutiérrez would continue to maintain a low public profile, publishing almost nothing that had a bearing on the troubled politics of the moment but continuing in his role as trusted advisor to Urquiza. In spite of reservations about some measures taken by the Paraná government, his support did not waiver. In 1859, on the eve of armed hostilities between Buenos Aires and the Confederation, he remained faithful to the analysis of Alberdi by berating Buenos Aires for its self-interested policies and its intent to maintain predominance over the other provinces.[175] He even went so far as to approve of the militant measures that the Confederation's government was now planning. He was confident that its superior military capabilities would lead to a decisive victory over Buenos Aires in an armed skirmish. He wrote to Benjamín Victorica, Urquiza's son-in-law and trusted advisor: "Here we have supported the prouncement and . . . I have complete confidence—and do thank the general on my behalf—in the course he has chosen to follow."[176] A week later he wrote to Alberdi: "Force is the only road left to us for changing an intolerable situation."[177] With the country again on the verge of civil war, Gutiérrez hastened back to Paraná, where he would celebrate the news of Urquiza's victory in the Battle of Cepeda.

VOICES OF CONCILIATION

During the latter half of the 1850s, Mitre, Mármol, and Sarmiento, on behalf of Buenos Aires, were squared off against Alberdi, Gutiérrez, and the other defenders of the Confederation. Meanwhile a few other former colleagues in the Asociación de Mayo attempted to situate themselves in a position ideologically equidistant from both extremes, advocating moderation and even conciliation. Perhaps most exemplary was the intervention of Félix Frías who, along with Luis Domínguez, founded the newspaper, *El orden* (Order), as a means of promoting this moderate view. In 1855 Frías returned to his native city, Buenos Aires, after eight years in Paris. Although his sympathies were more with the cause of the Confederation—and with his intimate friends Alberdi, Gutiérrez, and Dr. José Benjamín Gorostiaga—he realized that he could contribute most from the vantage point of Buenos Aires itself.

Through his daily columns in *El orden*, Frías heroically assumed the objective of steering an even path between the two embittered sides. "We do not wish to decide between two homelands—between the homeland with the port and that that does not have it; we want a single, united country."[178] Because he realized that few of his old friends in Buenos Aires or in Paraná were similarly disposed to follow the path of concord, many of his editorials had the task of toning down passions and encouraging rational dialogue. Such was the intent of his 1855 article criticizing Mármol's inflammatory rhetoric that excited "hatred and bitterness in certain unreflexive elements among the people; these excesses might stain the beautiful cause that we defend."[179] Similar was his objective in praising an editorial appearing in the Confederation government's official publication, *El nacional*, which severely repudiated the participation of provincial residents in the 1855 conspiracies of Coronel Ramón Bustos and General José María Flores.[180]

The opinions of this talented, principled, yet fervent Catholic, surrounded by intransigent Porteños, were bound to provoke conflict. In a letter of 1857 to Alberdi, Frías admitted: "I continue to lead a life removed from the turmoils of the day; I prefer isolation and have refused appointment to any post, although not having a position is worse than the one I had in exile; but I do not wish to belong to any faction that might have any importance."[181] With uncommon courage he persisted in his promotion of the national cause through both the press and as a member of the provincial legislature, in spite of frequent attacks and slander. But, in that same letter to Alberdi, he admitted that no effort on his behalf could sufficiently cool the hostilities exhibited on all sides: "I do not believe that unity will be achieved through the good will of the men involved. I see many things . . . that totally displease me."

The constant questioning of Porteño priorities from the pages of *El orden* provoked the verbal wrath of Sarmiento. From the columns of *El nacional*, the latter continually sought ways of criticizing this newspaper and its principal writer, Frías. Primarily at issue was *El orden*'s proclerical perspective, although several other stances also came under attack: that paper's promotion of laws against libelous journalism; its accusations of fraud, violence, and illegalities in recent elections; and, in general, "the unsound ideas" continually expressed in its pages about a possible resolution to the excruciating regional conflict that divided the nation.[182] According to historian Manuel Gálvez, most of these attacks totally lacked substance; they were the result of Sarmiento having found in Frías a convenient vehicle for expressing his characteristically vehement discourse.[183] As in his polemics with Alberdi a few years earlier, Sarmiento's attacks originating in political or ideological differences often ended in personal insults. The actions of "the friar" Frías, for him, served to "excuse political immoralities." In apparent reference to the latter's extended sojourn in Paris, he alleged that Frías "deserted his post in the hour of combat."[184]

Sarmiento's comments about other competitors were hardly more generous. Miguel Cané, who for several years had accompanied his brother-in-law, Florencio Varela, and other unitarians in the Montevidean struggle against Rosas, later became a supporter of Urquiza in Buenos Aires. Cané, according to Sarmiento, suffered from "*jaunisse* and his whole body that six years ago had its true color now appears quite yellow." Similarly, according to Sarmiento, "the learned Domínguez," in his public statements, was terribly confused: one never knew whether he spoke or wrote on the basis of his "ideas or his business interests—for him there's no difference."[185] One additional enemy of the pen was Nicolás Calvo, a talented young activist who, from the pages of *La reforma política* (Political reform), headed the group of "reformists" seeking a peaceful union of the country's two antagonistic sides. Calvo, in the words of Sarmiento, was "a groveling boaster"; as a journalist he practiced "the art of verbal homocide" as a means of political gain and self-advancement.[186]

In contrast to the decision of Frías and Domínguez to carry on the ideological struggle from the front lines, the intervention of V. F. López was far less frequent and less effective. After his stinging political defeat in the Buenos Aires legislature in 1853, he followed his father's advice of embracing the doctrines of Stoicism[187] and sought relative silence and seclusion in Montevideo. The fact that he wrote very few letters to his former allies in the struggle against Rosas suggests his profound disillusionment and perhaps growing cynicism about the new struggle engulfing his homeland. He occupied his time with responsibilities as professor of law in the university; the composition of his noteworthy historical novel, *La novia del hereje* (The bride of the heretic—1854); and historical research and writing. Indeed, at this very moment he was initiating the historical work that years later would be the crowning achievement of a studious life: his *Historia de la República Argentina* (History of the Argentine Republic).

Perhaps the most important influence on López's intellectual development was the intimate relationship that he always enjoyed with his father, Vicente López y Planes, the renowned statesman, poet, and author of the national anthem. As such, back in 1837 the ambitious youths of Buenos Aires had invited the elder López to preside over those inaugural sessions of the Literary Salon that marked their own entrance into public life. During the next few years, the elder López had followed closely the activities of his son and the other exiled militants. Perhaps he celebrated vicariously their rebellion against Rosas, even though his own commitment to the fatherland placed him for the most part above factional politics. Over the next few decades, father and son (and daughter-in-law), separated by the forty-mile wide estuary, wrote copious letters on a weekly or biweekly basis. This largely unstudied correspondence contains a wealth of data about the sentimental and family values of the close-knit clan and their time. On this level, it could provide a parallel reading for the son's ambitious narrative, *La novia del hereje*, the novelized history with the didactic mission of making explicit the link between the affectionate, trusting relationships within the family, and the success of a given society in engendering a social and political order based on harmony and liberty.[188]

The strong domestic and emotional attachment to his family was one factor contributing to the essentially conservative orientation of Vicente Fidel's republican ideals. He favored a "conservative" constitution and political regime, because they corresponded naturally to the antecedents of the nation's own history, the moral characteristics of its people, and the administrative tradition and social categories that had proven their worth over generations.[189] Ideally the new generation of national leaders would be able to build upon and improve this bedrock of social tradition, through their gradual introduction of republican principles and practices.

During the 1850s López found that his conservative republican ideals were best served by the promises of the Confederation legitimized by the 1853 Constitution (later he would prefer the Constitution of 1819— and its system of nationality concentrated in a unitarian parliamentary regime).[190] Although he had harbored since early childhood an abhorrence for the anarchy brought upon by the rural lower class that threatened to put asunder the enlightened traditions and values of the country's most illustrious citizens, he also realized the complete impotence of Buenos Aires to exert a positive influence over the development of events in the provinces of the interior. He agreed wholeheartedly with the analysis of Alberdi that the clique of Porteños, who wished to reestablish that city's predominance over the rest of the nation, were primarily motivated by the selfish goal of recuperating lost prestige. The Porteño leadership, in effect, raised to the level of offical political discourse the basest sentiments of the "localist, plebian street-educated" population, whose total indifference to the other provinces' misery or marginality was well known.[191] In effect it was that population that had sent him into voluntary exile in Montevideo after his legislative defeat over the San Nicolás Accord in 1852.

Many of these factors explain López's attraction to the cause of the Confederation, about which there was little mention in his personal correspondence. Although he and Alberdi rarely corresponded, their views about the troubling national question largely coincided. They also embraced a similar conception about the "philosophy of history," according to which the past customs and traditions of a society were held to be more powerful influences over the course of future change than voluntaristic, political action. Another possible influence over López were the ideas of his friend Gutiérrez, whose infrequent letters highlighted the scandalous state of affairs in Buenos Aires and the bellicose leaders there who eschewed a peaceful resolution to the crisis.[192] Another possible influence over his ideas was Francisco Pico, who as late as 1858, maintained a deep respect for Urquiza as "the most level-headed" person in the whole situation who continued to "inspire confidence"; Urquiza's leadership still promised relief from the present impasse, in spite of the mediocrity of other Paraná leaders.[193]

López, in Montevideo, either ruminated or remained largely silent before the growing hostilities between Buenos Aires and Paraná. His memory of defeat in the Buenos Aires legislature seemingly neutralized his desire for further intervention. As late as May 1858, when recent and more serious events occupied the thoughts of almost everyone else, he meekly sought from Luis Domínguez some words of consolation for his own part in those debates some six years earlier.[194] Gathering courage for a new entrance into the political foray, he wrote and had published a letter in the Buenos Aires press three months later. Then he called upon Domínguez once again to reassure him. "Follow your conscience, no more doubts" are the assuaging words that he needed to hear.[195]

Drawing upon these words of reassurance, López felt motivated to emerge even more confidently from his self-imposed silence and exert his moderating influence on both sides of the dispute. In a series of letters published in the Buenos Aires press in 1858, he criticized the Porteño Legislature for having exceeded its authority in provincial and external affairs. In words tinged with resentment, he attempted to minimize the contributions of Mitre and Sarmiento because their lack of formal training in law and jurisprudence had led them to misrepresent and attack the San Nicolás Accord and the Constitutions of 1812 and 1853.[196]

Such accusations in the charged Buenos Aires milieu could not go unchallenged. Sarmiento retaliated from the editorial columns of *El nacional*. López's fixation on the "inadequate" San Nicolás Accord was, for Sarmiento, evidence of a "posthumous stubbornness that undermined the self-confidence needed for one to effectively deal with issues relevant to the present."[197] With regard to his and Mitre's supposed incompetence in legal issues, Sarmiento retorted that López was the perfect example of one who was overschooled in the theory of law but who had no practical experience in its application. It was totally presumptuous for that "Mr. Nobody" in the public affairs of the region and author of only an insignificant novel to criticize the qualifications of one such as Mitre, who had already distinguished himself as leader in the provincial legislature and as the author of a ground-breaking historical study on Manuel Belgrano. According to Sarmiento the criticisms of López, as well as those emanating from Domínguez and Cané, exhibited little more than "plagerism of Alberdi's verbal trickery."[198]

Yet López's criticisms were not directed only at Buenos Aires. In a personal letter to Alberdi in November 1858, he expressed grave doubts about the advisors surrounding Urquiza, whose "provincial vanity" was assuming very harmful directions. They constituted "the darkest and most evil circle that you can imagine." With irrational hatred of Buenos Aires, they continually proposed measures that the Porteño leadership would find impossible to accept.[199]

López also criticized Alberdi himself. He found especially harmful the latter's recent pamphlet, *Las cosas del Plata explicada por sus hombres, escrito por . . . un vecino* (Events in the Plata, as explained by its citizens, written by . . . a neighbor—apparently published in French), because it provided a rationalization for the most destructive policies emanating from Paraná. He futilely urged Alberdi not to imitate the intransigence of Urquiza's other advisors but rather to defend a more "fertile" plan of action. López ended with a personal note that revealed the costs he had borne after attempting to steer a path midway between the two antagonist sides in the national conflict: "I have been slandered, I am detested; . . . [I have suffered] the silence . . . the opposition . . . and the bad intentions . . . of the two parties."

POLITICS IN BUENOS AIRES

By mid-decade the charged political scenario of Buenos Aires was divided between two groupings. First there was the Liberal Party, which, in fact, brought together unitarians, ex-supporters of Rosas, and several of the former members of the May Association in their common defense of Buenos Aires's autonomy from the Confederation. The principal members of this grouping were Mitre, Valentín Alsina, Rafael Obligado, Rufino de Elizalde, Sarmiento, Dalmasio Vélez Sársfield, and the Uruguayan Juan Carlos Gómez. Opposing them were the "reformists," led by Nicolás Calvo, who, as editor of *La reforma pacífica* (Peaceful reform), sought Buenos Aires's peaceful integration into the Confederation. Militating on the side of Calvo were the young José Hernández, Frías, and Domínguez. The former grouping was derogatorily called by their detractors the *pandilleros*, in reference to their street gangs that provoked disturbances and intimidated political foes with total impunity from the police. The latter were known as the *chupandinos* (the "bottle suckers" or "boozers") in reference to their custom of meeting together for wine drinking and speeches. The rivalry between the two groups slowly escalated into a heated conflict. Especially noteworthy were the periodic elections in Buenos Aires that either side attempted to win, sometimes at any cost. This was particularly so for the *pandilleros*, or *oficialistas*, whose zeal to retain governmental control led them to resort more and more to gangsterism and fraud.

Mitre's name was continually linked with the unruly climate that was becoming a feature of Porteño politics. His capacity for demagoguery in leading the more active elements of the city had already been demonstrated in the events of September 1852. During the provincial elections of early 1854, there were also many abuses: intimidation at the polls, the buying and robbing of votes, even violence in the streets. These disturbances, carried out by his supporters, served to fortify Mitre's influence all the more.

The growing disorder spread from the Buenos Aires streets and into the chambers of the provincial legislature. Sarmiento, from the editorial columns of El nacional, continually sounded his alarm at the disorderly public that more and more frequency interrupted its sessions.[200] He objected not only to the new role of passion and intimidation in deliberations of state but also to the grandstanding antics of his fellow leaders before Buenos Aires's most unruly citizens. Nevertheless he must have been aware of the contradiction in his own values. However much he disapproved of the disorderly "barras"—groups—in the legislative chambers, their presence fortified the virulent anti-Urquiza and anti-Confederation politics to which he was a full party.

The disintegrating moral climate in Buenos Aires fueled the anger of the province's leaders over the intentions and actions of the Confederation. On both sides inflamed words motivated the more radicalized elements to commit acts of violence. In the face of a mounting military threat, each side reallocated already scarce funds for arms purchases. In the latter months of 1855 the leaders of Buenos Aires reacted to the invasion of the province by a band of some one hundred forty soldiers headed by Colonel Jerónimo Costa—an enterprise apparently undertaken without the formal assistance or approval of the confederate government.[201] A formal declaration signed in late January 1856 by Obligado, Alsina, Norberto de la Riestra, and Mitre authorized the latter, in his capacity as colonel and minister of war, to mete out the most severe punishments possible to this "group of anarchists." Mitre then orchestrated a successful attack and captured the majority of the invading force without suffering a single casualty in his own ranks. In doing so his troops pursued the enemy for a short distance into the Province of Santa Fe and, as such, violated the declared truce. The subsequent execution of more than a hundred prisoners earned Mitre kudos from his belligerent followers in Buenos Aires but provoked the wrath of Confederation officials and sympathizers. Julio Victorica, secretary to Urquiza, undoubtedly exaggerated in calling that bloodbath one of the most terrible acts in the country's history.[202] Nevertheless those words communicate well the growing sentiment on the part of Paraná leaders that a violent confrontation between the two sides was becoming unavoidable.

As the conflict deepened, the level of intolerance of many groups in Buenos Aires rose accordingly: street gangs threatened Confederation defenders, and political moderates found it increasingly difficult to voice their views before an impassioned public. Leaders of the faction in power did little to discourage such behavior. Mitre must have realized the impossibility of thwarting that growing storm of passions, so he positioned himself at its front to guide its movement. In the atmosphere of growing tensions, those defending moderation lost visibility as more hardened leaders gained control. Gutiérrez, writing Alberdi from Paraná, shared his sense of impending doom:

> I have the bitter honor of informing you that that people [of Buenos Aires] have traveled along a path of errors and aberrations from which they will not exit in many years. I see not one man, not one head capable of producing the ideas that might save Buenos Aires or bring it back to a state of happiness. . . . That giant poppy, with all it wishes to embrace, crazily tries to absorb everything, and nothing can oppose it.[203]

Buenos Aires's political life, according to Gutiérrez, was little more than "a hell of dirty passions." Alberdi apparently shared that opinion. Writing from London to Alfonso Bulnes in Santiago, he stated that Buenos Aires was governed by a "Cabinet led by crazies: Alsina and Mitre."[204] Other observers expressed a similar opinion: the shameless *caudillo*-like actions of Mitre and company were "a hopeless case."[205]

These opinions were confirmed by Buenos Aires's continued descent into mob rule. Civil violence reached its peak in the 1857 provincial elections for governor, when open confrontations occurred between street gangs, which included assaults, confrontations with knives, and armed intimidation. In the two previous weeks, the theaters had to be closed due to the threat of violence, and a candidate chose to withdraw from the senate race after receiving a death threat. The government, partisan to its supporters, let an assassin escape when it came to light that he was a registered member of the Club Libertad. Calvo, from the pages of *La reforma pacífica*, compared the tactics of electoral intimidation used by "Mitre's *mazorca*" with those employed by Rosas's henchmen a decade before; in those same pages Governor Obligado, who oversaw those elections, was referred to as "the Argentine Nerón."[206]

Sarmiento, whose political future was at stake, did not hesitate to participate in illegal activities in order to bring about a favorable electoral result. In a letter to confidant Domingo de Oro, which was intercepted by Urquiza loyalists, he, as the province's newly designated director of Schools, provided a detailed description of his part in the electoral fraud:

> in various places we established deposits of arms and munitions, on several corners in every parish we placed groups of armed men, we imprisoned about twenty foreigners linked to an alleged conspiration; some bands of armed soldiers roamed the streets of the city at night, knifing and pursuing mazorqueros; in the end, such was the terror that we inspired in all those people— through these and other means—that on the 29th our party triumphed without serious opposition.[207]

The lesson that he drew from this valuable experience in civic disruption was that "fear is an endemic sickness of this community: it is the great lever which will always be used to govern the Porteños; used with skill, it will unfallibly bring about one's desired results."

It became clear to all concerned that the *oficialista* clique that exercised authority in Buenos Aires would go to almost any extreme to maintain power and thus continue unchanged its intransigent politics vis-à-vis the Confederation. The allegation that these individuals stood to gain financially from their control of the political machinery in Buenos Aires was perhaps misplaced,[208] but beyond doubt was the determination of Mitre, Sarmiento, and Alsina to hold onto the power and influence that they had acquired. This motivation apparently took precedence over their democratic and liberal persuasion; moral convictions were often sacrificed before the need to accommodate to social and political pressures. Safely in control of the provincial government, they vetoed suggestions of a possible plebiscite over the issue of reincorporating Buenos Aires into the nation. They forcibly silenced those opposed to their own view and answered a resounding negative to any peace initiative.[209]

THE ROAD TO DISSOLUTION IN PARANÁ

The defiant position adopted by the Buenos Aires leadership contributed to a growing intransigence on the part of the leadership in Paraná. In the next few years, this would lead to the disenchantment of key Confederation leaders and the withdrawal from public life by several of them: Gutiérrez, Guillermo Rawson, Marcos Paz, and others.

During this period even Alberdi would be the object of strident criticism on the part of influential confederate leaders. A key issue was the treaty with Spain for which he had dedicated long months and great care in promoting before the Madrid government. His great achievement was the Spanish legislature's recognition of the Confederation as a free, sovereign, and independent nation and, consequently, its denial of an equal status for Buenos Aires. It has been speculated that the tacit price for that great diplomatic coup was the treaty's article 9, which affirmed that Spanish natives accepting Argentine citizenship, as well as their children born in Argentina, would perpetually retain Spanish citizenship or the right to obtain it; the same right was automatically extended to Argentines who resided in Spain. In negotiating this article Alberdi ignored specific instructions from the foreign ministry, headed by his friend Gutiérrez. Was it arrogance or a blinding dislike of nationalist chauvinism that led him to personally promote that extraordinary stipulation? The reaction to that clause in Paraná and even in Buenos Aires was overwhelmingly negative. In the backbiting environment of Paraná politics, mention was made of Alberdi's possible "treason" to the homeland. With passionate and legal arguments, the legislative majority then overwhelmingly rejected the treaty in its entirety.

For some time, Alberdi had reason for suspecting that some of the Confederation's highest officials, whether out of jealousy for the privileged position he enjoyed as Urquiza's trusted advisor or out of petty ambition in anticipation of the coming presidential elections, were engaging in intrigues against him.[210] In his personal correspondence to a Chilean friend, he mentioned his suspicion that Vice President Salvador María del Carril, several months earlier, had released to the Buenos Aires press copies of his personal correspondence to Urquiza.[211] At about the same time, Alberdi shared his suspicion in a letter to Urquiza that del Carril had organized the "fabric of false statements and puerile pretexts" against the treaty with Spain with the intention of discrediting him.[212] Alberdi communicated the disquieting idea that, outside of Urquiza, the Confederation did not possess leaders of stature, commitment, and respect who could enhance its position in the struggle against Buenos Aires. Within two years, when Urquiza's term as president would expire, who was a likely candidate for replacing him as head of government? The prospect that the calculating del Carril or the mediocre Derqui would occupy that position hardly inspired his confidence.

Confederate leaders began to realize that if Buenos Aires could not be enticed to comply with the national constitution through peaceful means, then the only recourse left was military action. However this line of reasoning accompanied a growing sense of urgency: recent diplomatic setbacks, coupled with a stagnating financial situation, betrayed the Confederation's slow but steady process of dissolution. On the surface its military might was impressive. Since 1855 it had spent considerable funds to obtain foreign weapons and expand its already large standing army. At the end of May 1858 it sponsored an impressive military parade of sixteen thousand trained and disciplined troops in full regalia, with the obvious intention of intimidating the Buenos Aires leadership.[213] Informed observers knew that the Confederation still had a slight edge, even with Buenos Aires's plentiful armaments and a respectable military fleet (which that province had been able to purchase with the abundant monies obtained through the customshouse).[214] But even with a military victory, the Confederate leadership would face a nearly insurmountable problem: a prolonged military occupation might force Buenos Aires's compliance with the dictates of the Paraná legislature, but it would also inspire angry resistance.

Alberdi was fully in agreement with this analysis. Undoubtedly one of his goals in winning European recognition for the confederate cause had been to secure collaboration in the event of another military confrontation. In his letter of 1858 to Urquiza after the failure of his negotiations with France, he wrote:

> I believe that we have arrived at the point of needing to think of drastic measures. Diplomacy will be useful to us, but it will not provide us with the solution that will mean the salvation of our country. The integrity of the Argentine Nation cannot remain dependent upon the caprices or ignorance of European cabinets. . . . No other course is left to us than that which has served every other nation in establishing its own territorial integrity: the power of law backed by the power of arms. This course has become as necessary today as it was in 1851.[215]

Although his later publications would identify him clearly as a pacifist and antiwar activist, at this moment in time Alberdi still embraced armed conflict as a means for resolving regional and national disputes (the same belief that had motivated his support for the Lavalle campaign some decades earlier). If forceful action were not taken against Buenos Aires, then the Paraná leadership would risk losing everything. The economic strength of the rebellious province increased daily, especially after the European powers' resumption of commercial and diplomatic relations. For this reason there was a new urgency for the Confederation to take decisive action. His additional suggestion to Urquiza was that Paraná should seek the assistance of Brazil in a future military venture against Buenos Aires. In light of Alberdi's strident warnings throughout the past decade about the geopolitical ambitions of this neighboring power (and his opposition a decade hence to Argentina's alliance with Brazil in the Paraguayan War), this receptivity to military collaboration with Brazil must have shocked many informed followers. But the deteriorating position of the Confederation now demanded desperate measures that would have been been unthinkable five years earlier.

A POWDER KEG READY TO EXPLODE

The series of tragic events in the distant province of San Juan, which began toward the end of 1858, set tempers aflame and escalated the hostilities between the two competing sides in the national conflict. Since the overthrow of Rosas in 1852, San Juan had been the site of perhaps the most inflamed passions confronting the nation as a whole. The embittered conflict between liberals and federalists there might have been limited to the local level had it not been for the presence of San Juan natives, Salvador María del Carril and Sarmiento, in the highest circles of power for both the Confederation and Buenos Aires. As a consequence any local confrontation in the distant Andean province almost immediately became elevated to the status of a national event.

Since 1852 anger among the liberal leaders in San Juan had been high, following Urquiza's intervention to prevent the removal of Nazario Benavides as the province's governor. Early in 1858, following their party's electoral victory over Benavides, a small group of militant liberals orchestrated the arrest and then brutal murder of the ex-governor.[216] These actions were cause for celebration on the part of such extremist voices as Juan Carlos Gómez, the Varela brothers—sons of Florencio Varela—and others in Buenos Aires. Some examples of their strident yellow journalism were "The people of San Juan have been the first in Argentina to have the courage to bring down a caudillo!" "The epoch of caudillos has ended on the shores of the Plata and soon none of them will be tolerated. The people have begun with Benavides; with Urquiza they will soon conclude!"[217] Other opinion leaders in Buenos Aires demonstrated less enthusiasm for the tragic events in San Juan. Disfavor came from Nicolás Calvo in the pages of *La reforma pacífica;* Chilean liberal, Francisco Bilbao, indignantly inquired whether those events meant that both sides would now "grant sovereignty to destructive passions." Sarmiento's first reaction, in contradiction to later accusations on the part of his detractors, was to urge a suspension of judgment until more facts were available. He believed that the early versions of the killing were tendentious and that they might have been exaggerated in order to stain the reputation of fellow San Juan liberals.[218] Within weeks, however, he would abandon any idea of moderation, and would join the most intransigent of Porteños leaders in urging a total war against the Confederation.

Peaceful dialogue was no longer possible. *L'Union étrangère,* a French newspaper in Buenos Aires, captured the sentiment widely held throughout the Confederation: "Our pen shamefully admits it: the newspapers of Buenos Aires applaud only those crimes worthy of cannibals."[219] Informed observers were well aware that many of the same individuals dominating the press in that city were precisely those who controlled the political destiny of the province. General Urquiza, for his part, did not hesitate to link the extremist opinions emanating from Porteño newspapers with the bloody acts of the San Juan liberals: the former advocated, and the latter performed assassination as a means of furthering political objectives.

> The men of crime and discord who are the instruments of concealed interests have repeatedly bloodied this land; perhaps they were the same men who threatened the life of their liberating general after the Battle of Caseros, then the life of the president, and, even more recently, they who have sacrificed that victim in their lamentable passion for skirmish and revolt.[220]

In the provinces even former advocates of peaceful measures to bring Buenos Aires to comply with the constitution of 1853 now began to change their minds. The assassination of Benavides had angered many, causing them to unite against Buenos Aires. Citizen groups across the interior spontaneously met to urge a stern response.[221] After short debate both legislative bodies in Paraná approved of military measures in order to force Buenos Aires's incorporation into the nation and to conclude speedily the smoldering civil war. The governments of all the provinces then endorsed special resolutions in support of that decision.

Subsequent events unfolded accordingly. Writers and ideologues now yielded to the prerogatives of the generals, as the dramatic confrontation became the focus of universal attention. Mitre and Sarmiento, the Porteño protagonists in that struggle, now gave priority to direct action over propaganda or writing. More contemplative individuals—Gutiérrez, Alberdi, López, Frías, Cané, and others—now sank into unaccustomed silence, perhaps realizing that any analysis or judgment they might produce would quickly border on the irrelevant in a rapidly changing scenario.

In May, Buenos Aires mobilized its forces under the command of Mitre, recently ascended to general. The next month the Confederate government authorized the mobilization of the National Guard, headed by Urquiza. At the beginning of July the mutinied crew of "El Pinto" (Spotted horse) turned the Porteño warship over to Confederate forces and in doing so neutralized the naval advantage on the Paraná River previously enjoyed by Buenos Aires. On October 23 the Battle of Cepeda took place, with Confederate forces winning a decisive victory over the troops of Buenos Aires.

The Confederation's dramatic military victory in the Battle of Cepeda, and then their advance to the outskirts of the city of Buenos Aires, forced Porteño leaders to negotiate for peace. Over the opposition of Sarmiento and a few other intractable leaders, Valentín Alsina was forced to step down as governor. Through the effective mediating efforts of Francisco Solano López, son of the aging Paraguayan president, the two sides approved the Pact of Union, which granted generous capitulation terms to Buenos Aires. The province was allowed to retain all its arms and munitions and, for the time being, its control over the customshouses, which continued to be its main source of revenue. After the Porteño legislature pledged its compliance with Paraná directives for incorporation into the national union, Urquiza, at the head of his army, quit the siege and removed his troops from the defeated province.

The hope of the Confederate leaders was that the generous terms of peace provided for by this pact would lead to Buenos Aires's willing incorporation into the Union. This was not to be the case, however. In the December elections for Buenos Aires's constituent convention that would have as its mission the reconsideration of reforms to the 1853 Constitution, the *oficialista* candidates won a majority over those supporting conciliatory measures with Urquiza. Nevertheless the new congress was a most impressive group. Among its members were Mitre, Sarmiento, Mármol, Domínguez, Frías, V. F. López, Vélez Sarsfield, Obligado, Valentín Alsina, Adolfo Alsina, Wenceslao Paunero, Irineo Portela, Rufino de Elizalde, and Eduardo Costa.

The contemporary reader attempting to understand the series of events surrounding the conflict between Buenos Aires and the Confederation becomes accustomed to encountering wholly divergent accounts emanating from the two antagonistic sides. This problem becomes especially acute when considering the events following the Confederation's victory at Cepeda: the motives of the protagonists appear particularly clouded and their actions contradictory. Rather than give total credibility to one exclusive line of interpretation, the generous historian must grant to both sides the power of posthumous explanation.

From the point of view of Alberdi, Cané, Gutiérrez, and other witnesses partial to the cause of the Confederation, the Buenos Aires legislature of 1861 was characterized, from start to finish, by a sharp antagonism between the two groups. The liberal majority, led by Mitre and Sarmiento, was engaged in a game of deception that had as its goal the preservation of Buenos Aires's prerogatives before the demands of the Confederation. The liberals generally agreed that prolonged deliberation or debate worked to Buenos Aires's favor. They knew that the province's prosperous economic situation, in contrast to the Confederation's progressive decline would, in short order, tilt the military balance to their favor. This explains their stalling tactics and opposition to the petitions of Frías, López, Domínguez, and others to delimit discussion and to approve without delay the 1853 Constitution such as it then existed.

During the deliberations of the special constitutional convention, Mitre again assumed a leadership role. He chaired the commission assigned to study the most needed reforms, and he authored its final report to the convention. He had already expressed his ideas in a proclamation to the Porteño population a week after the signing of the Pact of Union. While acknowledging the prospects for peace that the accord signified, he urged his followers not to forget Buenos Aires's special position within the region, nor the liberal principles of the May Revolution that the Buenos Aires population—in apparent contrast with that of the interior provinces—so prized. Mitre, by now, was the undisputed leader of Buenos Aires opinion. Commentators provided divergent testimonies about his new public role. According to his detractors, Mitre's leadership merely contributed to the continuing spirit of Porteño intransigence and obstructed the movement toward conciliation that others were promoting. However historians partial to the Porteño cause have argued that Mitre, seconded by Sarmiento, sought the best of all possible means for Buenos Aires to assume its rightful place as leader in the national union that would soon emerge. This was the spirit of Sarmiento's distinguished address before the legislature on May 1, 1860. Without compromising with his intractable pro-Porteño views, he stated that the time had come for realizing the nation's reunification, the long deferred aspiration of its most respected leaders. The memorable conclusion to that address drove home his thesis: "We wish to unite the country; we want to become again the United Provinces of the Río de la Plata!"[222]

Largely guided by Mitre and Sarmiento, the Buenos Aires constitutional congress set forth a number of thorny conditions that would have to be fulfilled before that province would join the Confederation. Heading the list was their insistence that twenty-five articles of the national constitution be modified and that Urquiza step down as head of state. Not surprisingly the Confederation leaders felt this last condition to be insulting and unacceptable. The apparent impasse explains Cané's pessimism in several letters to Alberdi. He saw little hope for reconciliation given the predominance in Buenos Aires politics of the same men whose anarchical ideas had brought about the 1852 Revolution of September.[223] Gutiérrrez wrote to Urquiza in a similar vein about his doubts over Buenos Aires's good faith in cooperating further in the project of reunification, and he urged the general's intervention: "Public opinion is restless and will go astray unless men like yourself accept a decisive course of action in this great enterprise."[224] The reaction of Alberdi was similar. In a letter to Francisco J. Villanueva, in Chile, he identified Mitre, Vélez, and Sarmiento as those most responsible for Buenos Aires's disruptive politics. Their plan for constitution reforms was an attempt to obstruct the real work of reunification; it was "a miserable work of anarchy and disorder."[225] In another letter he communicated a growing disillusionment with the entire situation of the Plata region: "I place more faith in *things* than in *men.*"[226]

Alberdi's pessimism also responded to the disintegrating political situation of the Confederation. The federalists were faced with a true quandary in the presidential elections of February 1860. Although they recognized that only the continuation of Urquiza as president would assure strong Confederation leadership, they also realized that his reelection would provide additional evidence to Buenos Aires's criticisms of that leader's *"caudillo"* intentions of perpetuating himself in power. In the end Urquiza decided to step aside in favor of another candidate, in accordance with Alberdi's often repeated advice. With the vision of a true statesman, he undoubtedly realized that his withdrawal was the price he would have to pay for the nation to realize its unification. Santiago Derqui was subsequently elected; in March he was inaugurated as the Confederation's new president. Two months later Urquiza reassumed the governorship of his native province, Entre Ríos.

Meanwhile Buenos Aires celebrated provincial elections in May, with Mitre emerging as the new governor. He immediately designated Sarmiento as head of cabinet and foreign affairs, while Elizalde and General Juan Andrés Gelly y Obes were named to the ministry of the treasury, and war and maritime affairs, respectively. In April of the following year, Gutiérrez would be named to the prestigous position of dean of the newly reorganized University of Buenos Aires.

Derqui, as the Confederation's new president, enjoyed a long-standing friendship with Mitre. This was in spite of his recent past as leader in the Confederate legislature of the campaign against Buenos Aires and of having earned the reputation of "champion of hate toward Buenos Aires."[227] To the surprise of many, he chose to continue Urquiza's politics of dialogue upon assuming the presidency. This caused new dissention in the ranks of federalist supporters, whose alarm grew with every new concession to the Buenos Aires leadership. In July, Derqui and Urquiza visited Buenos Aires; Mitre and Sarmiento went out of their way to guarantee the success of this ground-breaking summit before the skeptical and potentially hostile Porteño public. For two weeks a spirit of reconciliation flavored the meetings between these four kingpins of national politics, while special ceremonies, banquets, and fiestas occupied their free time. The four leaders were further brought together by their joint allegiance under the Masonic pledge to seek "through all possible means the prompt and peaceful consolidation of a definitive national union." At Urquiza's urging, an additional pledge was required: the respective leaders of the two opposing sides pledged that neither would initiate armed hostilities unless as a last resort, and only after prior consultation with the others.[228]

Progress toward unification proceeded apace. In the month of September, the national convention in Santa Fe approved the constitutional reforms suggested by Buenos Aires. In October, Derqui's administraton began their implementation. Meanwhile the Buenos Aires legislature, under Mitre's special urging, pledged its allegiance to the revised constitution.[229] Shortly thereafter Sarmiento and other Porteño representatives demonstrated their own spirit of collaboration by visiting with Urquiza and Confederation officials at Paraná. In November, Urquiza reciprocated the gesture of conciliation by inviting Mitre and Derqui to his palace in San Juan, Entre Ríos, in order to celebrate the first anniversary of the signing of the Pact of Union. It was during that friendly meeting that all participants learned of the new outbreak of violence in the Province of San Juan. Those events precipitated a renewal of hostilities and brought to an end any remaining hope of a peaceful resolution to the national conflict.

END OF CONCILIATION

The new outbreak of violence in the Province of San Juan once again was the spark that ignited the smoldering conflict into flames. At the beginning of November 1860, Sarmiento published in *El nacional* an angry tirate denouncing the illegal acts of Coronel José Antonio Virasoro, a native of Corrientes, whom Urquiza had named governor shortly after the death of Benavides a few years before. He had remained in close contact with other liberals in his native province, in particular with his intimate friend, Antonino Aberastain, who was the leader of the liberal opposition. In one letter Aberastain had described his brief imprisonment and exile, in addition to other acts of tyranny on the part of Virasoro. Others, in addition to Sarmiento, were concerned about the deteriorating situation in the Andean province. As reports multiplied of Virasoro's illegal and unpopular acts and the growing anger of the San Juan population, the national government took unavoidable action. On the 16th of that month, Mitre, Urquiza, and Derqui signed a joint letter requesting that the provincial governor voluntarily step down. His removal from office had become a rallying cry for liberal groups across the region. *El mercurio* of Valparaíso announced his approaching fall on the 14th. On November 18, Sarmiento published a pamphlet entitled "The tyrant José Virasoro," in which he stated that San Juan had "the right to rid itself of its tyrant at any risk."

Two days earlier (although the news would not arrive to Buenos Aires until the 29th), the group of infuriated liberals in San Juan, apparently following the orders of their leader, Antonino Aberastain, seized and then executed the governor, his brother, and five other collaborators. Shortly thereafter the liberal majority in the provincial legislature invited Aberastain to return to San Juan and assume the responsibilities of governor.

Did Sarmiento take a direct role in this assassination? Although the opposition press in Buenos Aires accused him, in his capacity of leader in the Porteño government, of having facilitated one million and a half pesos to finance the San Juan uprising,[231] concrete evidence of this complicity was never presented. Before similar accusations that Urquiza made to Mitre, Sarmiento submitted his resignation as Ministro del Gobierno, even though Mitre continued insisting that neither Sarmiento nor any official of his government had taken part in the conspiracy. This being said there was no doubt that Sarmiento was fully sympathetic to the objectives of the San Juan liberals, with whom he enjoyed close friendships. Moreover those instigating the act were without doubt the loyalists of Aberastain, who, in turn, was Sarmiento's intimate friend and the closest thing to his political representative in the province.

Events in San Juan quickly developed a new turn, and once more civil war threatened to engulf the country. Derqui named Coronel Juan Saá, governor of San Luis and old Rosist supporter, as head of the national mission charged with restoring order in the convulsed province. This choice caused anger among liberal partisans in Buenos Aires, and even Urquiza registered his grave reservations. Buenos Aires loyalists, General Wenceslao Paunero and Emilio Conesa, were ordered to accompany Saá in the intervention but withdrew shortly thereafter upon learning of the heavy-handed tactics planned. Aberastain, as interim governor of San Juan, perhaps expected Buenos Aires's assistance for resisting what he considered to be the Paraná government's illegal intervention in provincial affairs. Is there any other reasonable explanation for the "insane and suicidal" decision to lead his small unit against the vastly superior forces commanded by Saá?[232] On January 11, 1861, Saá's victory was brutal and one-sided. Of the four hundred casualties to the San Juan forces, the majority died in battle, but after surrendering many had their throats savagely slit and their bodies pierced by lances. This politically inspired massacre, and then the execution of Aberastain, infuriated liberal sensitivities across the country.

The peaceful collaboration between Derqui, Mitre, and Urquiza to fulfill the Pact of Union was suddenly derailed. The governors of Santiago del Estero, Salta, Jujuy, and Buenos Aires angrily censored the assassination of Aberastain, thundering accusations about the resurgence of Rosas tyranny. Federalists had their own complaints. From their perspective the ruthless liberals were primarily at fault after having rebelled against two governors, Benavides and J. Antonio Virasoro. In an angry letter to Mitre, Urquiza called the San Juan revolutionaries "uncaged wild felines" and Aberastain a "caudillo of cowardly assassins."[233] Mitre, for his part, placed the blame for the sordid events on Urquiza for having perpetuated in power those groups or nuclei of persons who owed their ascendance to the Rosas regime a decade before. "The poor people of San Juan have been bathed in innocent blood, they have been barbarously punished because they dared to be free," Mitre argued in an indignant letter to Urquiza.[234] To Derqui he issued a heated protest of the national intervention in that province and demanded punishment for those guilty of the crimes committed. In effect the climate of peace and cooperation that had been painfully constructed through the Pact of Union abruptly came to an end.

Perhaps more significant for the Confederation was the crisis of leadership that these events triggered. Derqui did not possess the moral and intellectual stature necessary for dealing with such momentous happenings. In the first two years of his presidency, he had alienated many powerful federalist supporters throughout the interior provinces by accepting, and even exceeding, Urquiza's conciliatory measures in dealing with Buenos Aires; his inclusion of several liberals into his cabinet was viewed by many as totally selling out to Porteño prerogatives. The bloody overthrow of Virasoro by the liberal opposition in San Juan suddenly placed into doubt the wisdom of Derqui's and Urquiza's politics of compromise with Buenos Aires. Derqui, as head of the Confederate government, was now backed into a corner. On the one hand, if his government did not forcefully punish the liberal revolutionaries in San Juan, then he stood to lose whatever federalist support still remained. On the other a strong response was bound to antagonize even further the Buenos Aires partisans of Aberastain.

Meanwhile confederate politics became even more divided with the September 1860 decision of the national legislature, now dominated by the most intransigent members, to reject the newly elected Buenos Aires delegation on the basis of that province's failure to follow to the letter the national electoral procedures. In short order they officially sanctioned the Saá intervention in San Juan. Both of these measures provoked the wrath of Buenos Aires. Also both clearly were intended as a slap at the leadership of Derqui, whose recent actions had demonstrated his resolve to mend in whatever way possible the aggravated relations with Porteño leaders.[235]

At this time Derqui was in trouble. Perhaps motivated by the desire to establish a politics independent of the heavy influence of Uruqiza, or perhaps out of sincere pro-Buenos Aires convictions, he had granted concessions and powers to the Porteño leaders that went beyond what even Urquiza felt to be prudent. Shouldering responsibility for his terrible error of having named Saá as intervener in San Juan, Derqui then sought ways of appeasing the Buenos Aires leadership. These and other measures, in turn, were interpreted by Urquiza loyalists as part of a plan, in conjunction with Buenos Aires, to destroy completely the influence of Urquiza and the Federalist Party throughout the republic.[236]

During this period Urquiza still wielded enormous personal influence throughout the Confederation, but his official responsibilities were limited to the command of the Confederation's army, a capacity that placed him under the orders of the president and the legislature. He sincerely had intended to model his postpresidential politics after those of George

Washington by distancing himself from disputing factions and assuming the role of elder statesman.[237] The monument of his administration was the Constitution of 1853. To now adopt a course of action against any of its principles would merely add legitimacy to the arguments of his enemies, who continued to maintain that his robe of statesman barely covered over the *poncho* of his *caudillo* origins. Given his immense economic means and overall influence, Urquiza could hardly avoid being an obstacle to whatever independent politics that Derqui or the government might wish to forge. Yet he was totally opposed in principal to any sort of direct intervention in the affairs of state via channels not specifically condoned by the Constitution. This explains his choice of inaction in response to the plea by Gutiérrez and others that only his intervention at that time could save the honor of the Confederation from the "highly unpolitical" conduct of the Paraná government in its violation of the spirit, if not the letter, of the Pacto de Unión.[238]

The protagonists of the respective sides were subjected to intense pressures, given the unresolvable conflicts of the country and the searing passions they engendered. Predictably the historians treating those events have divided along ideological lines in either praising or vilifying their actions. According to his detractors Urquiza was hardly the model of abnegation and self-sacrifice, as painted above. They believed that his conciliatory acts toward Buenos Aires undermined his federalist supporters and brought about the collapse of the Confederation. The opinion widely embraced across the Confederation was that Buenos Aires leaders and the Masons, playing upon Urquiza's enormous "vanity," had manipulated his sympathies and won his allegiance to their own ends.[239] In the next decade Alberdi himself would add reasons for condemning the conduct of Urquiza: after stepping down from the presidency, Urquiza's lucrative commercial dealings with Buenos Aires interests corrupted his sense of responsibility to the Federalist Party and the government he had helped establish.[240]

Other commentators, while not denying Urquiza's motivations of economic self-interest and vanity before Buenos Aires leadership, have emphasized his recognition of the definitive weakness of the Confederation and his realism in accommodation to the criteria of the Buenos Aires elite that was emerging triumphant.[241] Urquiza-defender partisans—prime among them is historian Beatriz Bosch—emphasize Urquiza's sincere desire for peace at this juncture and his commitment to a course of action most beneficial to both his province and the country.

Much evidence supports this perspective of Urquiza, the pacifist. After his victory at Cepeda, Urquiza had generously refrained from disarming Buenos Aires, arguing that a lasting reunification of the nation could not be accomplished by force and that the Porteños had to be enticed to accept voluntarily their province's entrance into the folds of the Confederation. Yet Urquiza also had less altruistic reasons for not embracing a more belligerent stance. He recognized that the very precarious financial situation of the Confederation did not permit more than the shortest of military commitments for its men under arms; even though his forces had been victorious on the battlefield, they would be powerless to alter Porteño sentiments about collaboration with the Confederation. He had come to realize that the struggle between the Confederation and Buenos Aires could only be won through construction and not destruction and that the eventual winner would be the side that succeeded in extending its political and economic hegemony over the other.

Urquiza, perhaps alone among federalist leaders, realized that the increasingly desperate financial straits of the Paraná government made earlier objectives difficult, if not impossible, to achieve. Previously they had been wrong in projecting that peace and tranquility were all that were needed for the united provinces of the Confederation to catch up and then bypass Buenos Aires in terms of material wealth and prosperity. Contrary to those bullish predictions, by 1858 the economy of the Confederation was stagnating, while that of Buenos Aires was spiraling. This directly affected the financial status of the respective governments: the customshouses of Buenos Aires produced a steady supply of receipts while Paraná's level of funding had scarcely grown in the previous decade. In fact the employees of the Paraná government went several months unpaid, and its troops were in a state of misery and discontent.[242] Minister R. E. Luis José de la Peña wrote to Urquiza in April 1861 informing him of the Paraná government's inability to meet even its most routine expenses. In essence it was entering into the initial stages of bankruptcy: "Your Excellency well knows that financial resourses are the soul of any administration and the spring of its life. The revenues of the province don't even cover the cost of its most urgent needs."[243] The message was clear: regardless of the Confederation's success or failure on the field of battle, its long-range objective of establishing hegemony over Buenos Aires was growing more remote.

Sarmiento and Mitre implicitly agreed with Urquiza about the near parity of their respective military forces, and they correctly read in the latter's restraint at Cepeda the sign of the Confederation's terminal weakness. Their initial willingness to abide by the terms of the Pact of Union was probably motivated by the desire to stall for time. Each new month Buenos Aires gained in population and wealth, and the Confederation's star progressively declined. They were both seasoned warriors, and they knew the value of waiting for the proper moment to strike a new blow. It would have been out of character for them to have relinquished their liberal agenda at that time—in spite of Buenos Aires's narrow defeat at

Cepeda. They were not about to forget their long-standing antipathy to Urquiza and the Confederation, and they were not about to act against their lifelong conviction that the historical mission of Buenos Aires was to guide the nation into the approaching era of growth and prosperity. Sarmiento, in spite of his public acquiescence to the measures stipulated by the Pact, continued to preach in private correspondence the necessity of an all-out war in order to defeat once and for all the federalist forces. However—contrary to the opinion of writer and historian, Manuel Gálvez, and others[244]—Mitre was more peacefully inclined. In contrast to the belligerent Sarmiento, Mitre preferred to employ any possible means short of war in order to strengthen Buenos Aires's position.

According to Mitre's analysis Buenos Aires's militia, at present, was no match for the superior military forces of Entre Ríos. Consequently his politics between 1859 and 1861 aimed at buying time in order to permit his province to continue gaining strength and the Confederation to continue its financial dissolution. Mitre and Sarmiento were convinced that it was only a matter of months—or a few short years—before Buenos Aires, with its rapidly increasing population and bullish economic situation, would predominate over the rest of the nation. They knew that economic prosperity would translate into military might which, in turn, would lead to social and political predominance.[245] The key to their delay strategy was to isolate politically the main threat to Buenos Aires authority: the Province of Entre Ríos and its maximum leader, Urquiza. Mitre and Sarmiento therefore attempted to convince certain Federalist leaders in the interior who had publicly demonstrated dissatisfaction with the Paraná leadership that their provinces could gain even more under a national regime centered in Buenos Aires. They also sought ways to aid and encourage liberal partisans to ascend to positions of provincial authority, whether through electoral or violent means. To Mitre's and Sarmiento's satisfaction, the politics of Santiago Derqui, the Confederation's new president, seemed to favor their own strategy. At best Derqui's pro-Porteño stance would facilitate Buenos Aires's incorporation into a reunified nation on their own terms; at worse it would antagonize Urquiza and lead to a split in Confederate ranks. The latter turned out to be the case. By 1861 Derqui's political maneuvering, in addition to compounding problems besetting the Confederation, had led to a rebellion in the Paraná legislature. From the Porteño perspective Derqui now proved to be an expendable ally. But sufficient time had passed. In the intervening months, Buenos Aires had gained considerable strength, and the Confederation was on the brink of bankrupcy. Mitre realized that a future military confrontation, regardless of the short-term military consequences, could only strengthen Buenos Aires's position.

Reacting to the increasingly inflexible posture of the Paraná legislature, many previous confederate supporters began to experience a change in orientation. Gutiérrez, in a flurry of letters to Victorica, Mitre, and Urquiza, demonstrated a new disagreement with Alberdi when he maintained that the greatest impediment for national unification now lay with the leaders of the Confederation. The Paraná government's politics of continued hostility was, for him, leading "to ridicule, to a mocking of the Argentine name."[246] This means that by the beginning of 1860, Gutiérrez had experienced an abrupt change in his political sympathies from tepid Confederate supporter to disillusioned opponent. He was disgusted by Derqui's political ineptitude, and offended by inflexible, belligerent ideas of the leaders of the Paraná legislature. This led to his own realization of the moral and political bankruptcy of the Confederation: "In general, I have very little respect for the character of my countrymen, the Argentine people, but even worse are the Confederation supporters—to hell with them all."[247]

Perhaps the most important moment of Gutiérrez's public career was upon him. With his reputation intact for unquestionable honesty and disinterest and enjoying the trust of both Mitre and Urquiza, he was the catalyst for the important dialogue that was then to take place between these two protagonists of the two contending sides in the national conflict. Between May and July, in his letters to both Mitre and Urquiza (in addition to Urquiza's son-in-law and Confederate Minister Benjamín Victorica), he argued for the necessity of both sides continuing to strive for national unity and urged each of them to champion serenity and tolerance among their respective followings. He sensed the possibility of the two leaders reaching a personal understanding, over and above the flaired passions dividing their respective constituents. With this in mind he shared with Urquiza his pessimism about the motives of the Confederate legislative leaders and attempted to convince him that Mitre, over and above the latter's angry public postures, was a man of honor, high intelligence, and principles. He praised the "magnificent first steps" of the Porteño leader in his initial days in office but at the same time warned him of the hidden enemies and hypocrites who threatened to derail his project of national union.[248] At the same time Gutiérrez attempted to convince Mitre that his public image of provocateur or belligerent Porteño was now counterproductive and that it was now necessary to guard appearances and project an image of disinterested national leader sincerely concerned about the welfare and prosperity of all the provinces. If Mitre were to do this, then Buenos Aires itself would also benefit.[249] At Gutiérrez's urging the two leaders initiated a correspondence that testifies to the high principles that each defended as they led their respective armies toward the city of Pavón.[250]

Gutiérrez's clairvoyant perspective of the new alignment of regional interests was significant, as was also the wise council he extended to both Mitre and Urquiza about avenues for a desirable outcome to the approaching confrontation. Almost alone among Mitre's and Urquiza's advisors, he urged their close collaboration. Before Mitre he argued that Entre Ríos and Buenos Aires were "natural allies, being that their populations included the most capable individuals from any point in the Littoral." Likewise he understood that Urquiza, by promoting negotiations with Buenos Aires, had invited upon himself the wrath of Paraná's most powerful leaders. In the event of a new military confrontation, Gutiérrez predicted that Urquiza would welcome dialogue with the Porteño leader and would seek approval from public opinion in Buenos Aires.[251] In retrospect these valuable insights would inspire Mitre's acts as commander of Buenos Aires's military forces both before and after the dramatic events at Pavón. To Gutiérrez's credit it was he who first articulated what Urquiza perhaps only intuited at the time—that the alliance between Entre Ríos and the interior provinces, which until then had constituted the basis for the Confederation's power, was already in crisis. To his credit he foresaw that the newly emerging axis of hegemony, which would predominate in the next period of the nation's history, would join the provinces of the Littoral to the preponderant Buenos Aires.[252] Embittered Confederate sympathizer, Fermín Chávez, was correct in his observation, but confused as to the geopolitical considerations underlying Urquiza's actions, when he stated that that leader's behavior at Pavón "merely sealed with fire an agreement that had already been decided."[253]

Succeeding events reinforced the conclusion already reached by many that a new round of armed conflict was unavoidable: the imprisonment of General Paz in Córdoba on charges of disturbing the peace; the Paraná legislature's stamp of approval for the conduct of Saá in San Juan; the escape to Chile of Colonel Francisco Clavero, assassin of Aberastain; and the Confederation's interventions in San Juan, Santiago de Estero, and Córdoba with the objective of removing liberals from positions of authority.[254] The time for dialogue was now over. Both sides made preparations for war, although the respective leaders of the two armies did so with great reluctance. Mitre eloquently echoed this view in a letter to Urquiza. Both he and Urquiza were "answerable to superior authorities and, regardless of our own beliefs and faith in the benefits of peaceful means, we cannot, we must not subordinate our own sentiments to the line of conduct that our respective positions oblige us to follow." Mitre was correct: events beyond their control were propelling the two leaders into a conflict that neither desired. Nevertheless, each believed it his responsibility to assume control of his respective fighting force and lead it into battle.[255]

4

National Consolidation (1860–1880)

Pavón and its Aftermath

Conflict was in the air. Recalcitrant elements of both the Liberal Party in Buenos Aires and the Federalists dominating in Paraná obstructed the politics of reconciliation that both governments seemingly supported. Then tension turned to anger when the radicalized liberals of San Juan made their bloody power play. Any hope of a return to peaceful dialogue faded when the Federalist forces under Colonel Saá brutally massacred the San Juan liberals. Exalted Federalists in Paraná then rejected Buenos Aires's elected representatives to the confederate legislature and officially condoned Saá's severe form of justice. After these insults and provocations, extremist liberals sought a belligerent response. Both sides began preparations for another round of armed conflict.

Subsequent events have been treated in depth by historians. In the Battle of Pavón, Mitre, heading the forces of Buenos Aires, confronted the army of the Confederation led by Urquiza. According to most accounts the superbly mounted cavalry from Entre Ríos proved decisive as the Confederate forces once again defeated Buenos Aires. There then occurred perhaps the most controversial and misunderstood act in the nation's history: Urquiza withdrew his troops and returned to Entre Ríos, thereby ceding the field of battle to Mitre's forces. In subsequent months the confederate government, bankrupt and defenseless, dismantled whatever remained of its army and dismissed employees from its offices in Paraná. All avenues were now open for the Buenos Aires government, through the efforts of its diplomats and the might of its army, to impose its will over the entire country.

This was the long-awaited moment for the Buenos Aires leadership. For over ten years Urquiza had represented the incarnation of everything evil in their country's past. His very presence had justified violence on their part. Now his flight from power invited their own forceful response. The letters sent to Mitre by ministers and prominent personalities in Buenos Aires reflected this angry, vengeful attitude; they called for the convocation across the country of people sympathetic to the ideas of Buenos Aires and urged the military invasion of Entre Ríos "in order to finish with Urquiza and the national authority."[1]

Sarmiento, in his letters to Mitre during this same period, revealed an even more vindictive temperament. He angrily demanded severe military measures to eradicate completely the surviving focuses of federalist power. He would settle for nothing less than exile or hanging for Urquiza: "Don't let the wound of Pavón form scar tissue. Urquiza must disappear from the scene, whatever the cost. Southhampton [in reference to the site of Rosas's British exile] or the noose."[2] His rage over the recent assassination of his childhood friend Aberastain now found its target in every remaining stronghold of federalism: "Provoke Corrientes to rebellion, then send in 24 batallions of infantry." He prescribed military invasion in order to do away with Santa Fe as a province.[3] Giving flight to his pent-up emotions, he called for a scorched-earth campaign against all those opposing Buenos Aires's civilizing mission. "Don't try to economize with the blood of gauchos. It's a fertilizer that must be laid for the benefit of the country. Blood is the only thing human that those people have."[4] This was the terrible sentence that he cast for the country's inhabitants who were resolved to defend their traditional way against the advance of Mitre's conquering armies. Ricardo Rojas did not mince words about Sarmiento's vengeful view of the national situation at that time: it was "like an episode of 'Civilization and barbarism,' and, represented by him, civilization, in his fantasy, was exhalted to the point of delerium, as if it were the inspiration for a tragedy."[5]

Yet behind the scenes and largely unknown to the other protagonists of these very events, Mitre and Urquiza were participating in a dialogue of historical importance whose moderate tone contrasted dramatically with the strident exhortations of their respective colleagues. In long meetings over the previous months, they had apparently established a personal relationship based on mutual respect and trust. Their letters from May 1860 to the end of 1862 document the noble sentiments and disinterested motivations of both as they entered into the most controversial period of their respective historical roles and undoubtedly one of the most misunderstood chapters of the nation's history.

As governor of the Province of Buenos Aires and head of its army, Mitre was in a singular position to shape the outcome of events. Over the past months his views had changed considerably. According to V. F. López, Mitre was

a genuine product of the delirious exaltation of the period. He was capable of committing great injustices and employing resources in a most implausible manner if he were pushed to do so by local or partisan passions; but he was not capable of committing infamous acts which he was sufficiently intelligent to foresee and avoid.[6]

Mitre realized that his moment had come to oversee and conclude the process of transferring the nation's power center from Paraná to Buenos Aires. Given the heightened distrust and even hatred for Buenos Aires across the interior, Mitre sought every means possible for a peaceful and gradual reconciliation. In spite of the superior military force he now directed, Mitre realized—like Urquiza before him—that to recur to further military force at this time would be counterproductive. As far as possible he would seek peaceful means for bringing about a change of leadership in the different provincial governments. He would use forceful means only as a last result. As a symbolic measure he rejected the council of the most prominent members of his cabinet—Alsina, Obligado, Elizalde, De la Riestra, Sarmiento, and others—and affirmed the continued viability of Urquiza's Constitution of 1852 under the condition that it be amended in several areas.

Mitre assessed that in many provinces Buenos Aires's strong show of force, accompanied by a politics of restraint and respect for constitutional principles, would provide the necessary leverage for new leadership to arise without bloodshed or protracted struggle. He rejected the advice of his closest advisors, who urged Porteño armies to march straightforward to the provinces and remove through force the remaining vestiges of federalist power. If Buenos Aires had carried out this plan, according to V. F. López, "the Republic would have witnessed the most horrible degree of chaos. . . . at best, the crazy plan would have been risky and counterproductive."[7] Mitre's politics of moderation, when announced to the cabinet, met with a cold response. Sarmiento advocated a more forceful response: "Before and after the campaign you have demonstrated a predisposition to accommodate to the demands of the opposition in such a way as to make your best friends tremble. Buenos Aires is indifferent to the issue of a national union; but it knows of no other passion that its hatred for Urquiza."[8]

Urquiza was willing to cooperate with Mitre's plan. He realized the inability of the interior provinces to sustain a successful military campaign against Buenos Aires; even a show of resistance would result in a protracted civil struggle with the tragic consequence of thousands of casualties and a further hemmorhage of the interior's human and material resources. A peaceful separation that would allow for the "tranquil reconstruction" of the nation at a later date was far preferable for Urquiza.[9] Perhaps it will never be definitively resolved whether Urquiza was motivated more by self-interest or "supreme patriotism" at this time. Similarly inconclusive is the evidence about whether his monumental decision to withdraw voluntarily from the political scene was due more to a realistic appraisal of the Confederation's lost cause or an illusion of self-importance which Porteño influences had succeeded in instilling in his mind. Was it high-minded patriotism or narrow self-interest that motivated his decision to save Entre Ríos from Buenos Aires's intervention and in doing so abandon the rest of the republic to the prerogatives of the Liberal Party?[10] Whatever his reasons, he placed his trust in Mitre's willingness and ability to contain the more extreme voices of Porteño sentiment such as Obligado and Sarmiento, who advocated military reprisals against Entre Ríos, and Uruguayan General Venancio Flores, who would have been the most likely leader for such a vengeful campaign. The stakes were exceedingly high. In order to achieve a peaceful resolution to the national impasse, Urquiza was willing to sacrifice not only the government, on whose behalf he had struggled so hard to defend, but also the Federalist Party in the interior that looked to him as their undisputed leader.

At this time Mitre apparently was sincere in his application of a politics of conciliation as long as that served to accomplish his objectives. He was also disposed to a moderate show of force in the case of especially recalcitrant provinces. His military occupation of Córdoba, he stressed to Urquiza, would be carried out with "a constitutional and patriotic spirit."[11] To that end he instructed General Wenceslao Paunero to avoid involvement in local disputes and to respect the processes of provincial government as long as they were carried out according to existing laws.[12] Accompanying Paunero was Marcos Paz, whose liberal convictions and widespread prestige throughout the interior made him Mitre's ideal candidate for interim governor in that difficult moment of transition.

The case of Marcos Paz is perhaps representative of how recent events had prepared the way for Buenos Aires's assumption of leadership in a newly reorganized country. Paz, according to Cané in *Juvenilia*, was "one of the purest and most generous of men to have ever been born on Argentine soil." Hailing from Tucumán he shared many of the same educational experiences and political loyalties as Alberdi, who was one year his senior. After receiving the law degree in Buenos Aires in 1834, he returned to Tucumán and distinguished himself as Governor Heredia's personal secretary, military leader, and right-hand man in the project of establishing the federation that united the northern provinces. Several years later, after the Battle of Caseros, Paz formed part of the commission that wrote the national Constitution. His service on behalf of the Confederation in the capacity of national senator, and then as governor of Tucumán, earned him widespread respect. As late as 1858 his correspondence with Alberdi revealed a meeting of the minds in support of the Confederation and against Buenos Aires's overly preponderant role in the affairs of the Plata.[13] In 1859 he was the unsuccessful candidate for the vice presidency. But his liberal political ideals, combined with his commitment to the principle of provincial autonomy, increasingly brought him into conflict with the recalcitrant leaders of the Paraná legislature. In a letter to Derqui, he heatedly protested the "arbitrary actions" of Confederate forces in San Juan, arguing that their intervention had violated provincial rights. In 1861 he cast the only vote in the Paraná congress in favor of seating the Buenos Aires delegation. In a reaction to Paz's attempt at impartiality, Mitre wrote in June 1861, inviting his support for the project of constituting a "legal authority derived from constitutional truth and founded through the initiative of free people . . . it will have as its guiding objective to govern according to the law; its saving influence will be liberal ideas."[14] Derqui, learning about this communication, incarcerated Paz on the basis of his alleged conspiracy against the Confederation. Paz would be released on Urquiza's orders only after the Battle of Pavón.[15]

Paz's growing dissidence with the leadership of the Confederation was a sign of the times. Several important leaders from the interior provinces followed the same trajectory. First their initial support for the cause of the Confederation waned before provincial hatred toward Buenos Aires. Then their disillusionment with the Paraná cause led to a shift of loyalties to Buenos Aires. The cases of Guillermo Rawson and Juan María Gutiérrez, in addition to that of Marcos Paz, merit special attention here.

Rawson, born in San Juan in 1822 and ten years Sarmiento's junior, remained in that province during the 1840s. While sharing many of Sarmiento's liberal convictions he, nevertheless, tolerated the bland Federalism of the San Juan governor, Nazario Benavides, believing for several years that the latter and not Uruqiza would be the leader from the interior who would eventually lead the resistance to Rosas.[16] In 1852, when Urquiza overruled the San Juan legislature's vote to replace Benavides as governor, Rawson's protest brought about his incarceration for fifteen days, during which time he was also tortured. In 1854 he was elected as one of San Juan's representatives to the Paraná senate, but his disenchantment with Urquiza led him to delay assuming that position until 1856, whereupon he was immediately elected vice president. His fervent opposition to economic sanctions against Buenos Aires, added to his continuing dissatisfaction with Urquiza's leadership, led him to renounce that position a few years later and move definitively to Buenos Aires. In 1861 he was elected senator for the Province of Buenos Aires. His nationalist views about Buenos Aires's obligations before the rest of the republic placed him in the camp of Mitre and Sarmiento, in opposition to the autonomists led by Alsina and Obligado. After the Battle of Pavón, he was elected to the national congress as senator from San Juan. In the next two years, he lent firm support to Mitre and Urquiza in their decision to seek a peaceful solution to the national conflict. In 1862 he would be named to Mitre's cabinet as minister of the interior.

Also defecting from confederate ranks and embracing Mitre's movement toward national unification under Buenos Aires leadership was Juan María Gutiérrez. The previous chapter explained that he, like several important moderate leaders (Francisco Pico, Salvador María del Carril, Martín Zapata, and others), fully supported the project of the Confederation up through its victory in the Battle of Cepeda. However, Gutiérrez's rapid disenchantment after 1860 resulted from the inept politics of the new president, Santiago Derqui, and the increasingly inflexible anti-Porteño politics of the confederate legislature.[17] After moving to Buenos Aires, he dedicated himself to scholarly pursuits and avoided involvement in the turbulent political scene. In April 1861 Mitre appointed him dean of the newly reconstituted Universidad de Buenos Aires. By the time of the Battle of Pavón, his sympathies were totally with Buenos Aires. In his personal correspondence he depicted that battle as one between "gauchos of fortune" and the "youth of Buenos Aires":

> There it was patently demonstrated that the uneducated rabble, possessing no ideas of its own, is worthless on the battlefield, except when it has been subjected over time to the strict discipline required of foot soldiers on the line. The men dressed in topcoats have triumphed under the orders of General Mitre, himself a dignified and honorable man of the pen and principles; and this is the first time that the material power of this country is in the hands of this class. Everyone is enchanted with him.[18]

For the next few months, his faith in Mitre's unification project could not have been greater. He shared in the general euphoria over Mitre— whom hagiographers were calling "one of America's most exemplary figures."[19]

Even Alberdi, from his vantage point of Europe, had relatively positive things to say about Mitre's first steps in reconstituting the country. Alberdi's thought throughout this next period of the country's history would generally alternate between blindness and insight. After the presidency passed from Urquiza to Derqui, his letters to Urquiza dropped considerably in frequency and ceased altogether after January 1862.[20] Alberdi understood how the inherent weaknesses of the Confederation's political economy, added to the destructive politics of Derqui, would have motivated Urquiza to yield his battlefield victory to the defeated Porteño general. His immediate impression was to see Urquiza's actions as a defensive tactic, "as one of the only possible measures for saving and assuring the success of the national cause."[21] According to this perspective Urquiza yielded his battlefield victory in order to maintain intact the military potential of Entre Ríos and Corrientes with the objective of opposing Porteño localism under more favorable circumstances in the future. However Alberdi would change this perspective as events progressed and as information slowly filtered across the Atlantic to him.

Over the previous decade Alberdi had argued time and again about the destructive qualities of Mitre's politics, and he was now slow to appreciate that leader's break with extremist Porteño sentiment immediately after Pavón. What for others was evidence of Mitre's greatness as a leader was taken by Alberdi as calculated gestures of a demagogue, if not a hypocrite. But Mitre's commitment to a nationalist politics in the first several months after Pavón, over and above the fervid Porteño support maintaining him in power, led Alberdi to admit begrudgingly the positive aspects of Mitre's leadership.[22] He was willing to admit the possibility that Mitre did indeed have the intention of rising above Porteño localist sentiment and found a truly "national" government. In several writings of this period, he praised Mitre's efforts to end the disorder and establish a strong national authority[23] and urged converting only the city of Buenos Aires into the national center.[24] Mitre apparently responded favorable to Alberdi's support; as late as 1864 he is reputed to have accepted with "total enthusiasm" Alberdi's criticisms of Porteño localism and the latter's suggestions for constructing a national order that would benefit the interior provinces.[25]

MITRE'S ATTEMPT AT "PEACEFUL" CONQUEST

Mitre now sought the means for bringing to power throughout the interior provinces a political leadership favorably disposed to his own liberal program of national transformation. This was also the short-term goal of localist sentiment in Buenos Aires. But what separated him from the defenders of those neounitarian views, who nearly monopolized the organs of public expression in the port city, was his commitment to achieve these ends through peaceful measures as far as it were possible. Mitre firmly believed that a vindictive military intervention would be counterproductive for the long-range task of reconstituting the country. That goal would be realized only through the good will and willing compliance of all participating parties.

There was no clearer example of Mitre's peaceful intentions than his administration's actions with regard to Córdoba. It was essential to win this province's support for his nationalist politics given its key strategic position and its traditional role as leader among the provinces of the interior. Mitre projected that a firm show of military force under the disciplined authority of General Paunero, combined with the political savvy of Marcos Paz, would accomplish his ends while avoiding violence. Paz, who enjoyed widespread prestige among federalist loyalists, did what he could to pacify Córdoba's highly factionalized environment. He explained in a letter to Mitre at the end of 1861 that those provincials most adamantly opposing this plan were not Federalist diehards but rather were a rather unruly grouping of citizens calling themselves liberals and claiming allegiance to Mitre's cause: "They wanted me to be the instrument of their persecutions . . . I believe that they wanted to convert me into an arbitrator for satiating their hatreds.[26] Paunero also encountered problems with the feuding liberal leadership there; the city was for him a "Babel of stale gossip. . . . They are a highly educated rabble, none of them are capable of commanding the respect of the rabble of enemies that we have."[27] Subsequent events bore out this terrible prognosis as Córdoba, over the next decade, would witness a high degree of political violence and instability. As it turned out the political chaos unleashed in Córdoba as a result of the Battle of Pavón and its aftermath was but a microcosm of the fierce political passions at play throughout the republic.

In the provinces of the North, Mitre also confronted a liberal leadership bent upon retribution. For years Manuel Taboada and his brothers in Santiago de Estero had resisted threats to their authority through astute political maneuvering and intimidation by a well-armed militia that answered to them alone. Over the past decade their political loyalties had adapted to changing political fortunes. It was now expedient to demonstrate allegiance to the rising banner of liberalism. Pavón, the liberal pronouncement in Córdoba in November, General Venancio Flores's bloody victory over federalist forces in Cañada de Gómez later that month (more about this below), and the final dissolution of the confederate government weeks later provided an impetus for their own efforts to consolidate control in the north. For this reason they lent a deaf ear to the generous principles announced by Mitre administration officials. First they intimidated the Federalist governor in Santiago del Estero into retirement.[28] After marching upon Tucumán and defeating Federalist forces there, they resolved upon a similar plan of military force against Salta and Catamarca. However the unforeseen intervention of *montonera* troops from the neighboring province of La Rioja under the leadership of Angel "El Chacho" Peñaloza, the most prestigous leader of the region and a general of the national army, abruptly stalled this plan of military conquest. When at last Mitre and his representatives intervened, little could be done to soothe exasperated sensitivities between rival federalist and liberal groups. The bishop of Catamarca wrote to Mitre, "All the citizens of this province are desirous of peace, Mr. General, and they confidently await Your Excellency's measures—resulting from your prudence and patriotism—to end the ignoble plundering that is occurring daily."[29] Yet the die had been cast; the victories of the Taboada brothers and the rising belligerence of forces under Mitre's authority increasingly provoked Peñaloza and culminated in the violent events of 1863.

From 1861 to at least 1863, Mitre's actions, along with those of his able representatives Marcos Paz and General Wencesalo Paunero, were indeed directed toward achieving a peaceful transition to liberal rule throughout the interior. The one exception to this otherwise peaceful pattern had been the brutal massacre of Federalist troops in Cañada de Gómez, an event that was independently instigated by Venancio Flores, a general in Mitre's army who was Uruguayan by birth and a leader in the Colorado (liberal) Party there. This declaration is important, given the wrathful sentences emanating from embittered federalist supporters at the time and in recent decades from impassioned "revisionist" historians. Unfortunately many of the latter have confused the chronology of events or have projected distorted interpretations on the basis of the sordid events of Cañada de Gómez.[30] The existing documentation reveals that until 1863 Mitre ignored his ultraliberal supporters in attempting to implement a politics of conciliation leading to the peaceful transition of power from federalists to moderate liberals throughout the country. At this distance from those events, it is difficult, if not impossible, to know whether he sincerely attempted to contain the more bellicose inclinations of General Flores, the Taboada brothers, and his ideological cohort, Sarmiento.

1863: THE PEÑALOZA REBELLION

Ever since Buenos Aires's defeat in the Battle of Cepeda and possibly before, Mitre and the Porteño elite had been actively involved in seeking provincial support for their project of reinstating Buenos Aires as the "older brother" among the rest of the provinces. Their aim was to create political bases of support throughout the interior. To this end Mitre had written to the Taboadas in Santiago del Estero about Buenos Aires's willingness to provide the communities of the interior with the "power and wealth" necessary for legally emancipating themselves from "bastard influences" and organizing themselves democratically like truly federated provinces.[31] One letter ended with the vaguely worded statement that the liberal group headed by the Taboadas could count on all the resources that Buenos Aires was able to provide not only for its progress but also for its "internal security." With more direct language the Taboadas responded to Mitre requesting rifles, cannons, sabres, and munitions in addition to trained military officials. Obviously Buenos Aires's plan was to aid such pockets of liberal resistance and to encourage them to bring about the overthrow of federalist leaders independently. There is evidence that such assistance also made its way to the Aberastain faction in San Juan and to the liberals who successfully seized power in Córdoba during that same period.

In the months following Mitre's surprise victory at Pavón, the brutality with which the Buenos Aires armies established their control over the different provinces puts into question the sincerity of Mitre's articulated design for a "peaceful" conquest. Flores's bloody victory at Cañada de Gómez has already been mentioned. Although the Uruguayan general received a public reprimand for the throat-slitting execution of several hundred prisoners, he was given new and higher responsibilities shortly thereafter. Within weeks Mitre sent a personal letter to thank him for his assistance; at the same time Mitre acknowledged the personal and ideological ties between them: "You know, General, that my heart reaches out to you and your men as friends, as a former companion of arms and politics."[32] It is also probable that two years later Flores received arms and an unofficial nod of approval from the Mitre administration to carry out his invasion of Montevideo with the purpose of overthrowing the Colorado government there.[33] One person who believed Mitre's verbal postures of generosity were but smoke screens masking more severe intentions was Carlos Antonio López, president of Paraguay. López wrote to Uruguayan President Berro in 1862 about Mitre's promises to respect Uruguayan neutrality: "Friend! Don't believe a single word coming from Mitre."[34]

A second figure who had every reason to doubt the sincerity of Mitre's peaceful overtures was Angel "El Chacho" Peñaloza, who had served with distinction under Unitarian Generals Juan Lavalle and Gregorio de Lamadrid and who had also demonstrated loyalty to Juan Facundo Quiroga and Justo José Urquiza during different moments of a distinguished career. The seventy-year-old *caudillo* was at the height of his influence with entire provinces obedient to his gentle, stately will. Accounts differ about why such a man was driven to open rebellion. In the first place, federalist partisans have justifiably portrayed Peñaloza as a bonafide representative of the patriarchal society of the interior that desired a continuation of its peaceful, traditional life without the interference of Buenos Aires. In this respect little doubt exists about Peñaloza's peaceful objectives in spite of epithets of "bandit" and "robber," which came from his liberal opponents. For example General Rivas, in spite of his hatred of El Chacho, wrote to Paunero about the unanimously positive sentiment of the population of the Mediterranean provinces about their undisputed leader: "Without the Chacho the Republic is inconceivable."[35] Paunero, alternating between caution and fear, affirmed to Mitre that Peñaloza was the region's "best and only element of social order."[36] Of the same opinion was the bishop of Paraná, Monseñor Luis A. Gabriel, on a special mission for Mitre, who sincerely believed in Peñaloza's expressed desire for collaboration with Mitre's nationalist objectives.[37] At first the will of these individuals prevailed; they negotiated the Treaty of La Banderita (The little banner) with the respected *caudillo* in May 1862.

Yet, at the same time there were key liberal leaders enjoying the highest confidence of Mitre who adamantly opposed the peace overatures with Peñaloza. Foremost among these was Marcos Paz, former Federalist governor of Tucumán, now designated by the Buenos Aires government to head the liberal intervention in Córdoba and slated within months to become Mitre's vice president. In a steady stream of letters to Mitre in the first week of January 1862, he expressed in the strongest of terms his trepidations about Peñaloza's destabilizing influence in the region. He recommended the dispatch of Buenos Aires troops in order to hamper El Chacho's assistance to federalists resisting the invasion of the Taboada brothers in Catamarca. At the same time he informed Mitre of his decision to sent a militia unit from Córdoba: "I have already given the order for the invasion of The Plains [of La Rioja] by a unit of highlanders from this province. But this measure alone is not enough; I believe that we will have to take additional measures."[38] Paz's anti-Peñaloza sentiments indicate that the Federalist leaders in the interior were hardly a united lot: many of them must have realized, like Paz, the antiquated value of old federalist practices, as represented by Peñaloza, and now placed their hopes with the liberal program of Buenos Aires in order to resolve the country's political impasse.

Peñaloza was undoubtedly the key to the future politics of the Cuyan region. Immensely popular he effectively controlled the whole region surrounding the urban oasis of San Juan and, as such, possessed a veto power over any future initiatives of the Liberal Party. Although Mitre's advisors differed with regard to the advisability of collaborating with Peñaloza, all were in agreement about the need to begin by securing San Juan and from there work to bring the other provinces into the liberal fold. Who better than Sarmiento, a native of that province, was the person to carry out that important mission? These reasons account for the designation of Sarmiento as war auditor to accompany the Porteño troops northward and his subsequent assumption of the governorship of San Juan.

Sarmiento, like Paz, was irate to the limit over the recent treaty with Peñaloza, and he began to implement his own plan to undermine that accord. His almost daily letters to Mitre from San Juan stridently criticized the peaceful overtures of Generals Rivas and Paunero and urged severe reprisals against the *riojano* patriarch. According to Sarmiento, El Chacho was a social enemy in spite of any alleged peaceful intent. For him Peñloza was the maximum representative of an archaic social structure based on an artisanal production and a pastoral economy that was an impediment to the advance of modern institutions. Sarmiento's slogan of "Civilization versus Barbarism," which had originated sixteen years earlier as a catchy literary motif, had by now assumed the status of a war declaration against the foes of progress. The only treatment for El Chacho and his like was annihilation. In 1861 he had written to Mitre the wrath-filled death sentence for federalist leaders like Peñaloza: "It's not necessary to economize when it comes to the blood of gauchos."

But fear and caution for the time being took precedent over bold action. From San Juan, Sarmiento wrote: "This community lives sick with fear of the savage neighbors that surround it . . . ." With what he considered a wholly inadequate defense of the city against a possible attack by Peñaloza partisans, he communicated his grave preoccupation over the "moral depression" of the province.[39] There was no question in his mind that the Peñaloza menace had to be ended. But how, without endangering the entire liberal project in the interior?

Sarmiento and his followers therefore put into action a plan designed to provoke Peñaloza into violating the peace. The liberal press, following Sarmiento's lead, printed any number of allegations of federalist wrongdoings: "armed patrols, forays, invasions, saques, plundering, requisitions for weapons, robberies and assassinations, as much within La Rioja as in the border zones of nearby provinces . . . ."[40] Meanwhile Sarmiento encouraged Uruguayan Colonels Sandes and Arredondo, as well as the Chilean Major Pablo Irrazábal, to take as prisoners any men suspected of collaborating with the *riojano* leader and to confiscate or destroy their property.[41] According to historian Manuel Gálvez, Sarmiento "wanted war and, as was customary in his case, he did not lack pretexts for starting one."[42]

According to Peñaloza partisans, the Riojan *caudillo* was forced into a new rebellion for largely defensive reasons. El Chacho's letter of April 16, 1863 to Mitre angrily listed the abuses that his people were suffering at the hands of the Porteño armies: illegal seizure of property, the killing of respectable citizens for simply having been members of the Federalist Party, and persecution and execution of his loyalists. The Porteño army commanders, through their proclamations and provocations, were treating him and his followers like criminals at large. They had invited his assistance in pursuing law offenders, but Peñaloza proudly refused to become an agent for their "criminal intentions."[43] With his followers being eliminated one by one, Peñaloza announced to Mitre that the only honorable recourse was to take up arms in self-defense. In writing this he prefigured the tragic end that awaited his followers: "All men, when they reach the point of having nothing left to lose but their lives, resolve to lose that one remaining possession on the field of battle and in defense of their liberties, their laws, and the dearest of their interests that have been vilely trampled."[44]

Accounts differ about Mitre's role in all of these events. One view is that his articulated politics of "peaceful means" was, from beginning to end, nothing more than a smoke screen that hid the violent hatred he shared with Paz and Sarmiento for El Chacho and other *caudillos* of the interior provinces.[45] Less cynical was the perspective that Paz and Sarmiento ended up convincing Mitre of the need for a politics of extermination against Peñaloza.[46] A third perspective is given by historian and Mitre apologist, José Campobassi, who argues that the treaty of La Banderita was a sour disappointment to the Buenos Aires leader.[47] In this light it is possible that Mitre did defer to Sarmiento's and Paz's vengeful plan of provoking El Chacho into violent reaction. Whatever Mitre's original motivations, Sarmiento's plan worked to the letter; Peñaloza's call to arms provided a legal justification for the national army to suspend the peace and initiate hostilities.

At that point causes for the new outbreak of violence were rapidly forgotten. By March 1863 there was no doubt that the Peñaloza rebellion endangered Mitre's entire project of national unification. The uprising was not limited to a few thousand poorly armed gauchos from La Rioja and Catamarca; on the contrary, it mushroomed into a popular uprising across the Mediterranean provinces.[48] Mitre learned that Peñaloza, in his private correspondence, had urged Urquiza to lead the provinces of the Littoral into open rebellion. It was Peñaloza's hope that Urquiza's troops in the east, in conjunction with his own in the north, would be able to restore the vanquished Federalist Party to prominence and deliver a resounding defeat to the ambitious liberal leadership of Buenos Aires. Urquiza, however, demonstrated his continuing commitment to Mitre's plan of national consolidation by turning these letters promptly over to the Buenos Aires leader.

By April 1863 Mitre's views about Peñaloza had hardened considerably. His personal letter to Sarmiento would be interpreted by supporters as a cautious call for legality and moderation; his detractors would interpret those same words as a discrete call for extermination:

It is my desire that you carry out in La Rioja a policing function. La Rioja is a nest of robbers that threatens the neighboring provinces; its government, in disarray, provides no protection for its citizenry or for property. By labeling the *montoneros* as robbers, without granting them the honor of considering them members of the political opposition, and without elevating their pillaging to the status of reactions, what has to be done is very simple: you will simply move into the danger zone, you will simply carry out policing actions.[49]

This vague language has served Mitre well, for there are certain things that a head of state, mindful of the opinion of posterity, should not put into writing.

Sarmiento and the Uruguayan colonels, with these orders from Mitre, led Buenos Aires troops against El Chacho's campesino army. According to Sarmiento, Mitre's instructions authorized "a war to the death." It was not a "civil war" allowing for prisoners of war; it was, instead, a war against "vandals or pirates," in which the defenders of the social order were justified in killing their opponents whenever the opportunity presented itself.[50]

Meanwhile, El Chacho invaded Córdoba in July 1863—an action that caused a general panic. Paunero's response was efficient and decisive; his victory in the battle of Las Playas (The beaches) resulted in 300 deaths and 40 wounded to Peñaloza loyalists as opposed to only 14 deaths and 20 wounded to nationalist ranks. Sarmiento instructed Mitre's colonels to speed ahead with the onslaught: "Sandes has marched upon San Luis. He's eager to be sent to La Rioja to give a sound whipping to el Chacho. What regulations should be followed in this emergency? If he goes, let him go. If he kills people, simply keep quiet about it. [The people of La Rioja] are biped animals in such a pittiful physical state that I don't know what would be achieved if we treated them any different."[51]

The results of this terrible campaign are the stuff of history: the victory of Porteño forces in a series of battles; El Chacho's unsuccessful attack against the San Juan militia commanded by Sarmiento; and the dispersal of Peñaloza's *montonera* troops, his refuge in the small La Riojan town of Olta, and his surprise capture and brutal execution on November 12 by Major Irrazábal.

Sarmiento's well-known response to this extralegal execution was totally in keeping with his exalted furor: "I have applauded the measures taken, especially the style [of] their execution. If the head of that inveterate scoundrel had not been cut off and paraded publicly, then the scum of that province would not have quieted down in months."[52] Years later generational colleague Vicente F. López would compare Sarmiento's bloodthirsty profile with Rosas's paid assassins:

The head of El Chacho, stuck on the end of lance and exhibited in the plaza of Olta, demonstrated to the people there what was meant by the words culture, civilization, and humanity; and those who perpetrated the act kept on pretending that they felt horror before the spectacle of the the barbarisms committed by the crude montonera horsemen.

But if the author of *Civilización y Barbarie* copied from Rosas's hired thugs in piercing the head of a fallen enemy chief with a pike and exhibiting it in a plaza, he wins a prize for originality in the way he treated the wife of El Chacho. That poor woman, only on account of her being the wife of Peñaloza, was subjected to a series of vexations and the most unworthy treatment.[53]

Mitre, as head of state who was responsible for upholding the constitution, did little to punish those responsible for the extrajudicial execution.[54] His minister of the interior, Guillermo Rawson, did call Sarmiento to account for an alleged abuse of authority, when the latter, in his capacity as governor, had declared a state of siege before invading Peñaloza forces. But, in actual fact that issue was only indirectly related to the circumstances surrounding Peñaloza's brutal death and has largely obscured this more important issue. Although Mitre publicly criticized the form of Peñaloza's execution, he privately congratulated Sarmiento for having orchestrated a "death blow to the montonera, and for having saved the province from the claws of El Chacho and his rabble; and if any of his remaining followers are tenatiously and actively pursued, as it is to be expected, then we will obtain the complete pacification of La Rioja and the total dissolution of the montoneras."[55] However, toward the end of December when Mitre realized the furor that the brutal execution was causing throughout the country, he expressed to Sarmiento a mild note of disapproval.[56] Mitre was always careful to project the image of statesman untouched by the factional disputes of his lieutenants. Sarmiento's direct association with liberalism's highly unpopular policies in the interior, in addition to his overt challenge to the Mitre government's ruling over the application of state of siege, were the primary factors that contributed to Mitre appointing him ambassador to the United States and thereby removing him temporarily from the national scene.

REPORTING THE CIVIL WAR IN THE INTERIOR

News about the savage tactics used by the *proconsuls* of the Buenos Aires armies (a word that derogatorily compared the Uruguayan and Chilean field commanders to the foreign-born generals of the Imperial Roman Army) against the impoverished followers of El Chacho spread across the interior provinces, transforming the surprise and disappointment of Urquiza Loyalists and long-time Federalists into outright anger.

The venerated seventy-year old leader, named by Urquiza as general of the nation because of his distinguished military exploits during the civil wars and then for his loyal support after Caseros, enjoyed near universal respect throughout the interior; he was truly "a valued son of the Homeland."[57] The sordid circumstances of his extrajudicial execution and beheading obscenely clashed with his own proverbial reputation for magnanimity, generosity, and abnegation. Also disturbing was the miserable treatment afforded to Peñaloza's wife and child in the months after his murder.[58] And what could be said about the national leaders who openly or tacitly approved of such vengeful measures?

News also spread about the brutal treatment of individuals or dissident groups that were suspected of having collaborated with Peñaloza. A pattern was evolving: in battle after battle Buenos Aires's troops demonstrated a thirst for bloody vengeance against the vanquished Federalist troops that modeled the worst atrocities in the country's tragic history. Nationalist troops blatantly disregarded the practice of Urquiza who, since 1852, had pardoned those adversaries conquered in battle. In contrast the leaders of the Buenos Aires forces, upon emerging victorious, executed prisoners and confiscated or destroyed the properties of surviving family members. José Hernández's words of bitter sarcasm would be repeated endlessly throughout the interior: "The party that invokes the Enlightenment, decency, and progress, ends up perforating its enemies with daggar thrusts."[59] The high number of federalist casualties in Cañada de Gómez, Las Playas, Villamayor, Quinteros, Yatay, Salinas, and la Florida was evidence of a definite pattern and not merely of excesses committed by a few overly zealous commanders. The Buenos Aires *proconsuls* apparently had received written instructions to perform "exemplary" executions and to show no mercy with the prisoners and the wounded.[60]

Informed readers throughout the country were familiar with the terrible lesson learned by Peñaloza after signing the 1862 treaty at La Banderita. Buenos Aires's troops, in total disregard for humanitarian principles and whatever nationalist sentiment uniting opposing factions, had executed all the federalist troops captured in battle. The official report of Colonel Sandes, after the battle of Las Salinas, substantiated that death to prisoners taken in battle by the *degüello*, or throat-slitting, was done in accordance with the instructions received from the high command:

> Among the prisoners were to be found Sargent-Major Cicerón Quiroga, Captain Policarpo Lucero, Major Carmelo Rojas, Lieutenants Amoroso Molina, Ignacio Bilbao, Juan N. Vallejo and ensigns Ramón Gutiérrez and Juan de Dios Videla. All [of] them had been thrust through by bayonets, in accordance with the orders given by Your Excellency, in order that their exemplary pun-

ishment, performed according to the law, might deter others from rising up and threatening the public tranquility.[61]

The Buenos Aires commanders had their justification for these terrorist tactics. First, there was the precedent of more than two generations of civil conflict in the pampas where the *degüello* was commonplace and cruelty often knew no limit. Second, although his apologists portrayed El Chacho in humanistic colors, Sarmiento and the nationalist troops knew firsthand the great dangers of skirmishes or guerrilla conflict with Peñaloza's *montonera* loyalists: one either became a dehumanized fighting animal, or one learned to live with fear in anticipation of the enemy's next surprise attack. Third, even though the treatment of war prisoners by El Chacho was far more humanitarian than that afforded by other military leaders, his foes surely remembered the bloody beheading of liberals Avellaneda, Acha, and Castelli in recent years. Fourth, the stabbing death of Colonel Sandes only weeks earlier had shocked liberal commanders; fifth, the more hardened liberal combatants probably were enraged over the generous legal treatment that Mitre was disposed to guarantee for Clavero, the assassin of Sarmiento's lifelong friend, Aberastain. And last, the extraordinary resiliency of the Peñaloza movement, which continued to flare up even after several stinging defeats, convinced many that only an exemplary death of that leader would bring the bloody civil conflict to an end. For all of these reasons, Major Irrazábal might have believed his methods of dealing with Peñaloza to be justified, and Governor Sarmiento would have agreed, at least in part.

Ironically the people of Buenos Aires were hardly aware of the bloodbath that was being implemented throughout the interior in the name of the "Party representing Liberty." The near absence of commentary about those events in the writings and private correspondence of Juan María Gutiérrez, V. F. López, and Félix Frías, that is, those individuals who continued to be sympathetic to an Alberdian perspective and who might have reacted critically to the Porteño rendition of events in the interior, was striking. Indeed the greater part of the news that did get printed in Buenos Aires was hardly the type to elicit sympathy on behalf of Peñaloza and his followers. This was because the local press was still dominated by Velez Sarsfield, the Varela brothers, and other extremist voices who continued to urge harsh measures against the holdovers of *rosismo*. Their reports highlighted the "barbarian" nature of the uprisings and the attacks by "robbers" and "ransackers." In addition Sarmiento, who was Mitre's man of confidence at the scene of those uprisings, had by then won their confidence; the Porteño public knew that Sarmiento's excesses in words or deeds were surely committed on their own behalf. Finally there was Mitre, their leader, who at the time was enjoying unchallenged prestige and whose public image of equanimity had conditioned a positive reaction among his followers. In conclusion Peñaloza and his cause were destined to have few if any sympathizers in Buenos Aires:

> With the exception of Entre Ríos, where the newspapers—and not all of them—express federalist sentiments, it was difficult to find a single anti-Mitre page in the whole of Buenos Aires or the interior. One could say that the harmony enjoyed by Argentines was complete: only in the most isolated of cases did there appear a notice about *montoneros, barbarians, El Chacho's hordes,* that affirmed the existence of a reality completely unrepresented by the liberal press.[62]

Mitre, in short order, would assume the status of protagonist in this monopolistic monologue; he would found his own newspaper, *La nación argentina* (The Argentine nation), in which he would defend and justify his acts as President. Impartial observers were already drawing the distinction between two Argentinas: the one of lived events, and the one depicted in the country's "official" liberal press.

In this environment of censorship and biased reporting, Carlos Guido Spano, Olegario Andrade, Miguel Navarro Viola, Estanislao Zeballos, Agustín de Vedia, Francisco Fernández, and José Hernández were to play an important role. These individuals constituted the nucleus of what the liberal establishment would later call Argentina's "second romantic generation," a name that hardly suggests the political and polemical nature of their literary and political initiation.[63] Added to this list was Luis Alberto de Herrera, a representative voice among Uruguayan Blanco Party defenders. To this second generation fell the mission of recording the tragic struggles of federalist militants across Argentina's interior provinces who beat a steady retreat before the advance of Buenos Aires's armies and the task of combatting the official histories emanating from Buenos Aires with their own, sometimes lyrical, testimonies of federalism's final tragic days. These writers and publicists accepted the task of educating the people of the interior in the face of the news blackout or the disinformation campaigns that their adversaries promoted.

Polemic: José Hernández versus Sarmiento

José Hernández was undoubtedly the most talented of this young generation of writer-militants. Within a decade the first part of his widely disseminated poem, *El gaucho Martín Fierro* (1872) would lyrically capture the pain and tragedy of a rural population retreating before the expansive, oppressive urban culture. But in late November 1863 his initiation into public life was as author of a series of articles that passionately denounced the brutal slaying of Peñaloza. These articles were immediately united in book form under the title, *Rasgos biográficos del general Angel V. Peñaloza* (Biographical features of General Angel V. Peñalosa); since its 1875 reprinting the work has carried the shorter title, *Vida del Chacho* (Life of El Chacho).

The work's initial section (approximately eleven pages) called attention to discrepancies in the official reports treating Peñaloza's death (these discrepancies were subsequently corrected). Hernández also emphasized the act of betrayal on the part of an ex-Chacho loyalist that made the assassination possible—a theme later popularized in much of the oral poetry and folklore treating the event.

The second and final section, about twenty pages long, presented a brief biography of Peñaloza. Hernández traced Peñaloza's rise to prominence as lieutenant to Facundo Quiroga, Lavalle, and Lamadrid; Loyalist of San Juan Governor Benavides; and finally supporter of Confederate President Urquiza. He portrayed Peñaloza as "a brave, generous, and gentlemanly *caudillo* . . . he has the type of heart that has never known hatred or fear, has never held a grudge, and has never sought revenge."[64] Hernández argued that the savage treatment by his enemies of this noble, generous leader revealed the true character of the Liberal Party that was consolidating its bloody predominance throughout the country. In this regard one of his most memorable statements became part of the catechism of federalism's continuing rage and resentment: "The savage unitarians are dancing in the streets."

A new and surprising theme that this short book introduced to the discourse of embattled federalism was the indictment of Urquiza. Hernández, who only months before had been a Urquiza loyalist, now unerringly predicted that the former Confederation president would never again defend the federalist cause through arms:

> Urquiza will never again lift arms in its defense. He can avoid lending his sense of personal responsibility to the struggle, if he so chooses, or like an innocent lamb he can give his body over to the knives of the assassins who are waiting for the moment to give him a fatal blow; but he cannot prohibit that act of revenge from occurring, but he cannot contain for much longer the rush of indignation that bursts forth from the heart of the people.[65]

The uncanny prediction of Urquiza's future assassination erred in only one detail: the authors of the future crime would be disgruntled federalists instead of enraged untarians.

Hernández's book had an instant and fervorous reception with a wide sector of the population of the interior, who quickly elevated Peñaloza to the status of martyr for the fallen federalist cause. The myth Hernández helped to perpetuate of the generous La Riojan leader obviously spoke to their psychological needs of the moment. With their cause defeated in battle and their supporters either killed, dispersed, or in disarray, they eagerly grabbed at this positive version of the *montonera* and its maximum patriarch. This new literary symbol fueled their social and political imagination; it helped them to deal with their disappointment over the rapid dissolution of the federalist project and the horror they experienced upon witnessing firsthand the inhumanity of their new liberal conquerors.

The report that Sarmiento immediately sent to Mitre about the Peñaloza execution provoked criticism on all sides. The major issue was the extrajudicial execution of Peñaloza, a general of the National Army, who was obviously not a common criminal. General Paunero and Minister of War Gelly y Obes charged that Sarmiento had intentionally placed himself above the law in ordering Irrazábal to perform that act. (Sarmiento seemed to confirm this accusation several months later when he wrote that he would have been the last to embrace the highly impractical "new legal forms in favor of individual guarantees" and that he wished to save the country from the "ugly spectacle" of a drawn-out public trial.[66]) Rawson also criticized Sarmiento's declaration of state of siege in the Andean provinces. These, among other factors, led to Sarmiento's renunciation of the governorship of San Juan in April of the following year and his departure for Chile and then to the United States shortly thereafter. But the issue of his role in the war against El Chacho continued to provoke angry polemic. This accounted, in part, for his decision, while in the United States, to defend himself in writing. Such was the origin of his long biography, *El Chacho: último caudillo de la montonera de los llanos* (El Chacho: last *caudillo* of the montonera of the plains—1866).

The work was vintage Sarmiento. Like *Campaña en el Ejército Grande* (Campaign in the Great Army) and *Vida de Aberastain* (Life of Aberastain), his text generously copied from the existing body of correspondence, proclamations, and official reports in presenting a one-sided view of those events that already were the stuff of history and legend. Like *Facundo* and *Aldao*, his *El Chacho* combined biography with ethnography and sociology as a means of substantiating his politicized thesis that the *caudillo* protagonist represented the most retrograde of tendencies. For the uninformed reader the work assumed an aura of impartiality as Sarmiento-author carefully unfolded the setting, introduced the actors, and discussed in third-person narrative the acts and decisions of Sarmiento-governor who had been a protagonist in those events. However, for the reader informed about the issues in question, the work was transparent in its objective of rationalizing and justifying the author's own role in those controversial events.

The work revealed that Sarmiento's world vision of a national universe divided between the antagonistic forces of civilization and barbarism had changed little, if at all, in the intervening two decades since his 1845 masterpiece. Or, more generously considered, the work revealed the romantic, literary quality of his thought in its reduction of a multifaceted historical actor into his one-dimensional literary protagonist. Sarmiento depicted Peñaloza as "agent of disorder," "perturber" of the peace, protector of bandits, and epitome of immorality. As in *Facundo* the writer took pains to link his novelized protagonist to the "sterile" natural environment of the Llanos, which was underpopulated and underdeveloped because of its centuries-ingrained indigenous traditions. Although the work is of questionable historical value, it does reveal much about the author himself. Ricardo Rojas's appraisal of Sarmiento, the military commander who waged the extermination war against El Chacho and his followers, was just as applicable to Sarmiento, the author, who chronicled those events: "Such is the disconcerting psychology of this man whose sensitivity bordered on raptures of a primitive being, even though his mind illuminated noble ideals."[67]

One aspect of Sarmiento's world vision that now occupied foreground status was the *social* configuration of the Peñaloza conflict. Sarmiento returned to the standard thesis of his generation that the countryside, by accosting the city, threatened to put asunder the civilizing project so arduously promoted by the educated, urban element of the country. Added to this was his emphatic description of the struggle as pitting society's "haves" against the "have-nots." The conflict originated

> in a conspiracy of dark-skinned faces, of ignorant masses who scandalously terrorize the countryside, or in the basest social classes of the cities, without ideas, without newspapers, without audible means of expression; . . . whatever happens among peons and country folk does not reach the ears of the lettered society that lives of other ideas and interests.[68]

Sarmiento correctly noted that in the provinces affected by the struggle, whatever "written declaractions" emanating from the federalists were "rational or intelligible . . . because nowhere did there participate men of a a certain level of education. This is the most plebian, barbarian movement that has taken place to date in these countries."[69] In conclusion, he depicted it as a war between the educated city dwellers and illiterate, impoverished rural workers. The former had the providencial obligation to defend themselves and their glorious cause of Progress from the threats mounted by the latter: "It fell to the common people, in the name of human dignity, to save the civilization that was threatened by these shameful uprisings by the most backward sector of the population who gave total vent to their own destructive instincts."[70]

Reacting to these words, Manuel Gálvez was wrong in stating that the author "hasn't understood, or has not wanted to understand" that the conflict was a form of "social war" between La Rioja's rural workers and the invading forces of the city.[71] But Gálvez's words did express his and others' discomfort before Sarmiento's condemnation of rural culture. In the *Cartas quillotanas* (Letters from Quillota) of 1853, Alberdi had criticized *Facundo* for a similar reason: Sarmiento's mistaken argument about civilization's origins in the cities ignored the fact that Buenos Aires itself had produced some of the most "barbaric" and cruel acts in the region's history.

Sarmiento's disdain for lower-class rural culture went hand-in-hand with his strong racist and ethnic prejudices against the bronze-skinned gauchos, *mestizo* campesinos, and the Indians of the Llanos. We have criticized these ideas earlier. Clearly illustrated here was the man's deepseated fear of the lower classes. For the enraged activist of the mid 1860s, the mark of poverty, the garb of the rural proletariat, and the ignorance resulting from a lack of school education were the equivalent of the sinister birthmark of Cain. Sarmiento's condemnation of human beings because of a marginal social and economic situation cannot be passed over; there is no apology possible. The chapter of Sarmiento's career that had to do with El Chacho Peñaloza is undoubtedly the darkest. It is a small consolation to acknowledge that when the man would return to Argentina as president-elect five years later, his orientations, if not his ideas, would be substantially changed.

MITRE: URUGUAY AND THE WAR WITH PARAGUAY

Mitre's closest advisors celebrated these initial victories over their long-time federalist foes. With internal opposition well on the way to being vanquished, they turned their attention to Uruguay and Paraguay, the only remaining vestiges of federalist power in the region. In this, were they the victims of self-delusion? The liberal circle controlled the press, and the foremost intellectuals and writers of the country shared their biases on behalf of progress and civilization. However they did not count on the widespread protests and uprisings throughout the country that their interventions in those two neighboring countries would provoke. Added to that was the protracted struggle in Paraguay that caused thousands of Argentine casualties in addition to the massacre of Paraguay's majority population. The Mitre presidency, which had begun on such a propitious note, ended—in Alberdi's words—with the triumph of the principles of death, dissolution, and rebellion.[72]

Briefly considered here are the major events. In April 1863—only days after El Chacho's letter to Mitre announcing his suicidal rebellion—Venancio Flores, a general in Mitre's army and head of the Uruguayan Colorado (liberal) Party, crossed into his country and ignited an insurrection against the Blanco government. Shortly thereafter the newly installed liberal administration in Brazil, with expansionist politics, came to the assistance of the Colorado insurgents. Then began the Mitre administration's politics of duplicity. Although steadfastly proclaiming neutrality, its secret support for the Brazilian intervention included the supply of munitions to the joint Colorado-Brazilian forces in its siege of Paysandú.[73] Although Mitre was always careful to avoid the direct association of these unpopular policies with his own name, an abundant documentation substantiates the existence of secret agreements and the overt involvement of the leading members of his cabinet.[74] Tempers arose across the country, because many Argentines considered Uruguay, with close historical ties, to be their sister country; Brazil, in contrast, was the country's historical rival on the subcontinent, in spite of moments of cooperation.

In Entre Ríos, the Flores invasion triggered angry demonstrations among federalist loyalists still smarting from recent defeats. They felt close links with the Blanco Party in power in Montevideo that had supported the objectives of the Confederation and had provided a haven for federalist exiles. In September 1863 Waldino Urquiza, son of the ex-president, crossed the Río Uruguay at the head of a small force intent upon assisting the beleaguered Blanco government. The widespread anti-Mitre sentiment in Entre Ríos, now fueled by its pro-Uruguayan militancy and its historical suspicion of Brazilian intentions, peaked in October when militant groups were on the verge of rising up to renew their war with Buenos Aires. All that was lacking was the word of their standard bearer, Justo José Urquiza.[75]

The elder Urquiza, however, was of another mind. He continued in his efforts to quell rebellious sentiment in Entre Ríos and steer the province on the path of peace and conciliation. In April 1864 he assured the victory of a new provincial leadership that supported his overtures to Buenos Aires.[76] Throughout the next year he overruled his own pro-Blanco sentiments and lent personal prestige to the task of containing the furor of his fellow Entrerrians after Brazil's invasion of Uruguay, the Brazilian-Colorado seige and mortar bombing of Paysandú, and Flores's victory in Montevideo. After Paraguay's invasion of Corrientes in April 1865, he closed ranks with Mitre but failed to contain the mutinous sentiment of provincial troops when they were ordered to join Brazil in marching upon Paraguay. This last gesture marked the beginning of the end to his political influence in Entre Ríos. His relative and former aide, Ricardo López Jordán, wrote to him at this time:

> You call us up to fight in Paraguay. Never, General: those people are our brothers. Call us up to fight against Porteños or Brazilians. We are ready. They are our enemies. We still hear in our ears the canons of Paysandú. This, I'm sure, is the true sentiment of the *entrerriana* people.[77]

Reasons for Urquiza's conciliatory position with Mitre up through about 1862 have already been discussed. After that date, through at least 1866, new factors came into play. Urquiza had steadfastly attempted to steer a middle course between the pro-Uruguayan, pro-Paraguayan sentiments of his fellow Entrerrians and Buenos Aires's pursuit of hegemony over the nation. As months passed this middle position became harder to sustain given the rising exasperation of opinion leaders in his province, least of whom was his son, Waldino, in response to the emergence of Buenos Aires's anti-Blanco and anti-López politics with respect to Uruguay and Paraguay. Urquiza, meanwhile, continued counseling the strictest neutrality for the country before Brazil's developing hostilities with Uruguay and Paraguay and sternly censored any idea of an "odious alliance" that might involve Argentina in those affairs.[78]

In all this Urquiza was obviously the victim of Mitre's deceptions as well as his own wishful thinking. On this first point the record is clear. The secret agreement between members of Mitre's cabinet (totally independent of the National Congress) and Brazilian governmental representatives was reached sometime in May 1864 for united action against the Blanco government of Uruguay; this agreement was formalized in writing on August 22, 1864.[79] Yet as late as February 17, 1865, Mitre was still arguing in his correspondence with Urquiza that any alliance between Brazil and Argentina was, in his opinion, unacceptable and not in the best interest of the country.[80] Urquiza apparently accepted Mitre's assurances at face value. While other federalist voices were denouncing Buenos Aires's complicity with the Flores insurrection and its passive support for Brazil's intervention, Urquiza stubbornly continued defending the neutrality of the Mitre government.[81] At this time he was intent upon neutralizing Porteño hostility toward himself with the apparent motive of creating the conditions conducive to his own future election as the country's president. Later, documentation would be published about another factor possibly contributing to Urquiza's continued acquiescence to Buenos Aires's evolving politics, that is, his lucrative financial dealings with both Brazilian and Porteño interests. Most important was the deal arranged by wealthy Brazilian banker, the baron of Mauá, between October and December 1863, for Urquiza to supply the Brazilian army with thirty thousand horses.[82]

Explanations differ about the reasons for the Argentine government's involvement in the Paraguayan war. All sides agree that Solano López sorely misjudged the reactions of the Brazilian and Argentine leaders, and then the respective military potential of those two countries', when he declared war on the first and invaded a border town of the second. Few Argentines argued over the legitimacy of the Mitre administration's subsequent declaration of war. Far more polemical was the country's further involvement that led to the widely protested alliance with Brazil and then the massive slaughter of Paraguayan troops and citizens over the course of the next six years. Although Estanislao S. Zeballos—later followed by historians Zinny and Cárcano[83]—was to describe a situation of regional instability due to Paraguay's massive military buildup, the Buenos Aires leadership at the time did not believe that López and his armies offered a credible threat to Argentina's territorial integrity.[84] Argentina's reasons for involvement were primarily ideological rather than geopolitical. For the members of Mitre's cabinet, Paraguay was one of the two surviving foci of federalist power and influence in the region (the other was Urquiza's Entre Ríos) that had to be eliminated. In the words of Sarmiento, the war against Solano López was justified because his government was the direct heir to the "shocking despotism of Dr. Francia, leader of a laical republic with an indio-Jesuit system."[85] Solano López had to be eliminated because his anachronistic system stood in obscene contradiction to their litany of sacrosanct liberal institutions: free trade, private property, liberty of the press, and importation of European capital and ideas.

Federalist sympathizers, together with revisionist historians, have emphasized wholly different aspects of the Paraguayan experience. According to them, Solano López repeatedly demonstrated his support for the beleaguered Blanco government in Uruguay and interpreted Brazil's invasion as a threat to the equilibrium of the entire region. Solano realized that a Colorado victory in Uruguay would subject his own country to enemies on all sides. Not only did Brazil wish to expand its control over Paraguayan territory, but the liberals in Argentina and Uruguay were hostile to the Paraguayan government as well. Also the British minister in Buenos Aires was making it very clear to all parties concerned that Her majesty's government opposed the trade restrictions that Paraguay applied to British commercial agencies.[86] Federalist ideologues refused to grant due credence to Solano's illusions of imperialist grandeur or territorial expansion. They interpreted Paraguay's military build-up only as a response to Brazilian provocation. According to this analysis Solano's declaration of war against Brazil was a self-defense measure in response to the danger confronting his government after the Colorado defeat in Uruguay.

Urquiza, along with most informed observers from Entre Ríos and Uruguay, accepted this latter explanation almost to the letter. Responding to the authentic and widespread sympathy in his province for Paraguay's predicament and Uruguay's violated sovereignty, in addition to its shared fear of Brazilian territorial ambitions, Urquiza requested official permission from the Mitre administration to permit the transportation of Paraguayan troops across Argentine territory. This, to his way of thinking, would be in line with the country's position of strict neutrality because Brazilian naval forces had already been allowed passage along the Río Uruguay to carry out its attack of Paysandú. This request, repeated weeks later in a letter from Solano López to Mitre, was denied. One reason for the Mitre administration's denial was that it already had secretly pacted to collaborate with Brazil in its belligerencies against Uruguay.[87]

Paraguay was not named in that pact but Argentina's alliance against Uruguay was implicitly directed against that former country whose government considered the invasion of Uruguay by foreign troops to be a bona fide cause for declaring war on Brazil. At this point, some contemporaneous observers criticized Solano López for his "impatience."[88] Others understood his reaction in the light of a defensive strategy of attacking first instead of succumbing to slow strangulation;[89] still others point to López's "political folly"[90] in not understanding that Federalist opinion leaders such as Urquiza and José and Rafael Hernández would shelve intraparty rivalries and support the Mitre administration in a moment of unprovoked aggression. Nevertheless most of the Argentine commentators who were sympathetic to Solano's predicament admit his lack of vision and mistaken leadership in what followed, that is, declaration of war of the Paraguayan congress against Argentina and that country's invasion of Corrientes in mid-April. Argentina's formal declaration of war against Paraguay followed in short order. The War of the Triple Alliance (Argentina, Brazil, and Uruguay against Paraguay) had begun.

Mitre's Argentina: "Dissolution and Rebellion"

Mitre vastly miscalculated two essential issues: first, the degree of unpopularity that his pro-Blanco, pro-Brazilian, and anti-Paraguayan politics would provoke throughout the country; and second, the dedication of the Paraguayan people to their leader and the depth of their resolve to resist the threat from their enemies. The first miscalculation led to widespread mutinies of provincial troops ordered to the Paraguayan war, massive uprisings across the interior with the resulting massacres of Argentine citizens by national troops, and the hateful imposition of a state of siege throughout the country with the censorship, imprisonment, and human rights violations that this entailed. The second miscalculation led, in the final result, to the death through battle and disease of thousands upon thousands of Argentine troops and perhaps half of the Paraguayan population.

Here is a brief chrolonology of the events up through 1867. In April 1865 the Argentine government declared war against Paraguay and began recruitment efforts across the country. At the beginning of July, whole divisions of Entrerrian troops deserted in protest of the unpopular war, forcing Urquiza, their battlefield commander, to disband temporarily the provincial force. There was a second mass desertion of Entrerrian troops at the beginning of November, even under the threat of Urquiza's most severe punishment. During those same months revolts and desertions from other provincial contingents bound for service in Paraguay occurred in Córdoba, Santiago del Estero, and Tucumán. In November 1866 a force of 280 men recruited for the war against Paraguay overthrew the provincial governor of Mendoza, motivating the national government to order the first of another round of bloody interventions. A month later Colonel Felipe Varela announced his rebellion against the national government under the banner of peace toward Paraguay, friendship with Argentina's sister nations, and strict observance of the principles of the May Revolution a half-century earlier. The rebellion quickly spread to almost all of the interior provinces. After a massive effort on the part of the national army, which precipitated the hurried return of Mitre from Paraguay at the head of twenty-five hundred crack troops, Varela was defeated in the Battle of Pozo de Vargas (Vargas's spring) in April 1867, and insurgent activity was snuffed out by October. The national government imposed a state of siege in the initial months of 1867 that remained in force for nearly a year. Militants were persecuted, newspapers were closed, and writers and journalists who held critical views of national policy were incarcerated.

Tragic civil strife returned to the interior, this time between disciplined national troops and poorly armed federalists. Repression by the conquering army was denounced. One writer, who suffered imprisonment because of his dissident opinions, called attention to the intolerable conditions of the state of siege:

> Lives, liberties, possessions: all suffered during that long period of transgressions. And with the war continuing without any hope of ending, the state of siege became onerous and intolerable. [. . .] During General Mitre's presidency these abuses were directed against even the best minds of the capital city.[91]

The war itself was also cause for angry criticism. Mitre's boastful promise of victory after three months of heroic struggle was sadly mistaken. The end of the war would only occur in 1870, two years into Sarmiento's administration. It is calculated that of Paraguay's population of one million five hundred thousand at the beginning of the conflict, only two-hundred fifty thousand survived. Estimates of Argentine casualties due to battle and disease were around thirty thousand, with perhaps an equal number of victims for Brazil. The terrible curse to Argentina would continue even after the trumpets of its sad victory had sounded on the plains of Paraguay: yellow fever, born by Argentina's returning soldiers, scourged whole cities in the worst epidemic in the nation's history.

One other sad legacy of Mitre's war was the country's resultant indebtedness to British banking interests. The British Crown had been a silent protagonist in the Triple Alliance. Its representative in Argentina, Edward Thornton, had encouraged the leaders of the three allied countries and had facilitated the financing of their interventionalist plans. It can be argued that although Great Britain played no active role in the entire struggle, it emerged as the only clear winner. Its goal of opening Paraguay to British investment and trade was achieved, as well as its long-term objective of protecting the integrity of Uruguayan territory from annexation by either Argentina or Brazil. Furthermore the huge loans granted by English banking houses to fund the costly military campaigns and reconstruction of all the countries concerned assured a high profile for British interests in all commercial and governmental affairs in the Rioplatense region well into the next century.[92]

Further complaints were launched against Mitre throughout the interior provinces because of his party's incursions into the practices of electoral fraud. If Mitre's intention was to bring about a radical change in the political composition of the differing provinces, then his methods were heavy-handed and manipulative. In province after province the state of siege gave full reign to the imposition of unpopular governments that would faithfully follow Mitre's initiatives. Nicasio Oroño, governor of Santa Fe, angrily wrote to Mitre at the time:

It would seem that you were little affected by the many violent revolutions that throughout the period of your government continued to bleed the country. La Rioja and Catamarca, Córdoba, Salta, and Tucumán, San Luis, Mendoza, San Juan, and Corrientes, each of these names conjures up memories of movements that, although ignited by local circumstances, were also acts expressing a resistance to to the very enlightened government headed by you.[93]

Carlos D'Amico, cabinet head for the Province of Buenos Aires during this period, was equally condemnatory: "If we pass from the provincial dynasties to the succession of power in even the National Government, we find in the latter, during Mitre's administration, a similar abuse of republican practices."[94]

The historical record is clear about the deep disillusionment of the country with Mitre—with the exception of his closed circle of liberal defenders in Buenos Aires and in the capital cities of the interior—as his term as president came to a close. The candidacy of the *provinciano* Sarmiento, in fact, arose in great part as a protest against the Porteño orientation of Mitre, and Mitre's bitter opposition to Sarmiento was predictable. The fact that Elizalde—presumed to be Mitre's favored successor—had been virtually defeated even before the final voting was indisputable evidence of the unpopularity of the administration's alliance with Brazil and its conduction of the war with Paraguay. Adding to the discontent in the interior was the national army's intervention in Corrientes led by Mitre's brother, General Emilio Mitre, that many feared would bring about a repression even more severe than the conflict it pretended to suffocate.[95] One of Mitre's critics called attention to the fact that not one day passed during the entire six years of his presidency when the country enjoyed peace without social turbulence.[96] Given the state of continual conflict and uprisings throughout the country and given the accumulated effects of heavy casualties and indebtedness that resulted from the very unpopular war, public unease was high. One newspaper wrote, "Will we be happier with the new government? This is the question that all are posing. Much is hoped from the government of Mr. Sarmiento. We hope to God that we won't suffer continued disillusionment on his account."[97]

Criticisms of Mitre's character were also beginning to be heard. At first many people had been captivated by his florid rhetoric, but actions now spoke louder than words. Sarmiento, upon witnessing Mitre's efforts to preserve influence through any possible means after the conclusion of his presidency, called him "simpleton . . . [without] moral sense . . . his only achievement was to figure as the most recent of generals and politicians who have controlled the country."[98] Another former liberal supporter, Juan Carlos Gómez, lashed out at Mitre because of the moral bankruptcy of his administration's politics; an additional concern was the disastrous condition of the country which made it ripe for a resurgence of federalism. Juan María Gutiérrez had also experienced a growing bitterness over Mitre's destructive policies with regard to Brazil and Paraguay. With the benefit of another half-decade of observing Mitre's corrosive ambitions in politics and the press, Gutiérrez would later write:

> Bartolomé Mitre is the most ambitious man who has ever existed; he is greatly unaffected by the spilling of blood. There you have the man of principles

who trampled those same principles under his feet when he saw that power and wealth threatened to escape from his and his cronies' hands. . . . Everything else being said, believe me my friend when I tell you that I have never respected the politics of Don Bartolo, his friends or his admirers, and I felt sorry for the man on account of his vanity and pedantic attitude. . . . It is truly pitiful to see him sinking to the point of crawling through the mud— this, the same man who is acclaimed by a sizable portion of my countrymen as a wise man and a hero. It is truly a shame that he is neither one nor the other. Now, he is only the most recent scoundrel in our parade of political scoundrels; in democracies, garbage floats ot the top in accordance with the law of gravity.[99]

These opinions of Sarmiento, Gómez, and Gutiérrez were wholly endorsed by Paul Groussac, writing a few decades later, who reproached Mitre for "the impotent fury of a leader who has destroyed his armed contingency by leading it from defeat to defeat. . . . The blood of the Republic that was spilt on account of his banal fraseology and verbose rhetoric has not yet dried." Mitre and others converted "the pen into an instrument of terror or an arm of revenge . . . his hatreds are as black as Africa and nothing appeases them once his vanity has been pricked . . . he is a pathological case."[100] This was the image of Mitre that has been recorded for posterity by some of his most respected contemporaries.

On the basis of the above paragraphs, the negative image of Mitre that has predominated in several different groups is wholly understandable. For Uruguayan and Paraguayan nationalists, Mitre is remembered as a master of duplicity who was careful to cultivate a magnanimous image in "external forms," but the policies he actually pursued reeked of sectarianism and hatred. Mitre, "unmoved by grand sentiments," was the cynical architect of the butchery of a neighboring country.[101] According to his nemesis Alberdi, Mitre was "the Tartuff of the principles of civilization and liberty" in word; in deed he was a dangerous, egotistical warmonger, a *caudillo in topcoat,* who relied on the army to suppress true democracy violently, ruin the peace of the country, and destroy liberty in favor of a new social and political system that was *antipopular* and *antipueblo.*[102]

Julio Victorica fittingly described the tragic gap separating the Buenos Aires leader's words and deeds. Victorica had served briefly in the ministry of foreign relations in the latter months of the Confederation and then as private secretary to General Urquiza during the 1860s. He recounted that Mitre, after reputedly proclaiming that there would be neither victors nor vanquished, "threw legions of soldiers against the weak provinces of the interior in order to subject them; those legions, captained by foreigners, left desolation and extermination in their wake."[103] Another commentator provides a summary for all of the above:

"There never before had existed in the Littoral or the interior a resentment as accentuated against Buenos Aires, as that existing in the decade of the 1860s."[104] This is hardly an exaggeration. That anger and hatred has been imprinted onto the collective memory and preserved in the region's folklore; traces of that historical bitterness survive even to the present day.

A DIVIDED COUNTRY

By the end of his presidential term in 1868, Mitre's name evoked feelings of disillusionment and hatred across the interior provinces. In Alberdi's caustic words the principal sin of Mitre's inner circle was their unfettered egotism. They had continually demonstrated an inability to comprehend or appreciate anything outside the confines of their own group or class: "His political party revolves around his own person, his politics, and the people dependent upon him for their daily bread."[105] Their type of "combat-line democracy" favored a minority group that was educated and relatively wealthy; it displaced a rival political system that was supported by the less-educated masses of the country who enjoyed fewer material benefits. They achieved this hegemony at no small cost: a bitter social and regional struggle with thousands of victims.

Yet the liberal supporters in Buenos Aires hardly embraced this view. Liberal ideologues dominated the written culture of that city and granted little attention to opinions other than their own. An "official" history had been born. The liberal group's ascent to power accompanied a totally new set of legitimizing myths for which Mitre and Sarmiento were the principal agents and protagonists. Henceforth these new myths would engage in ideological battle with the images corresponding to the social order in the interior that, although militarily defeated, nevertheless continued to thrive. Like his cohort Sarmiento, Mitre was undoubtedly aware of the power of the appropriate public gesture and the magnifying effect of select words spoken in the public plaza, as both their critics and acolytes have repeatedly documented. Mitre's own words as the country's leader were the most eloquent source for the folklore that has arisen on his behalf.

For the first time the country's leaders cultivated a politics whose motor was the information media. They were adroit in the enterprise of cultivating public images, which many times took precedent over truth. In Mitre's correspondence with Urquiza, the cultivated lie or half-truth ably served in his task of carrying out state policy. This was also the case with his administration's treatment of Peñaloza and the pacification of the Andean provinces, as well as their official dealings with Uruguay and Brazil. In many instances words or stated intentions contradicted acts. In the eyes of posterity, Mitre's association with the legacy of Machiavelli, the clever and manipulative prince, is inevitable.

For this reason the function of the press during those eventful years merits close study. Given the social and class divisions in the country, as depicted by Alberdi, it stands to reason that the vast majority of newspaper writers and readers were firm supporters of Mitre's governmental project. Simply stated, what individuals from official circles chose to write was what the Buenos Aires public had the opportunity to know. This accounted for Victorica's observation that the near silence (if not the conspiracy) of the press to hide the truth about the 1865 tragedy of Paysandú caused "great indignation" across country.[106] Córdoba's representative to the National Congress corroborated this opinion when he called attention to the ignorance of his fellow representatives about the causes and terrible effects of the civil struggle then raging across the interior: "They ignore that some provinces have been reduced to rubble; they ignore that many communities enjoying prosperity a few years back have now been reduced to the status of beggars."[107] Guido y Spano also denounced in impassioned tones the complicity of the press with the government's policies in Paraguay: "The writers for the Buenos Aires's press, in their great majority, were like frenzied, dissheveled drunkards jublilantly engaging in a brutal orgy, in the way they tore to pieces the rights of a sister nation."[108]

The government took stern efforts to intimidate or censor the oppositional press. In July 1866, for example, it ordered the closing of *La América* and the imprisonment of its leading writers and publisher.[109] The following year it did the same with the four leading newspapers of Entre Ríos and the oppositional press in Buenos Aires itself.[110] In light of these actions, one understands Estanislao S. Zeballos's severe condemnation that Mitre's most censurable act of tyranny was his attempt to "drown . . . the echoes of four-fifths of public opinion in Argentina."[111]

The written record is incomplete or nonexistent about the semiliterate majority population of the interior and the indignation they felt toward the Mitre administration. Sarmiento, in *Vida del Chacho* (Life of El Chacho), had noted the almost complete absence of newspapers in the entire Province of La Rioja, a condition that probably varied little throughout the interior, with the possible exception of the provincial capitals. As it was liberal interests sympathetic to Mitre's program owned and managed the great majority of newspapers in the interior. At least one case has been reported of the national government granting a generous subsidy to a federalist newspaper in the city of Córdoba. Was its editors' "scarce support" for Felipe Varela's popular insurrection against the pro-

Brazilian and anti-Paraguayan politics of the Mitre administration a direct result of that financial support?[112] In brief Mitre's struggle on behalf of the city, liberal ideals, and progress found a formidable ally in the regional press: to own the written word was to exercise control over the type of news published. This, in turn, empowered the liberals in their quest of elevating their own set of social myths to the position of prominence in the region's cultural discourse.

ALBERDI: NEMESIS OF BUENOS AIRES

Alberdi's guarded optimism in the first few months following Pavón quickly dissolved as evidence accumulated about the violation of rights and the Porteño armies' brutal conquest of the interior. He became convinced that Mitre would correct only the first of what he believed to be the two primary causes for social and political instability in the country, that is, the lack of a strong central authority. But the early acts of the Buenos Aires leader made it abundantly clear that he would only aggravate the second of those fundamental causes of instability: Buenos Aires's monopoly over the country's resources and governing institutions. Alberdi and other learned observers from the interior coincided in their opinion that Mitre's rhetoric of a national politics could not obscure the acts of his administration that aimed at the preservation and consolidation of Buenos Aires's control. In this light Alberdi, as the interior's faithful interpreter, felt compelled to renew his antagonistic role before Buenos Aires initiatives.

During the next decade Alberdi wrote much and published several important pamphlets that circulated widely. But his views now exhibited areas of blindness inextricably linked with profound insight. Some writings demonstrated his customary detachment and impartiality while others were marred by inconsistencies and contradictions. In the opinion of an important biographer, Alberdi did not find himself in the best disposition to perceive correctly the political reality of Argentina because his mind was clouded by the pain he felt over the human suffering experienced in the interior provinces and in relation to the events in Uruguay and Paraguay.[113] According to another biographer an excessive devotion to his homeland accounted for some opinions that bordered on the unjust and for judgments that were skewed at times because of "his overexcited imagination that was flamed by the heat of polemic."[114] Here it is necessary to untangle some of his written statements and reconstruct as nearly as possible Alberdi's views at the time.

A first issue of concern was Alberdi's position with regard to Buenos Aires's scorched-earth campaign against Peñaloza. Since his earliest works his defense of the "great man" or *"caudillo"*—be it Rosas, Urquiza, or Peñaloza (who provided order and stability to society)—was constant. In the 1860s and 1870s, Alberdi returned to this theme in those writings which would be published only after his death. The *"caudillo,"* he argued, was the imperfect representative of a truly democratic sentiment because his prestige was based on a wide popularity among the rural masses. Peñaloza was the best of the lot. In an obvious overstatement Alberdi stated that he was an "angel of goodness" when compared to Facundo Quiroga: "The truth about El Chacho's life is that it revealed not a single act of barbarism; about his death by assassination one could affirm the same."[115] But this did not mean that Alberdi unambiguously supported the rebellion of Peñaloza against Buenos Aires. His position was more complicated than that. David Viñas writes that Alberdi "neither defended nor mythified El Chacho. The latter was, like others, a man of his class, a bourgeois conquistador, and imbued to his roots in the ideology of that class, even though he might have disagreed with some specific aspects of its actions."[116] Alberdi's support for the national state under Roca after 1880—with the corollary stand against anarchistic rebellions of society's marginal areas or groups—makes clear the truth of Viñas's view.

But in the mid-1860s, when it came to the Peñaloza issue, Alberdi must have been tormented by intense contradictions. On the one hand the authoritarian in him silently celebrated the victory of national forces over this and any outbreak of localized violence. Alberdi was definitely a supporter of firm action by the country's newly constituted central government in defense of the principles of security and authority. In addition the positivist in him—as Viñas suggested—celebrated the defeat of the retrograde social, political, and technological values that Peñaloza represented. On the other hand the humanitarian in Alberdi reacted furiously against the directors of that war effort because of their brutal imposition of Porteño priorities over the defeated and demoralized people of the interior. In addition the provincial in him recognized in Peñaloza a folk hero who defended the cause of the people against the unjust foreign policy initiatives of the Porteño oligarchy. These contradictory impulses stung Alberdi deeply; in future publications he would give vent to the rage he felt against Buenos Aires and the utter disgust he held for Mitre. Yet noticeable for its absence in his published writings at the time was any concerted defense of Peñaloza and the rural rebellion of that leader's intrepid followers.

A second area of confusion was Alberdi's advocacy of monarchy and European intervention as remedies for Spanish America's perennial ills of civil war and government by megalomaniac *caudillos*, military leaders, lawyers, and demagogic newspaper writers. These views had their fullest expression in *Del gobierno en Sud-America* (About governing in South America), which was written in the early 1860s but never published during his lifetime. These views undoubtedly corresponded to his disillusionment with Mitre and the latter's clique of national leaders and, *por ende*, the reforms they were carrying out in the name of political liberalism. Alberdi's thesis was that the goal of establishing truly democratic institutions was utopian and, therefore, unrealizable, given the backwardness of South American institutions and the lack of preparation of its people. His solution was for South American societies to abandon such unproductive projects and instead embrace a European-styled parliamentary monarchy that would better guarantee a desperately needed stability. With internal peace those countries could then attract the European ideas and capital that were the sine qua non of progress: "For these reasons, [South] America ought to embrace Monarquism, not because Monarquism is, in itself, better than Republicism, but rather because it is the form of Government that prevails in civilized Europe, and it is with the latter that we have to unite with in order for us also to enjoy the fruits of civilization."[117] Although *Del gobierno* was never published in his lifetime, Alberdi's promonarchy views were well known because they figured in the justifications he gave for the treaty he negotiated with Spain and for his defense of French imperial pretensions in Mexico during the 1860s. These retrograde opinions provoked the ire of many committed republicans in Argentina and somewhat undermined the credibility of his views on the war with Paraguay.

Alberdi's fierce opposition to Mitre's war with Paraguay demonstrated the height of his brilliance and the depths of his blindness. In his passion to attack Mitre and the Brazilian government, he refused to treat seriously the imperial ambitions—however ill-founded—of the young Paraguayan despot, Francisco Solano López, against Argentine sovereignty. A logical result was Alberdi's mistaken support for Paraguay against his homeland. His critics were at least partially justified in calling this "treason." Herein lay the chasm separating Alberdi, the mistaken maestro, from José Hernández, his most illustrious disciple. Hernández, while accepting almost to the letter Alberdi's reasoned analyses for the roots of that conflict, understood more clearly that Solano López's aggression was "a formidable accusation against our Nation."[118]

Added to his mistaken allegiance were troublesome exaggerations. Paraguay hardly defended free commerce along the continent's rivers, nor did it represent the principle of civilization before the imperial pretentions of Buenos Aires, as the heat of polemic led Alberdi to argue in 1865. Similarly mistaken was his argument that the Paraguayan president, Solano López, was largely free from blame in precipitating the events that led to the bloody war.

In spite of these distortions, nobody saw more clearly or argued as passionately as Alberdi about a related point, that is, Brazil's historical territorial ambitions in its bellicose activities with both Uruguay and Paraguay and the danger that that country represented for Argentina's own sovereignty and leadership in the Plata region. In several important pamphlets published in the next five years,[119] Alberdi would return time and again to the issue of Argentina's dangerous and potentially destructive alliance with Brazil. At the same time he would defend the principle of Paraguayan territorial sovereignty as a safeguard for Argentina's own position on the subcontinent vis-à-vis Brazil. His opponents unjustly saw in this protest the motivations of a traitor, but Alberdi believed his pro-Paraguayan sympathies to be the legitimate position of a patriot observing from afar the destructive effects of a terrible war that his country was inflicting on a "natural ally." Only after 1872, with four fifths of Paraguay's adult-male population dead and hostilities at an end, would the truth of his stand come home to Buenos Aires's leaders. Brazil's leaders would violate the terms of the previous accord and do everything possible to advance their own narrow interests at the expense of the defeated country. The near fiasco of the Sarmiento administration in dealing with the territorial ambitions of Brazil had its earliest prophet in the irksome attacks of Juan B. Alberdi.[120]

Alberdi was to leave an indelible mark on the conscience of his compatriots in a related area: his antiwar sentiment, which flowered into the most eloquent statement of Argentine pacifism of all times, *El crimen de la guerra* (The crime of war).[121] Although the work remained unpublished in his own lifetime, it is this Alberdian work that, after *Bases*, has seen the greatest number of reprintings and has circulated the most widely. Until a decade before undertaking its writing in 1870, Alberdi hardly embraced pacifism; at the time of the Lavalle campaign, he had been one of the foremost advocates of war as a means of ousting the discredited dictator, Rosas. Similarly, toward the end of the 1850s, it was he who led the way in urging the Confederation's leadership to take bellicose measures to force Buenos Aires to rejoin the union. But in the 1870 pamphlet, Alberdi's arguments stood in contradiction to his previous advocacies. Here he argued against any supposedly "just" or "legitimate" war—concepts that for him were entirely devoid of content and reason:

Just war cannot exist because no war is judicious. . . . [I]n a state of war, men only commit crazed acts, there is only evil and ugliness, there is nothing worthy of a good man. Wherever one might look, the only ambition of men in war is to advance through cruel, barbarous, and obscene acts their savage ambitions and interests, which they cloak in the language of rights.[122]

Although this work addressed a public not circumscribed by any single nationality, Alberdi, in writing it, was undoubtedly motivated by his very negative reaction to the liberal state under Mitre and Sarmiento. In its pages Alberdi warned against demagogic leaders who used patriotic rhetoric to promote destructive wars as a means for furthering personal ambitions. The blame for all wars, he argued, lay entirely upon the shoulders of megalomaniac, vainglorious leaders who manipulated public opinion on behalf of their own selfish interests. The wars that had been waged in South America during his lifetime had as their sole objective the occupation and possession of power.[123] Little had to be said about the disastrous consequences of war on the defeated country. He did not have to look beyond the case of Argentina in its recent conflict with Paraguay for irrefutable evidence of war's harm to even the "victorious" side. First, the growth of the army and increased powers of the state led to a general militarization of society, the debasement of individuals now transformed into masses, and the general loss of liberty in all aspects of life. Second, militarism consumed the resources that could otherwise be directed toward the construction of civic institutions and the promotion of individual wealth. Third, war caused a loss of population, a factor with even more serious implications than a loss of territory upon the strength of the state. Fourth, the waging of war distorted the economic life of the country by creating monopolistic fortunes for the few while contributing to the general impoverishment of the majority; it also encumbered future generations with the burdens of an increased national debt. And fifth, war campaigns contributed to the increase in corruption and served to sanction violence as a legitimate means for resolving disputes. Perhaps even more destructive for the moral fabric of society was the reacceptance into the fold of the family, at war's end, of members with twisted sensitivities formed under the stress and brutality of the battlefield. In all of this Alberdi's caustic commentary could be read as his indictment of the state of affairs in Argentine public life that Mitre and his successor Sarmiento had brought about since 1862.

One last area of confusion for many readers of those essays composed by Alberdi during the Mitre and Sarmiento presidencies arises from the emphasis placed alternatively upon two contrasting reasons for the South American countries' continuing experience with rebellion and social anarchy. First there was the "moral" factor that arose from the mistaken directions chosen for the country by its principal leaders, and second there were the region's "material" deficiencies or, in Alberdi's words, the "constitution of things"—that is, factors relevant to the region's population and productive infrastructure.

Alberdi communicated the first view—the "moral" weaknesses of Argentine or regional leaders—in many of the essays and pamphlets already considered above in addition to two longer works: the historico-philosophical fiction, *Peregrinación de Luz del Día o viajes y aventuras de la verdad en el Nuevo Mundo* (Pilgrimage of Light of Day, or travels and adventures of truth in the New World—1874), and *Grandes y pequeños hombres del Plata* (Great and small men in the River Plate), a work first appearing posthumously in *Escritos póstumos* (Posthumous writings—1895–1901) and then under separate title in 1912. The hardly transparent objective of these works was to lambast the ideas and acts of both Mitre and Sarmiento and to denounce liberalism's deformations in doctrine and practice.[124]

In the first few decades after its publication, many of Alberdi's contemporaries praised *Luz del Día*. J. M. Estrada, for example, admired the work's fictional qualities, such as movement and colorful characterization (judgments that subsequent generations of readers have not embraced so enthusiastically), as well as the penetrating insights into national reality that Alberdi communicated through "his powerful, cutting satire."[125] No informed reader of the time would have erred in associating actual public figures with Alberdi's caricatures. Leading the list was Tartuff (from Molière's comedy), modeled after Sarmiento, for whom liberty, progress, and education were but "his pin-action rifles, steel canons, mortars, exploding canon charges." A second figure was Basilio de Sevilla, the stand-in for Mitre, who combined traits of soldier and poet, newspaper writer and historian, and who claimed to be a disciple of Italian liberals Mazzini and Garibaldi but in fact earned his living as the servant of governments enriching themselves through the slave trade. De Sevilla was "talented in any sort of operations that were as ·warped in purpose as his body was in form, purged of any high principle or ideal." Although the rich and varied themes of this satirical novel can never be reduced to one general thesis, Alberdi's bitter indictment of the liberal leaders of the country stood out. Those most exalting liberalism proved to be, in practice, the country's worst enemies. Mitre and Sarmiento headed this list for having fortified an oppressive oligarchy which committed horrendous acts of barbarism and then absolved itself of any wrongdoing. According to their warped sense of justice, "he who scorches the earth to further his civilizing plan and promote progress, does not commit crimes, but only meritorious acts."[126]

The second work attacking Mitre and Sarmiento, *Grandes y pequeños hombres del Plata*, was never published in Alberdi's lifetime, but generations of readers, nevertheless, have distilled from it the principal tendencies of his thought at the time. One biographer excused in part the work's "libel and angry sarcasm [in] unexpectedly lashing out at times with uncontrolled passions and violent hatreds,"[127] because of the persecutions Alberdi suffered at the hands of both Mitre and Sarmiento throughout the forty years of his self-imposed exile. In truth a careful reading of this work reveals inconsistencies, contradictions, and exaggerations that one does not find in the *"public* texts" which Alberdi chose to publish in his lifetime. One therefore understands the decision of Martín García Merou, Natalio Botana, and others to leave entirely aside these tainted pages in their own authoritative studies. The decision of Bernardo Canal Feijóo to devote only a few short paragraphs to these "attempts to write polemical criticism that [Alberdi] abandoned in their initial stages" was similar.[128]

The main thrust of these writings was to criticize the recent publications by both Mitre and Sarmiento (the former's *Historia de Belgrano*— History of Belgrano—and the recent appearance in French translation of *Facundo*, by the latter), but Alberdi's criticisms of the ideas and acts of both in their capacity as national leaders generally overshadowed literary or historiographical judgments. Here polemical furor sometimes usurped reasoned judgment; an example is Alberdi's argument that Mitre united the worst aspects of regional *caudillos*, José Gervasio Artigas and Juan Manuel de Rosas, and that he was the bloody defender of separatism, federalism, and provincial feudalism. Rather than represent any great cause or national vision, Mitre and his clan were "bastard offspring not respecting the parentage of any form of government. They are only interested in their own gain. The totally control their *party*; their *program* is that enterprise that earns the most for them."[129]

Sarmiento was the target of similar treatment. He was the author of a wholly mistaken thesis: "To say that Buenos Aires represents civilization and that the Argentine provinces represent barbarism, is an extravagance that can only be explained in light of the fanatism of [the Liberal P]arty."[130] Alberdi went on to accuse Sarmiento and other liberals of having utilized this erroneous duality as justification for some of the worst crimes ever committed by the liberal Porteño establishment against the rest of the country: "His whole program as public writer and statesman since the fall of Rosas, is to absolve and then reconstruct the same state of things that before he had condemned in the name of liberty and Argentine civilization."[131] In essence Alberdi's arguments in this work lent support to a "moral" interpretation that argued that the root cause for the country's recent conflicts lay in the incorrect interpretations fielded by the country's two past presidents and in their destructive leadership that followed from those tragically erroneous interpretations.

Rivaling this "moral" or political interpretation was Alberdi's longstanding view of the deep or long-term causes for the country's recent problems. This general view had received its earliest expression in his *Fragmento* (1837), which offered an "organic" interpretation for the Rosas dictatorship, according to which the phenomenon of the "great man" was only the most visible expression of a whole network of interrelated structural causes. In the 1850s Alberdi provided a new "materialist" elaboration to this same general perspective, as explained in a previous section. Whatever remained of his previous "idealism" was now over-shadowed by "economic facts." A further installment of this focus was to be found in *Del gobierno en Sud América*, in which he emphasized "the force exerted by material factors," meaning that the country participated in a course of development that was largely independent of the decisions taken by the men who administered its political affairs: "Material factors are those governing and at the same time condemning the country. Their power is situated precisely where one finds Argentina's greatest concentration of interests and economic forces: in its nominal center, in Buenos Aires."[132] Because Sarmiento and Mitre served the same economic interests, the two defended in practice the same geopolitical policies as their former foe, Rosas. For all their ideas and intents to the contrary, Mitre and Sarmiento, during their respective presidencies, ended up supporting in deed the predominant socioeconomic interests of the nation's hegemonic group, the cattle-exporting oligarchy of Buenos Aires.

Throughout this whole period Alberdi continued defending a liberal economy for the developing Argentine state. However some publications dating from the late 1860s or early 1870s evidence a slight waivering on the issue. On one page he attacks "protectionism" in general, and on the next he defends a brand of "intelligent protectionism" that he never attempts to define.[133] Further on he intelligently recognized that England's liberal trade policies were "transitory and depended upon the circumstances of the moment," meaning that if the country were not to possess a strong manufacturing plant, then free trade might have destructive, rather than beneficial, results. Inconsistencies in this text abound. On one page he attacks a publication in which José Victorino Lastarria equated the economic situations of North and South American countries—an implicit argument for different economic policies. Then, pages later, Alberdi returns to his now decades-old litany of the need for the South American countries to remove any and all impediments to European trade and investments and even to offer guarantees for attracting that commerce.[134] Well into the next decades, when the national legislature would consider the benefits of selective protectionism for stimulating the growth of the country's infant industries and an incipient agriculture, Alberdi's name would head the list of those thinkers most staunchly opposed to any modification of the country's strict free-trade policies.

The trip to America of Alberdi's novelistic figure, Luz del Día, prefigured his own brief return to Argentina in 1879 after more than forty years of absence. The political significance of his presence in Buenos Aires was understandably confused. From one direction old Buenos Aires foes, led by Mitre, continued their opposition to the ideological warrior because of his opposition to the Liberal Party's war in Paraguay and his propagandistic battle over decades against Porteño egotism and domination. From another direction liberal leaders from the interior, with Sarmiento as their standard-bearer, could not forget Alberdi's decade-long support for Urquiza, whose Confederation had as its pillars of support the very *caudillos* who had come to power under *rosismo*. These two liberal groupings would view with suspicion what had appeared to be Alberdi's political support for the embittered survivors of the *criollo, caudillo*-led Argentina that had already ceased to exist. But they found consolation in Alberdi's unceasing promotion of progress: technology, railroads, immigration, commerce, and the institutionalization of the state. It did not take the Buenos Aires oligarchy long to comprehend the ideological affinities uniting their world vision—soon to be realized in the post-1880 state headed by Julio A. Roca—and the tightly argued opinions of Alberdi: state protection for private property and guarantee of totally unfettered free trade, the consolidation of a centralized state with its capital in Buenos Aires, and the political control of the country firmly in the hands of a social class uniting patrician and aristocratic elements.[135]

Official Justification of Liberalism

Not all historians have interpreted Mitre's and Sarmiento's contributions in such a negative light as did Alberdi. During his whole term as president, Mitre enjoyed the unquestioned loyalty and support of the Buenos Aires economic and political elite. Honorable men, such as Guillermo Rawson and Marcos Paz, served him faithfully. If he had indeed engaged in a politics of deception with regard to what liberals regarded as the very dangerous presence of Urquiza, then the favorable end he achieved totally justified in their eyes the questionable means employed. And Mitre did succeed in limiting federalism's influence and making Urquiza subservient to Porteño objectives. The liberal press (*La tribuna, [La] nación argentina, El nacional*) was solidly behind his war against the *montoneras* of the interior and the Paraguayan despot Solano López, whom they called "The American Attila."[136] Although detractors continued to question Mitre's military competence, the great majority of public figures in Buenos Aires and elsewhere did not doubt his integrity and competence as the nation's leader. This explains, at least in part, the political folklore that has grown up around his name.

Indeed the historians partial to Buenos Aires and liberalism offer a generally and sometimes highly positive view of the social, political, and institutional transformations that occurred across the country during Mitre's and Sarmiento's administrations. This view is predicated on the belief that the country's entrance into modernity had two prerequisites: first, the successful emergence of a strong national government obedient to the democratic sentiment of the people and the authority of a constitution; and second, the definitive disappearance of an "aggressive" federalism, defended by autocratic *caudillos*, whose retrograde notion of provincial "autonomy" gave license to a personalist exercise of power exempt from external influences. Liberal historians have recognized Urquiza's precursor contribution with regard to the first of these conditions: his inspiration for the Constitution of 1853, which established the guidelines for organizing the provinces and establishing a strong, centralized republican government. But they were equally convinced that Urquiza had not even attempted to act upon the second need. Early on that leader had decided not to work for the removal of the provincial leaders who had risen to prominence under the protection of Rosas but rather to base his own authority upon their continued support.

This, in essence, was the basis for the theoretical dispute throughout the 1850s between Mitre and Sarmiento, on the one hand, and Alberdi on the other. Although the first two sought the removal of Urquiza and the other federalists from positions of power in the interior provinces, Alberdi supported Urquiza's efforts to construct the new order upon the foundations of the old. After the Porteño victory at Pavón and well into the 1860s, this same dispute would continue to define the principal line of ideological cleavage separating the country's liberal leadership, now situated in Buenos Aires, from the defenders of traditionalism and federalism, who resided throughout the interior. Liberal historians, then and afterward, have praised both Mitre and Sarmiento, whose firm presidential leadership brought about the formation of a national authority that was able to squelch rebellious, anarchistic elements in the provinces and support the practices of parliamentary government and electoral succession.

The Mitre administration also placed the country firmly on the road to progress. Buenos Aires, which for decades had experienced steady, moderate growth, now witnessed an intoxicating prosperity. The high profits for the region's wool exports led to a dramatic surge in economic activity and improvement in living standards for even trade workers and house servants. The country's reality slowly began to measure up to the grandiose dreams of its liberal leaders. They could begin to boast of

progressive educational and cultural practices and the country's incipient infrastructure of railroads, agriculture, and technology. Even in the
interior it was apparent to all that the country had emerged into a
new age; the traditional patriarchical society, with roots in the region's
Hispanic colonial past, slowly yielded to a system more conducive to
progress.[137]

What was the value of Alberdi's position in light of the liberal conquest
of the 1860s? In other words what was the nature and promise of that
traditional society which—according to Alberdi—these energetic liberal
leaders, with unfettered egotism, had brutally put asunder? It is difficult
to explain the federalist cultural ideal because no *caudillo* has been able
to project a program with the verbal mastery of liberal writers such
as Sarmiento. Félix Luna, hardly a liberal apologist, suggests that the
homeland envisioned by the *caudillos* was one where courage and loyalty
(as exemplified by Facundo Quiroga or Peñaloza) would prevail, where
the provinces, with all their defects and anachronisms, would have a
more resonating voice, and where the communities of the interior would
be left in tranquility and not be swept away by the forces of change:

> It is difficult to conceptualize the homeland of the "bárbaros": it would be
> the vision that they dreamed about in the sleepless nights of a pampean
> campaign or the raging anger that led them to rise up in rebellion. Perhaps
> it would be a country with the scent of rawhide and range cattle, a people
> rejoicing in their traditional celebrations with a few ounces of the fierceness
> that they exhibited from time to time when affirming their manliness.[138]

The *caudillos*, who nobly defended the traditional system of provincial
autonomy, possessed some undeniably admirable qualities, but they
could not resist the forces of change. The rapidity and thoroughness of
their defeat merely underline the inherent weakness of the system that
they had defended. Luna concludes, "Before those served by the Rem-
ington, the telegraph and the railroad, the men dressed in hides were
destined to lose. That is precisely what occurred, and we should not
lament their passing." In short the *caudillos* were the victims of history's
relentless progress. They attempted to impede an evolution that was,
in essence, undetainable. Herein lies the ambiguity experienced by the
impartial observer. The citizen of the present celebrates the passing of
that archaic society because it prefigured the triumphed of a modern
society, but that passing also evokes lament because of the defeat of
those heroic rural leaders who tenaciously struggled against such unfavorable odds.

This being said, it would be a mistake to equate Alberdi's perspective
with the federalist cultural ideal, as presented above. Although he accepted the legitimacy of the interior's *criollo*, *caudillo*-led society for the

time being, he also worked unceasingly on behalf of measures that would bring about its rapid transformation. For this reason he placed such importance on his efforts while in Europe to attract immigrants and foreign capital to Argentina. He wrote of the need to "littoralize" the interior, to create foreign interests in the heart of the provinces that would act as agents for cultural and institutional change.[139] The society of the interior was far from static in his eyes. In *Bases* he called attention to the significant transformations that had already occurred in the ideas and actions of the leaders of the interior. Those leaders, "before crude and uncivilized, have cultivated their spirits and character in the school of leadership."[140] Now those leaders could provide for a needed stability in the face of the material changes that would inevitably occur. Alberdi optimistically believed that the interior's traditional leadership would welcome and promote the institutional change inherent in the modernization process.

The liberal victories across the interior definitively ended any possibility for Alberdi's ideas to be put into practice. Mitre's lieutenants, possessing the might and the will, forcibly removed the federalist leaders in order to promote their own version of institutional change. New priorities were sometimes brutally imposed against majority sentiment. The new regimes would not tolerate dialogue with what they considered to be defenders of the decrepit, retrograde past. Even Alberdi believed that the objectives of that imposition were admirable. But more important for the moment were the dramatic short-term costs of a brutal military occupation and the interior population's dislocation and trauma.

Historians treating this period have dealt in different ways with these events. In their great majority they have chosen to remain silent about the deep resentment and even hatred that Mitre's policies inspired throughout the interior. Hardly mentioned is the near universal opposition outside of Buenos Aires to Mitre's unpopular alliance with Brazil against Uruguay and his war against Paraguay. Even the most respected of historians have recurred to half-truths or falsehoods in this regard. Ramón J. Cárcano, for example, distorts the truth by depicting Mitre as constant in respecting the "strict neutrality" in his administration's dealings with Uruguay: "In no moment did he waiver from this firm and loyal position."[141] However convincing evidence as well as Mitre's own words demonstrate that the members of Mitre's cabinet had carried forth a deliberate and decisive plan to support Brazil's Imperial politics. Again Cárcano writes a half-truth: "Mitre stood out in these preliminary episodes of the coming war. He avoided falling under the influence of either the powerful lobbyists promoting the position of the [Brazilian] Empire nor the exhalted passions of his own country. He was firm and unyielding in his political and legal position; he was as rational, level-headed, and calm as a mathematician."

Typical of the liberal historiographic tradition is the portrayal of Mitre after 1852 as having outgrown his violent, rebellious past and having become a model of moderation and pacifism in a career at "at the service of liberty."[142] Historians of this mold, having recognized the undeniably admirable traits of Mitre during the early 1860s, treat the electoral disturbances orchestrated by Mitre loyalists a half-decade later in a similar fashion. One writer hypocritically argues that Mitre's 1874 leadership of the bloody rebellion in protest of Avellaneda's election to the presidency was the act of a "great citizen in whose breast all the noble passions of the homeland had their home."[143] Mitre himself escaped censure because he accepted the responsibility for all the "miscalculations and errors of his party." A pattern emerges in these hagiographic biographies. The narration is constructed around quotes from Mitre's florid and self-apologetic statements, while the negative or more damning chapters of his performance as president or national leader are totally ignored, treated ambiguously, or represented only with a spattering of favorable details.

Another aspect of the liberal historiography is its selective treatment of Mitre's conquest of the interior. "Official" historians have underlined Mitre's proverbial and largely verbal opposition to a violent, military imposition. However they have ignored or treated lightly the fierce and often cruel treatment by the armies under his supreme command. Few texts have mentioned that state of siege was the rule and not the exception and that hardly a day passed during his six years as president that did not witness uprisings or conflict directed against the Buenos Aires armies stationed in the interior. Those historians do not deny that there were abuses committed against El Chacho's dedicated followers or soldiers captured in battle; instead they justify those abuses as resulting from the excessive verve of a few liberal leaders—Flores, Sarmiento, Paunero, Gelly, Elizalde, and Costa—and allege that those military leaders ignored the moderate directives of Mitre himself:

In many cases Mitre took decisive measures in response to problems created by his friends. Excluding the necessary course of action in the Littoral, it is possible to establish that the only action resulting directly from Mitre's own spontaneous decisions, was that carried out in Córdoba through the leadership of Paunero. However, the other two theaters of governmental action, Cuyo and the northern provinces—even with all that went wrong in the latter—were orchestrated in Buenos Aires before Mitre even had an opportunity to resolve them.[144]

In brief one finds little documentation in liberal histories about what was perhaps the most far-reaching event of the entire period of Mitre's administration: the bitter civil struggle across the interior.

The most widely accepted view in liberal circles is that the Porteño military campaigns in the provinces, led by Paz, Rawson, Mitre, and Sarmiento, were models of restraint and moderation. Early on Mitre had decided to leave Entre Ríos and Urquiza alone and to yield to the initiatives of the powerful Taboada brothers in the provinces of the north. In the remaining provinces Mitre ordered a demonstration of military might but with moderate and limited ends. Given the breakdown of local authority in many areas, the Mitre administration recognized its responsibility for reestablishing peace and order. With this goal in mind, the reformed Constitution justified his armies' interventions in Santa Fe, San Luis, Mendoza, San Juan, Catamarca, Córdoba, Tucumán, and La Rioja. In brief liberal historians have applauded the Mitre administration's restrained application of the constitutional power of intervention.

What was Mitre's track record with regard to the promotion of democratic practices in the interior provinces? Given the absence of a tradition of electoral participation, all parties to some degree recurred to fraudulent practices as a means of influencing voter outcomes. Practices of printing counterfeit votes, ballot-box stuffing, intimidation of opposition supporters, and the mustering of peons or public employees in order to vote for official candidates were common. Local elections, even with the relatively "civilized" population of Buenos Aires, often obeyed the "law of the strongest," according to which the party with the greatest number of voters often had to yield before an armed minority that did not stop at assaulting voting tables and taking into their control the ballot boxes.[145]

Over and above the common practices of vote fraud and intimidation, most elections were easy to control through quasi-legal means because they rarely involved more than a small nucleus of voters. While the constitution granted suffrage to all adult males, the actual number of voters rarely exceeded 2 percent of the total population even in Buenos Aires. The "decent" people, meaning the landowners and the educated middle sectors, often refrained from participating. This meant that elections favored the party in power, which had the means for inducing employees of the railroad, the customshouse, or any other branch of the rapidly expanding state bureaucracy to vote for its own slate.[146] Even though they had the support of only a minority of the population, liberal candidates held the edge in provincial elections because of restrictions against federalist candidates or voters who had participated in recent uprisings.[147] Another important factor in favor of the Liberal Party was the vote by soldiers who generally followed the dictates of their commanding officers.

Although the written record provides evidence that both Mitre and Sarmiento, during their respective presidencies, attempted to correct

the most flagrant of violations, there is reason to believe that they responded to many electoral abuses with guarded applause. This was
the first time that elections of any type had ever been held, and the
elections, in spite of fraud, provided for a relatively peaceful resolution
to political conflicts among local elites. In addition the manipulation of
electoral results guaranteed the Liberal Party's monopoly of political
power during the difficult transition to a new order. Only well into the
next decade would it become a concern of Sarmiento and the budding
Nationalist Autonomist Party to assure the voice and vote of the new
middle class and, as such, to mount a challenge to liberal partisans, led
by Mitre, who would defend the interests of the Porteño cattle oligarchy.
But throughout the 1860s the political system brought into practice
under the tutelage of Mitre accomplished two objectives cherished by
liberal thinkers during the previous half-century of national life: the
unification of all the provinces under one single authority and the return
of government and social leadership to the hands of a small educated
minority.[148] According to the liberal view, the long postponed liberation
of the country from its feudal and colonial past was now on the path
toward realization. The defeats of Peñaloza and Varela (and later,
Urquiza) meant that the country's long line of powerful rural *caudillos*
was now liquidated. All of this signified the approaching victory for the
forces of "civilization" and the definitive absorption or transformation
of the country's ignominious centers of "barbarism."

Liberal historians, when taking all the above into account, have
granted high marks to the Mitre presidency. Campobassi praises Mitre's
predications as well as practices of honest civic behavior that were "essential for laying the foundation for a solid democratic political regime.
[. . .] In no moment did he compromise with elements of disorder,
rebellion, or mutiny."[149] Cárcano portrays Mitre as a paragon of civic
virtue: "He succeeded in imposing his own moderate temperament,
respect for sovereign rights, and judicious application of principles and
well-founded convictions upon a country still traumatized by provincial
disturbances. In accomplishing this, he ushered in a wholly new political tradition in the republic."[150] Sommarivia offers a fitting summary of
Mitre's prime accomplishment:

> The chief infused in all a praiseworthy and persistent spirit of moderation,
> and tempered the inevitable excesses of others without dampening their en-
> thusiasm. And credit is due primarily to him for the country finally achieving
> its unification, after a long history of frustrations. This time, neither side
> attempted to impose demands benefitting exclusively its interests; instead,
> the goal was to reconcile the old ideal of the undivided homeland, as held
> by the exiled militants, with the aspirations for autonomy that the provinces
> tenaciously defended.[151]

The only qualification that must be added to these three views is that while they are accurate with regard to Mitre's contributions in the period between Pavón and the end of his presidency in 1868, less and less would this be the case after that year.

The Sarmiento Presidency

Sarmiento won the election to succeed Mitre as the country's president in spite of being absent from the country (he was in the United States serving as Argentina's ambassador) and having no political party working on his behalf. Several factors explain that unlikely victory:

(1) Mitre, who enjoyed unrivaled prestige in liberal circles, had doomed the candidacies of Urquiza and Alsina in his important "political testament" and refused to support actively his preferred successor, Elizalde.

(2) Liberal provincial leaders respected Sarmiento because of his provincial roots and firm leadership in the Peñaloza uprising.

(3) Sarmiento's distinguished service during four years as Mitre's lieutenant in Buenos Aires neutralized the potential hostility there because of his provincial links.

(4) many individuals saw Sarmiento as the peace candidate who would bring an end to Mitre's unpopular war in Paraguay and the odious alliance with Brazil.

(5) Army officials throughout the country, for many of the above reasons, supported Sarmiento's candidacy and marshalled their troops to vote in his favor.

(6) Sarmiento's progressive ideas on any number of issues that he had incessantly promoted through the press in Chile and Argentina for over a quarter century were embraced by a growing sector of the population now intent upon modernizing the country.

(7) Given the high level of discontent throughout the interior and the repeated uprisings against provincial and national authorities, many believed that Sarmiento's strong will, demonstrated competence and energy, and commitment to principled executive action were precisely what the nation needed in its next president.

In spite of these recognized strengths, many other observers expected the worse because of Sarmiento's legendary egocentricity, coarseness or insensitivity in social situations, and long history of personal animosities.

Sarmiento had been in training for the nation's presidency since his first public experiences as an intrepid youth in San Juan. To his immense credit the new president attempted to place old loyalties aside and act in the interest of as broad a public as possible. In this spirit he broke with the Masonic Lodge and the Liberal Party and thereby provoked the ire of his former friend, ex-president Mitre. He included in his first cabinet Nicolás Avellaneda and José Benjamín Gorostiaga, who enjoyed wide support in the interior. This was merely the anticipation of the most surprising political event of his administration, that is, his fence-mending with Urquiza. In many instances he attempted to put minor political and ideological disputes aside in order to concentrate on his lifelong causes: the spread of public education, construction of the railroad, promotion of industry and European immigration, and land distribution to stimulate agricultural activities and to weaken *latifundia* cattle interests.

The new administration's efforts on behalf of national conciliation found an unlikely supporter in the figure of José Hernández, who now projected his widely respected opinion from the pages of the Porteño newspaper *El Río de la Plata*. The first part of Hernández's monumental poem, *El gaucho Martín Fierro*, which would be published four years into the new presidency, seemingly blamed Sarmiento for the sufferings of the *gaucho* protagonist (although Sarmiento is never named in the poem, General Martín de Gainza, then serving as minister of war in Sarmiento's cabinet, is playfully implicated). However the important series of articles and editorials written by Hernández between 1869 and 1870,[152] which are—surprisingly—largely unknown to even the nation's historians, identify Mitre, and not Sarmiento, as responsible for the most serious of those abuses in recent years. According to Hernández the previous administration had trampled the rights of the people of the interior through its military interventions and opprobrious states of siege; brought upon the country the the tragic war with Paraguay due to Mitre's egotism and "detestable ambition" for a perverse type of glory; and dishonored the country with the treaty with Brazil. The danger that Mitre offered to the country was hardly a thing of the past; it was in the best interests of the country to continue containing the evil inclinations of that hypocritical conspirator.

In contrast to the venomous criticisms emanating from the extremist liberal press, Hernández depicted the Sarmiento administration as working seriously to end the politics of dissolution and to put the country back on the path of peace and progress.[153] Hernández applauded Sarmiento's accord with Urquiza as a bold initiative on behalf of national conciliation. Hernández's magnanimity in forgiving an old political foe and putting the sad, tragic past behind him was evident here; only eight years before his fury could not have been greater as a result of Sarmiento's central role in the persecution and then murder of "El Chacho" Peñaloza. This new spirit of conciliation also revealed the distance Hernández had come in only a matter of months, from enraged opponent of the Porteño political world to tepid, even enthusiastic supporter. For some critics these changes have been an indication of ideological inconsistency; for others, however, they document Hernández's accurate assessment of the great changes that were occurring in his midst and his courage to seek new solutions for the problems inadequately addressed by the existing political parties. Mitre, with his divisive tactics, belonged to the sordid past; Sarmiento, with his energetic plans for peace and progress, was now the most qualified individual for leading the country in the turbulent years ahead: "Speaking with total impartiality about the present administration, we have recognized its patriotic zeal and its constancy in struggling on behalf of progress and social improvement. . . . The situation at present is extraordinary, we repeat."[154]

When the Sarmiento administration decided to intervene militarily in the Province of Entre Ríos following the April 1870 assassination of Urquiza, Hernández closed *El Río de la Plata* and made his way to Paraná to join López Jordán in resisting the national government's military intervention of Entre Ríos. This was a difficult time for Hernández: his newfound generosity toward Sarmiento was temporarily shelved. Yet his return to the schisms of old proved to be short-lived. By the end of 1874, he was again declaring public support for Sarmiento, and he joined the president in supporting the candidacy of Avellaneda for the country's next president. By 1876 Hernández's followers would find in the second part to his monumental poem the definitive proof of his commitment to national reconciliation and the Sarmiento-Avellaneda brand of liberalism. The *"poeta gauchesco"* no longer urged rebellion against the established system. Instead his reformist message was that the *gaucho* could avoid mistreatment by leaving aside past rebelliousness and assimilating himself to the now hegemonic system. If the *gaucho* wanted an improved life, he had to earn it through moral reform, hard work, and education. Hostile critics have interpreted Hernández's new message as an abandonment of the old federalist standard and a sellout to liberalism. In contrast more generous critics have applauded Hernández's realism in recognizing federalism's definitive demise and the positive alternatives offered by both the Sarmiento and Avellaneda administrations in the face of ultra-Porteño objectives. Hernández, the peacemaker, saw in Avellaneda's candidacy the country's best hope for a reconciliation of the nation's previously warring factions.

Did Sarmiento, while president, fulfill in practice this optimistic prognosis for Argentina's social peace? At the outset it must be stated that Sarmiento's theoretical pessimism about the fitness of the *gaucho* and *mestizo* for civilization never softened. Throughout the period of his presidency he continued to oppose the *caudillos* and the retrograde society they represented. In this last respect the heatedly contested interventions that he ordered against San Juan, Mendoza, and especially Entre Ríos were but the continuation of Mitre's policies, which had as their aim the fortification of the national state centered in Buenos Aires and the liquidation of *caudillo* anarchism. Inevitably diehard federalist voices in the interior interpreted these actions in the most negative manner imaginable.

Yet, in spite of Sarmiento's theoretical condemnation of the *gaucho* and the *mestizo* and his administration's decisive military measures against peasants and rural workers rising in rebellion, he continued to promote a type of social and institutional progress that would benefit those precise groups. Indeed Hernández, renowned defender of the *gaucho*, probably was not disappointed. In Sarmiento's noteworthy speech to the residents of Chivilcoy only weeks before commencing his presidential term, he had argued that technological advances in agriculture usually brought about an even more important social objective: property ownership and economic sulf-sufficiency of a previously impoverished *gaucho* population. He argued that other poor people, when given the opportunity, would leave aside their "pathetic role of bandits" and their confusion of "violence with patriotism" in order to become active citizens and producers. During the next six years, Sarmiento struggled untiringly, although without unqualified success, to bring about new laws that would build upon Chivilcoy's successes.

In contrast to Sarmiento's positive efforts to find a humanistic solution to the problems associated with rural poverty and social disorder, his legacy with regard to democratic practices continues to be a debated issue. He was never a supporter of universal suffrage, and his letter of June 1857 (quoted in the previous chapter) documented his willingness to participate in electoral fraud in order to guarantee the victory at the polls of his preferred candidates. According to one detractor President Sarmiento "from the first had the intention of indicating with his finger who his successor would be and placing the weight of his office solidly behind that candidate. [. . .] Sarmiento did what he could to influence the situation in various provinces, with the goal of bringing favorable elements to power who would assure the victory of his designated candidate."[155] According to Gálvez,

> Nobody doubts the merits of the winner [Avellaneda]. . . . But nor does anybody doubt that he has been elected through fraud and co-option. Although Sarmiento might be innocent, as he attempts to make people believe, he will always have against him the fact that he tolerated that voting fraud and the maneuvering of the league of governors.[156]

According to this interpretation the primary complaint of the leaders of the destructive revolution of 1874—among them a reluctant Mitre—was Sarmiento's role in orchestrating the national army's support across the interior in order to secure Avellaneda's election.

In the area of institutional reform and promotion of material progress, Sarmiento's accomplishments were indisputable. However his initiatives as president were constantly thwarted by a number of weighty obstacles: the rebellions in Entre Ríos, Mendoza, and other provinces that required costly interventions; the war with Paraguay that for three more years continued to provoke public dissension and drain the country of needed manpower and capital; severe epidemics of typhoid and yellow fever that ravaged Buenos Aires and other areas of the country; and the continuation of Indian attacks all along the frontier in several provinces. Added to these was the increasing opposition from the vested interests of the country's cattle oligarchy that, through Mitre and its other agents in the Liberal Party, all but dominated the national congress and continued to define the course for the nation's development. Sarmiento's track record in combatting this powerful group was mixed. He registered small gains in his efforts to modernize the country but at a price of short-term accommodation and postponement of eventual confrontation.

In spite of its important political implications, the growing animosity between Mitre and Sarmiento has received clear treatment by only a handful of historians. Undoubtedly the two leaders were of one mind with regard to several important issues: the desire to bring the costly Paraguayan War to an honorable conclusion; the need to continue fortifying the function and authority of the national government; the imperative of uprooting *caudillo* influence throughout the interior and fostering liberal political institutions; the commitment to material and technological progress, immigration, public education, and unfettered trade; and the conviction that only through foreign investment and the imitation of North European and Anglo-American ideas and institutions could Argentina take its rightful place in the community of civilized nations. However a decisive factor in the growing split between the two men was Sarmiento's generally populist orientation in contrast to Mitre's increasingly pronounced role as defender of the Porteño oligarchy.

SARMIENTO VERSUS MITRE: 1874–1880

Many of Sarmiento's initiatives while president were stymied in large part by the fierce opposition of Mitre and Porteño localists in the national congress, the heavy drain on the national treasury occasioned by the war in Paraguay and costly interventions in Mendoza and Entre Ríos, and the scourge of yellow fever. Nevertheless his ideas continued to define the parameters of the national political dialogue well into the next decade.

His election to the presidency marked a new split in Liberal Party ranks and would generate the emergence of the National Autonomist Party. This new political grouping responded in part to the old regional cleavage in that Sarmiento and his group defended provincial or national priorities in opposition to narrow Porteño interests. In addition there were vaguely defined social distinctions. Many from autonomist ranks hailed from the new urban middle class or were small landowners of the littoral with nationalist orientation.[157] Autonomist objectives reflected these groups' concerns: greater independence of the municipality; administrative decentralization; reform of judicial power, especially in rural areas; free and universal education; political representation of minorities; encouragement for industry; and a public lands policy benefiting those actually working the soil. Mitre's armed rebellion of 1874, and to a lesser extent the revolution of Mitre loyalist, Carlos Tejedor, in 1879, found a partial explanation in the electoral threat that these new groups posed to traditional vested interests.

As it was the autonomists never developed into a political force capable of launching a credible opposition to the *latifundia* cattle ranchers of the region. The 1860s witnessed the publication of several articles in the local newspapers that attacked the "feudal lords" of the cattle industry and called for governmental intervention to protect nascent industries and agriculture. But by 1880 it became apparent that the ruling elite did not prioritize industrialization in its plans for the country's development and that it welcomed new agricultural initiatives only as a complement to the region's already predominant cattle raising activities.

The political elite of the country—regardless of differing political affiliations—was now united behind a common vision for the country's future that accepted the central role of a modernized cattle and agrarian sector with close ties to European financial and commercial concerns. No substantive social or economic issues divided autonomists from liberals; "no principles are in dispute," wrote one observer.[158] Political parties were short-lived because no significant ideological issues divided them. "Avellaneda was as liberal as Mitre, Alsina or Alem."[159] The very fluid situation allowed for a leader such as Mitre to oppose Avellaneda one day and then to join with him the next in overriding the protest of a large group of Porteño youths, led by Dardo Rocha and Aristóbulo del Valle, who sought a more open political process. Political groupings pledged loyalty to individual leaders, not to ideological or social orientations. A united governing class was coming into existence with growing agreement among its members over economic and political options. Its "liberal" orientation affirmed the central role of cattle production in the nation's development in conjunction with an open economy, close ties to Europe, and defense of European investment and immigration.

However Sarmiento's continued presence on the political scene meant that real ideological issues would, on occasion, continue to be discussed. No serious student of history can in good faith reduce the differences now separating Mitre from Sarmiento to a dispute between two personalistic leaders. From the time of his presidency until his death in 1888, Sarmiento at times assumed the role of Mitre's and the Porteño oligarchy's most impassioned critic. Unfortunately, he never achieved a coherent articulation of these radical, antioligarchical ideas in his writings. Somewhat confusing for the contemporary reader is the fact that this radical orientation was accompanied by his unswerving support for social order and a conservative political regime. All of this explains his defense of the national government when faced with the rebellions that were either led or inspired by Mitre in 1874 and 1880.

Only a few biographers or historians have told of the anguished (but not altogether coherent) struggle that Sarmiento, accompanied by a few enlightened voices, waged against the region's cattle oligarchy from the assumption of the presidency until his death some twenty years later. Ever since he was a young man, Sarmiento had been convinced that the prerequisite for the country's development was the curtailment of the cattle *latifundia's* economic and social power and the agricultural transformation of the pampa's immense underpopulated expenses by industrious European immigrants. For that reason he had always granted immense importance to the study of land-tenure realities and public land policies in Argentina and elsewhere (but especially in the United States).

Sarmiento's experiences in this important struggle for equal access to the land were especially revealing. Advancing into the 1870s fewer and fewer influential political leaders continued to share Sarmiento's view of the need for developing independent sources of productive wealth in agriculture and industry as a means of counterbalancing the region's powerful cattle interests. In contrast to the folklore that has grown up around the event (a la Ricardo Rojas and Félix Weinberg), his speech before the neighbors of Chivilcoy shortly before assuming the presidency was not warmly received.[160] According to several accounts even the former colonists benefiting from the progressive laws that Sarmiento earlier had helped to pass now recognized the degree to which those ideas hardly spoke to the socioeconomic and geographic realities of the region. In short early agriculturalists had, in the intervening decade, forcibly realized that expensive transport in fickle climatic conditions made wheat growing a precarious economic undertaking; cattle and wool production, in contrast, offered a sure and healthy return on investments. In short, the majority of immigrant farmers in Chivilcoy had, by 1868, largely abandoned agriculture as their predominant productive activity in favor of cattle raising.

In contrast to the tepid reception given to Sarmiento, the Chivilcoy colonists, joined by large landowners, warmly applauded Mitre a few weeks later. In his speech Mitre demonstrated a more accurate understanding of the regional economy and criticized the "doctos" (corruption of "*doctores*" in reference to those city folk with university degrees) from the city—like Sarmiento—because of their impractical, utopian ideas and their mistaken condemnation of cattle ranching.[161] In contrast Mitre offered a most favorable interpretation of the large cattle ranchers' historical role. Their early presence in the outlying regions had provided a first line of defense against the marauding Indians and, therefore, a semblance of security for the settler population. Given the Plata region's peculiar geography and demography, cattle ranching had proven to be the most indicated and appropriate means for the spread of civilization.

Although Sarmiento would alternate between supporter and foe of the region's powerful cattle interests, Mitre's position was more constant. Throughout the 1850s his views had been generally undistinguishable from those of Sarmiento; both had supported an activist state to promote European immigration and assure a division of public lands in order to favor small agricultural interests.[162] Yet, by the end of the 1860s, Mitre's views had largely changed. Whether due to a greater commitment to realism or a strategy calculated to win the support of the region's power-elite, his politics now revolved around the defense of large cattle-producing interests. In their name he defended free trade policies and obstructed proposals for governmental regulation or control over productive activity. He defended their search for favorable markets in Europe in exchange for unrestricted importation of consumer goods.[163]

It was only toward the end of his presidential term that Sarmiento finally succeeded in advancing through the national legislature the much debated law empowering the central government to distribute public lands to agricultural immigrants. But that proposal, after receiving approval by the House of Representatives, met with defeat in the Senate. As to be expected those representing the economically entrenched oligarchy opposed the bill; additional opposition came from provincial leaders Patricio Cullen and Nicasio Oroño, both from Santa Fe, who objected to the national government's continued control over lands located in their province.[164]

Sarmiento's activity in support of progressive land policies continued after his presidency. His frustration grew with the passage of regressive legislation between 1877 and 1879 that limited the state's function in the distribution of public land, protection of nascent industries, and promotion of agriculture.[165] The oligarchical state was now entrenched; in spite of Sarmiento's efforts to the contrary, *latifundia* cattle interests now reigned supreme with their conservative brand of laissez-faire liberalism and financial dependence on Great Britain. Highly favorable international markets momentarily favored this New Argentina. The unbridled prosperity of the region (except at the beginning of the 1870s) served to muzzle most critics. Few joined Sarmiento in looking beyond the glitter of momentary prosperity in order to perceive the country's structural problems that would cause stagnation in the future. Sarmiento's perspective of his homeland in the last decade of his life was, in retrospect, agonized and distraught, many would even say profound. For Sarmiento it was a country with enormous potential but unfulfilled promises.

OTHER PARTICIPANTS

During the Mitre and Sarmiento presidencies, other members of the 1837 generation continued to be active. Regardless of their previous stances over the dispute between Buenos Aires and the Confederation, by 1862 almost all of them had returned to Buenos Aires. Only Alberdi chose to remain distant; his reasons for remaining in Europe would multiply as Mitre progressively eliminated former focuses of opposition to Buenos Aires's hegemony. Juan María Gutiérrez, seeking an escape from the vicissitudes of the public forum, continued dedicating his energies to the study of literature and culture and directed the fledging Universidad Nacional. José Mármol and Félix Frías first served as provincial senators in the months after Pavón and were then elected, respectively, to the nation's Senate and House of Representatives. Miguel Cané and Vicente Fidel López, having returned to Buenos Aires after their long residence in Montevideo, attempted to channel accumulated bitterness into public service. López, in short order, would be elected to the national House of Representatives where he would serve long years with distinction; Cané, with aggravated physical ailments in addition to an "mortal bitterness" as a result of Mitre's definitive victory over the Confederation, died in 1862.[166]

With the attention of the nation's historians riveted primarily on Mitre, Sarmiento, and the epic events of their respective administrations, the activities and beliefs of López, Frías, Mármol, and Gutiérrez during this same period have been largely obscured. There is little evidence of a conscious plot. But it is understandable that these and other critics of

Buenos Aires found little opportunity to express their views through the Porteño press. For this reason a brief reconstruction of their positions is in order here.

Estranged from Buenos Aires politics since his political defeat in 1852, López maintained a distrustful distance during the Mitre presidency. He continued with his pedagogical activities in Montevideo while administering his extensive land holdings near Chivilcoy from afar. As with most he initially celebrated Mitre's apparent sincerity in striving for a "peaceful" reintegration of the country. His information about the heated conflict with Peñaloza was limited almost entirely to that provided by the exalted Porteño clique monopolizing the local press. In general his perspective about Peñaloza differed little from that of official circles, but his long-time sympathies with the goals of the Confederation and his opposition to ultraunitarian sentiment in Porteño circles made him more sensitive to the criticisms of the new national government that emanated from points in the interior.

In 1871 López ended his self-imposed Montevidean exile of nineteen years and returned to Buenos Aires. Almost immediately he began teaching courses in politics and economics at the University of Buenos Aires. Within a year he was elected provincial senator, and in 1873 he became a national representative. He immediately assumed a leadership role in the legislative movement against the war with Paraguay, which unfortunately never gained significant support.[167]

In the early 1870s López came to play an important role as legislative and political leader in the national legislature. To this writer's knowledge no biographer has treated these outstanding contributions in depth. He collaborated with José Hernández and other former "exiles" from Buenos Aires politics, and several of his articles on historical topics were published in the latter's *El Río de la Plata*. Approaching 1874 López and his associates—Leandro N. Alem, Aristóbulo del Valle, Carlos Pellegrini, Miguel Goyena, Vicente G. Quesada, and Dardo Rocha—had become the backbone of the newly formed Partido Autonomista Nacional that supported the candidacy of Nicolás Avellaneda in opposition to the Mitre clique that defended Buenos Aires's *latifundia* cattle interests. As senator of the province, national representative, and then president of the Banco de la Provincia—in addition to his growing fame as historian[168]—López was one of the principal activists of this political grouping in spite of his advancing age. In 1876 the party named him its second vice president. He would culminate this distinguished career of public service as minister of the treasury under President Ricardo Pellegrini in 1890.

The legislative debates of 1873–76 saw López leading congressional forces in favor of tariff protection for the country's incipient industries.[169]

This was not a deliberate challenge to the region's prepotent cattle interests. In fact López's views did not differ substantially from what was emerging as a near unanimous opinion that cattle raising was the preferred industry of the region. But López did argue that a healthy economic development for the future required a diversification in the country's productive capacities. This put him at odds with proponents of a totally laissez-faire economy. According to López, "with free-trade we will never emerge from the state of barbarism . . . the principles of political economy practiced by the European do not and could not yield the same results if applied by American states."[170] Yet even his moderate attempts at legislative reform failed. Like Sarmiento, López suffered frustration over the cattle oligarchy's hegemony over the region,[171] while he simultaneously celebrated the liberal Porteño oligarchy that was successfully leading Argentina forward in public education, immigrant colonization, and economic prosperity benefiting rural and urban sectors alike. His disenchantment with the Roca regime was over the increasing autonomy of the state guided by an oligarchy that marginalized intellectuals such as himself from governing circles. His "reinvented Whig ideology" sought a coherent oligarchical liberalism, much like what was practiced in England, Imperial Brazil, and Chile. He advocated a parliamentary regime that would give effective power not to a broadly based public opinion but rather to those citizens with the independence of criterion and intellectual formation that would permit wise council.[172] His historical writings expressed a complementary theme: a negative assessment of the historical role of the *caudillos* of the interior whose retrograde cultural values and anarchistic politics faithfully reflected the barbarism of their setting.[173]

* * *

Félix Frías, like López, tepidly supported Mitre's efforts at the beginning of the 1860s to unite the country, but afterword he became a vocal critic in reaction to the resurgence of Porteño extremism. Given his staunch conservative views, Frías welcomed measures to strengthen the country's central authority, restrict the political liberty of the masses, and condition the values and conduct of the citizenry through shared religious beliefs.[174] This orientation accounted for his opposition to the armed uprisings of El Chacho, Felipe Varela, and López Jordán, although his pacifist sentiments led him to question the harsh measures utilized by the Mitre and Sarmiento administrations to gain their desired ends.[175] With regard to foreign policy, he emerged as one of Mitre's most outspoken critics. In June 1866 he and several other representatives followed Alberdi's lead in protesting the government's support for Brazil's belligerency against Uruguay and Paraguay: "It is my opinion that had our country followed a wise course of action in dealing with Uruguay, then we would have saved Brazil, Uruguay, and our own country from the calamaties of the war which we are presently suffering; the consequences of this war, as I see it, will be deplorable for all concerned, including the victors."[176] Particularly offensive was the Mitre administration's apparent violation of its professed neutrality, which Frías compared to an act of sedition.[177] In a letter to Alberdi, he expressed pessimism over the growing immorality in government: "Fortunate are those like yourself who can contemplate from afar so many blunders, so many shortcomings, and so many misguided decisions."[178]

Beginning in 1868 Frías, in the capacity of Argentina's ambassador, carried out delicate negotiations with Chile over the disputed possession of the Straits of Magellan and successfully steered the country away from armed conflict. In 1874, he vociferously opposed Mitre's armed revolt and denounced the widespread practices of electoral fraud in the provinces. In 1878 his name circulated briefly as the Liberal Party's candidate for the nation's vice presidency on a ticket headed by Carlos Tejedor and supported by Mitre. Later, although denouncing the military interventions of the new administration headed by president Julio Argentino Roca,[179] he must have applauded its successes in fortifying the nation's central authority. Meanwhile, his conservative values and links with the Catholic Church progressively brought him into conflict with Roca over another important issue: the secularization of public education.

* * *

Also active in public affairs throughout the Mitre presidency was José Mármol. In the late 1850s his independence in the Buenos Aires-Confederation dispute had progressively led to his association with the autonomist faction: those who defended the independence of the province against a more nationalist orientation. This meant that he and Mitre came into frequent conflict. One biographer incredulously suggests that Mármol's activities with the *pandilleros*—or "street-gang members," which was his group's derogatory nickname—were not entirely honorable. Along with Nicolás Calvo, Francisco Bilbao, Juan José Soto, and others, he was reported to have strolled the steets seeking confrontations with the police.[180] Later, as director of the public library and senator in the provincial legislature, he continued to align himself with Adolfo Alsina in heatedly confronting Mitre's politics.

However this record of opposition did not prevent Mitre from calling upon his old friend from exile days in Montevideo to represent the newly reunified government before the Blanco administration in Montevideo in 1863 and then a half-year later before the imperial court of

Brazil. Was the Mitre administration—or more specifically Rufino de Elizalde, the minister of foreign relations—using Mármol as a pawn in its secret political dealings? Mármol's public admiration for the Blanco Party in Montevideo clashed with Elizalde's passionate support for Colorado General Flores.[181] When they named Mármol to that important post, Elizalde and other members of Mitre's cabinet were already providing secret support for Brazilian intervention in Uruguayan affairs. Their deceptions would lead to several instances when Mármol suffered serious public embarrassment: first in March 1865, when he was forced to admit his ignorance to the Montevideo government about the Mitre cabinet's pro-Brazilian and anti-Uruguayan actions; second in June, when Elizalde refused to share with him a copy of the secret treaty signed months earlier with Brasil; and third—a month later—when details of Argentina's secret role in supplying arms for Brazil's siege of Paysandú were announced to the Brazilian senate.[182] Throughout this series of events, Mármol continually defended Mitre's patriotic sentiments and sincerity in carrying out a state policy of neutrality. When the deception later became apparent, he blamed Elizalde, not Mitre.[183]

In the parliamentary debates of July 1868 over Argentina's role in the Paraguayan War, Mármol harshly criticized the Mitre administration's double dealings with Uruguay and the secrecy with which the cabinet had proceeded in its negotiations. It was then becoming clear that the war was highly unpopular with the Argentine people and was also going to cost the country dearly in lives and resources. Along with other representatives he stressed Argentina's historical links with Uruguay and questioned the wisdom of the administration's recent agreements with the Brazilian government. He angrily censored the administration's violation of the constitution in not having sought parliamentary approval for its important foreign policy initiatives: "Congress has been informed of utterly nothing . . . even though it holds the power to determine public policy, it receives no official information about, for example, the status of the war."[184]

A year later, when the stormy polemic erupted between Uruguayan Juan Carlos Gómez, Mitre, and Elizalde over the causes and effects of the Paraguayan War, Mármol was a protagonist. Gómez's critical role was a surprise, given his close collaboration with Mitre over the years and his role as intellectual architect for a pan-Rioplatense republic uniting all the former colonies of the Spanish crown. Indeed Gómez's own ultraliberal vocation, his close association with the leading intellectuals of Buenos Aires, his "repudiation" of the people of the interior, the association in his writings of the pampas with barbaric or infernal influences, and his "aristocratic" conception of the civilizing role for the men of culture seemingly placed him among the ranks of Mitre's most enthusiastic supporters.[185] But the Mitre government's alliance with arch-rival Brazil and the resulting annihilation of Paraguay were too much for even this defender of exalted liberal principles. These reasons help to explain Gómez's willingness to engage Mitre in angry polemic over the origins of the Paraguayan War.

The 1869 polemic provided the pretext for Mármol to set forth publicly his privileged view of key events three years before. In an anonymous public letter (informed observers immediately identified his authorship), he largely exonerated the former president in spite of the harmful acts perpetrated by his administration. According to Mármol, Mitre yielded to the pressure of all five of his ministers and only reluctantly agreed to lend support for Brazil's intervention in Uruguay. Mármol suggested that Elizalde's secret agreement with Brazilian representatives went back to at least the first days of May 1864. As such Mármol suggested that the administration's play at neutrality involved either the deception of the Blanco government in Uruguay or the deception of Mitre by his own cabinet.

* * *

The last figure to be considered here with regard to the national political situation during the Mitre and Sarmiento presidencies is Juan María Gutiérrez. For a decade, beginning in 1861, he exercised the responsibilities of dean of the National University. He enjoyed immense prestige in all circles because of his dedication and demonstrated competence in cultural, educational, and literary matters. One of his many important services was the 1871 plan he authored for reforming the provincial system of public education. The plan embraced a middle position, incorporating both Sarmiento's idea of free and obligatory schooling for all children and Alberdi's emphasis on technological and industrial training for instruction on the secondary level.[186] At this early moment in the growing dispute between conservative Catholics and proponents of secular public education, this dignified gentleman and scholar is reputed to have celebrated the burning of the Jesuit Cathedral of El Salvador by radicalized opponents of "the religious restaurations."[187] Regarded as the custodian of the nation's cultural heritage, he performed other important cultural services, among them the organization for publication of Echeverría's complete works. In 1876 he provoked a noisy polemic in cultural circles when his somewhat inflexible nationalistic criteria led him to reject the invitation of the Real Academia Española to become a corresponding member.[188]

Gutiérrez's total dedication to scholarly tasks after 1864 was but a balm against the deep disillusionment that he would feel for the rest of his life about the country's course of development under Mitre's and

Sarmiento's leadership. For him the entire chapter of the country's history having to do with the Paraguayan war was a terrible, tragic mistake. That "monstrous" war, in his opinion, left both countries permanently scarred: Argentina, in the moral sense, because tens of thousands of its soldiers had stained their honor by participating in the genocide of Paraguay's population and the destruction of its wealth; and Paraguay, in the social and material sense, because "adult men have all but disappeared, and women and children fall victim to hunger, sickness, and prostitution."[189] In a letter of 1874, he vindicated Alberdi's valient opposition to that atrocity even though it had earned the permanent oprobium of Elizalde, Mitre, and the Liberal Party in Buenos Aires: "The Paraguayan War"—he wrote Alberdi—"is a disgrace that nobody wishes to remember."[190]

The terrible doubts Gutiérrrez harbored about the wisdom and contributions of Mitre were confirmed by the latter's seditious uprising in 1874. Gutiérrez, on this occasion, wrote that Mitre was "the most ambitious man that one can imagine."[191] Here was a man who put principles aside when he saw the power and wealth of the nation's highest office escaping from his grasp. It was hypocritical for Mitre to denounce as illegitimate the election that had resulted in his own defeat. Most perverse was Mitre's sorry attempt at a military coup which led to the death of hundreds of his partisans. This was but one more instance of his tragic indifference over the spilling of his countrymen's blood. Although Gutiérrez never disliked Mitre as a person, he believed that "vanity and pedantry" played a greater role in that leader's public actions than sound political judgment. It was deeply unfortunate for the country that Mitre's reality was so distinct from his popular reputation as "scholar and hero." The events of 1874 revealed that Mitre was just one more "scoundrel" leader in the sorry succession of "putred administrations" that predominated the country's short history.

Three years later Gutiérrez's opinion would hardly alter about Mitre and the political party he led. Political parties, Gutiérrez observed, competed only for the power to distribute jobs and had little concern for formulating policy on the basis of high principles. Mitre's continued pursuit of power was a sure symptom of the country's "sick democracy."[192] Gutiérrez harbored similarly negative opinions about Mitre's successor to the presidency, Sarmiento, whom he likened to "a small-town pedant dominie" presiding over a governmental farce.[193]

1880 AND BEYOND

The year 1880 stands as a watershed in Argentina's development. The victory of national forces over the rebellious provincial troops of Buenos

Aires, led by Carlos Tejedor, cemented the central government's authority. The forceful interventions of the previous two decades had brought about the final defeat of the Federalist Party and an end to more than sixty years of bloody conflicts between the interior and the port city. Now, the capitalization of Buenos Aires signified the attainment of a new social peace throughout the country. Indeed for the first time since the late colonial period, there was no serious split or division among those constituting the region's socioeconomic elite. Their liberal-positivist ideology reigned supreme. With internal peace and order assured and the authority of the central government now unchallenged, the road was clear for realizing the most ambitious dreams of material progress.

Historians point to Buenos Aires's impressive progress in the previous two decades, compared to the sluggish growth of the interior provinces, as one of the underlying causes for that province's emerging supremacy in the country. To most observers the advance of Buenos Aires was irrepressible; neither the economic sanctions of the Confederation nor the costly Paraguayan conflict had significantly slowed the steady push forward on all fronts. Signs of wealth and progress were evident in the modernized port and recently completed railroad lines to distant points of the province and cities of the interior. The wealth and power of the country's emerging oligarchy was evident to all in the exuberant buildings of the Jockey Club and the Club del Progreso—that "dreamy mansion" for which "not all mortals are allowed entrance" (in the words of Lucio V. López)—and the luxurious mansions in the neighborhood of San Telmo. Aristocratic taste characterized the Race Track and Palermo Park. The new prosperity primarily benefited the large landowners, but all other classes also shared it to some degree. Whether through speculation or enterprise, fraudulent dealings or hard work, prosperity and material improvement were within reach of even the most humble *gaucho* or impoverished immigrant. A thirst for fortune and material comfort touched all social classes.

In the countryside the social structures that would predominate for the next century were now evident. The bullish world demand for the region's meat, wool, and cereal exports accounted for the unprecedented prosperity of rural producers. Land values doubled overnight in many regions, leading to widespread real estate speculation and the creation of instant fortunes. The "Desert Campaign" of 1879—the euphemism given to Roca's military expedition that resulted in the slaughter of thousands of Indians—proved to be a bonanza for the small group of powerful landowners. The fifteen thousand leagues of pampa plains, with abundant pastures for fattening range cattle, fell primarily into their hands and would undergo little, if any, development.

But in areas close to urban centers and accessible to national and international markets, the transformations were profound. Here, the wealthy landowning class quickly adjusted to the new demands of rural production. They invited foreign interests to construct railway lines, to raise sheep to benefit from bullish world prices for wool, and to modernize traditional cattle-raising operations through new techniques in sanitation and mestization with British breeds. Immigrant sharecroppers or migrants from the interior tilled their soils for wheat harvests. These changes brought about the domestication or disappearance of the *gaucho* population, the settlement of Italian and Basque immigrants, and the rise of totally new occupations: fencers, blacksmiths, builders, carpenters, and mechanics.

In other key aspects the development of the country gave definite reason for pride. Sarmiento, in the latter years of his long and fruitful life, oftentimes viewed the proverbial glass as ambiguously half-full: "Within the ranks of the world's most backward of countries, Argentina rates as the most advanced," he wrote.[194] In this respect, Aníbal Ponce was correct in describing "Sarmiento's golden years" as a period of celebration over the "new homeland" that was now emerging.[195] Thanks to the grandiose civilizing effort since the fall of Rosas, the country had much to brag about: Buenos Aires was the "high point of activity, force, and progress"; the "prodigious extension" of the region's press had no comparison even in Europe; the central government had put on the market over twenty thousand square leagues of land suitable for colonization; and provinces like Santa Fe had benefited extraordinarily from the settlement of a large immigrant population, the spread of agriculture, the emergence of Rosario as commercial entrepot of the interior, and the creation of thousands of medium-sized farms owned by immigrants of humble means. Another source of pride was education: the Province of Buenos Aires compared favorably to Europe's most advanced countries in the number of educational institutions and the proportion of literate citizens. There illiteracy had been almost eradicated, even among former Black slaves and *gaucho* squatters. No one was more critical than Sarmiento of the country's slow emergence from underdevelopment, yet even he had to admit that in spite of many obstacles his countrymen were well on the way toward creating the "future Argentine citizen" who would regenerate the country.

The political dimensions of the Roca state also provided much basis for a new and widespread optimism. Initially many observers—Alberdi included—had erroneously interpreted Roca's ascent to the presidency as signifying the definitive dislodging of Buenos Aires from the leadership position in the nation's politics. However it soon became apparent that the Roca epoch signified, instead, the consolidation of an oligarchy, based primarily in the Province of Buenos Aires but also with membership in the neighboring provinces, that legitimized its control over the political and economic institutions throughout the country.[196] In spite of the fact that one of Roca's primary bases of electoral support had been the league of provincial governors, the authority of his regime was anchored in the hegemonic province; this was the reality that soon came to flavor the decisions and actions of his administration that affected the entire nation. The assertive interventionalist policies of Mitre, Sarmiento, and Avellaneda—and now culminating with Roca—resulted in the definitive repression of the *caudillos* with federalist orientation and the coercive domination of the most rebellious or anarchistic groups in the interior. In short the Roca administration signaled Buenos Aires's definitive and undisputed domination over the entire nation.

The most remarkable aspect of the Roca period was the almost total conformity that now existed among the nation's elite with regard to the socioeconomic reality of the country and the most desirable course of development for the future. Incredible as it might seem, the anger and resentment that had exploded periodically throughout the previous two decades were now largely forgotten, repressed, or overcome. This is seen in the ideological trajectory of some of the country's most important writers who, only a short time before, had been the spokespersons for the tragedy of the interior.

José Hernández's ideological trajectory in this regard was noteworthy. His vibrant protest over the treatment of the *gaucho* by a corrupt urban society in the first part of *Martín Fierro* (1872), in addition to his anguished support for López Jordán against the intervention of national troops in Entre Ríos, became transformed by 1876—in the second part to his monumental poem—into the poetic exhortation for the *gaucho* to bury the mystique of his past freedom on the ranges, change his ways though education, and resign himself to the newly predominant system in his role as domesticated ranch hand. Then, by 1881 Hernández, through his publication *Instrucción del estanciero* (Cattle rancher's manual), would be educating the landed oligarchy in the efficient use of land and *gaucho* labor. Through his contributions as national senator, he would promote the cattle industry that represented Argentina's most appropriate route to achieve material progress and "civilization."

A similar transition in ideological orientation would occur with Carlos Guido y Spano. His father, General Tomás Guido, had fought in the struggles for independence as one of General San Martín's most trusted supporters; later, in his long and distinguished service to the young country, the general had been able to distance himself from the repressive politics of the Rosas regime by accepting diplomatic responsibilities in the imperial court of Río de Janeiro. Carlos Guido, born in 1827, passed his adolescent years in that idyllic Brazilian setting while nurturing an intense commitment to his homeland that he inherited from his father. The son's enthusiasm upon returning to Buenos Aires after the fall of the dictator in 1852 quickly soured as a result of the separatist movement of September 11 that was led by Mitre, Valentín Alsina, and others. Beginning in 1854 his opposition to Buenos Aires localism took the form of journalistic activism in Paraná; toward the end of that decade, he briefly served the Confederation in the capacity of undersecretary for foreign relations. After 1862 he bitterly opposed the alliance with Brazil that was negotiated by Mitre's minister, Rufino de Elizalde. Along with José and Rafael Hernández, he hastened to Paysandú in January 1865, but he could not save that city from the siege and tragic massacre by the Empire's navy. That event inspired in him the epic resonances of several wrath-filled essays that circulated widely across the interior.[197] In 1866 Guido y Spano authored *El gobierno y la alianza* (The government and the Alliance), which angrily denounced the actions of the Mitre administration in Uruguay and Paraguay. In addition his poem, "Nenia," was one of the most memorable of the period, with its funeral lament over the death and destruction of Paraguay by the armies of Argentina and Brazil. During that period no other voice was more enraged than his over the unjust treatment by Buenos Aires of the people of the interior.

Within a decade the politics of the country would change dramatically. Guido's unselfish service during the yellow fever epidemic of 1871 brought him into personal contact with the foremost members of the Buenos Aires elite, causing him to reassess his previously rebellious relationship with that group. In 1872 he accepted the directorship of the newly established National Department of Agriculture, and two years later he eagerly took up arms against Mitre's bloody insurrection. In subsequent years he served as director of the Provincial Archives, while his reputation as a poet spread. His *Autobiografía* (Autobiography) of 1879 revealed a newly positive assessment of national reality that was based on the oblivion of the bitter past. In his own words, he had decided to "quit living the life of desperation. . . . I began to realize that worldly existence was not so detestable, nor my fellow men so perverse."[198] Having made peace with the established powers, his poetic trajectory after 1880 rarely treated issues relative to the country's social reality. But this was precisely the type of literature that would earn him, after that date, recognition as the country's poet laureate.

A similar trajectory can be seen in the ideas and actions of Olegario Andrade. He was born in Brazil in 1839. As a student in Entre Ríos, he fervently defended Urquiza and the Federalist Party while assimilating liberal ideas that spoke to the need for opening the province and the region to Europe's modernizing influences. Following Caseros his articles in *El porvenir* (The future) of Gualeguaychú stridently attacked the Mitre administration's politics of "extermination" in the interior provinces and its opprobrious alliance with Brazil in the war with Paraguay. His long years of anger and disillusionment would fade, however, before the growing realization that the moment for national reconstruction was at hand. In 1876, with Avellaneda as the nation's president, he moved to Buenos Aires. From this moment on the tone and themes of his romantic poetry were decidedly different; he became known as one who "sang praise of the country's new democracy." His patriotic poetry henceforth spoke to his optimism in Argentina's "Promethean race" and the brilliant future awaiting his country in the coming positivist age.[199] Like Hernández, Guido y Spano, and others, the anguished protest of two decades before totally yielded to an effervescent hymn to the Roca state.

What were the respective positions of the now aged warriors of 1837 before the new state that took definitive form under Roca? Frías, V. F. López, Sarmiento, and Mitre continued to provide distinguished public service, in spite of the advancing age of the first three. In relation to the most important issues, these four—in addition to Alberdi—found themselves in general agreement about the most important issues. Their long struggle against tyranny had successfully ended, and the new political order would henceforth guarantee the peaceful transition of power through institutionalized elections. Formerly they had lashed out at the usurpation of social, economic, and political power by the unruly and anarchistic masses; now they took solace in the fact that society's direction was firmly in the hands of a small elite whose conservative social and political ideas generally coincided with their own. If they had been perturbed over the displacement of power from the educated urban elites to the barbaric *caudillos* of the countryside before, they now could rejoice about the new and important role of writers and intellectuals in country's public affairs. And last, if their complaint had previously targeted the "closed," localist, petty-nationalist, and "Americanist" system perpetuated by their *caudillo* foes, now they could applaud the acceptance of their liberal, cosmopolitan, pro-European outlook by the most active sectors of society. In this regard the Roca regime represented precisely the realization of their long-deferred dreams of order, progress, and civilization.

This conservative, celebratory view is precisely what now predominated in the important writings on Argentine history by Vicente F. López that began to appear in print after 1881.[200] Surprisingly his pro-Confederate sympathies and the influence of Alberdi, manifest in his thought throughout the 1850s and early 1860s, now waned in front of the dramatic changes throughout the country. Some readers have suggested López's irrelevance in that new age by linking his worldview with that of his father's generation and the inspired group of Porteño leaders at the outbreak of the revolutionary struggle.[201] This view however, fails to take into account the recurring expression in his historical writings of pro-Porteño sentiments and his scathing criticisms of the *caudillos* in the interior; this last perspective decidely links his perspective with the worldview of the liberal Porteño oligarchy in its new predominance.

Indeed López's mature historical interpretation of the country's recent past hardly differed from Sarmiento's views in *Facundo* or Mitre's perspective in *Historia de Belgrano* (History of Belgrano). According to López the retrograde *gaucho* leaders of the countryside and the interior— whose representative figures were Ramírez and Artigas—had waged war against Buenos Aires and had cast the country into destructive anarchy. This caused an unnatural "retrogression" in the region's historical development," because its "traditional hierarchy," headed by authoritarian leaders, favored their own class interests at the expense of the public good. Instability and stagnation resulted when unitarian governments, representing progressive urban groups, attempted to dismantle those traditional hierarchies through the implementation of radical democratic reforms. Those extremist measures clashed not only with rural society's retrograde institutions and practices but also with the foundation of long-standing administrative traditions that had weathered the test of time.[202] López's dramatic interpretation of the nation's recent past read like historical romance (for this reason he has been called an "imaginative synthesizer" of events). In his narrative one reads how a more responsible generation of Porteño leaders than the early unitarians patiently awaited the appropriate historical moment and then succeeded in finding allies within the ranks of the oppressed masses in order to overcome the social threat offered by the *montoneros;* they succeeded in reestablishing their ties with "the old community, and reclaiming their rightful position as the nation's ruling class."[203] The sense of prophecy that one reads in these words is striking. For V. F. López, writing in the 1880s, the inspired actions of liberal presidents (Mitre, Sarmiento, Avellaneda, and now Roca) finally succeeded in reconstituting a semblance of that "ancient community" of enlightened Porteño leaders and restoring them to the center and head of the nation.

UNITY AND DECEPTION

The surviving militants from the 1837 generation joined with the reigning popular opinion in embracing the view that Argentina's times of civil war and material want were in the past and that only prosperity, order, and progress lay ahead. All had sacrificed long years and untiring service in the construction of the new national state that was firmly under the influence, if not control, of the Porteño liberal oligarchy. Yet while they supported the presidency, they all had reservations about the president. Such was the nature of political life that these seasoned, consummate politicians—Mitre, Sarmiento, and López—quickly claimed for themselves a distinct segment of the ideological terrain to continue their debates.

Into and beyond the 1880s, Mitre's reputation altered dramatically according to the viewer. Many could not forget the acute deficiencies in his character that twice in seven years had led to his leadership and then military defeat of seditious rebellions against the very government he had done so much to consolidate only decades earlier. Interestingly his surviving generational cohorts—Gutiérrez, López, Sarmiento, Alberdi—emphasized these deficiencies when they considered his contributions. But for a majority of the elitist Porteño circle, Mitre remained a venerated elder statesman as well as a literary and journalistic maestro. Martín García Merou communicated his youthful "blind admiration" for Mitre and the "prestige of his triumphant genius." "[E]veryone would vouch for the integrity of his character and the power of his intelligence."[204] This was a widespread sentiment. Paul Groussac also confirmed that positive view: "Few ignored the magnanimity of his character and the personal prestige that he enjoyed among the people."[205]

Mitre's opposition to Roca was understandable given the recent defeat of the Tejedor rebellion that he had supported. For the Porteño elite, Roca's victory, coupled with the federalization of Buenos Aires, had initially assumed the proportions of their city's definitive defeat by the internal provinces. But within a few years, that view would be radically revised. Nevertheless that initial perspective flavored Mitre's politics and determined his decision to assume the role of parliamentary and journalistic detractor before the new president's policies. From the pages of *La nación*, he repeatedly attacked the growing moral decadence of the Republic, which was manifest in an electoral system endemic with fraudulent practices. He also denounced the growing militarism in government that resulted from the new executive's network of loyalists in the armed forces. Another target of attack was Roca's authoritarian will which allowed for no rival within the government. In spite of his two unsuccessful rebellions against the constitutional government, Mitre's hagiographers have nevertheless characterized him as the country's maximum defender of democratic ideals and practices.[206]

A more impartial historiography calls attention to the links that Mitre continued to enjoy throughout the period with the powerful cattle interests that thrived because of their lucrative commercial and economic relations with Great Britain. His writings and political stands continued to demonstrate an essential agreement with the interests of the Porteño cattle oligarchy and the governing program that Roca and Pellegrini were in the process of realizing: "Our program is Free Trade." Mitre celebrated the close ties existing between the economic powerbrokers of Argentina and the financial and commercial interests in Great Britain. He believed Argentina's limitless potentiality for agricultural and cattle production deserved the total confidence of British investors.[207] Few members of the Porteño economic and political elite took exception to this view at the time; they reasoned that if free trade had led to the enrichment of the region's most potent economic sector, that practice had also helped to bring about an enviable prosperity for society as a whole. However more critical minds (foremost among whom was Sarmiento) clearly saw the distortions in the country's development that such policies were causing and even predicted the dire economic crisis that would engulf the country in the near future. Mitre's detractors, both then and now, view his pact with the cattle *latifundia* to be a result of his own lack of political vision or a consequence of an intelligence blinded by self-interest. His "truly Basque-like stubbornness," according to Carlos D'Amico, was manifest in how he always placed egotistical objectives before the happiness of his fellow Argentines.[208]

After 1880 Mitre's political influence continually declined as did his possibilities for reassuming the position of national leadership. Nevertheless he continued his strident criticism from the columns of *La nación*.[209] In 1891 his name briefly figured as candidate for the presidency under the banner of the newly constituted Unión Cívica Party. His program, in opposition to the conservative order that become implanted under Roca, called for the implementation of universal suffrage, an objective that would not be realized until 1912, some six years after his death.[210]

* * *

In surveying Sarmiento's writings between 1880 and his death in 1888, one is struck by the coexistence of two apparently contradictory perspectives. On the one hand, he strongly affirmed many aspects of the Argentine state that had emerged in the thirty years since the fall of Rosas; with so much progress and material improvement, Buenos Aires totally resembled Europe or North America. With pride he admitted, "This is proof enough that our struggle of 30 years against a tyrant was not in vain."[211] On the other hand, one finds in essay after essay, in addition to Sarmiento's copious correspondence with political intimates José Posse, José Victorino Lastarria, and others, perhaps the most reasoned and developed critique of the grave ills besetting the young country in the latter decades of the nineteenth century.

Although Sarmiento joined Mitre in raising points of contention against Roca—for example his fury in 1885 over Roca's attempts to impose Júarez Celman as successor to the presidency—his most enduring criticisms were of more systemic or structural issues. Among these three topics merit further commentary: the mixed results of Argentina's decades-long experience with European immigration, the detrimental contribution of the powerful cattle-exporting oligarchy, and the inferior racial stock of Amerindians, *mestizos*, and Blacks who constituted a significant proportion of the country's population.

Sarmiento was among his country's earliest and most persistent advocates of encouragement for European immigration to colonize the vast expanses of range land, initiate an agricultural industry to rival the predominant cattle interests, and invest and develop the country's latent industrial potential. Yet by the end of the 1870s—after nearly a quarter-century of heavy immigration—he was beginning to realize the great gap between those early promises and the actual results. The White emigrants from the more advanced societies of northern Europe tended to prefer the United States and Canada, whereas Argentina received primarily the impoverished and uneducated peasantry from Southern Europe. Among those that did find their way to Argentina, only a relatively small number succeeded in occupying their own land and tilling the soil. Instead the majority of immigrants came to constitute an uneducated mass populating the country's urban areas. His early writings, primarily of the 1850s, incessantly argued the benefits of an immigrant population whose industry and work habits would foster industry and agriculture in the country. He foresaw that the prosperity of immigrant producers would lead to the creation of a new middle class that would eventually come to rival the economic and political power of the regime's oligarchy, which was given over to cattle production.[212] Although his fears would grow over the threat to the established social order that came about as a result of the ever-expanding conglomeration of unassimilated immigrants on Argentine soil, he celebrated how their enterprising spirit was rapidly displacing antiquated *criollo* practices in retail commerce and small industrial production. Until his death Sarmiento would continue to defend the central role of the immigrant in the development of the country. But at the same time he repeatedly expressed his growing concerns over the threat they posed to the newly consolidated social and political order.[213]

In apparent contradiction to his earlier advocacies, Sarmiento now argued against the electoral enfranchisement of foreign-born residents. He argued that voting privileges would grant the immigrant population effective control over the Argentine government, a situation with totally unforeseeable consequences. Here his xenophobic pride, combined with a fear of radical change and civil disorder, led Sarmiento to support the very position defended by the *criollo* oligarchy of the province.[214] His verbal consolation for the foreign-born residents whom he wished to continue excluding from political participation was one more example of his uncanny prophetic power; he argued that within a generation the immigrants and their descendants would enjoy the uncontested advantage of numbers and wealth, and even the government would pass to their hands.[215]

Although Sarmiento joined hands with the oligarchy over the need to restrict the immigrant's political participation, he continued to sound criticisms about the retrograde role of that same oligarchy in the country's ongoing development. However—contrary to the impression communicated by Milcíades Peña, Anderson Imbert, and others—the 1880s saw little of the verve and passion that his attacks had manifested in earlier decades. By this time his profound disillusionment over the unchallenged predominance of the *latifundia* cattle exporters in the country's power structure—that "aristocracy smelling of cow dung," as he had called it[216]—had become transformed into a "deaf antagonism."[217] Sarmiento was becoming bitterly resigned to the socioeconomic reality of a country with a few hundred very large landowners who allowed only the temporary settlement by agricultural sharecroppers and who completely controlled the country's social and political institutions.

Martínez Estrada and Halperín Donghi[218] communicate the extent of this disillusionment in the aged Sarmiento, which found expression in dispersed passages of his correspondence and writings but never in the form of a sustained elaboration. A new target for Sarmiento's muffled criticisms was the very group to which he belonged: the cadre of intellectuals and politicians who had provided leadership for the country in the post-Rosas period. In fleeting passages he suggested his generation's collective treason before the great promises of the country, but more prevalent was the depiction of his generation as victim of a widespread decadence affecting the country as a whole. This new, sober realization brought about a reevaluation of the generally favorable image of the region's colonial elite that he had offered thirty years earlier in *Recuerdos de provincia*. The desolate testimony of this growing pessimism was *Conflicto y armonías de las razas in América* (Conflict and harmonies of the races in America—1883), a collage of historical and ethnographic excerpts that was Sarmiento's halfhearted attempt to document the inferior genetic stock of the South American nations.

In the work's prologue (a letter to Mrs. Horace Mann, wife of the Boston educator and English translator of *Facundo*), Sarmiento attempted to imbue with authority the racist message of *Conflictos* by characterizing it as his "*Facundo* having grown old." He was correct about one factor here: there was a continuity to his thought, from his earliest publications to the last, with regard to the inferior biological status with which he viewed the Indian race. Yet in this view he was hardly alone; all the members of his generation—from Echeverría to Alberdi and Mitre—believed the Indian to be an obstacle for the country's realization of a glorious future. In addition all of them implicitly, if not explicitly, defended a politics of genocide in order to end once and for all the threat of terrifying Indian raids against White settlements along the frontier. Even the pro*gaucho* José Hernández, Sarmiento's most vociferous detractor in the 1860s, did not differ substantially with regard to this rabidly negative view of the Indian. This was hardly a mere theoretical concern. From the fall of Rosas until Roca's "Desert Campaign" of 1879, White settlement of the underpopulated pampas had been severely restricted because of "the Indian problem."

Yet Sarmiento carried his pseudoscientific onslaught even further by condemning even the Spanish and their new-world descendants for the truncated progress of his continent. He argued that the Inquisition had eliminated Spain's most progressive elements and then acted to stunt the intellectual growth of those who remained. As a consequence the Spanish empire in the Americas could only offer retrograde, confused leadership. In several passages he indiscriminately grouped social and psychological behaviors with genetic and physiological traits. Specific political ideas were arbitrarily correlated with specific racial groups. According to this analysis that was heavily tainted with bias and racial prejudice, the blame for the country's destructive civil wars fell upon three likely culprits: the Indians, the Jesuits, and the *gaucho*-barbarian, Artigas.[219] One need not catalog any further the deeply flawed methodology of this work and the highly skewed conclusions it produced. More important here is to call attention to the deep pessimism in the spirit of the man who wrote it. Gone was his faith in the educated elite that had guided Spanish America in colonial times and in which he had deposited his faith for steering the country into a new republican era. The septuagenarian stubbornly continued to defend the goals that had inspired him throughout a fertile lifetime of public service. He continued to dream of an egalitarian society in which all citizens had the opportunity to improve their station through meaningful labor and access to education and to promote the goals of grass-roots democratic participation and a political economy favoring agriculture over cattle raising. Thoroughly disillusioned with the directions indicated by the Roca state, Sarmiento could only find solace in returning to the utopian politico-cultural ideals that he had defended in his youth.

Notes

CHAPTER 1. THE FORMATIVE YEARS

1. Domingo Faustino Sarmiento, *Obras completas* vol. VII (Buenos Aires: Luz del Día, 1948–56), p. 62.

2. Tulio Halperín Donghi, "Liberalismo argentino y liberalismo mexicano: dos destinos divergentes," in *El espejo de la historia: problemas argentinos y perspectivas latinoamericanas* (Buenos Aires: Sudamericana, 1987), p. 150.

3. Leonardo Paso, *Los caudillos y la organización nacional* (Buenos Aires: Futuro, 1965), pp. 51–53.

4. Sarmiento, *Obras completas*, vol. VII, p. 46.

5. Arturo Ardao, "Interpretaciones de Rosas," in *Estudios latinoamericanos: historia de las ideas* (Caracas: Monte Avila, 1978), p. 78.

6. Ibid., p. 84.

7. Echeverría, "Cartas a un amigo," in *Obras completas de Esteban Echeverría*, ed. and prol. Juan María Gutiérrez (Buenos Aires: Zamora, 1972), p. 401.

8. Ibid., pp. 144, 222.

9. Juan B. Alberdi, *Estudios económicos* (Buenos Aires: 1934), p. 118.

10. Ibid., p. 127.

11. Sarmiento, *Obras completas*, vol. VII, p. 100.

12. Tulio Halperín Donghi, *Economics and Society in Argentina in the Revolutionary Period*, trans. Richard Southern (Cambridge: Cambridge University Press, 1975), p. 166.

13. Paso, *Caudillos*, pp. 271–72.

14. M. Núñez, *Bustos: el caudillo olvidado* (Buenos Aires: Cuadernos de Crisis, 1975), p. 23, quotes V. F. López, *Manual de Historia Argentina*.

15. Halperín Donghi, *Politics*, p. 352.

16. Ibid., p. 361. Halperín argues that Rivadavia's measures only hastened the dissolution of civil authority, which was already in crisis as a result of the dislocations of the independence struggle.

17. José María Paz, as quoted by José Luis Romero, *A History of Argentine Political Thought*, trans. Thomas F. McGann (Stanford: Stanford University Press, 1963), p. 100.

18. Jorge Mayer, *Alberdi y su tiempo* (Buenos Aires: Editorial Universitaria de Buenos Aires, 1963), p. 35, quotes Paul Groussac, "El desarrollo constitucional" (1902). Groussac undoubted exaggerates here: both Ibarra and Quiroga were well educated and could hardly be considered "poncho-clad barbarians."

19. Vicente Fidel López, *Historia de la República Argentina. Su origen, su revolución y su desarrollo político hasta el gobierno del general Viamonte. Continuada hasta 1910 por Emilio Vera y González y ampliada desde el descubrimiento hasta nuestros días por Enrique de Gandia. Nueva edución profusamente ilustrada*, vol. IV (Buenos Aires: Sopena, 1964), pp. 352n, 353. Although López blamed Artigas, in actual fact the

Battle of Cepeda and the subsequent march upon Buenos Aires were directed by that leader's lieutentants, Francisco Ramírez and Estanislao López, the strongmen respectively of Entre Ríos and Santa Fe, who would shortly break with the Banda Oriental leader.

20. A. Belin Sarmiento, *Sarmiento anecdótico (ensayo biográfico)* (Saint Cloud: Imprenta Belin, 1929), p. 20.

21. Sarmiento, *Obras completas*, vol. VII, p. 52.

22. Carmen P. de Varese and Héctor D. Arias, *Historia de San Juan* (Mendoza: Spadoni, 1966), p. 234.

23. Jonathan C. Brown, "The Bondage of Old Habits in Nineteenth-Century Argentina," *Latin American Research Review* 21, no. 2 (1986), p. 12, quotes Magnus Mörner, "Economic Factors and Stratification in Colonial Spanish America with Special Regard to Elites," *Hispanic American Historical Review* 63, no. 2 (1983): 356.

24. Brown, "Bondage," p. 11.

25. Domingo Faustino Sarmiento, *Obras completas*, vol. III (Buenos Aires: Luz del Día, 1948–56), p. 186.

26. George Reid Andrews, *The Afro-Argentines in Buenos Aires, 1800–1900* (Madison: University of Wisconsin, 1980), reports that Blacks accounted for over 50 percent of all enlistees in the wars for independence between 1810 and 1820 and constituted 26 percent of Buenos Aires's total population of sixty-three thousand in 1836.

27. David Viñas, *Literatura argentina y realidad política*, vol. 1, *De Sarmiento a Cortázar* (Buenos Aires: Siglo Veinte, 1971), pp. 20–21, 146–47, 166–74. Metaphorically speaking Viñas suggests that the annihilation of the Indian was necessary in order to make way for the railroad.

28. Félix Luna, *Los caudillos* (Buenos Aires: Peña Lillo, 1984), p. 157, copies from Facundo Quiroga's letter to General José María Paz of January 10, 1830.

29. Two examples—in addition to Sarmiento—of influential historians who totally pass over the positive contributions of Facundo Quiroga are Adolfo Saldías, *Historia de la Confederación Argentina* (Buenos Aires: Editorial Universitaria de Buenos Aires, 1968), and Ramón J. Cárcano, *Juan Facundo Quiroga: simulación, infidencia, tragedia* (Buenos Aires: López, 1933).

30. Luna, *Los caudillos*, p. 170.

31. Roberto Etcheipareborda, *Rosas: controvertida historiografía* (Buenos Aires: Pleamar, 1972), pp. 77–96, offers a balanced account of the terror administered by both factions participating in the intermittent civil struggles that consumed the energies of the republic between 1810 and 1852.

32. Luna, *Los caudillos*, pp. 155–58, copies the letter from Facundo Quiroga to General Paz dated January 10, 1830.

33. E. F. Sánchez Zinny, *Los ciento diez jinetes de la gloria* (Buenos Aires: Linari y Cía, 1944), p. 212 (from his essay, "Juan Facundo Quiroga era unitario").

34. David Peña, *Juan Facundo Quiroga* (Buenos Aires: Hyspamérica, 1986), p. 161.

35. Luna, *Los caudillos*, pp. 169–70, copies from Quiroga's letter to Rosas, January 12, 1832.

36. The most passionate advocates of this view are Peña, *Juan Facundo Quiroga*, pp. 169–90, and Antonio Zinny, *Historia de los gobernadores de las provincias argentinas*, vol. 2, *Provincia de Buenos Aires, 1810–1853* (Buenos Aires: Huemul, 1942), p. 286. The notes are by Eduardo F. Sánchez Zinny.

37. See Enrique Barba, "Estudio Preliminar," *Correspondencia entre Rosas, Quiroga y López*, ed. Barba (Buenos Aires: Hachette, 1958), pp. 7–21. See also

chapter 2 to Etchepareborda's *Rosas: controvertida historiografía* entitled "Trayectoria del revisionismo argentino," for a balanced review of the historiographic literature of the past sixty years that has been partisan to the Rosas legacy.

38. Cárcano, *Juan Facundo Quiroga*, p. 19.

39. Juan Bautista Alberdi, *Escritos póstumos* (Buenos Aires: Imprenta Juan Bautista Alberdi, 1900). Vol. XV, p. 430.

40. Ibid., p. 292.

41. Juan Bautista Alberdi, *Grandes y pequeños hombres del Plata* (Buenos Aires: Plus Ultra, 1974), pp. 149, 157. In contrast with this generally positive treatment of the nation's great *caudillos,* Alberdi also rendered a more critical view. For him they were retrograde representatives of a historical period that had to be superseded and of a race and social grouping that had demonstrated inferiority vis-à-vis the rest of the world. According to David Viñas, [*Rebeliones populares argentinas*], vol. I, *De los montoneros a los anarquistas* (Buenos Aires: Carlos Pérez, 1971), p. 31, Alberdi "neither defended nor rehibilitated El Chacho. [Alberdi] is also a man of his class, a bourgeois *conquistador,* and profoundly steeped in its ideology even though he quibbles about specific aspects of its actions."

42. Juan María Gutiérrez, *Epistolario,* ed. and prol. Ernesto Morales (Buenos Aires: Instituto Cultural Joaquín V. González, 1942), p. 13, copies the letter of April 25, 1835.

43. Vicente Fidel López, *Panoramas y retratos históricos,* prol. Joaquín V. González (Buenos Aires: W. M. Jackson, n.d.), pp. 256–63.

44. Vicente F. López, *Historia de la República argentina. Su origen, su revolución y su desarrollo político hasta el gobierno del general Viamonte. Continuada hasta 1910 por Emilio Vera y González y ampliada desde el descubrimiento hasta nuestros días por Enrique de Gandia. Nueva edición profusamente ilustrada.* 10 vols. Buenos Aires: Sopena Argentina, 1964, Vol. VI, pp. 159–70.

45. Gutiérrez, *Epistolario,* p. 57.

46. Alberto J. Masramón, *Urquiza: libertador y fundador* (Buenos Aires: Plus Ultra, 1982), pp. 46–54.

47. Norma L. Pavoni, *El noroeste argentino en la època de Alejandro Heredia,* vol. 1, *Política* (Tucumán: Fundación Banco Comercial del Norte, 1981), p. 87.

48. Ibid., p. 115. The novel mentioned is Jorge Söhle, *Chavela (novela histórica argentina)* (Rosario: La Velocidad, 1903), pp. 6–9. I am indebted to Olga Fernández Latour de Botas for having obtained for me a xerox copy of this novel from the original owned by Profesor Bruno C. Jarovella.

49. Antonio Zinny, *Historia de los gobernadores de las provincias argentinas,* vol. III, *Córdoba, Tucumán, Santiago de Estero, San Luis* (Buenos Aires: Vaccaro, 1920), pp. 283–98.

50. López, *Historia,* vol. VI, pp. 160–61.

51. Alberdi, *Escritos póstumos,* vol. XV, p. 286.

52. Juan Bautista Alberdi, *Cartas inéditas a Juan María Gutiérrez y a Félix Frías,* ed. and introd. by Jorge M. Mayer and Ernesto A. Martínez (Buenos Aires: Luz del Día, 1953).

53. Alberdi, *Escritos póstumos,* vol. XV, p. 228, reproduces the letter from Brígido Silva to J. B. Alberdi, September 26, 1836.

54. Juan M. Méndez Avellaneda, "¿Quién mató a Alejandro Heredia?" *Todo es historia* 126 (November 1977): 78–94, persuasively argues in the light of all the contradictory evidence that the assassination of Heredia was probably an act of personal revenge by a low-grade officer, Gabino Robles, whom Heredia had dressed down in front of a body of troops. However, Juan Pablo Oliver, *El*

verdadero Alberdi: génesis del liberalismo económico argentino (Buenos Aires: Biblioteca Dictio, 1977), pp. 150–52, reproduces popular ballads from the period linking Alberdi to Heredia's killing. Oliver's unconvincing argument is that Heredia's refusal to break with Rosas's Pacto Federal highly displeased Alberdi, who then instigated Marcos Paz and Marco Avellaneda to rebel against his ex-protector.

55. Gutiérrez, *Epistolario*, p. 29, copies the letter from Gutiérrez to Alberdi, December 28, 1838.

56. Although Avellaneda followed in the political footsteps of Heredia, his predecessor in the governorship of Tucumán and as leader of the coalition of northern provinces, his May 1839 letter to Pío Tedín (shortly before his own brutal death) revealed his very negative sentiments toward Heredia at that time. Méndez Avellaneda's authoritative conclusion in *Alejandro Heredia*, p. 177, is that Avellaneda's letter condemning Heredia "can be used to legitimately accuse him of being ungratious and hasty or unguarded in his opinions, but it in no way substantiates that he was Heredia's assassin, nor that he was accomplice or instigador of that deed."

57. These quotes are taken from Carlos Machado, *Historia de los orientales*, vol. II (Montevideo: Banda Oriental, 1987), p. 14.

58. Zinny, *Historia de los gobernadores*, vol. II, p. 292, copies from Rosas's proclamation of April 13, 1835.

59. Ibid., pp. 300–304.

60. Félix Weinberg's "Estudio preliminar" to Marcos Sastre, et al., *El Salón Literario* (Buenos Aires: Hachette, 1958), pp. 9–101, provides much of the information for the following paragraphs.

61. Paul Groussac, "El doctor don Diego Alcorta," in *Estudios de historia argentina* (Buenos Aires: Jesús Menéndez, 1918), p. 259.

62. Vicente Fidel López, *Autobiografía*, in *La Biblioteca*, vol. 1 (Buenos Aires: [n.p.], 1896), pp. 325–55.

63. Quoted by Weinberg, "Estudio preliminar," p. 24.

64. Ibid., p. 28. Gutiérrez's essay appeared in *Diario de la tarde*, October 3 and 4, 1837.

65. Bartolomé Mitre, "Literatura americana: *Rimas* de D. Esteban Echeverría" (1837), in Adolfo Mitre, Manuel Conde Montero, and Juan A. Farini, *Apuntes de la juventud de Mitre y Bibliografía de Mitre* (Buenos Aires: Academia Nacional de la Historia, 1947), p. 218.

66. Alberto Palcos, "Prólogo" to Esteban Echeverría, *Dogma socialista*, critical edition (La Plata: Universidad Nacional de la Plata, 1940) p. xxvii, affirms the correctness of this date in spite of V. F. López's assertion that the Salón met between 1835–36. See also Palco's *Echeverría y la democracia argentina* (Buenos Aires: Imprenta López, 1941).

67. Marcos Sastre, *Compendio de la historia sagrada, seguido de un diccionario latino-español* (Montevideo: La caridad, 1832), 162 pp.

68. From an announcement of July 1835, according to Weinberg, "Estudio preliminar," p. 39.

69. D. Marcos Sastre, "Ojeada filosófica sobre el estado presente y la suerte futura de la Nación Argentina," in Weinberg, *El Salón Literario*, pp. 106–7.

70. Echeverría, *Obras completas*, p. 102, from "Discurso de introducción a una serie de lecturas pronunciadas en el 'Salón Literario' en setiembre de 1837."

71. Sastre, "Ojeada filosófica, p. 111.

72. Letter from Miguel Cané to Juan B. Alberdi, [n.d., Montevideo], no. 302 in Alberdi Archives (see also Cané's letter to Alberdi, n.p., n.d., no. 298).

73. Weinberg, "Estudio preliminar," p. 50n.

74. Alberto J. Masramón, *Urquiza: libertador y fundador* (Buenos Aires: Plus Ultra, 1982), p. 155, quotes Antonio Sagarna (in *Medio siglo entrerriano: entre dos cruces*, [Nogoyá, 1964]): "Sastre's contribution was admirable, and it alone constitutes a luminous page in the history of public education in Entre Ríos, since he occupied himself with the founding of schools, supervision of instructional programs and texts, teacher assemblies, school construction, and student fields and farms."

75. A fine biography of works by and about Sastre is included in Héctor Adolfo Cordero, *Marcos Sastre: el propulsor de la educación y las letras desde Rivadavia a Sarmiento* (Buenos Aires: Claridad, 1968).

76. Juan Bautista Alberdi, *Obras completas*, vol. 1 (Buenos Aires: "La tribuna nacional," 1886), p. 111.

77. Ibid., p. 111.

78. Bernardo Canal Feijóo, *Constitución y revolución: Juan Bautista Alberdi* (Buenos Aires: Fondo de Cultura Económica, 1955), p. 132.

79. Alberdi, *Obras completas*, vol. 1, p. 112.

80. Ibid., p. 125.

81. Ibid., p. 265, in the essay, "Discurso pronunciado el día de la apertura del Salón Literario."

82. Ibid., pp. 119–20, from *Fragmento*.

83. Miguel Canè reported from Montevideo, for example, that very few people understood the ideas expressed in Alberdi's inaugural address. Furthermore, "Yours I liked but . . . parts are hard to comprehend or are incomplete . . . you must write more clearly in order for your readers to understand." Letter from Cané to Alberdi, n.p., n.d., no. 302 of Alberdi Archives.

84. Cané reported in a letter to Alberdi that "Florencio [Varela] doesn't like your address in the slightest; he laments that you have passed to the side of the Federalists and that you praise Rosas." Montevideo, n.d., Alberdi Archives.

85. Andrés Lamas, "Impugnación a la obra del Sr. D. J. B. Alberdi," *El nacional*, July 27, 1838. Marta E. Peña de Matsushita, *El romanticismo político hispanoamericano* (Buenos Aires: Docencia, 1985), pp. 335–84, offers a detailed analysis of the contribution of Lamas and his relationship to Alberdi and the other Argentine militants.

86. Sarmiento, *Obras completas*, vol. VII, p. 39.

87. José Ingenieros, *La evolución de las ideas argentinas*, vol. II, *La restauración* (Buenos Aires: L. J. Rosso y Cía, 1920), p. 624.

88. Juan María Gutiérrez, "La vida y la obra de Esteban Echeverría," in Echeverría, *Obras completas*, p. 23.

89. Quoted by Gutiérrez, "Esteban Echeverría," p. 24.

90. This letter is published in the appendix to Palco's edition of Echeverría, *Dogma Socialista*.

91. Gutiérrez, "La vida," p. 34. However Abel Cháneton, *Retorno de Echeverría* (Buenos Aires: Ayacucho, 1944) and Ingenieros, *Evolución*, pp. 708–9, 720–21, present significant evidence in arguing that the two texts were composed at a later date.

92. Echeverría, *Obras Completas*, pp. 98–116, copies "Discurso de introducción a una serie de lecturas pronunciadas en el 'Salón Literario' en Setiembre de 1837." According to Weinberg these addresses by Echeverría remained unpublished until 1873.

93. Ibid., p. 103, from "Discurso."

94. Ibid., p. 115, from "Segunda lectura."
95. Ricardo Piccirilli, *Los López: una dinastía intellectual. Ensayo histórico literario, 1810–1852* (Buenos Aires: EUBA, 1972), p. 58, quotes the letter by Florencio Balcarce to Féliz Frías, Paris, 1837.
96. Ibid., p. 68, quotes Vicente López y Planes's letter to Vicente Fidel López, Montevideo, 1837.
97. Alberdi, *Escritos póstumos*, vol. XV, p. 297.
98. Vicente Fidel López, *Evocaciones históricas: Autobiografía, La gran semana de 1810, El conflicto y la entrevista de Guayaquil* (Buenos Aires: El Ateneo, 1929), p. 55. In these pages López mentioned nothing about the two "discursos" of Echeverría.
99. Palcos, "Prólogo" to Echeverría's *Dogma socialista*, p. xxvii, authoritatively argues that Echeverría, in the *Ojeada*, had erroneously attributed the founding of Joven Argentina to 1837; similarly Gutiérrez erroneously sustained that it was created in 1835.
100. This act of rebaptism occurred in Echeverría's hundred-page essay of 1846, the *Ojeada*, which accompanied the second edition of *Dogma socialista*.
101. This "Palabra" was listed tenth of the fifteen on the first list but was moved to last for the reprinting of 1846.
102. Paul Groussac, "Esteban Echeverría: La Asociación de Mayo y *El dogma socialista*," in *Crítica literaria* (Buenos Aires: Jesús Menéndez e hijo, 1924), p. 295; José Ingenieros, *La evolución de la ideas argentinas*, Vol. II, *La restauración* (Buenos Aires: Rosso y Cía., 1920), pp. 605–754, discusses the early oeuvre of the young generation in the chapter entitled, "Los sansimonianos argentinos."
103. Cháneton, *Retorno*, p. 102; and Palcos, *Echeverría y la democracia*, and "Prólogo" to Esteban Echeverría, *Dogma socialista*, edición crítica y documentada (La Plata: Universidad Nacional de la Plata, 1940). Other noteworthy studies are Tulio Halperín Donghi, *El pensamiento de Echeverría* (Buenos Aires: Sudamericana, 1951); Raúl A. Orgaz, "Echeverría y su doctrina," in *Obras completas*, vol. II, (Córdoba: Assandri, 1950), pp. 343–52; and Pablo Rojas Paz, *Echeverría: el pastor de soledades* (Buenos Aires: Losada, 1951).
104. Canal Feijóo, *Constitución y revolución*, pp. 183, 192.
105. Chaneton, *Retorno*, p. 104.
106. Ingenieros, *Evolución*, pp. 635, 637–38.
107. Quoted from Canal Feijóo, *Constitución*, p. 189.
108. Alberto Palcos, "Prólogo," p. 65; Romero, *History*, p. 133.
109. Ingenieros, *Evolución*, p. 647.
110. Alberdi, *Escritos póstumos*, vol. XV, p. 435.
111. Weinberg, "El salón literario," p. 90.
112. Alberdi, *Escritos póstumos*, vol. XV, p. 298: "Supe que Don Pedro de Angelis—Rosas's close advisor—me daba como perdido, por causa de [el Fragmento]."
113. There are several important writers who have depicted Echeverría during this key period as hardly willing to continue the active opposition to the Rosas regime that he had passionately inspired in the other youths only months before. See Sarmiento, *Obras completas*, vol. V, pp. 53–54; Martín García Merou, *Ensayo sobre Echeverría* (Buenos Aires: W. M. Jackson, 1944; reprint from 1895): 129–30; and José Ingenieros, "La filosofía social de Echeverría y la leyenda de la 'Asosiación de Mayo,'" *Revista de filosofía, cultura, ciencias* 4 (1914): 239–40, 244. Two historians who have opposed these three writers in interpreting Echeverría's actions during this period as a continuation of his commitment to the struggle

against Rosism are Alberto Palcos, *Historia de Echeverría* (Buenos Aires: Emecé, 1960); and José Luis Lanuza, *Echeverría y sus amigos* (Buenos Aires: Paídos, 1967). I attempt to make sense of these different interpretations in "Echeverría: la personificación sarmientina de una nación ultrajada por la barbarie," *Cuadernos americanos* 255 (1984): 165–85.

CHAPTER 2. EXILE: A NEW SET OF PRIORITIES (1838–1852)

1. Juan Bautista Alberdi, *Escritos póstumos*, vol. XV (Buenos Aires: La Facultad, 1920), pp. 701–2, copies the letter of March 4, 1839 from Félix Olazabal to Alberdi.

2. *Antecedentes de la Asociación de Mayo, 1837–1937* (Buenos Aires: Consejo Deliberante, Comisión de Biblioteca, 1939), pp. 123–27, copies Manuel Quiroga Rosas's letters to Alberdi, dated January 25, 1839 and February 15, 1839.

3. Juan María Gutiérrez, *Epistolario de Don Juan María Gutiérrez* (Buenos Aires: Instituto Cultural Joaquín V. González, 1942) transcribes seven such letters from Gutiérrez, written from December 1838 to late 1839.

4. Juan Bautista Alberdi, *Escritos póstumos*, Vol. VI, pp. 25–26. (Buenos Aires: La Facultad, 1920).

5. Gutiérrez, *Epistolario*, p. 25, copies the letter of December 28, 1838 to Alberdi.

6. Ibid., p. 30, copies Gutiérrez's letter of December 28, 1838 to Alberdi.

7. Ibid., p. 35, copies Gutiérrez's letter of February 25, 1839 to Alberdi.

8. Ibid., p. 37, copies Gutiérrez's letter of [1839] to Alberdi.

9. Ibid., p. 33, copies Gutiérrez's letter of February [1839] to Alberdi.

10. Alberdi, *Escritos póstumos*, XIII, pp. 12–13, and *Antecedentes*, pp. 128–29, copy letters from Gutiérrez to Alberdi, December 28, 1838 and February 14, 1839.

11. Echeverría's letter [n.d.] to "Señor Vice-Presidente de la Asociación de la Joven Generación Argentina," reprinted in *Antecedentes*, p. 116.

12. Letter from Quiroga Rosas to Alberdi, February 15, 1839 [no place], Furt Archives. My personal inspection of this letter makes obvious the errors in the transcription printed in *Antecedentes*, p. 126.

13. Domingo F. Sarmiento, *Obras completas*, vol. III (Buenos Aires: Luz del Día, 1948–56), p. 172.

14. Ibid., vol. VII, p. 103.

15. Leoncio Gianello, *Florencio Varela* (Buenos Aires: Guillermo Kraft, 1948), p. 265, quotes Ricardo Rojas.

16. Florencio Varela, *Escritos políticos, económicos y literarios*, ed. Luis L. Domínguez. (Buenos Aires: Orden, 1859), offers an important preliminary essay about Varela's activities. Essential for understanding Varela's relationship to the ideological and political issues of the time is the collection of essays united by Félix Weinberg, ed., *Florencio Varela y el 'Comercio del Plata'* (Bahía Blanca: Universidad Nacional del Sur, Instituto de Humanidades, 1970).

17. Vicente Fidel López, *Historia de la Revolución argentina. Su origen, su revolución y su desarrollo político hasta el gobierno del general Viamonte. Continuada hasta 1910 por Emilio Vera y González y ampliada desde el descubrimiento hasta nuestros días por Enrique de Gandia. Nueva edición profusamente ilustrada*, vol. VI (Buenos Aires: Sopena Argentina, 1964), p. 334n.

18. Varela's antiquated literary ideas were the implicit focus of Alberdi's essay on "Certamen Poético de Mayo" (1841), in *Obras selectas*, vol. 1, pp. 115–38.

19. Gianello, *Florencio Varela*, pp. 263–64, does not provide convincing evidence when he argues against several of the issues mentioned here.

20. Félix Weinberg, "Florencio Varela ante la encrucijada política de su tiempo," in *Florencio Varela*, ed. Félix Weinberg pp. 11–54. Undoubtedly Mitre read into this "aristocratic vision" the implication that Varela favored the preservation of the colony's hierarchical social system when he wrote—perhaps unjustly—about Varela: "And he died still perhaps doubting the worth of the ideas generated by the May Revolution!" (Quoted in Juan Baustista Alberdi, *Grandes y pequeños hombres del Plata* [Buenos Aires: Plus Ultra, 1974], p. 86.)

21. Gianello, *Florencio Varela*, p. 238.

22. According to Alberto Blasi Brambilla, *José Mármol y la sombra de Rosas* (Buenos Aires: Pleamar, 1970), p. 44: "Mármol collaborates assiduously with [*El comercio del Plata*]; Varela reciprocated that favor by authoring a magnificent essay on [Mármol's] *Cantos del peregrino* (Songs of the wanderer), that appeared in 1846, which revealed penetrating reflection and sagatious literary sensitivity."

23. Félix Frías, *Escritos y discursos*, vol. II (Buenos Aires: Librería de Mayo, 1884), p. 453, copies from "Don Florencio Varela," originally published in *La religión*, June 19, 1858.

24. In *Escritos póstumos*, Alberdi consistently mentions F. Varela in a favorable context: vol. VII, p. 93, comparing him to Washington and Belgrano; vol. VIII, 143; vol. XII, pp. 40–47; vol. VI, p. 57, links him with Rivadavia, Alvear, Gutiérrez, V. Alcina, and Belgrano. On p. 119 of that same volume, Alberdi praises Varela for having come around to embracing many of the Association's doctrines.

25. Aldolfo Saldías, *Historia de la Confederación Argentina*, vol. II, *Rozas y su época* (Buenos Aires: Editorial Juan Carlos Granda, 1967), p. 406. Saldías, for unexplained reasons, elevates Rivera Indarte to the status of major protagonist in the struggle against Rosas by dedicating thirty pages (pp. 406–36) to attacking him.

26. López, *Historia*, vol. VI, pp. 278–79n.

27. Among José Rivera Indarte's works are *El voto de América* . . . (Buenos Aires: Comercio, 1835), pp. 40; *Apuntes sobre el asesinato del general Quiroga: su secretario Ortiz y demás comitiva en el parage de Barranca-Yaco, territorio de Córdoba* (Buenos Aires: Comercio, 1835), p. 43; *Rosas y sus opositores* ([Montevideo]: Nacional, 1843), p. 72; *La intervención en la guerra actual del Río de la Plata* (Río: Mercantil de Lopes, 1845), p. 61; *Demonstración de la legitimidad de la independencia de la República del Paraguay* . . . (Montevideo: Nacional, 1845), p. 61; and *Poesías* . . ., introd. Bartolomé Mitre (Buenos Aires: Mayo, 1843), p. 406.

28. Saldías, *Historia*, p. 275n, explains the events surrounding the infamous *máquina infernal* (infernal machine).

29. Alberdi, *Escritos póstumos*, vol. VIII, p. 145.

30. An unlikely critic of Rivera Indarte's journalistic distortions, Sarmiento wrote in *Viajes*: "Rivera Indarte succumbed [to the temptation] of returning injury for injury in that struggle in which reason and principles were thrown against coarse passions and violence." Quoted by Gianello, *Florencio Varela*, p. 387.

31. Bernardo Canal Feijóo, *Constitución y revolución: Juan Bautista Alberdi* (Buenos Aires: Fondo de Cultura Económica, 1955), p. 263.

32. Alberdi, *Escritos póstumos*, vol. XV, p. 562.

33. Juan Bautista Alberdi, *Cartas inéditas a Juan María Gutiérrez y a Félix Frías*,

ed. and introd. Jorge M. Mayer and Ernesto A. Martínez (Buenos Aires: Luz del Día, 1953), p. 53, copies Alberdi's letter of September 22, 1845 to Gutiérrez.

34. Mitre, "Biografía de José Rivera Indarte," *El nacional,* September 11, 1845; *Biografía de José Rivera Indarte* (Valparaíso: Mercurio, 1845 [copy in Biblioteca Nacional, Montevideo]). His bibliographers completely ignore Mitre's pamphlet, *Estudios sobre la vida y escritos de D. José Rivera Indarte* (Studies on the life and writings of D. José Rivera Indarte) (Buenos Aires: Imprenta de Mayo, 1853), pp. lxxxv (Bodlean Library: no. 23178 e 39).

35. Bartolomé Mitre, *"Profesión de fe" y otros escritos publicados en "Los debates" de 1852,* prologue Ricardo Levene (Buenos Aires: Universidad de Buenos Aires, 1956), pp. 17–18.

36. Gutiérrez, *Epistolario,* p. 37, copies from the [1839] letter to Alberdi.

37. Alberdi, *Escritos póstumos,* vol. XV, pp. 654, 658.

38. Historians have been kinder to Lavalle than were the 1837 militants. Saldías, *Historia,* p. 218, portrays him as a noble warrior making the best of a desperate situation after being abandoned by the French and his erstwhile allies, Pedro Ferré and Frutuoso Rivera. Antonio Emilio Castello, "Lavalle frente a todos," *Todo es historia,* no. 94 (1975): pp. 8–43, provides a convincing, sympathetic portrait of the pathetic Lavalle. Castello quotes Generals Paz and Iriarte, who testified to Lavalle's tenuous position that had been weakened by meddling, rancorous unitarian politicians. Similarly sympathetic is the perspective offered by E. F. Sánchez Zinny, "El General Juan Lavalle bajo la cruz de la adversidad," in *Los ciento diez jinetes de la gloria* (Buenos Aires: Linari y Cía., 1944), pp. 187–208, who argues that Lavalle's decision not to march on Buenos Aires was the result of a reasoned assessment of the dangers that his forces might have encountered (pp. 199, 206).

39. Gianello, *Florencio Varela,* pp. 188–89, quotes important paragraphs from Varela's letter of October 4, 1840.

40. Echeverría, *Obras completas,* p. 546, copies the epithet to his long narrative poem, *Avellaneda.*

41. Alberdi, *Escritos póstumos,* vol. XIII, pp. 339–349, describes how after his trip to Tucumán in 1834 he kept in close contact with his friends and fellow Joven Argentina associates there: Brígido Silva, Santiago Zavalía, and Marco Avellaneda. His letter of February 28, 1839 invited their declaration of open rebellion against Rosas. Alberdi would later write about Avellaneda: "I initiated him in the trials of our political agitation at that time" (*Escritos póstumos,* vol. XV, p. 289).

42. Juan B. Terán, "Prólogo" to Marco M. de Avellaneda, *Reflejos autobiográficos, 1813–1841* (Buenos Aires: Coni, 1922), p. xxv, quotes from this correspondence.

43. Echeverría, *Obras completas,* pp. 582–83 (in a footnote to *Avellaneda*), copies the letter written by Colonel Sandoval to his superior, Manuel Oribe, and then the letter sent by Oribe to Rosas, which explained Avellaneda's role in these events. In *Avellaneda,* Echeverría provides only a rhetorical rebuttal to the charge of Avellaneda's complicity in the death of Heredia. He has Avellaneda say to an interrogator that the accusation of his involvement in Heredia's death is an attempt to "defame" his name, that it is based on nothing other than "lies . . . a crude distortion of the facts," and that "history will do justice by me/as it will by you and the Tyrant" (pp. 569–70).

44. Echeverría, *Obras completas,* p. 814.

45. Mayer, *Alberdi y su tiempo,* p. 249, copies from Alberdi's letter of January 27, 1841 to Echeverría.

46. Canal Feijóo, *Constitución y revolución,* pp. 240–42, copies from *El nacional* of January 16 and 23, 1841.

47. Alberdi, *Escritos póstumos,* vol. XV, p. 437.

48. Ibid., pp. 446–47.

49. Ibid., p. 504.

50. José Luis Romero, *Latinoamérica: las ciudades y las ideas* (Buenos Aires: Siglo XXI, 1976), pp. 210–11, 243–44, is wrong in equating the Portales regime to that of Rosas in Argentina.

51. Ibid., p. 243.

52. Tulio Halperín Donghi, *El espejo de la historia: problemas argentinos y perspectivas latinoamericanas* (Buenos Aires: Sudamericana, 1987), pp. 25, 200.

53. Echeverría, *Obras completas,* p. 151.

54. The following pages copy from my article, "Sarmiento frente a la Generación de 1837," *Revista iberoamericana,* no. 143 (1988): 525–49, which is reprinted in *Sarmiento de frente y perfil* (Geneva and New York: Peter Lang, 1993), pp. 35–62.

55. Juan Bautista Alberdi, *Obras completas,* vol. I (Buenos Aires: "La Tribuna Nacional," 1886), p. 251 (from *Fragmento preliminar*).

56. Ibid., p. 273.

57. Sarmiento, *Obras completas,* vol. I, 248.

58. Juan María Gutiérrez, *La literatura de Mayo y otras páginas críticas,* prologue by Beatriz Sarlo; notes by Hebe Monges (Buenos Aires: Centro Editor de América Latina, 1979), p. 15 (from "Fisonomía del saber español: cual deba ser entre nosotros").

59. Ibid., p. 20.

60. Sarmiento, *Obras completas,* vols. IV, 1–227; XI, 362–400.

61. For a discussion of Sarmiento's contradictory baggage of liberal ideas, see Noël Salomon, "El *Facundo:* manifiesto de la preburguesía argentina en las ciudades del interior," *Cuadernos americanos* 39 (1980): 121–71; and Natalio A. Botana, *La tradición republicana: Alberdi, Sarmiento, y las ideas políticas de su tiempo* (Buenos Aires: Sudamericana, 1984).

62. Sarmiento, *Obras completas,* vol. VII, 218.

63. Alberdi, *Obras completas,* vol. I, 303 (from an article signed by "Figarillo" in *La moda*).

64. Sarmiento, *Obras completas,* vol. I, 310.

65. Echeverría, *Obras completas,* p. 350 (in "Clasicismo y romanticismo").

66. Sarmiento, *Obras completas,* vol. V, p. 51.

67. Echeverría, *Obras completas,* p. 716.

68. Adolfo Mitre, Manuel Conde Montero y Juan A. Farini, *Apuntes de la juventud de Mitre y Bibliografía de Mitre* (Buenos Aires: Academia Nacional de la Historia, 1947), p. 218, copies from Bartolomé Mitre, "Literatura americana: *Rimas* de E. Echeverría," (November 7, 1837).

69. Echeverría, *Obras completas,* p. 150.

70. Alberdi, *Obras completas,* vol. I, pp. 115–38 ("Certamen poético").

71. Juan María Gutiérrez, *Colección Doctor Juan María Gutiérrez: Archivo-Espistolario* (Buenos Aires: Biblioteca del Congreso de la Nación, 1979), p. 281, copies the letter of August 7, 1844 from Gutiérrez to Echeverría.

72. José Rivera Indarte, *Rosas y sus opositores* (Montevideo: "El nacional," 1843), p. 363, with the appendix titled, "Es acción santa matar a Rosas," p. 75.

73. See Bartolomé Mitre, *Estudios sobre la vida y escritos de D. José Rivera Indarte* (Buenos Aires: Imprenta de Mayo, 1853), p. 85.

74. Gutiérrez, *Archivo del Doctor*, p. 275, copies the letter of June 7, 1844 from Luis L. Domínguez.

75. Alberdi, *Escritos póstumos*, vol. VIII, p. 157 (this volume includes Alberdi's unpublished notes from 1871–76).

76. In Sarmiento's papers there is no copy of this letter signed in the pseudonym, García Román, and he—in the light of his fierce polemics with Alberdi after 1852—denied ever having written it. The transcription of this and Sarmiento's subsequent letter can be found in Alberdi's *Escritos póstumos*, vol. VIII, as well as Domingo Faustino Sarmiento, *Sarmiento: cartas y discursos políticos* (Buenos Aires: Ediciones Culturales Argentinas, 1965), vol. III, pp. 3–4.

77. See my "Reading *Facundo* as Historical Novel," in *The Historical Novel in Latin America: A Symposium* ed. Daniel Balderston (Gainesville, Md.: Hispamérica, 1986), pp. 31–46; and reprinted in Spanish as "*Facundo* como novela histórica" in *Sarmiento de frente y perfil*, pp. 105–20.

78. Sarmiento, *Obras completas*, vol. VII, p. 221.

79. Antonio Pagés Larraya, "La 'recepción' de un texto sarmientino: *Facundo*," *Boletín de la Academia Argentina de Letras*, vol. 49, nos. 193/194 (1984): 233–85.

80. Pedro de Paoli, *Sarmiento: su gravitación en el desarrollo nacional* (Buenos Aires: Theoría, 1964), p. 87.

81. Echeverría, *Obras completas*, p. 82.

82. Alberdi, *Escritos póstumos*, vol. XV, p. 786.

83. Gutiérrez, *Epistolario*, p. xx, copies the letter of August 6, [1845] to Alberdi.

84. Juan Bautista Alberdi, *Obras completas*, vol. IV, pp. 70, 50.

85. Ibid., p. 55.

86. Twentieth-century critics calling attention to the distortions inherent in the civiilzation-barbarism opposition are Gaspar P. del Correo, *Facundo y Fierro: la proscripción de los héroes* (Buenos Aires: Castañeda, 1977); Alfredo L. Palacios, "Civilización y barbarie: dualismo simplista inaceptable," *Cuadernos Americanos* 105, no. 4 (1959): 162–202; Ricardo Rojas, *El profeta de la pampa: vida de Sarmiento* (Buenos Aires: Losada, 1945), pp. 205–10; and Alfredo E. Ves Losada, "Campo y ciudad en *Facundo*," *Cuadernos americanos*, 15, no. 6 (1956): 185–200.

87. See Françoise Pierre Guillaume Guizot, *The History of Civilization in Europe*, trans. William Hazlitt (New York: A. L. Burt, n.d.), pp. 50, 65, 372. I discuss the similarity between Sarmiento's and Guizot's perspectives in *Domingo F. Sarmiento, Public Writer (Between 1838 and 1852)* (Tempe: Center for Latin America, Arizona State University Press, 1985), pp. 114–15.

88. See C. L. B., "Des Rapports de la France et de l'Europe avec l'Amérique du Sud," *Revue des deux mondes*, Series 4, 31, no. 15 (1838): 54–69; Un Voyageur, "Les Deux Rives de la Plata: Montevideo, Buenos-Ayres, Rivera, Rosas," *Revue des Deux Mondes*, 50, Year 13, no. 2 (1843): 5–49; and Francis B. Head, *Rough Notes Taken during Some Rapid Journies across the Pampas and among the Andes* (Boston: Wells and Lilly, 1827).

89. Sarmiento, *Obras completas*, vol. XXI, pp. 86–87.

90. Ibid., vol. VII, part II, ch. 5, p. 3.

91. Salomon, "El *Facundo*," pp. 150–57.

92. Frías, *Escritos y discursos*, vol. II, pp. 26–30.

93. Andrés Lamas, *Escritos políticos y literarios durante la guerra contra la tiranía*

de D. Juan Manuel Rosas . . ., foreword Angel J. Carranza (Buenos Aires: Cangallo, 1877), p. 128.

94. Ibid., p. 41.

95. Ibid., p. xviii, quoted from Sarmiento's *Campaña en el Ejército Grande.*

96. See the correspondence between the Lamas and Mitre, dating from 1847, in General Bartolomé Mitre, *Correspondencia literaria, histórica y política* (Buenos Aires: Coni Hermanos, 1912), vol. I, pp. 47–62.

97. Alberdi, *Escritos póstumos,* vol. VIII, pp. 160–66 (comments written at the beginning of the 1870s).

98. Félix Frías, *La gloria del tirano Rosas y otros escritos políticos y polémicos,* prologue Domingo F. Sarmiento (Buenos Aires: El Ateneo, 1928), pp. 138, 170, 176.

99. Quoted from Miguel Angel Speroni, *Que fue Alberdi* (Buenos Aires: Plus Ultra, 1973), p. 121. Critics have taken diametrically opposed positions with regard to Echeverría's commitment to the anti-Rosas struggle at that moment. Sarmiento, in *Facundo,* portrays Echeverría, a *cajetilla*—or "city dude"—as entertaining mesmerized *gauchos* with his guitar in 1839 at more or less the same time when Alberdi and others in Montevideo were organizing the military force that would march against Rosas (Sarmiento, *Obras completas,* vol. VII, 39). José Ingenieros followed Sarmiento's general view: "Echeverría didn't seem to be much interested in the political spirit that Alberdi was infusing in the younger members of the group; and while it is unknown if his motives were to avoid complications, he did distance himself from the group, moving away from Buenos Aires." Quoted from "La filosofía social de Echeverría y la leyenda de la 'Asociación de Mayo,'" *Revista de filosofía, cultura, ciencias,* no. 4 (1914), pp. 239–40, 244. Here I differ with José Luis Lanuza, *Echeverría y sus amigos* (Buenos Aires: Paídos, 1967), and Alberto Palcos, *Historia de Echeverría* (Buenos Aires: Emecé, 1960), who interpret the decision of Echeverría to remain in Argentina as a continuation of the commitment he had demonstrated before the Salón Literario and the Young Argentina to struggle against Rosas in any way possible. I discuss all these points of view in "Echeverría según Sarmiento: la personificación de una nación ultrajada por la barabarie," *Cuadernos americanos,* 255, no. 4 (1984): 164–85; reprinted in *Sarmiento de frente y perfil,* pp. 125–50.

100. Quoted from Lanuza, *Echeverría y sus amigos,* p. 165.

101. Esteban Echeverría, *Páginas autobiográficas* (Buenos Aires: EUBA, 1962), p. 76, copies Echeverría's letter of April 6, 1844 to Melchor Pacheco y Obes.

102. Ibid., pp. 81–82, copies the July 10, 1844 letter to Alberdi.

103. José Ingenieros, *Evolución de las ideas argentinas,* vol. II, *La restauración* (Buenos Aires: L. J. Rosso, 1920), p. 679, quotes Echeverría's letter of December 24, 1844 to Gutiérrez.

104. Pedro de Angelis, "Examen del folleto publicado en Montevideo con el título de 'Dogma Socialista de la Asociación de Mayo,' etc." *Archivo Americano,* 1st series, no. 32 (January 28, 1847). Echeverría's letters to De Angelis were first published in Montevideo in 1847 by the "18 de Julio" Press.

105. Ingenieros, *Evolución,* vol. I, pp. 690–91.

106. Sarmiento, *Obras completas,* vol. VII, p. 103.

107. Echeverría, *Obras completas,* p. 195.

108. Ingenieros, *Evolución,* p. 682, quotes the October 1, 1846 letter from Echeverría to Gutiérrez and Alberdi.

109. Esteban Echeverría, *Dogma socialista,* critical edition, ed. Alberto Palcos (La Plata: Universidad Nacional de la Plata, 1940), p. 433n.

110. Ibid., p. 158.
111. Ibid., p. 88.
112. Ingenieros, *Evolución*, p. 682.
113. James R. Scobie, *La lucha por la consolidación de la nacionalidad argentina, 1852–1862*, trans. Gabriela de Civiny (Buenos Aires: Hachette, 1964), p. 19, states that before 1852, 45 percent of those residing in Buenos Aires were citizens of other countries and even a greater proportion of the commercial establishments were owned and operated by European (primarily British) interests.
114. Rojas, *El profeta*, pp. 633–39.
115. Juan Bautista Alberdi, *Sobre la nueva situación de los asuntos del Plata*; [V. F. López,] *Vindicación de la República Arjentina en su Revolución y sus guerras civiles, por A. y X., emigrados arjentinos* (Santiago, 1841), p. 31 [document cup 405 b. 25 in Bodlean Library]; Domingo F. Sarmiento's articles were published between October 1841 and August 1842 in *El progreso* of Santiago; see *Obras completas*, vol. XIII, pp. 305–29; [Florencio Varela,] *Observations on Occurrences in the River Plate as Connected with ther Foreign Agents and the Anglo-French Intervention*, (Montevideo, 1843), p. 30 [document 8179 aaa 77 in Bodlean Library].
116. [Varela], *Observaciones*, p. 8.
117. Esteban Echeverría, *Páginas autobiográficas* (Buenos Aires: EUBA, 1962), p. 87, quotes from the letter of October 1, 1846.
118. Ibid., p. 89, from the letter of November 1, 1846.
119. Canal Feijóo, *Constitución y revolución*, pp. 241–42.
120. I develop this perspective in greater detail in "Echeverría según Sarmiento."
121. Sarmiento, *Obras completas*, vol. V, p. 54.
122. Ibid., vol. VII, pp. 216, 221, 222.
123. Ibid., vol. V, p. 208.
124. Ibid., XIII, 305–20, copies from Sarmiento's "Colonización inglesa en el Río de la Plata," *El mercurio* November 1, 1841; August 19 and 23, 1842. The editors most probably assembled a series of shorter essays written by Sarmiento and joined them under one title for their publication in the *Obras completas*. In *Domingo F. Sarmiento: Public Writer (Between 1839 and 1852)* (Tempe: Center for Latin America, Arizona State University, 1985), pp. 167–96, I discuss in greater detail the views of Sarmiento with regard to Europe's civilizing role in the Río de la Plata.
125. Sarmiento, *Obras completas*, vol. XIII, p. 312.
126. Ibid., pp. 307–8.
127. Ibid., p. 314. In his own correspondence, Gutiérrez would demonstrate another brand of moral denunciation. In a letter to Alberdi, he revealed his fear of their movement obtaining only fickle support from the French: "The French as we know them through books and the written word are hardly the same as those who embark on their ships—similarly, those in Paris are hardly the same when in the Río de la Plata." At times the "powerful and sublime Nations" are represented by "rudiments of men, pathetically interested only in gold." (See his December 28, 1838 letter to Alberdi, as reprinted in Juan Maria Gutiérrez, *Epistolario de Don Juan Maria Gutiérrez*, prologue and ed. Ernesto Morales [Buenos Aires: Instituto Cultural Joaquin Gonzalez, 1942], p. 29).
128. Sarmiento, *Obras completas*, vol. VI, pp. 276–95.
129. Alberdi, *Obras selectas*, vol. V, p. 27 ("Acción de la Europa en América"; "Notas de un español americano"; "A propósito de la intervención anglo-

francesa en el Plata," published in *El mercurio* of Valparaiso on August 10 and 11, 1845).

130. Alberdi, *Escritos póstumos*, vol. IV, p. 653 ("Del gobierno en Sud-América"—1867).

131. This was the opinion of Paul Groussac, "Esteban Echeverría: la Asociación de Mayo y *El dogma socialista*," in *Crítica literaria* (Buenos Aires: Jesús Menéndez, 1924), p. 308.

132. Ingenieros, *Evolución*, vol. I, pp. 684–85.

133. Echeverría, *Obras completas*, p. 231.

134. Ibid., p. 204.

135. Ibid., p. 151.

136. Sarmiento, *Obras completas*, vol. V, p. 54.

137. Domingo Faustino Sarmiento, *Viajes en Europa, Africa i América* (Santiago: Julio Belén y Co., 1849), vol. II, p. 463; this appendix reprints the speech of July 1, 1847 in Paris.

138. Botana, *La tradición republicana*, pp. 339, 348, points out the grave contradictions in Sarmiento's advocacies after 1852. Combined with his support for a centralized republic of monarchical inspiration, he defended an aggressive agrarian policy and free, public education that would benefit even the poorest of the country's citizens.

139. Juan Pablo Oliver, *El verdadero Alberdi: génesis del liberalismo ecónomico argentino* (Buenos Aires: Biblioteca Dicta, 1977).

140. Tulio Halperín Donghi, "En el trasfondo de la novela de dictadores: la dictadura hispanoamericana como problema histórico," in *El espejo de la historia: problemas argentinos y perspectivas hispanoamericanas* (Buenos Aires: Sudamericana, 1987), p. 26.

141. Botana, *La tradición republicana*, pp. 303–16.

142. Mayer, *Alberdi y su tiempo*, p. 338, quotes Alberdi, *Biografía del general Don Manuel Bulnes, Presidente de la República de Chile* (1846).

143. Ibid., p. 338.

144. Ibid., p. 331, in reference to Alberdi's "Los americanos ligados al extranjero," in *El mercurio*, November 15, 17, and 30, 1846.

145. Ibid., pp. 350–51, quotes from Alberdi's prospectus for *El comercio de Valparaíso*, 28 August 1847.

146. Ibid., p. 327.

147. Ibid., p. 371.

148. Ibid., pp. 311–12.

149. Ibid., p. 367, quoting from Alberdi, *El comercio de Valparaíso*, April 7, 1849.

150. Alberdi, *Obras completas*, vol. III, p. 80 ("Acción de la Europa en América" and reproduced in *Bases*).

151. Canal Feijóo, *Constitución y revolución*, p. 312.

152. Botana, *La tradición republicana*, p. 303.

153. Canal Feijoo, *Constitución y revolución*, p. 308.

154. Ibid., p. 310.

155. Américo A. Tonda, *Don Félix Frías: el secretario del General Lavalle. Su época boliviana (1841–1843)* (Córdoba: Ediciones Argentina Cristiana, 1956), pp. 37, 41.

156. Félix Frías, *La gloria del tirano Rosas y otros escritos políticos y polémicos*, prologue Domingo Faustino Sarmiento (Buenos Aires: El Ateneo, 1928), p. 23.

157. Echeverría, *Obras completas*, p. 60.

158. Sarmiento, *Obras completas*, vol. V, p. 54 (*Viajes*).

159. José Ingenieros, *La evolución de las ideas argentinas*, vol. II, *La restauración* (Buenos Aires: Talleres Gráficos Argentinos, 1920), pp. 685, 674.

160. Mayer, *Alberdi y su tiempo*, p. 341, quotes from Echeverría's letter of October 1, 1846 to Alberdi and Gutiérrrez.

161. Ibid., p. 358, quotes from Alberdi's letter of April 26, 1848 to Echeverría.

162. Ibid., p. 344.

163. Ibid., p. 345.

164. Ibid., pp. 345–46, provides the quotes and documentation for the entire paragraph.

165. Echeverría, *Obras completas*, pp. 295–98 ("Revolución de febrero en Francia," July 22, 1848).

166. Ibid., pp. 298–308: "Sentido filosófico de la revolución de febrero en Francia."

167. Ibid., p. 500, reproduces Echeverría's letter of January 28, 1849, which later would serve as introduction to his short narrative poem, "Insurrección del Sud de la Provincia de Buenos Aires."

168. Félix Frías, *Escritos y discursos*, vol. 1 (Buenos Aires: Librería de Mayo, 1884), pp. 3–10, quotes Frías's letter to Juan Carlos Gómez, Paris, 9 June 1849.

169. Ibid., p. 105, copies Frías's letter to Juan Thompson, Paris, March 21, 1851.

170. Ibid., pp. 22–23, copies Frías's letter to Alberdi, Paris, July 9, 1851.

171. Ibid., p. 108, copies Frías's letter to Thompson, Paris, March 21, 1851.

172. Mayer, *Alberdi y su tiempo*, p. 389, copies from Alberdi's letter to Frías of September 24, 1851.

173. Tulio Halperín Donghi, "El espejo de la historia," *Contorno* 9/10 (1959), p. 79.

174. Echeverría, *Obras completas*, p. 542. Other quotes in the paragraph are from pages 686, 581, and 232.

175. Palcos, *Historia de Echeverría*, p. 135, quotes Sarmiento.

176. Echeverría, *Páginas autobiográficas* (Buenos Aires: EUBA, 1962), p. 73.

177. Echeverría, *Obras completas*, p. 71.

178. Significantly the text quoted most frequently by Juan María Gutiérrez in his *Pensamientos, máximas, sentencias de escritores, oradores y hombres de estado de la República Argentina (1859)* is Echeverría's *El dogma socialista*.

179. Oliver, *El verdadero Alberdi*, provides details about this trying chapter in Alberdi's personal life.

180. Echeverría, "Ojeada," *Obras completas*, p. 84.

181. Letter from Luis Domínguez to Frías, Montevideo, September 12, 1843, as copied in Oliver, *El verdadero Alberdi*, p. 188.

182. Alberdi, *Obras completas*, vol. I (Buenos Aires: "La Tribuna Nacional," 1886), p. 125.

183. Quoted from Julio Irazusta, "Alberdi en 1838: un trascendental cambio de opción práctica," in *Ensayos históricos* (Buenos Aires: La voz del Plata, 1952), p. 162.

184. The suggestion by Irazusta in "Alberdi en 1838" that Alberdi was a "mental prisioner" (p. 204) and that his position favoring European interests over national ones was "embarazosa" (p. 199) seems more applicable for the period beginning about 1855. The same could be said about Halperín Donghi's opinion about "the almost supernatural ineptitude [of Alberdi] in understanding the effective political mechanisms in the River Plate" ("1880: un nuevo clima de

322   NOTES TO CHAPTER 3

ideas," in *El espejo de la historia: problemas argentinos y perspectivas hispanoamericanas* [Buenos Aires: Sudamericana, 1987], p. 242).

185. Vicente Fidel López, *Historia de la República Argentina . . .*, vol. VI, continuada por Emilio Vera y González (Buenos Aires: Sopena Argentina, 1964), p. 543n, labels Alberdi "a sick man," "victim of painful bouts of disequilibrium and nervous fatigue, that almost always caused in him brusk changes in energy level, from lucidity and contentness to intellectual incapacity and physical deterioration; his bouts of sadness reached such extremes that they sometimes tempted suicide." López went on to quote Alberdi's letter to Urquiza in 1852 declining appointment to the position of minister of finances for the Confederation, because of his "very fragmented and poor state of health. . . . I am capable to a certain degree of activity and labor, but it must be the type of activity that is free from all rules and timetables."

186. I defend this thesis in the Epilogue of *Sarmiento: Public Writer.*

187. Tulio Halperín Donghi, "El espejo de la historia," *Contorno* 9/10 (1959): 76–91.

188. Raúl A. Orgaz, *Obras completas*, vol. II, *Sociología argentina*, introd. Arturo Capdevila, (Córdoba: Assandri, 1950), p. 412, copies from the 1849 letter that Echeverría wrote to Alberdi.

189. Ibid.

190. Alberdi's written opinions about *Facundo* date from 1853, beginning with the third of his letters included in *Cartas quillotanas*. See *Obras completas*, vol. IV (Buenos Aires: "La Tribuna Nacional," 1886), p. 61.

191. Sarmiento's letter is reproduced in Palcos, *Echeverría*, p. 88.

192. Mayer, *Alberdi y su tiempo*, p. 388, quotes the letter from Alberdi to Frías, Valparaíso, May 24, 1851.

193. Carlos D'Amico, *Buenos Aires: sus hombres, su política (1860–1890)* (first edition 1890; Buenos Aires: Americana, 1952), p. 114, wrote about the mature Mitre both as a warrior and as a statesman: "He resembles a child who begins to carry out his responsibilities in life before fully attaining maturity."

194. José Campobassi, *Mitre y su época*, p. 31.

195. Sarmiento, *Obras completas*, vol. V, p. 57.

CHAPTER 3. BUENOS AIRES VERSUS THE CONFEDERATION (1852–1860)

1. Juan Bautista Alberdi, *Obras selectas*, vol. 5 (Buenos Aires: La Facultad, 1920), p. 73.

2. Aldo Ferrer, *The Argentine Economy*, trans. Marjory M. Urquidi (Berkeley and Los Angeles: University of California Press, 1967), p. 57.

3. James R. Scobie, *Argentina: A City and a Nation*, 2d ed. (New York and London: Oxford University Press, 1971), pp. 76–87.

4. Ferrer, *Argentine Economy*, p. 54, estimated a 100 percent growth in the value of Argentina's exports between 1800 and 1850, from 5 to 10 million pesos fuertes. He suggested that the growth in the value of the litoral's imports kept apace with the growth in the value of exports.

5. Tulio Halperín Donghi, "¿Para qué la inmigración? Ideología y política inmigratoria en la Argentina (1810–1914)," in *Espejo de la historia*, p. 204.

6. Alberdi, *Obras selectas*, p. 64.

7. Ibid.

8. Tulio Halperín Donghi, "Liberalismo argentino y liberalismo mexicano: dos destinos divergentes," in *Espejo de la historia*, p. 159.

9. Jorge M. Mayer, *Alberdi y su tiempo* (Buenos Aires: Editorial Universitaria de Buenos Aires, 1963), pp. 379–83.

10. Ricardo M. Ortiz, *Historia económica de la Argentina, 1850–1930* vol. 1 (Buenos Aires: Raigal, 1955), pp. 50–68.

11. Domingo F. Sarmiento, *Obras completas*, vol. VI (Santiago: Luz del Día, 1948–56), pp. 397–409, 430–33, copies "Movimiento en las provincias: escuelas, periódicos"; and "'La Regeneración', diario de Entre Ríos" (*Sud América*, April 1, 1851).

12. Leonardo Paso, *Los caudillos y la organización nacional* (Buenos Aires: Sílaba, 1970), p. 216.

13. César Díaz, *Memorias*, prologue Juan E. Pivel Devoto (Montevideo: Departamento de Investigaciones del Museo Histórico Nacional, 1968), p. 258. Díaz, a Uruguayan general serving in the Ejército Grande under Urquiza, provided an authoritative—but partisan—account of the "true cruelty" and "repugnant spectacle" of these executions.

14. This is the informed opinion of Urquiza loyalist, Julio Victorica, *Urquiza y Mitre: contribución al estudio histórico de la organización nacional*, 1st ed., 1906; Buenos Aires: Hyspamérica, 1986), p. 25.

15. León Rebollo Paz, *Historia de la organización nacional: treinta años en la vida de la República, 1850–1880*, vol. I, *De octubre 1850 a octubre 1852* (Buenos Aires: Librería del Plata, 1951), has particularly interesting chapters on the attitudes and events in the interior provinces after the fall of Rosas.

16. José A. Campobassi, *Mitre y su tiempo* (Buenos Aires: EUBA, 1980), p. 60.

17. Ibid., p. 61.

18. Bartolomé Mitre, *"Profesión de fe" y otros escritos publicados en "Los debates" de 1852*, foreword Ricardo Levene (Buenos Aires: Universidad de Buenos Aires, 1956), pp. 26–27. "Profesión de fe"—wrongly dated here as April 1, 1852—was published on March 31.

19. Unsigned editorial, *Los debates*, May 7, 1852.

20. This and the following speechs are reproduced in Bartolomé Mitre, *Arengas de Bartolomé Mitre: Colección de discursos paralmentarios, políticos, económicos y literarios . . . desde 1848 hasta 1888* (Buenos Aires: Librería de Mayo, 1889).

21. Victorica, *Urquiza y Mitre*, p. 32.

22. Letter of June 24, 1852 from Gutiérrez to Luis Barros Borgoño, in Juan María Gutiérrez, *Don Juan María Gutiérrez: a través de una correspondencia*, ed. Luis Barros Borgoño (Santiago: Prensas de la Universidad de Chile, 1934), p. 94.

23. Examples of Sarmiento's doubts about Urquiza's objectives are found in the two letters he sent to Alberdi on September 16 and 27, 1852, in which he expressed his high praise for *Bases* but asserted that because of this book, "Urquiza, on its account, will never forgive him." Copied from Ricardo Rojas, "Introducción," in Juan Bautista Alberdi, *Bases y puntos de partida . . .*, ed. J. Francisco V. Silva, 2d ed. (Cordoba: Imprenta de la Universidad, 1928).

24. *El nacional*, October 8, 1852, which reprints Mitre's speech of the previous day to the legislature. Mitre served as editor of the newspaper from October 9, to November 2.

25. Vicente Osvaldo Cutilo, *Nuevo diccionario biográfico argentino, 1730–1930* (Buenos Aires: Elche, 1975).

26. José Mármol, *Amalia: novela histórica americana* (Buenos Aires: Sopena, 1944), p. 156 (III, 5); and *Asesinato del Sr. Dr. D. Florencio Varela. Manuela Rosas*.

prologue Juan Carlos Ghiano (Buenos Aires: Casa Pardo, 1972), p. 50. In his excellent introduction Ghiano refers to Mármol's deep admiration for Varela.

27. Mármol, "El guardia nacional," *El Paraná*, October 29, 1852. The Biblioteca Nacional's collection of *El Paraná* is found (without any indication in its indexes) at the end of the bound volume of *Los debates* for 1852. Although *El Paraná* published a total of forty-four issues between October 26 and December 22, 1852, this collection contains only the numbers between October 29 and November 30. Only one of Mármol's articles from *El Paraná* has been reprinted: "Ultima palabra en *El Paraná*," November 12, 1852, in Liliana Giannangeli, *Construcción a la bibliografía de José Mármol*, with essay-prologue "La fama de JM," by Juan Carlos Ghiano (La Plata: Universidad Nacional de la Plata, 1972). Giannangeli, although offering the most complete bibliography of Mármol to date, does not provide a list of his articles in this short-lived newspaper. Future bibliographers should at least include the following: "Al *Nacional*," October 29; "El Guardia Nacional," October 29; "La provincia," October 30; "Una ojeada sobre la historia de la República Arjentina," November 2, 3, and 4; "Una palabra nueva sobre un asunto viejo," November 5; "El Congreso," November 6; "Publicidad," November 8; "La Sala y el Gobierno," November 9; "[Editorial without title]," November 8; and "Ultima palabra en *El Paraná*," November 12.

28. Mármol, "Al *Nacional*," *El Paraná*, October 29, 1852.

29. The editorials written by Mitre for *El nacional* in 1852 have not been republished, and the most complete bibliography on Mitre completely ignores their existence. See Guillermo Furlong, S.J., "Bartolomé Mitre: El hombre, el soldado, el historiador, el político," in *Investigaciones y ensayos* (Buenos Aires: Academia Nacional de Historia, 1971), II, pp. 325–522. The only bibliographical source I have found that lists these articles is Cutilo, *Nuevo diccionario*, vol. V, p. 576, but he mistakenly gives the year as 1854. In spite of this error, Cutilo does correctly identify the dates and titles of these editorials: they appeared October 25, 26, 27, 29, and 30 and November 2 under the respective titles of *"El Paraná* por don José Mármol," "La túnica de Mesías," "Nacionalidad," "Aislamiento," "La revolución y la Sala," and "El aislamiento ante la historia." (However, Cutilo invents an additional editorial of November 2, "Ultima palabra en la cuestión," that he ascribes to Mitre.)

30. On September 17 Mitre received the charge of organizing the provincial guard. On November 3, he left the leadership of that body in order to assume the portfolios for minister of state and foreign relations. Between 1853 and 1860 Mitre's writing production was minimal. Furlong, "Bartolomé Mitre," lists only two articles published in the local press for 1853, one for 1854 (a letter addressed to J. M. Gutiérrez), and only the reprint of a letter to Tezanos Pinto published in the press of Lima, Perú, for 1860. In *Arengas*, several of Mitre's speeches from March to May 1854 are copied.

31. Mayer, *Alberdi y su tiempo*, p. 427, copies from letter of [V. F.] López to General Alvear, October 5, 1852.

32. Letter of April 19, 1853 from Luis José de la Peña in San Nicolás de los Arroyos, to Juan B. Alberdi, number 1170 in Furt Archives.

33. Manuel E. Macchi, *Urquiza: última etapa*, 3d ed. expanded (Santa Fe: Castellvi [sic], 1971); and Victorico, *Urquiza y Mitre*, who present favorable accounts of Urquiza's actions.

34. Mayer, *Alberdi y su tiempo*, p. 413.

35. According to Mayer, ibid., pp. 430–31, the new materials added to the original *Bases* included chapter IX, that referred to the Constitution of Uruguay;

X treating that of Paraguay; XII, that of California; XXI, the politics of the Constitution; XXII, the aphorism "En América gobernar es poblar"; XXXIII, a governmental program dealing with the "desierto," or great extentions of unsettled land; XXXIV, organic laws; XXXVI, the political future; XXXVII, an analysis of the Constitution; and XXXVIII, the project of the Constitution conceived according to materials treated in *Bases*.

36. Ambrosio Romero Carranza, Alberto Rodríguez Varela, and Eduardo Ventura Flores Pirán. *Historia política de la Argentina* Buenos Aires: Pamedille, 1971. vol. II, *Desde 1816 hasta 1862* (Buenos Aires: Pamedille, 1971), p. 1005.

37. Mayer, *Alberdi y su tiempo*, p. 432, copies from Sarmiento's letter of September 16, 1852 to Alberdi.

38. Carranza, *Historia*, p. 1004.

39. Juan Bautista Alberdi, *Bases y puntos de partida para la organización política de la República argentina*, prologue Francisco Cruz (Buenos Aires: Talleres Gráficos Argentinos, 1933), p. 211.

40. Ibid., p. 213.

41. Ibid., p. 79.

42. Canal Feijóo, *Constitución y revolución*, p. 362.

43. Alberdi, *Bases*, p. 211.

44. Ibid., p. 211.

45. Canal Feijóo, *Constitución y revolución*, pp. 347, 346. For a more philosophical treatment of Alberdi's thought and writings, see Canal's *Alberdi y la proyección sistemática del espíritu de Mayo* (Buenos Aires: Losada, 1961).

46. Alberdi, *Bases*, p. 199.

47. Natalio Botana, *La tradición republicana: Alberdi, Sarmiento, y las ideas políticas de su tiempo* (Buenos Aires: Sudamericana, 1984), p. 340. No one better than Botana has pointed out the contradiction in Alberdi's ideas with regard to its conservatism. Alberdi "knows that nobody can escape the past and, at the same time, he condemns that history as an intolerable hinderance" (p. 297). Alberdi argued that "the political order had to be established over the foundation of existing customs, even knowing that those customs contained the germ of slavery" (p. 300). With his "willingness to totally erradicate the decrepit social order . . . his theory about a vital transplant from Europe to America [. . .] satisfied his obsession for progress and his conservative reservations" (p. 303).

48. Alberdi, *Bases* (cap. XIV).

49. Dardo Pérez Guilhou, "Repercusiones de Pavón en Mendoza (1859–1870)," in *Pavón y la crisis de la Confederación* edited by Armando R. Bazán (Buenos Aires: Equipos de investigación histórica, 1965), pp. 569–70.

50. Canal Feijóo, *Constitución y revolución*, p. 329.

51. Carranza, *Historia*, p. 1012, quotes from Alberdi's *Bases*.

52. See William H. Katra, "Sarmiento en los Estados Unidos," *Todo es historia*, 255 (1988): 6–45, and reprinted in *Sarmiento de frente y perfil* (Geneva and New York: Peter Lang Publishers, 1993), pp. 151–224.

53. Alberdi, *Bases*, p. 179.

54. The ideas and quotes for this paragraph come principally from Canal Feijóo, *Constitución y revolución*, pp. 361, 394–95.

55. Alberdi, *Bases*, p. 80.

56. Juan Bautista Alberdi, *Cartas inéditas a Juan María Gutiérrez y a Félix Frías*. eds. Jorge M. Mayer and Ernesto A. Martínez. (Buenos Aires: Luz del Día, 1953), p. 257, copies from Alberdi's Valparaíso letter of July 1852 to Frías.

57. Canal Feijóo, *Constitución y revolución*, p. 401.

58. Domingo F. Sarmiento, *Obras completas*, vol. XIV (Buenos Aires: Mariano Moreno, 1895–1900), pp. 321, 80 (my emphasis).

59. Botana, *Tradición republicana*, pp. 263–65, 296; and William H. Katra, *Sarmiento: Public Writer (Between 1839 and 1852)* (Tempe: Center for Latin American Studies, Arizona State University, 1985), pp. 16–18.

60. Alberdi, *Bases*, p. 199.

61. Domingo F. Sarmiento, *Campaña en el Ejército Grande Aliado de Sud América* (Mexico: Fondo de Cultura Económica, 1958), p. 12.

62. Tulio Halperín Donghi, "Una nación para el desierto argentino," in *Proyecto y construcción de una nación (Argentina 1846–1880)*, ed. Halperín Donghi (Caracas: Biblioteca Ayacucho, 1980), p. xliii.

63. Mayer and Martínez, *Cartas*, p. 268, copy from Alberdi's letter of December 13, 1852 to Frías.

64. Alberdi, *Obras selectas*, vol. V, p. 103, copies from *Cartas quillotanas*.

65. Ibid., pp. 208–9.

66. Canal Feijóo, *Constitución y revolución*, p. 409.

67. Pablo Rojas Paz, *Alberdi: el cuidadano de la soledad* [1941] (Buenos Aires: Losada, 1952), p. 100.

68. Canal Feijóo, *Constitución y revolución*, p. 380.

69. Mayer, *Alberdi y su tiempo*, p. 468, quotes from Sarmiento's *Argirópolis*.

70. Sarmiento, *Obras completas*, vol. VIII, p. 287.

71. Sarmiento, "Examen crítico de un proyecto de Constitución de la Confederación Argentina, por Juan B. Alberdi," *La crónica* (Santiago, November 19 and 26 and December 3, 10, and 17, 1853), and reproduced in *Obras completas*, vol. VIII, pp. 329–74.

72. Quoted from Mayer, *Alberdi y su tiempo*, p. 471.

73. Frías, *La gloria*, p. 190, quotes from his article "Golpe de estado en Francia," *El mercurio*, December 11, 1851.

74. Félix Frías, *Escritos y discursos*, vol. I (Buenos Aires: Librería de Mayo, 1884), p. 108, copies Frías's Paris letter of March 21, 1851 to Juan Thompson.

75. Frías, *La gloria*, p. 214, quotes from Frías's article, "Mis opiniones religiosas y políticas," *El mercurio* of April 26, 1852.

76. Ibid., p. 223.

77. Letter from Tomás Frías to Alberdi, Lima, February 15, 1852, in Furt Archives.

78. In "Echeverría según Sarmiento: la personificación de una nación ultrajada por la barbarie," *Cuadernos americanos* 255 (1984): 165–85 (and reprinted in *Sarmiento de frente y perfil*, pp. 125–50), I discuss the differences in perspective between Sarmiento and Echeverría.

79. Roberto Zalazar, *Pedro Ferré y el federalismo* (Corrientes: Facultad de Derecho, 1963), p. 15.

80. Leonardo Paso, *Historia del origen de los partidos políticos en la Argentina (1810–1918)* (Buenos Aires: Centro de Estudios, 1972), pp. 186–89.

81. Campobassi, *Mitre y su época*, p. 89.

82. Mayer, *Alberdi y su tiempo*, p. 460.

83. Paso, *Partidos políticos*, pp. 186–87, copies from Pico's letter of November 13, 1853 to Urquiza.

84. Leonardo Paso, *Raíces históricas de la dependencia argentina* (Buenos Aires: Cartago, 1975), p. 115; Luis Franco, *De Rosas a Mitre: medio siglo de historia argentina 1830/1880* (Buenos Aires: Astral, 1977), p. 48, states that the new ruling elite in Buenos Aires, constituted by Mitre, Alsina, and others, had "exactly the same

class interests" as had Rosas. See also Ricardo M. Ortiz, *Historia económica de la Argentina, 1850–1930*, vol. I (Buenos Aires: Raigal, 1955), p. 68.

85. José Luis Romero, *A History of Argentine Political Thought*, trans. Thomas F. McGann (Stanford: Stanford University Press, 1963), p. 131.

86. Tulio Halperín Donghi, "La expansión ganadera en la campaña de Buenos Aires (1818–1852)," in *Los fragmentos del poder: de la oligarquía a la poliarquía argentina*, edited by Torcuato S. di Tella and Tulio Halperín Donghi (Buenos Aires: Jorge Alvarez, 1969), pp. 21–74.

87. Noël Salomon, "El *Facundo* de Domingo Faustino Sarmiento: manifiesto de la preburguesía argentina de las ciudades del interior," *Cuadernos americanos* 39, no. 5 (1980): 121–76.

88. Sarmiento, *Obras completas*, vol. XV, p. 166.

89. Ibid., vol. XVI, p. 75, copies the article, "Estado de las repúblicas sudamericanas a mediados del siglo" (a "memoria" presented to the Instituto Histórico de Francia in May 1853).

90. Mitre, *Arengas*, p. 83.

91. Justo José Urquiza, "Mensage del Presidente de la Confederación Argentina al Primer Congreso Legislativo Federal," *El nacional*, November 4, 1854.

92. [Bartolomé Mitre], unsigned editorial in *El nacional*, November 8, 1854. Mármol's response, appearing in a signed letter printed in the very same issue of *El nacional*, underlined Urquiza's "most uncalled for insults . . . he has attempted to stain the honor, authority, and institutions of Buenos Aires in his message. . . . Urquiza, with his hot-headed irritability . . . has slandered [Buenos Aires], he has slighted her glories."

93. [Bartolomé Mitre], unsigned editorial in *El nacional*, November 9, 1854. On the following day Mitre turned the direction of the newspaper over to Sarmiento and once again dedicated his full energies to the military defense of the province.

94. [Bartolomé Mitre], [unsigned article], *El nacional*, December 9, 1856, pp. 1–2.

95. The editorials published in *El nacional* on December 17 and 18 (Sarmiento's authorship?) ridiculed the idea of the Republic of the Río de la Plata. One specific reservation with the idea concerned the unresolved issue of the extent of authority that would be exercised by such a government. Sarmiento's point seems to have been that before any talk of national unity was possible, it was first necessary to decide whether the country should have either a weak government with limited power for provincial intervention or a strong unitarian authority that could protect broadly defined rights and principles in the face of local abuse.

96. José Mármol, *Carta del Ciudadano Arjentino José Mármol a los S. S. D. Salvador María del Carril, D. Mariano Fragueiro y D. Facundo Zubiría, Delegados al Sr. Director Provisiario, en la República Arjentina* (Montevideo: Imprenta del Nacional, 1853).

97. Mármol, *Carta*, p. 11.

98. In a letter published in the November 8, 1854 issue of *El nacional*, Mármol responded to Urquiza's October 22, speech to the National Legislature in Paraná. Here he repeated many of these same points, while continuing to defend the September Revolution and the Buenos Aires constitution. Like Mitre he was extremely irritated by Urquiza's intent to wound the honor of Buenos Aires. But in contrast to Mitre's recourse to insults and name calling, Mármol's letter was characterized by respectful indignation.

99. Alberto Blasi Brambilla, *José Mármol y la sombra de Rosas* (Buenos Aires: Pleamar, 1970). See especially the chapter "El representante," pp. 63–81.

100. Unsigned editorial in *El orden*, October 25, 1855.

101. Un amigo del Coronel Mitre, "Carta al Sr. Senador D. José Mármol," Luján, in *El nacional*, December 20, 1856.

102. [Unsigned editorial], [Sarmiento], *El nacional*, May 6, 1857.

103. Ibid.

104. In 1854 Mármol was elected to the provincial Senate, to which he was reelected two years later. That last year he was also elected member of the first Municipalidad de Buenos Aires and served at the convention charged with revising the Provincial Constitution of 1853. In 1858 he was appointed director of the National Library. In 1859 he took part in the Santa Fe convention for revising the National Constitution. In 1860 he was again reelected Senador, as well as representative to the National Congress. After that year, he would serve in several capacities in the country's diplomatic core. He died in 1871.

105. Although a fragment of the novel was published in the Montevidean press in 1844, the first edition is considered to be the text published by installments in Montevideo's *La semana* in 1851. The 1855 text included some relatively minor revisions to the 1851 text and added eight additional chapters to the end (after chapter 12 of the fifth part). This was the text that first circulated widely in Buenos Aires and Argentina.

106. *El Paraná*, October 25, 1852, as copied from Carlos Dámaso Martínez, "Nacimiento de la novela. José Mármol." In *Historia de la literatura argentina*, vol. 1, *Desde la colonia hasta el romanticismo* (Buenos Aires: Centro Editor de América Latina, 1980/1986), p. 281. An example of the acrid reaction by former Rosist supporters to the contents of the novel borders on literary folklore. On an afternoon in June 1856, Lucio V. Mansilla, future author of *Una excursión a los indios ranqueles* (1870), verbally assaulted Mármol in front of a theater full of spectators, accusing him of defaming his father in the chapter, "Quinientas onzas" (five hundred ounces of gold), and challenging him to a duel. Mármol's response was to calmly censure the impertinence of his young detractor.

107. *Amalia*, IV, ch. 5.

108. Ibid., ch. 9.

109. Dámaso Martínez, "Nacimiento," p. 287.

110. *Amalia*, IV, 8; III, 3. The problem of Porteño individualism is highlighted several other times: III, 17; IV, 16; and V, 11.

111. Ibid., V, ch. 11.

112. Cited in Manuel Gálvez, *Vida de Sarmiento*, 3d ed. (Buenos Aires: Editorial Tor, 1957), p. 200.

113. Sarmiento's letter, written toward the middle of 1854 to Damian Hudson, a known sympathizer of the Confederation, was quoted in the June 14, 1854 letter from Hudson to J. M. Gutiérrez, as cited in *Archivo del Doctor Juan María Gutiérrez. Epistolario* (Buenos Aires: Biblioteca del Congreso de la Nación, 1982), vol. III, p. 35.

114. Ibid., p. 141, copies the Valparaíso letter of December 31, 1854 from Carlos Lamarca to Gutiérrez, in which Lamarca refers to the "manoeuvering of Sarmiento, Sarratea and Zoluaga [*sic*] from Mendoza." In the April 8, 1855 letter Juan Ignacio García in Mendoza describes to Carlos Lamarca, in Valparaíso, the attempts of Sarmiento—"this famous anarchist"—to pass through the *aduana* of Santa Rosa a box of rifles in order to promote an armed revolution against the federals still in power there (p. 217). Gregorio Beeche, writing from Valparaíso

to Gutiérrez, also had reasons for suspecting Sarmiento's less than peaceful motives for visiting San Juan the year before; "as long as he is around, the social stability of that region will be in question" (letter of April 30, 1855, p. 239).

115. Beatriz Bosch, *Urquiza y su tiempo* (Buenos Aires: EUBA, 1980), p. 377, quotes from Urquiza's letter from San José of April 16, 1855 to de Carril.

116. Ricardo Rojas, *El profeta de la pampa: vida de Sarmiento* (Buenos Aires: Losada, 1945), p. 405.

117. The editors of Sarmiento's *Obras completas* have united those writings under several headings: vol. XVI: *Provinciano en Buenos Aires;* vol. XVII: *Unión nacional;* vol. XXI: *Discursos;* vol. XXIII: *Senador;* vol. XXV: *Organización: Estado de Buenos Aires;* vol. XXVI: articles in *La nación;* and vol. XXV: *Política: Estado de Buenos Aires, 1855–1860.*

118. Gálvez, *Vida de Sarmiento,* p. 206, where Gálvez quotes Benjamín Vicuña Mackenna's letter in which reference is made to Sarmiento: "One day he will awake with a San Juan disposition and will write against Buenos Aires; the next day he will awake with a Porteño spirit and will write against Urquiza; on yet the next day he will get up with the disposition of a horse-back rider, galloping across the pampa, and no one will escape his virulent criticisms except for his own sacred self."

119. Sarmiento, *Obras completas,* vol. XVI, p. 301.

120. Ibid., p. 364.

121. Ibid., pp. 366–67.

122. Ibid., vol. XVII, p. 147; vol. XXVI, p. 266.

123. Ibid., vol. XVII, p. 24.

124. Ibid., pp. 24, 45.

125. Ibid., p. 81.

126. Ibid., pp. 219–21, 224.

127. Ibid., vol. XXV, p. 347.

128. Ibid., vol. XVII, p. 144.

129. Two studies treating the topic of public lands are Miguel Angel Cárcano, *Evolución histórica del régimen de la tierra pública (1810–1916),* with an essay by María Susana Taborda Caro on "La legislación de tierras públicas nacionales y el régime legal vigente en las nuevas provincias (1950–1970)," 1st ed. 1917; Buenos Aires: EUDBA, 1972); and Romain Gaignard, *La pampa argentina: ocupación, población, explotación. De la conquista a la crisis mundial (1550–1930),* trad. Ricardo Figueira (Buenos Aires: Solar, 1989).

130. *El nacional,* August 9, 1856. Sarmiento's articles and speeches on the topic of public lands are divided among volumes XVIII, XXI, XXIII, XXIV, XXVI, and XXXVI, of his *Obras completas.*

131. Two authors studying Sarmiento's ideas and actions with regard to pubic lands are Luis Franco, "La democratización del agro," in *Sarmiento entre dos fuegos* (Buenos Aires: Paídos, 1968), pp. 175–206; and Natalio J. Pisano, *La política agraria de Sarmiento: la lucha contra el latifundio* (Buenos Aires: Depalma, 1980).

132. *El nacional,* January 26, 1857; reprinted in Sarmiento, *Obras completas,* vol. XXI.

133. *El nacional,* September 11, 1856.

134. Juan Bautista Alberdi, *Obras completas* (Buenos Aires: "La tribuna nacional," 1886), vol. IV, pp. 147, 145 (from *Sistema económico y rentística de la Confederación Argentina según la Constitución de 1853).*

135. See, for example, the May 16, 1854 letter from V. F. López to J. M. Gutiérrez, in *Archivo del Doctor Juan María Gutiérrez,* vol. III, p. 17: "You must not

forget the axiom that any government attempting to impose systems a priori, as good as the latter might be, will sink with the debris from those same systems, after the destruction wielded upon them by the conglomerate of personal interests opposing them. Those organized governments experiencing most success are those for which the law never was a *mold* but rather an *objective,* never enclosed like a *fence,* but rather opened possibilities like a *program.*"

136. In this regard one has to criticize the interpretation of Enrique de Gandia, for whom Sarmiento's consistent defense of "liberty" went hand-in-hand with a continuous opposition to all forms of statism, whether it were absolutism, socialism, or communism. On the contrary the examples given here demonstrate that Sarmiento forcefully argued for a more active role for the state in financial and commerical affairs. See Gandia's updated version of Vicente Fidel López, *Historia de la República Argentina* . . . (Buenos Aires: Sopena, 1964), vol. VIII, pp. 262, 272.

137. Gaignard, *La pampa argentina,* p. 114, explains that the land law of 1857 ended up granting new protection to the property rights of the small group of provincial *latifundistas.* In addition it accelerated, rather than impeded, the trend toward concentrated land holdings by placing over 3.25 million hectares in the hands of only 333 owners. It is these that "constitute the small number of family groups that have possessed the greater part of pampean space up to the present."

138. Pisano, *La política agraria,* correctly states that Sarmiento "did not serve the dominant party line of the liberal Porteño group, as did Vélez Sarsfield . . . he probably learned that he had to *concede* in order to *not be eliminated* all together" (p. 115). Similarly Luis Franco, *Sarmiento entre dos fuegos,* redeems Sarmiento for posterity because of his failure: he defended "the interests of the common people against the interests of the priveliged class" (p. 197).

139. Sarmiento's support for the French and British alliance against Rosas dated only as far back as 1843. Contradicting this stance were a series of articles he published in Santiago's *El mercurio* between October 1841 and August 1842: "El aprendizaje de la civilización," "Colonización inglesa en el Río de la Plata," and "Lo que gana el extranjero con nuestra anarquía," (vol. XIII, 305–29). In these articles he strongly denounced the British for their new strategy—what he called "modern colonialism" (vol. XIII, 310)—of supporting dictators such as Rosas with the intent of gaining a stranglehold on the economic activities of the region. I discuss these articles in "Sarmiento y el *americanismo,*" in Saúl Yurkievich, ed. *Identidad cultural de Iberoamérica en su literatura* (Madrid: Alhambra, 1986), pp. 67–74 (reprinted in *Sarmiento de frente y perfil,* pp. 23–34) and in *Sarmiento: Public Writer,* pp. 169–74.

140. Sarmiento, *Obras completas,* vol. VII, pp. 216, 221, 222. I discuss this topic in "Sarmiento y el *americanismo*" and *Sarmiento: Public Writer,* pp. 174–82.

141. These twelve or so articles are collected in Sarmiento, *Obras completas,* vol. XXXVI, p. 13–56.

142. Ibid., vol. p. 15.

143. Ibid., vol. p. 43.

144. Alberto Palcos, *Sarmiento: la vida, la obra, las ideas, el genio* (Buenos Aires: El Ateneo, 1938), pp. 123–39, argues that during the decade of the 1850s Sarmiento was among most respected and conciliatory voice in very difficult times.

145. Gálvez, *Vida de Sarmiento,* p. 212, quotes from the letter of June 17, 1857 that Sarmiento wrote to Domingo de Oro.

146. *El nacional,* April 26, 1856.

147. Gutiérrez, *Archivo del Doctor,* vol. III, p. 196, reproduces the March 14, 1855 letter from Gregorio Beeche in Valparaíso to Gutiérrez, in which reference is made to the situation in San Juan: "those people [are] capable of inconsiderate acts; they don't have any qualms nor interest other than that of personal engrandisement. Sarmiento has said that . . . he needs social chaos to exist in order that people call upon him to assume a position of leadership. That's his brand of patriotism."

148. Alberdi, *Bases,* p. 227.

149. Oscar Terán, "Alberdi póstumo," in Juan Bautista Alberdi, *Alberdi póstumo* (Buenos Aires: Puntosur, 1988), p. 18.

150. This is the inciteful observation of Canal Feijóo, *Constitución y revolución,* p. 455.

151. Ibid., p. 457.

152. Dardo Pérez Giulhou, *El pensamiento conservador de Alberdi y la Constitución de 1853* (Buenos Aires: Depalma, 1984), p. 41.

153. Terán, "Alberdi póstumo," quotes *Escritos póstumos* (edition of 1873), vol. XII, 179–81.

154. Ibid., pp. 35, 80.

155. Ibid., p. 77.

156. Ibid., p. 45.

157. José Hernández, "La división de la tierra," September 1, 1869, as copied from Antonio Pagés Larraya, *Prosas del Martín Fierro, con una selección de los escritos de José Hernández* (Buenos Aires: Raigal), p. 195.

158. Terán, "Alberdi póstumo," p. 77, cites Alberdi's *Escritos póstumos* (1873), vol. XIV, pp. 469, 470, 472.

159. Mayer, *Alberdi y su tiempo,* p. 480, quotes from Alberdi, *Sistema económico.*

160. Alberdi, *Escritos póstumos,* vol. V, p. 269.

161. Alberdi, *Bases,* p. 242 (section XXXV).

162. Ibid., p. 239 (section XXXIV).

163. Pagés Larraya, *Prosas del Martín Fierro,* pp. 141–50, presents convincing evidence affirming the authorship of Andrade. Surprisingly Enrique de Gandia, *José Hernández: sus ideas políticas* (Buenos Aires: Depalma, 1985), did not take this evidence into account when he credited the pamphlet to Hernández, even though he recognized that other critics, most notable among them Beatriz Bosch, believed Andrade to be its author.

164. José Hernández [sic], "Las dos políticas," as copied from Gandia, *José Hernández,* p. 89.

165. Ibid., p. 95.

166. Letter from Juan María Gutiérrez in Paraná, to V. F. López in Montevideo, April 27, 1853, López Archives.

167. Letter from Juan María Gutiérrez, to V. F. López in Montevideo (1854), López Archives.

168. Letter from Juan María Gutiérrez in Santa Fe, to V. F. López, May 6, (1854?), López Archives.

169. Letter from Juan María Gutiérrez in Paraná, to V. F. López, July 30, (1854), López Archives.

170. Antonio Sagarna, "Juan María Gutiérrez y la organización nacional," *Boletín de la Academia Nacional de Historia,* vol. 11 (1937–38), pp. 169–207.

171. Ibid., p. 200. The "differential rights" plan was finally approved by the Paraná legislature in 1857.

172. Mayer, *Alberdi y su tiempo,* p. 534. Liliana M. Brezzo, "El Doctor Juan

María Gutiérrez en Rosario: entre Cepeda y Pavón," *Res Gesta*, 19–20 (1986): 9–19, mentions that Gutiérrez personally favored de Carril as Urquiza's successor and that Derqui's election to that office caused his deep disillusionment.

173. Beatriz Bosch, "Juan María Gutiérrez al servicio de la Confederación Argentina," *Revista de la Universidad de Buenos Aires*, 5th epoch, 4, no. 4 (1955): 543–70.

174. Letter from Alberdi to Gutiérrez dated December 7, 1856, from Paris, as copied in Mayer, *Alberdi y su tiempo*, p. 535.

175. Gutiérrez, *Epistolario del Don Juan María Gutiérrez*, p. 79, quotes the May 25, 1860 letter to B. Victorica, in which Gutiérrrez wrote that Alberdi, with "reasoned propriety . . . views the temperament of the men from Buenos Aires as those who always want to be in the center of everything."

176. Brezzo, "El Doctor J. M. Gutiérrez," p. 10, quotes the letter from Gutiérrez to Victorica, April 11, 1859.

177. Letter of April 20, 1859 from Juan María Gutiérrez to Juan Bautista Alberdi, Furt Archives.

178. Copied from Ambrosio Romero Carranza, Alberto Rodríguez Varela, and Eduardo Ventura Flores Pirán. *Historia política de la Argentina* vol. II, *Desde 1816 hasta 1862* (Buenos Aires: Pannedille, 1971), p. 1078. The authors of this work, with obvious Catholic bias, feature the contributions of "the friar" Frías on pp. 1076–81, 1112–16, and 1154–56.

179. *El orden*, October 25, 1855.

180. *El orden*, November 21, 1855.

181. Letter from Frías to Alberdi, Buenos Aires, November 2, 1857, Furt Archives.

182. Sarmiento, *Obras completas*, vol. XXIV; vol. XXV, pp. 242–44, 278–84.

183. Gálvez, *Vida de Sarmiento*, p. 205, states that Sarmiento and Frías differed little if at all about the fundamental conflict dividing the Confederation and Buenos Aires and that the former's attacks were almost always "without basis, since Sarmiento's interpretations change the sense of the written words or obscure their context by focusing on parts at the expense of the whole."

184. Sarmiento, *Obras completas*, vol. XXV, p. 298.

185. Ibid., vol. XVII, p. 389.

186. Gálvez, *Vida de Sarmiento*, p. 210.

187. Letter from Vicente López y Planes to V. F. López, July 28, 1854, in López Archives.

188. Elizabeth Garrels, "El 'espíritu de la familia' en *La novia del hereje* de Vicente Fidel López," *Hispamérica*, 16: 46/47 (1987): 3–24.

189. Vicente F. López, *Historia de la República Argentina. Su origen, su revolución y su desarrollo político hasta el gobierno del general Viamonte. Continuada hasta 1910 por Emilio Vera y González y Ampliada desde el descubrimiento hasta nuestros días por Enrique de Gandia. Nueva edición profusamente ilustrada* (Buenos Aires: Sopena, 1964), vol. IV, p. 276.

190. Ibid.

191. Ibid., pp. 359, 361.

192. Letter from J. M. Gutiérrez to V. F. López, Rosario, January 21, 1860, López Archives.

193. Letter from F. Pico to V. F. López, September 2, 1858, López Archives.

194. Letter from Luis Domínguez to V. F. López, Buenos Aires, May 27, 1858, López Archives.

195. Letter from Luis Domínguez to V. F. López, Buenos Aires, July 16, 1858, López Archives.

196. Vicente Fidel López's letter was published sometime in April or May of 1858, with another article in January or February 1859, as judging from Sarmiento's responses of May 14, 1858, July 5, 1858, February 27 [no year given], and ff. See Sarmiento, *Obras completas*, vol. XIII, p. 344, 352–58.

197. Sarmiento, *Obras completas*, vol. XVII, p. 351, in articles published in *El nacional* on May 14 and July 5, 1858; and February 27, [1859?].

198. Ibid., p. 355.

199. Letter from V. F. López to Alberdi, Montevideo, November 29, 1858, Furt Archives.

200. Sarmiento, *Obras completas*, vol. XXV, pp. 25–29, 52–56, 214, 234, 341.

201. Victorica, *Urquiza y Mitre*, pp. 99–109.

202. Ibid. p. 102.

203. Alberdi, *Escritos póstumos*, vol. XIV, p. 453, copies the letter of January 24, 1856 from Gutiérrez to Alberdi.

204. Juan Bautista Alberdi, *Epistolario, 1855–1881*, ed. Alfonso Bulnes (Santiago: Editorial Andrés Bello, 1967).

205. Mayer, *Alberdi y su tiempo*, pp. 538 and 523, copies the letter from Higuera to Alberdi, February 17, 1856; and from José Cayetano Borbón to Alberdi, May 14, 1856.

206. Ramos, *Revolución*, vol. I, p. 225.

207. Gálvez, *Vida de Sarmiento*, p. 212, copies from Sarmiento's letter of June 17, 1857 to Domingo de Oro.

208. Ibid., p. 552, copies the letter from General Guido to Victorica, October 25, 1857.

209. López, *Historia*, vol. VI, p. 563.

210. Mayer, *Alberdi y su tiempo*, p. 559, refers to the letters written by Carlos M. Lamarca to Alberdi on September 23 and October 15, 1857; January 30, February 28, March 25, and September 23, 1858, that reveal details of these intrigues.

211. Alberdi, *Epistolario*, copies the letter from Alberdi to Francisco Javier Villanueva, dated October 31, 1857.

212. Mayer, *Alberdi y su tiempo*, p. 560, copies from the letter from Alberdi to Urquiza, Paris, December 7, 1857.

213. Victorica, *Urquiza y Mitre*, p. 111.

214. Ibid., p. 116.

215. Canal Feijóo, *Constitución y revolución*, p. 470, copies from the letter from Alberdi to Urquiza, Paris, May 7, 1858.

216. Gálvez, *Vida de Sarmiento*, p. 222; Victorica, *Urquiza y Mitre*, pp. 119–20.

217. Copied from Victorica, *Urquiza y Mitre*, pp. 122–23.

218. Gálvez, *Vida de Sarmiento*, p. 222, refers to the letter Sarmiento published in *El nacional*.

219. Victorica, *Urquiza y Mitre*, p. 122, copies from "Apología del asesinato," an article published in French in *L'Union étrangère* in Buenos Aires.

220. Copied from Victorica, *Urquiza y Mitre*, p. 121.

221. Ibid., p. 126.

222. Sarmiento, *Obras completas*, vol. XXV, pp. 142–44.

223. Letters from Miguel Cané to Alberdi from Buenos Aires, February 27, 1860 and March 28, 1860, Furt Archives.

224. Liliana M. Brezzo, "El Doctor Juan María Gutiérrez en Rosario: entre

Cepeda y Pavón," *Res Gesta* 19–20 (January–June and July–December 1986), p. 14, copies from Gutiérrez's letter to Urquiza dated May 4, 1860.

225. Alberdi, *Epistolario,* p. 185, copies the letter from Alberdi to Alfonso Bulnes, Madrid, June 6, 1860.

226. Ibid., in the letter from London dated September 30, 1859.

227. Letter from Miguel Cané to Juan Bautista Alberdi from Buenos Aires, dated February 27, 1860, Furt Archives.

228. Campobassi, *Mitre y su época,* p. 110.

229. Ibid., p. 113.

231. Victorica, *Urquiza y Mitre,* p. 202, quotes historian Pelliza about Sarmiento's complicity in the assassination of Virasoro. According to Gálvez, *Historia de Sarmiento,* p. 338, there was no doubt: "Does Sarmiento work against the government of his province? Most assuredly." In the otherwise admirably complete biography of Sarmiento written by Sarmiento hagiographer, Ricardo Rojas, *El profeta de la pampa,* the issue of Sarmiento's alleged complicity in these events is not even discussed (p. 420).

232. Gálvez: *Historia de Sarmiento,* p. 342.

233. Copied from Campobassi, *Mitre y su tiempo,* p. 119.

234. Quoted in ibid., p. 119.

235. Beatriz Bosch, *Urquiza y su tiempo* (Buenos Aires: EUBA, 1980), p. 527.

236. Ibid., p. 72, quotes from the letter of April 14, 1861 written in Paraná by Diógenes J. de Urquiza to his father.

237. Victorica, *Urquiza y Mitre,* p. 155, quotes Urquiza's proclamation to the people of Buenos Aires on the eve of the Battle of Cepeda: "I have not come to subject you to the arbitrary will of a man. . . . At the end of my political career, my sole ambition is to contemplate from the doors of my tranquil home a united and tranquil Argentine Republic, that has cost me long years of rough, hard labor. I have come to offer you a lasting peace under the banner of your elders, under the protective and wonderful law that we share."

238. Sagarna, "Juan María Gutiérrez," p. 203, quotes the letter from Gutiérrez to Urquiza dated May 4, 1860. See also Brezzo, "El Doctor Juan María Gutiérrez."

239. Fermín Chávez, *Vida y muerte de López Jordan* (Buenos Aires: Theoría, 1957), p. 57.

240. Alberdi, *Escritos póstumos,* vol. IX, pp. 107–8.

241. See the letters written by Gutiérrez to Mitre, as quoted below. David Viñas, *(Rebeliones populares argentinas),* vol. I, *De los montoneros a los anarquistas* (Buenos Aires: Carlos Pérez, 1971), pp. 48–49, while censoring Urquiza's seduction by Buenos Aires, nevertheless suggests the realism of Urquiza's new position, that is, he was "seduced by the idea of posthumous glory before the new elitist concensus that was emerging triumphant."

242. Palmira S. Bollo Cabrios, "Diferencias financieras en la lucha de la Confederación y Buenos Aires, 1857–1862," in *Pavón y la crisis de la Confederación,* pp. 167–251.

243. Ibid., p. 210.

244. Quoted by Gálvez, *Historia de Sarmiento,* p. 347.

245. César A. García Belsunce, "Mitre y la política de Buenos Aires, 1859–1862," in *Pavón y la crisis,* edited by Armando R. Bazán (Buenos Aires: Equipos de Investigacion Historica, 1965), p. 125.

246. Letter from J. M. Gutiérrez to V. F. López, Rosario, June 21, 1860, López Archives.

247. Brezzo, "El Doctor Juan María Gutiérrez," p. 16, quotes the letter from Gutiérrez to Alberdi, Rosario, June 17, 1860.
248. Gutiérrez, *Epistolario*, p. 80, quotes the letter from Gutiérrez to Mitre, July 12, 1860.
249. Sagarna, "Juan María Gutiérrez," p. 205.
250. This important correspondence between 1860–61 consisting of some eighty-six letters, is reproduced in Bartolomé Mitre, *Archivo del General Mitre*, vol. VII, *Antecedentes de Pavón* (Buenos Aires: Biblioteca de "La nación," 1911), pp. 105–280. William H[artley] Jeffers, *Mitre and Argentina* (New York: Library Publishers, 1952), totally misreads Mitre's letter of February 4, 1861 to Urquiza when he charactizes its content as reflecting "little except bitter insults and accusations between the two" (p. 156).
251. Sagarna, "Juan María Gutiérrez," p. 205, quotes from Gutiérrez's letters of July 2 and September 12, 1860 to Mitre.
252. Oscar Oszlak, *La formación del estado argentino* (Buenos Aires: Belgrano, 1982), p. 70, calls attention to the relatively marginal role of the interior provinces in the conflict between the government of the Confederation and Buenos Aires.
253. Chávez, *López Jordan*, p. 57.
254. Campobassi, *Mitre y su época*, p. 122.
255. *Correspondencia Mitre-Urquiza*, pp. 60, 41, quotes the letters from Mitre to Urquiza, Buenos Aires, July 5, 1861; and from Urquiza to Mitre, Concepción del Uruguay, April 30, 1861.

CHAPTER 4. NATIONAL CONSOLIDATION (1860–1880)

1. Vicente Fidel López, *Historia de la República Argentina. Su origen, su revolución y su desarrollo político hasta el gobierno del general Viamonte. Continuada hasta 1910 por Emilio Vera y González y ampliada desde el descubrimiento hasta nuestros días por Enrique de Gandia. Nueva edición profusamente ilustrada*, vol. VI (Buenos Aires: Sopena Argentina, 1964), p. 623n.
2. Manuel Gálvez, *Vida de Sarmiento: el hombre de autoridad* (Buenos Aires: Emecé, 1945), p. 352.
3. Ricardo Rojas, *El profeta de la pampa: vida de Sarmiento* (Buenos Aires: Losada, 1945), p. 642.
4. Gálvez, *Vida de Sarmiento*, p. 351.
5. Ibid.
6. López, *Historia*, vol. VI, p. 625.
7. Ibid., pp. 624, 625.
8. Gregorio Araoz Alfaro, *Rawson: ministro de Mitre* (Buenos Aires: Coni, 1938), p. 77, copies letter from Sarmiento to Mitre, December 1861.
9. Isidoro J. Ruiz Moreno, "El Litoral después de Pavón (septiembre-diciembre 1961)," in [Armando R.] Bazán, et al., *Pavón y la crisis de la Confederación* (Buenos Aires: Equipos de Investigación Histórica, 1965), pp. 440, 442.
10. Ibid., p. 439.
11. Quoted from Roberto I. Peña, "Córdoba en el plan político de Pavón, 1852–1863," in Bazán, *Pavón y la crisis de la Confederación*, p. 473; no date indicated.
12. Ibid., p. 477.
13. Letter from M. Paz to Alberdi, Rosario, April 29, 1858, Furt Archives: "The peace process continues and the government of Buenos Aires loses terrain

with each new day. Our triumph will be beautiful and how I hope and desire that the mere threat of our arms alone can convince them to follow the path of reason. Alsina has lost, and the opposition declares itself nationalist. Don't doubt it: truth and justice will triumph in the end."

14. Ramón J. Cárcano, *Guerra del Paraguay: orígenes y causas* (Buenos Aires: Domingo Viau, 1939), pp. 422–23, copies from the letter of June 1, 1861.

15. Carlos Heras, "El vicepresidente de Mitre, Coronel Doctor Marcos Paz," *Boletín de la Academia Nacional de Historia* 35, no. 29 (1958): 206–45. Heras writes nothing about Paz's beliefs about or possible involvement in the earlier assassination of Heredia and the Avellaneda-led rebellion.

16. Gregorio Araoz Alfaro, *Rawson: ministro de Mitre* (Buenos Aires: Coni, 1938), p. 19. Araoz writes nothing about Rawson's beliefs about or possible involvement in the assassination of Benevides and the Aberastain-led rebellion.

17. Juan María Gutiérrez, *Epistolario de Don Juan María Gutiérrrez* (Buenos Aires: Instituto Cultural Joaquín V. González, 1942), p. 75, copies from the letter by Gutiérrez to Urquiza, May 4, 1860. Liliana M. Brezzo, "El Doctor Juan María Gutiérrez en Rosario: entre Cepeda y Pavón," *Res gesta* 19–20 (1986): 14, errs in suggesting that Gutiérrez was perturbed over Buenos Aires's noncompliance with the Pacto de Unión.

18. Luis Barros Borgoño, *A través de una correspondencia: Don Juan María Gutiérrez* (Santiago: Prensa de la Universidad de Chile, 1934), p. 151, copies from Gutiérrez's letter to him of January 23, 1862.

19. Héctor F. Varela, *La situación de la República Argentina: su gobierno, su comercio y su política. Carta dirigida al Sr. D. Eduardo Asquerino* (Paris: Walder, 1863). This pamphlet is located in Brochure 30603 of Biblioteque de L'Arsenal, Paris. Varela, the son of assassinated Unitarian leader Florencio Varela, practiced journalism in Buenos Aires on behalf of the autonomist faction.

20. Ramón J. Cárcano, *Urquiza y Alberdi: intimidades de una política* (Buenos Aires: La Facultad, 1938), has compiled Alberdi's correspondence to Urquiza, which is accompanied by an excellent introduction by Cárcano himself.

21. Cárcano, *Urquiza y Alberdi*, p. 621, cites the letter from Alberdi to Urquiza, January 24, 1860.

22. Ibid., p. 627, cites the from Alberdi to Marcos A. Arredondo, Paris, April 24, 1862.

23. Juan Bautista Alberdi, *Obras completas* (Buenos Aires: La Tribuna Nacional, 1886), vol. VI, pp. 151–218, copies the pamphlet, "De la anarquía y sus dos causas principales, del gobierno y sus dos elementos necesarios en la Repúbica Argentina con motivo de su regorganización por Buenos Aires."

24. This was a slight modification of his proposal a year earlier, in "Condiciones de Unión," Paris, 1861, in which Alberdi argued that the Province of Buenos Aires's disproportionate size and power constituted an obstacle to national reunification and that the interests of the nation could best be served by dividing that large province into two or more new ones. One can imagine the strident opposition in Buenos Aires to such a proposal.

25. Letter from José María Zuviría to Alberdi, Rosario, October 1, 1864, Furt Archives: "[I']f there is one man in Buenos Aires who is trying to win back for the provinces what is rightfully theirs, that man is Mitre."

26. Peña, "Córdoba," p. 480, cites the letter from Paz to Mitre, December 31, 1861.

27. Ibid., p. 484, copies from Paunero's letter to Mitre, February 14, 1862.

28. Ramón Rosa Olmos and Armando R. Bazán, "Pavón y Catamarca (1852–

1868)," in *Pavón y la crisis de la Confederación*, edited by Armando R. Bazán (Buenos Aires: Equipos de Investigación Historica, 1965), p. 533.

29. Ibid., p. 530, copy from the letter from Bishop Segura to Marcos Paz and Mitre, January 13, 1862.

30. An example of this type of distortion is José María Rosa's *La guerra del Paraguay y las montoneras argentinas* (Buenos Aires: Peña Lillo, 1985), pp. 77–78, in which it is erroneously stated: "The Porteño army's actions to cleanse the countryside of creoles between 1861 and 1862 constitutes the saddest page of our nation's history."

31. Félix Luna, *Buenos Aires y el país* (Buenos Aires: Sudamericana, 1985), pp. 145–46, indicates that the letters are from April 1860.

32. Rosa, *La guerra del Paraguay*, p. 100, quotes from Mitre's letter of October 20, 1861.

33. Ibid., pp. 107–113.

34. Ibid., p. 101.

35. Ibid., p. 84.

36. Peña, "Cordoba," p. 493, quotes the Paunero letter of June 17, 1862.

37. Ibid., p. 494, copies part of Gabriel's January 13, 1862 letter to Mitre.

38. Dardo de la Vega Díaz, *Mitre y el Chacho: La Rioja en la reorganización del País* (La Rioja: Testori, 1939), pp. 21, 61, quotes from letters of January 3 and 7, 1862 sent by M. Paz to Mitre.

39. Ibid., p. 73.

40. Campobassi, *Mitre y su época*, p. 147.

41. Rosa, *La guerra del Paraguay*, p. 84.

42. Gálvez, *Vida de Sarmiento*, p. 368.

43. Copied from Fermín Chávez, *Vida y muerte de López Jordán* (Buenos Aires: Theoría, 1957), p. 93.

44. Peña, "Cordoba," p. 496–97, copies part of the proclamation but gives no date, which is presumed to be between March and May 1863.

45. Ricardo Mercado Luna, *Los coroneles de Mitre* (Buenos Aires: Plus Ultra, 1974), p. 79.

46. Rosa, *La guerra del Paraguay*, p. 82.

47. Campobassi, *Mitre y su época*, p. 147, obviously refers to Sarmiento: "This strange arrangement converted Peñaloza's defeats into victories. Mitre as well as the outstanding leaders of the the national army who were stationed near the scene of the struggle were intimately stung by the accord and the dishonorable situation that resulted."

48. Jorge Abelardo Ramos, *Revolución y contrarrevolución en la Argentina. II. Del patriciado a la oligarquía, 1862–1904*. 6th ed. revised (Buenos Aires: Plus Ultra, 1976), p. 26.

49. Rosa, *La guerra del Paraguay*, p. 83.

50. Ibid., p. 82.

51. Ibid.

52. Ramos, *Del patriciado*, p. 27.

53. López, *Historia*, vol. VI, p. 629n.

54. Ibid., where López is incorrect in stating that Mitre condemned the execution in energetic terms.

55. Campobassi, *Mitre y su época*, p. 167, quotes from this correspondence.

56. Ibid.

57. José Hernández, *Vida de "El Chacho,"* as included in the appendix to Antonio Pagés Larraya, *Prosas del Martin Fierro, con una selección de los escritos de*

José Hernández (Buenos Aires: Raigal, 1952), p. 163. Hernández's text was first published in installments in the Paraná newspaper, *El argentino*, in November 1863.

58. Julio Victorica, *Urquiza y Mitre*, p. 230, quotes the pathetic letter written by Victoria Romero de Peñalosa to Urquiza, La Rioja, August 12, 1864, which acknowledged the receipt of monies sent by the latter for her immediate needs after the government had confiscated all her possessions.

59. Hernández, *Vida de "El Chacho,"* p. 153.

60. Gálvez, *Vida de Sarmiento*, pp. 447–48, recounts the angry polemic triggered by *La nación argentina* (José María Gutiérrez was the editor, with Mitre as owner) in November 1869, in which Sarmiento falsely claimed responsibility for Peñalosa's murder. His was an "act of generosity" to cover up the actions of his friends in the army and to disguise the fact that he, as "simple provider of supplies," hardly exercised authority over the war effort at that time.

61. Herrera, *Buenos Aires, Urquiza y el Uruguay*, p. 148fn, gives neither the date nor the name of the person to whom this communication was directed.

62. Rosa, *La guerra del Paraguay*, p. 121.

63. Typical is Claude L. Hulet, "La segunda generación romántica argentina: ensayo de apreciación histórico-política," *Cuadernos americanos* 108, no. 1 (1960): 232–48, who states that the majority of these participants were sons of intransigent Federalists from Buenos Aires; were associated during the 1850s with the Porteño newspaper, *La reforma pacífica;* and later emigrated to Paraná to defend the Confederation. They were "more idealists" in comparison to the 1837 generation (who were "more realist"), because "they weren't interested in historicism in itself, but in its most immediate and mystical aspect: humanism." They were "untiring and persevering in their defense of the cause of the oppressed." Only with the presidencies of Avellaneda and Roca did they again reintegrate themselves with national life, primarily as militants in the new Partido Nacional Autonomista.

64. Hernández, *Vida del Chacho*, p. 163.

65. Ibid., p. 154.

66. Domingo F. Sarmiento, *El último caudillo de la montonera: El Chacho*, included in *Los caudillos* (Buenos Aires: El Ateneo, 1928), p. 194.

67. Rojas, *Profeta de las pampas*, p. 446.

68. Sarmiento, *El Chacho*, p. 121.

69. Ibid., pp. 129–30.

70. Ibid., p. 136.

71. Gálvez, *Vida de Sarmiento*, p. 369.

72. Juan Bautista Alberdi, *Grandes y pequeños hombres del Plata* (Buenos Aires: Plus Ultra, 1974), p. 191.

73. Herrera, *La diplomacia oriental*, pp. 75, 111.

74. Rosa, *La guerra del Paraguay*, p. 112, states in relation to Mármol's remarks of 1869 about Mitre's supposed opposition to the actions of his cabinet members: "Mármol, upon defending Mitre, honed in on the essential dilemma: either Mitre in 1863 played the fool in order to trick the Uruguayans, or he really did ignore the truth of the matter and was deceived by his associates."

75. Ibid., p. 132.

76. Ibid., pp. 143–44, quotes from the letter from Urquiza to Mitre informing him of the April 30, 1864 ascension of José Domínguez as Entre Ríos governor: "He is at present obedient to my will. You can count on the support of my influence. Your Excellency can count on his firm collaboration."

77. Ramos, *Del patriciado*, p. 52.

78. Beatriz Bosch, *Urquiza y su tiempo* (Buenos Aires: EUBA, 1980), pp. 603–33; in *Presencia de Urquiza, con una selección documental* (Buenos Aires: Raigal, 1953), pp. 295–300, the same author copies from documents in support of this position.

79. J. Natalicio González, *La guerra al Paraguay: imperialismo y nacionalismo en El Plata* (Buenos Aires: Sudestada, 1968), pp. 60, 43. This is a shortened version of González's prologue to Bartolomé Mitre and Juan Carlos Gómez, *Cartas polémicas sobre la guerra al Paraguay* (Asunción-Buenos Aires: Guaranía, 1940)—a work that copies in full the important letters written by Gómez, Elizalde, and Mármol, in addition to the relatively insignificant letters by Mitre. Campobassi, *Mitre y su época*, p. 196, chose to ignore entirely the Mitre-Gómez-Mármol-Elizalde polemic of 1869, and totally confuses the issue by stating that the secret document was that signed after the Paraguayan attack of Corrientes and that Urquiza and Flores, in addition to representatives from the Argentine and Brazilian governments, were present.

80. Bosch, *Urquiza y su tiempo*, p. 620, copies from this letter.

81. Ibid., p. 611, quotes from Urquiza's letter of December 25, 1865 to this effect. Carlos Guido Spano, in *El gobierno y la alianza* (1866), provided a documentation of the Mitre administration's complicity. This information is repeated by Herrera, *Buenos Aires, Urquiza y el Uruguay*, p. 111; and Rosa, *La guerra del Paraguay*, p. 181.

82. Rosa, *La guerra del Paraguay*, pp. 184, 143; Fermín Chávez, *El revisionismo y las montoneras. La "Unión Americana." Felipe Varela. Juan Saá y López Jordán* (Buenos Aires: Theoría, 1966), p. 38, quotes López Jordán to this effect. Chávez, in this discussion, follows the perspective later emitted by Alberdi, that "Urquiza and Mitre developed a politics of mutual commmitments that can only favor Buenos Aires" (p. 45).

83. Estanislao S. Zeballos, *El tratado de alianza* (Buenos Aires: Cook, 1872); Cárcano, *Guerra del Paraguay*, pp. 466–67, quoting Antonio Zinny, writes that Solano López, Paraguay's "solitary feudal lord," built up his country's military capacity with the idea of annexing Matto-Grosso and Misiones and establishing a protectorate in the Argentine provinces of Entre Ríos and Corrientes.

84. Witness Mitre's tragically mistaken boast at the initiation of that conflict that Argentine troops would be celebrating a victory march in Buenos Aires within three months; witness Juan Carlos Gómez's claim, *Cartas polémicas*—in his second letter of the polemic—that López's advance to Corrientes was easily repelled by an Argentine force consisting of less than a tenth of her military power in the zone.

85. Domingo F. Sarmiento, *Obras completas*, vol. 37 (Buenos Aires: Luz del Día, 1953), p. 51.

86. Rosa, *La guerra del Paraguay*, pp. 147–48, 160–64.

87. Ibid., pp. 111, 160. Mármol's letter dated December 14, 1869 and signed with the initials XX (see Mitre and Gómez, *Cartas polémicas*, pp. 109–17), argued perhaps ingenuously that of all Mitre's advisors, there was only one (presumably himself) who counseled opposition to the violation of the country's declared neutrality against Uruguay. In an attempt to absolve Mitre of wrongdoing, he argued that the president could do little "against the secret manoeuverings of the cabinet members" (p. 116)—in particular, Elizalde.

88. Victorico, *Urquiza y Mitre*, p. 251.

89. Herrera, *La diplomacia oriental*, pp. 364–66; and Carlos Guido [y] Spano,

El gobierno y la alianza: consideraciones políticas [no title page], prol. Estanislao Zeballos (Buenos Aires: Biblioteca de la Revista de los FFAA de la Nación, n.d.), pp. 75, 78.

90. According to Horacio Zorraquín Becú, *Tiempo y vida de José Hernández, 1834–1886* (Buenos Aires: Emecé, 1972), p. 102, these are the words of pro-López historian, Carlos Pereyra, *Francisco Solano López y la Guerra del Paraguay* (Madrid, 1919, and Buenos Aires, 1958), p. 75.

91. González, *La guerra al Paraguay*, pp. 30–31, quotes from Estanislao Zeballos. Another documentation of these abuses is found in Miguel Navarro Viola, *El despotismo del estado de sitio de la República Argentina en 1866 y 1867* (Buenos Aires: Imprenta de Mayo, 1867). This short pamphlet of forty-eight pages unites letters and articles written by the author, his wife Concepción, and Juan José Soto.

92. According to González, *La guerra al Paraguay*, pp. 90–102, Argentina's public debt in 1870, which had resulted primarily from the pacification campaigns in the interior and the Paraguayan War, passed $39,740,538 pesos—or in excess of £10,500,000, half of which was held by English financial interests. Comparable figures are given for Brazil—over £12,720,700—as for Uruguay. Ramos, *Del patriciado*, p. 70, tells that England immediatelly issued a reconstruction loan of £200,000 to the new government of Paraguay, which figured in its total debt of £1,438,000. Shortly thereafter this total was reduced in exchange for 300,000 hectars of land. By 1908 Paraguay's total debt had grown to £7,500,000.

93. Nicasio Oroño, *Intervención nacional en la Provincia de Santa-Fe. Correspondencia privada entre el general D. Bartolomé Mitre, Presidente de la República, y D. Nicasio Oroño* (Rosario: Imprenta de "El Ferro-carril," 1868), p. 19 (pp. 28; the notes handwritten in the margins of this pamphlet were supposedly written by M. Navarro, secretary to Oroño, who—according to him—was the actual author of the letters sent to Mitre under the name of Oroño). In the Bodleian Museum (shelf 2345, document no. 354), this pamphlet is accompanied by a book of 296 pages: [Nicasio Oroño and Miguel Navarro], *Intervención nacional en la Provincia de Santa Fe* (Buenos Aires: Comercio del Plata, 1868).

94. Carlos D'Amico, *Buenos Aires: sus hombres, su política* (Buenos Aires: Americana, 1952), pp. 107–8. Another witness of the time, F. Armesto, *Mitristas y Alsinistas*, originally 1874 (Buenos Aires: Sudestada, 1969), affirms the same sordid history of electoral abuses but partially absolves Mitre by explaining that Mitre's Buenos Aires political foes, the Alsinistas, were fully a party to the violent encounters and fraudulent tactics used for emerging victorious in the elections of the time.

95. Félix Weinberg, "El presidente electo Sarmiento en Buenos Aires: testimonios del periodismo porteño de 1868," in *Las ideas sociales de Sarmiento* (Buenos Aires: EUDBA, 1988), pp. 169–70.

96. D'Amico, *Buenos Aires*, p. 111.

97. Weinberg, "El presidente electo," p. 176n, quotes from *Intereses Argentinos*, but gives no date of publication.

98. Jorge M. Mayer, *Alberdi y su tiempo* (Buenos Aires: EUBA, 1964), p. 755, quotes from Sarmiento's letter to Sarratea, March 17, 1869.

99. Ibid., p. 814, quotes from the letter by Gutiérrez to Sarratea, November 30, 1874,

100. Ibid., p. 770, quotes from Groussac, *Sudaméricana*, January 5, 8, 12, 14, 16 and 19, 1886.

101. Herrera, *La diplomacia oriental*, pp. 109–10, 113.

102. Juan Bautista Alberdi, *Escritos póstumos*, vol. 10 (Buenos Aires: Juan Bautista Alberdi, 1900), pp. 44, 316; *Grandes y pequeños hombres*, pp. 161, 205; *Del gobierno en Sud-América* (Buenos Aires: Luz del Día, 1954), pp. 132–33.

103. Victorica, *Urquiza y Mitre*, p. 223. This work was initially published in 1906, months before the death of the author.

104. Félix Luna, *Buenos Aires y el país* (Buenos Aires: Sudamericana, 1985), p. 152.

105. Alberdi, *Grandes y pequeños hombres*, p. 205.

106. Victorica, *Urquiza y Mitre*, p. 239.

107. Efraín U. Bischoff, "La toma de Salta por Varela y la prensa de Córdoba," *Revista de la Junta Provincial de historia de Córdoba*, 10 (1982), p. 90, quotes Luis Vélez, *El eco de Córdoba*, October 14, 1867.

108. Guido y Spano, *El gobierno y la alianza*, p. 58.

109. Mayer, *Alberdi y su tiempo*, p. 717.

110. Ibid., pp. 726–27, 733.

111. Estanislao S. Zeballos, "Juicio preliminar," in Guido y Spano, *El gobierno y la alianza*, p. iv.

112. Bischoff, "La toma de Salta," pp. 92–95.

113. Enrique Popolizio, *Alberdi* (Buenos Aires: Losada, 1946), p. 171.

114. Martín García Mérou, *Alberdi: ensayo crítico* (Buenos Aires: Rosso, 1939), pp. 177–78.

115. Alberdi, *Grandes y pequeños hombres*, pp. 247, 254.

116. David Viñas, *Rebeliones populares argentinas*, vol. I, *De los montoneros a los anarquistas* (Buenos Aires: Carlos Pérez, 1971), p. 31.

117. Juan Bautista Alberdi, *Del gobierno en Sud-América* (Buenos Aires: Luz del Día, 1954), p. 55.

118. Zorraquín Becú, *Tiempo y vida*, p. 103, copies from Hernández's article in *El Río de la Plata*, August 21, 1869.

119. Other pamphlets by Alberdi treating the Paraguayan War are *Las disensiones de las Repúblicas del Plata y las maquinaciones del Brasil* (1865), *Los intereses argentinos en la guerra del Paraguay con el Brasil* (1865), *El Imperio del Brasil ante la democracia de América* (1866), *La crisis de 1866 y los efectos de la guerra de los aliados en el orden económico y político de las repúblicas del Plata* (1866), and *Las dos guerras del Plata y su filiación en 1867* (1867).

120. Miguel Angel Scenna, "Argentina-Brasil: cuatro siglos de rivalidad." 4th part: "El equilibrio," *Todo es historia* 79 (December 1973): 62–76, deals with this issue which no Sarmiento biographer, to my knowledge, treats in the rigor it deserves.

121. Alberdi began this pamphlet in 1870 with the intention of submitting it as an entry in a competition sponsored by the "Liga Internacional y Permanente de la Paz." However he never finished the work. It was first published postumously in the second volume of *Escritos póstumos* (Buenos Aires, 1895–1901), and then as a separate title in an edition by La Cultura Argentina in 1915.

122. Juan Bautista Alberdi, *El crimen de la guerra* (Buenos Aires: El Tonel, 1956), pp. 20–21.

123. Ibid., p. 16.

124. Hugo E. Biagini, "Alberdi y su ficción histórico-filosófica," in *Filosofía americana e identidad: el conflictivo caso argentino* (Buenos Aires: EUDEBA, 1989), pp. 83–90.

125. García Mérou, *Alberdi*, pp. 217–18, copied from an article written by Estrada and published in an unidentified number of *Revista del Río de la Plata*.

All the quotes in this paragraph are taken from García Merou's excellent chapter treating this work, pp. 205–22.

126. Biagini, "Alberdi y su ficción," p. 88, quotes from *Luz del Día*.

127. Popolizio, *Alberdi*, pp. 173, 193.

128. García Mérou, *Alberdi*; and Natalio R. Botana, *El orden conservador: la política argentina entre 1880 y 1916* (Buenos Aires: Hyspamérica, 1985). Bernardo Canal Feijóo, *Constitución y revolución: Juan Bautista Alberdi* (Buenos Aires: Fondo de Cultura Económica, 1955), p. 531, refers to the two parts to *Grandes y pequeños hombres*, which are *Belgrano y sus historiadores* (Alberdi's criticism of Mitre's *Historia de Belgrano*); and *Facundo y su biógrafo* (which criticized the fourth edition of Sarmiento's famous work in French translation).

129. Alberdi, *Grandes y pequeños hombres*, pp. 205, 186.

130. Ibid., p. 275.

131. Ibid., p. 290.

132. Quoted from Terán, "Alberdi póstumo," p. 73, who cites Alberdi's *Escritos póstumos*, vol. VIII, p. 582.

133. Juan Bautista Alberdi, *Obras selectas*, vol. XVII, *Estudios políticos*. Rev. for Joaquín V. González (Buenos Aires: La Facultad, 1920), pp. 334–35.

134. Ibid., pp. 347–48.

135. Botana, *El orden conservador*, pp. 87–93.

136. Mayer, *Alberdi y su tiempo*, p. 692, quotes from Mitre's articles of December 8 and 26, 1964.

137. This view has even been incorporated into contemporary social scientific orthodoxy, which views the consolidation of the state as the culminating experience of a people or a nation. In this light Oscar Oszlak, *La formación del estado argentino* (Buenos Aires: Belgrano, 1982), p. 33, justifies the Mitre administration's "bureaucratic repressive apparatus" that achieved through force the adhesion of the provinces to an enlightened plan of material advancement and the definitive consolidation of the Argentine state. Tulio Halperín Donghi, "Liberalismo argentino y liberalismo mexicano: dos destinos divergentes," in *El espejo de la historia: problemas argentinos y perspectivas latinoamericanas* (Buenos Aires: Sudamericana, 1987), pp. 161, 162–63, presents a similar argument when he compares Argentina to Mexico with respect to the institutionalization of democratic practices:

> That liberalism confidently open to the future, but at the same time loyal to a past that has moulded a society that is far from egalitarian, that liberalism that aspires to be everything for all people, can present itself at the same time to the masses as that instrument that will assist them in consolidating the political hegemony that is within their grasp. . . . The exceptional success of other aspects of the liberal program [is evidence] that the expectations of Mitre were largely realized, especially with regard to the giddy democratization of the lowest social levels, a process whose effects were beginning to be felt in the equilibrium of social forces.

138. Félix Luna, "Los bárbaros y nosotros," *Los caudillos* (Buenos Aires: Peña Lillo, 1984), p. 26.

139. Bernardo Canal Feijóo, "Introducción" to Juan Bautista Alberdi, *Sistema ecónomico y rentístico de la Confederación Argentina, según su Constitución de 1853* (Buenos Aires: Raigal, 1954), pp. vii–ix.

140. Alberdi, *Bases*, p. 199.

141. Cárcano, *Guerra del Paraguay*, pp. 479–80.

142. Examples of pro-Mitre historiography are Cárcano, *Guerra del Paraguay*

and Jorge Newton, *Mitre: una vida al servicio de la libertad* (Buenos Aires: Claridad, 1965), p. 72.

143. F. Armesto, *Mitristas y alsinistas*, (1st ed. 1874; Buenos Aires: Sudestada, 1969), p. 155.

144. Luis H. Sommariva, *Historia de las intervenciones federales en las provincias*, vol. I (Buenos Aires: El Ateneo, 1929), p. 167.

145. Armesto, *Mitristas y alsinistas*, pp. 15–16. Gálvez, *Historia de Sarmiento*, p. 523, quotes Sarmiento's writings of 1874, which detail Mitre's personal role in electoral abuses in Buenos Aires from the 1850s on.

146. Hilda Sábato, "La revolución del 90: ¿prólogo o epílogo?" *Punto de vista* 39 (December 1990), p. 29.

147. Sommariva, *Historia de las intervenciones*, pp. 174, 267, 276.

148. Ibid., p. 321: "The educated minorities were reclaiming for themselves the power formerly held by forceful means by the upstart caudillos. Their actions in this march to power always appealed to the authority of a republican and democratic Constitution."

149. Campobassi, *Mitre y su época*, p. 206.

150. Cárcano, *Guerra del Paraguay*, p. 80.

151. Sommariva, *Historia de las intervenciones*, p. 168.

152. Several of Hernández's articles published in *El Río de la Plata*, which urged reforms to benefit the *gaucho* and the country's rural population, have been reprinted in José Hernández, *Prosas de José Hernández, autor de "Martín Fierro,"* prologue Enrique Herrero (Buenos Aires: Futuro, 1944), and Antonio Pagés Larraya, *Prosas de "Martín Fierro" con una selección de los escritos de José Hernández* (Buenos Aires: Raigal, 1952). However, to my knowledge, the other articles in *El Río de la Plata*, in which Hernández praises Sarmiento and criticizes Mitre, were reprinted for the first time by Ayucucho Press (Venezuela) in 1988— that is, in Tulio Halperín Donghi, ed. *Proyecto y construcción de una nación (Argentina 1846–1880)* (Caracas: Biblioteca Ayacucho, 1980), pp. 257–94. Also, to my knowledge, the only biographer of José Hernández who gives an accurate (but very brief) consideration of these last articles is Pedro de Paoli, *Los motivos del "Martín Fierro" en la vida de José Hernández* (Buenos Aires: Huemul, 1968).

153. María Amalia Duarte, "Sarmiento frente a la revolución jordanista de 1870," Humanidades (Facultad de Humanidades, Universidad Nacional de la Plata) 37, vol. 2 (1961): 279–90.

154. Halperín Donghi, *Proyecto y construcción*, pp. 267, 269, which copies Hernández's article of October 16, 1869.

155. Miguel Angel Scenna, "1874: Mitre contra Avellaneda," *Todo es historia* 167 (April 1981): 10–11.

156. Gálvez, *Historia de Sarmiento*, p. 513.

157. Fernando E. Barba, *Los autonomistas del 70: auge y frustración de un movimiento provinciano con vocación nacional. Buenos Aires entre 1868 y 1878* (Centro Editor de América Latina, 1982), pp. 19–25, perhaps overstates the case of this new social division. Natalio J. Pisano, *La política agraria de Sarmiento: la lucha contra el latifundio* (Buenos Aires: Depalma, 1980), p. 255, mentions the names of several of these leaders in addition to that of José Hernández, who came together around 1870 to found the Club de los Libres in opposition to the agrarian politics of the Mitre-backed Liberal Party.

158. Roberto Etchepareborda, "La estructura socio-política argentina y la generación del ochenta," *Latin American Research Review* 13 (1978), p. 129, quotes the 1891 letter of Leopoldo del Campo to Tucumán governor, Justaniano Posse.

Carlos D'Amico, *Buenos Aires: sus hombres, su política (1860–1890)* (Buenos Aires: Americana, 1952), pp. 120, 105, affirmed generally the same idea.

159. Miguel Angel Scenna, "1874: Mitre contra Avellaneda," *Todo es historia*, no. 167 (April 1981), p. 14.

160. Pisano, *La política agraria*, pp. 239–47.

161. Bartolomé Mitre, *Arengas*, vols. 20–22 (Buenos Aires: Biblioteca de la Nación, 1902), pp. 261–62.

162. Halperín Donghi, *Proyecto y construcción*, pp. 388–99, copies from Bartolomé Mitre, "El arrendamiento y el enfiteusis," *Los debates*, September 16, 1875; "La tierra y el trabajo," *Los debates*, September 20, 1857; "Lotes de tierra," *Los debates*, October 29, 1857.

163. Pisano, *La política agraria*, pp. 240–44, 255–64, documents the differences separating Sarmiento from Mitre at this time and demonstrates how the latter's views, from 1868 on, were firmly in line with the interests of the large landowning estancieros in their opposition to any attempt to "replace cattle ranching with agricultural enterprises" (p. 245).

164. James R. Scobie, *Revolutión en las pampas: historia social del trigo argentino, 1860–1910* (Buenos Aires: Hachette, 1968), p. 149.

165. Barba, *Los autonomistas*, pp. 128–30.

166. Ricardo Saenz Hayes, *Miguel Cané y su tiempo (1815–1905)* (Buenos Aires: Kraft, 1955), p. 103, quotes the 1875 letter written to Sarmiento by the son of the 1837 militant.

167. D'Amico, *Buenos Aires*, p. 129, blames López's ineffective leadership for the failure of the antiwar movement at that time.

168. A good bibliography of Vicente Fidel López's publications is found in Ricardo Piccirilli, *Los López: una dinastía intelectual. Ensayo histórico literario, 1810–1852* (Buenos Aires: EUDBA, 1972), pp. 189–91. López's highly regarded *Historia de la República Argentina* and other works became the target of Mitre's criticisms in the famous 1881 polemic on historical writing. Mitre, not without reason, called attention to the defects resulting from López's "philosophy of history": the tendency to fall into an impassioned style and the frequent disregard for documentary evidence.

169. José Carlos Chiaramonte, *Nacionalismo y liberalismo económico en Argentina, 1860–1880* (Buenos Aires: Solar/Hachette, 1971), provides a detailed discussion of López's contributions in these debates.

170. *Estrategia*, serie documentos 2, *Protección a la industria nacional. Debate de 1876, Cámara de Diputados de la Nación* (Buenos Aires: Instituto Argentino de Estudios Estratégicos y de las Relaciones Internacionales, n.d.), pp. 116, 125.

171. Barba, *Los autonomistas*, p. 77.

172. Tulio Halperín Donghi, "Un nuevo clima de ideas," in Gustavo Ferrari and Ezequiel Gallo, eds. *La Argentina del Ochenta al Centenario* (Buenos Aires: Sudamérica, 1980), pp. 13–24.

173. Margarite B. Pontieri, "Concepción de la historia nacional: V. F. López y B. Mitre," in *Historia de la literatura argentina*, vol. 1, *Desde la colonia hasta el romanticismo* (Buenos Aires: CEAL, 1986), pp. 457–80.

174. Tulio Halperín Donghi, "Una nación para el desierto argentino," in Halperín, *Proyecto y construcción*, p. xxvi.

175. Ambrosio Romero Carranza, "Un precursor: Don Félix Frías," in Ambrosio Romero Carraliza, editor. *La política de ochenta* [cover title: *Controversias políticas del ochenta*] (Buenos Aires: Club de lectores, 1964), pp. 35–65.

176. González, *La guerra al Paraguay*, pp. 46–47, quotes from Frías's senate speech of June 19, 1866.

177. Mayer, *Alberdi y su tiempo*, p. 717, quotes from Frías's senate speech of June 12, 1866.

178. Ibid., quotes from Frías's letter of January 28, 1866 to Alberdi.

179. Romero, "Un precursor," p. 56, quotes Frías as having criticized Roca for having "backed with arms the constitutional right of intervening in the provinces and declaring state of seige; armed, what's more, with remingtons and canons, they made the federal system appear [nothing more] than a hateful comedy."

180. Alberto Blasi Brambilla, *José Mármol y la sombre de Rosas* (Buenos Aires: Pleamar, 1970), p. 84.

181. Bartolomé Mitre and Juan Carlos Gómez, *Cartas polémicas sobre la guerra al Paraguay*, prologue J. Natalicio González (Asunción-Buenos Aires: Guaranía, 1940), p. 294, quote Elizalde's published letter of December 20, 1869, in which he defended the Flores revolution as "the most noble and sacred of revolutions." Mármol, in his letter of December 21, 1869, defended the Berro government which had been "marching to the cadence of the constitution" and attacked the Flores revolution as "damned in the eyes of any honorable man . . . criminal . . . containing the most serious of errors." (pp. 331–36).

182. Mármol's letters in the polemic are the source of most of this information. See also Blasi, *José Mármol*, pp. 94–95; and Rosa, *La guerra del Paraguay*, pp. 185–86.

183. Mitre and Gómez, *Cartas polémicas*, p. 113, record Mármol's praiseworthy words about Mitre's "patriotism . . . his political honesty places him far above the common level"; Mitre was "sincere, loyal, conscientious." See also Rosa, *La guerra del Paraguay*, p. 186n.

184. González, *La guerra al Paraguay*, p. 54, quotes from Mármol's speech of July 24, 1868.

185. Herrera, *Buenos Aires, Urquiza y el Uruguay*, pp. 188, 195–96.

186. Barba, *Los autonomistas*, pp. 108, 123.

187. Tulio Halperín Donghi, "1880: un nuevo clima de ideas," in *El espejo de la historia: problemas argentinos y perspectivas latinoamericanos* (Buenos Aires: Sudamericana, 1987), p. 243.

188. See Juan María Gutiérrez, *Cartas de un porteño: polémica en torno al idioma y a la Real Academia Española, sostenida con Juan Martínez Villergas, seguida de "Sarmienticidio,"* prologue and notes D. Ernesto Morales (Buenos Aires: Americana, 1942). In his public letter refusing the invitation to join the Real Academia de la Lengua, Gutiérrez harkened back to some of the impassioned anti-Spanish rhetoric that had characterized the polemics on romanticism and language in Santiago and Montevideo at the beginnning of the 1840s. He argued that he could not comply with the Academia's objective of "fix" the purity and elegance of the Spanish language given that the political independence of the American republics from Spain signaled their receptivity not only to Spanish linguistic influences but also to those from other parts of Europe and North America as well.

189. Mayer, *Alberdi y su tiempo*, p. 768, quotes the letter from Gutiérrrez to Sarratea, January 9, 1870.

190. Ibid., p. 806, quotes the letter from Gutiérrez to Alberdi, February 9, 1874.

191. Ibid., p. 814, quotes the letter from Gutiérrez to Sarratea, November 30, 1874.

192. Ibid., p. 841, quotes the letter from Gutiérrez to Pío Tedín, August 9, 1877.

193. Ibid., p. 769, quotes the May 18, 1870 letter from Gutiérrez to Sarratea.

194. Sarmiento, *Obras completas*, vol. XXXVI, pp. 324, 258, 311, 332, 325.

195. Aníbal Ponce, "La vejez de Sarmiento," in *La vejez de Sarmiento. Amadeo Jacques, Nicolás Avellaneda, Lucio V. Mansilla, Eduardo Wilde, Lucio V. López, Miguel Cané* (Buenos Aires: J. Héctor Matera, 1951), p. 25.

196. Botana, *El orden conservador*, pp. 29–37.

197. According to Beatriz Sarlo Sabajanes, *Carlos Guido y Spano* (Buenos Aires: Centro Editor de América Latina, 1984), p. 23, these essays were later published in *Ráfagas. Colaboración en la prensa. Política y literatura*, 1 vols. (Buenos Aires: Igón Hermanos, 1979).

198. Carlos Guido y Spano, *Autobiografía*, preliminary study by Irma Cuña (Buenos Aires: Kapelusz, 1969), p. 113.

199. Beatriz Sarlo, "La segunda generación romántica. Gutiérrez, Andrade," in *Historia de la literatura argentina*, vol. 1, Desde la Colonia Hasta el Romanticismo (Buenos Aires: CEAL, 1986), pp. 433–56.

200. López's most important historical works are *Historia de la Revolución argentina* . . . (Buenos Aires, 1881), which also known under a subsequent title: *Introducción a la historia de la Revolución argentina* . . ., 10 vol. (Buenos Aires, 1883–93); and *Compendio de historia argentina*, 2 vol. (Buenos Aires, 1889–90)—a work adopted as the official text by the nation's secondary schools.

201. Pontieri, "Concepción de la historia nacional," p. 469, quotes from an unidentified source about López's spiritual and ideological link with that post-revolutionary group, "cuyos ideales han muerto con ellos."

202. López, *Historia*, vol. IV, pp. 361, 354, 276.

203. Ibid., p. 362.

204. Martín García Mérou, *Recuerdos literarios*, introd. Ricardo Monner Sans (Buenos Aires: La Cultura Argentina, 1915), p. 30.

205. Paul Groussac, *Los que pasaban: selección*, prologue Luis Alberto Romero (Buenos Aires: CEAL, 1980), p. 72.

206. Campobassi, *Mitre y su época*, p. 329, quotes Mitre's flowering rhetoric in portraying him as the country's maximum proponent of "the popular will" and "full direct participation" of the common people.

207. Milcíades Peña, *Alberdi, Sarmiento, el 90: límites del nacionalismo argentino en el siglo XIX* (Buenos Aires: Fichas, 1973), p. 34, quotes Mitre's letter to Bernardo de Irigoyen.

208. D'Amico, *Buenos Aires*, pp. 63, 103.

209. Tulio Halperín Donghi, "La imagen argentina de Bolívar, de Funes a Mitre," in *El espejo de la historia*, p. 133. *El espejo de la historia: problemas argentinos y perspectivas hispanoamericanas* (Buenos Aires: Audamericana, 1987). p. 133.

210. Natalio Botana, "Mitre en 1891: entre el acuerdo y la revolución," *La nación* (October 27, 1991), sect. 7a, p. 1.

211. Sarmiento, *Obras completas*, vol. XXXVII, p. 12, quotes from the January 1, 1883 letter to Mrs. Horace Mann, which constituted the prologue to the work included in this volume, *Conflicto y harmonías de las razas en las Américas*.

212. Ibid., pp. 15–25.

213. Ibid., (the quote is from *Condición del extranjero en América*).

214. Ibid., pp. 334–35, where Sarmiento, in an earlier moment, argued for

the nationalization of immigrants. Tulio Halperín Donghi, "¿Para qué la inmigración? Ideología y política inmigratoria en la Argentina (1810–1914)," in *El espejo de la historia*, pp. 189–238, discusses Sarmiento's change of views in the 1880s.

215. Sarmiento, *Obras completas*, vol. XXXVI, p. 287.

216. Peña, *Alberdi, Sarmiento, el 90*, p. 63, quotes A. Belín Sarmiento, *Sarmiento anecdótico*.

217. Ibid., p. 65.

218. Ezequiel Martínez Estrada, *Meditaciones sarmientinas* (Buenos Aires: Ediciones universitarias, 1968); *Radiografía de la pampa* (Buenos Aires: Losada, 1968), and Tulio Halperín Donghi, "Sarmiento: su lugar en la sociedad post-revolucionaria," *Sur* 341 (1977): 121–35.

219. Sarmiento, *Obras completas*, vol. XXXVII, p. 295.

Bibliography

Archives

Academia Nacional de Historia (Buenos Aires)
Alberdi Archives (Luján, Biblioteca Jorge Furt)
Archivos de la Nación (Buenos Aires)
Biblioteca Nacional (Montevideo)
Biblioteque d'Arsenal (Paris)
Bodleian (Oxford)
British Museum (London)
Museo Mitre (Buenos Aires)

Periodicals

Los debates (Buenos Aires, 1852)
El nacional (Buenos Aires, 1852–1858)
El orden (Buenos Aires,1856–1859)
El Paraná (Buenos Aires, 1852)
Revista del Río de la Plata (1871–1877)
Revue de Deux Mondes (Paris, 1838–1845)

Books, Articles, and Monographs

Alberdi, Juan Bautista. *Bases y puntos de partida para la organización política de la República argentina*. Prologue by Francisco Cruz. Buenos Aires: Talleres Gráficos Argentinos, 1933.

———. *Cartas inéditas a Juan María Gutiérrez y a Félix Frías*. Edited and introduction by Jorge M. Mayer and Ernesto A. Martínez. Buenos Aires: Luz del Día, 1953.

———. "Doble armonía entre el objeto de esta institución, con una exigencia de nuestro desarrollo social; y de esta exigencia con otra general del espíritu humano." In *El Salón Literario*, by Marcos Sastre, Juan Bautista Alberdi, Juan María Gutiérrez, and Esteban Echeverria. Prologue and edited by Félix Weinberg. Buenos Aires: Hachette, 1958.

———. *El crimen de la guerra*. Buenos Aires: El Tonel, 1956.

———. *Epistolario, 1855–1881*. Edited by Alfonso Bulnes. Santiago: Editorial Andrés Bello, 1967.

———. *Escritos póstumos.* 17 vols. Buenos Aires: Imprenta Juan Bautista Alberdi, 1900.

———. *Estudios económicos. Interpretación ecónomica de la historia política argentina y sud-americana, con un estudio sobre las doctrinas sociológicas de Alberdi, por José Ingenieros.* Buenos Aires: Talleres Gráficos Argentinos, L. J. Rosso, 1934.

———. *Grandes y pequeños hombres del Plata* Buenos Aires: Plus Ultra, 1974.

———. *Obras completas de J. B. Alberdi.* 8 vols. Buenos Aires: La Tribuna Nacional, 1886–87.

———. *Obras selectas.* 6 vols. Revised edition, Joaquín V. González, Buenos Aires: La Facultad, 1920.

———. *Obras selectas.* Vol. VIII. Buenos Aires: Luz del Día, 1954.

Andrews, George Reid. *The Afro-Argentines in Buenos Aires, 1800–1900.* Madison: University of Wisconsin, 1980.

Antecedentes de la Asociación de Mayo, 1837–1937. Buenos Aires: Consejo Deliberante, Comisión de Biblioteca, 1939.

Araoz Alfaro, Gregorio. *Rawson: ministro de Mitre.* Buenos Aires: Coni, 1938.

Ardao, Arturo. "Interpretaciones de Rosas." In *Estudios latinoamericanos: historia de las ideas.* Caracas: Monte Avila, 1978.

Armesto, F. *Mitristas y alsinistas.* 1874; Buenos Aires: Sudestada, 1969.

Barba, Enrique. "Estudio Preliminar." *Correspondencia entre Rosas, Quiroga y López,* Edited by Enrique Barba. Buenos Aires: Hachette, 1958.

Barba, Fernando E. *Los autonomistas del 70: auge y frustración de un movimiento provinciano con vocación nacional. Buenos Aires entre 1868 y 1878.* Buenos Aires: Centro Editor de América Latina, 1982.

Barros Borgoño, Luis. *A través de una correspondencia: Don Juan María Gutiérrez.* Santiago: Prensa de la Universidad de Chile, 1934.

Bazán, [Armando R.] et al. *Pavón y la crisis de la Confederación.* Buenos Aires: Equipos de Investigación Histórica, 1965.

Biagini, Hugo E. "Alberdi y su ficción histórico-filosófica." In *Filosofía americana e identidad: el conflictivo caso argentino.* Buenos Aires: EUDEBA, 1989.

Bischoff, Efraín U. "La toma de Salta por Varela y la prensa de Córdoba." *Revista de la Junta Provincial de historia de Córdoba* 10 (1982): 37–48.

Blasi Brambilla, Alberto. *José Mármol y la sombra de Rosas.* Buenos Aires: Pleamar, 1970.

Bollo Cabrios, Palmira S. "Diferencias financieras en la lucha de la Confederación y Buenos Aires, 1857–1862." In *Pavón y la crisis de la Confederación,* edited by Armand R. Bazán (Buenos Aires: Equipos de Investigacion Historica, 1965).

Bosch, Beatriz. "Juan María Gutiérrez al servicio de la Confederación Argentina." *Revista de la Universidad de Buenos Aires* 5th epoch, IV, no. 4 (1955): 543–70.

———. *Urquiza y su tiempo.* Buenos Aires: EUBA, 1980.

Botana, Natalio. *El orden conservador: la política argentina entre 1880 y 1916.* Buenos Aires: Hyspamérica, 1985.

———. *La tradición republicana: Alberdi, Sarmiento, y las ideas políticas de su tiempo.* Buenos Aires: Sudamericana, 1984.

———. "Mitre en 1891: entre el acuerdo y la revolución." *La nación* (October 27, 1991): p. 1.

Brezzo, Liliana M. "El Doctor Juan María Gutiérrez en Rosario: entre Cepeda y Pavón." *Res gesta* nos. 19–20 (1986): 9–19.

Brown, Jonathan C. "The Bondage of Old Habits in Nineteenth-Century Argentina." *Latin American Research Review* 21, no. 2 (1986): 3–31.

C. L. B., "Des Rapports de la France et de l'Europe avec l'Amérique du Sud." *Revue des Deux Mondes* series 4, 31, no. 15 (1838): 54–69.

Campobassi, José A. *Mitre y su tiempo.* Buenos Aires: EUBA, 1980.

Canal Feijoó, Bernardo. *Alberdi y la proyección sistemática del espíritu de Mayo.* Buenos Aires: Losada, 1961.

———. *Constitución y revolución: Juan Bautista Alberdi.* Buenos Aires: Fondo de Cultura Económica, 1955.

Castello, Antonio Emilio. "Lavalle frente a todos." *Todo es historia* 94 (1975): 8–43.

Cárcano, Miguel Angel. *Evolución histórica del régimen de la tierra pública (1810–1916).* Includes essay by María Susana Taborda Caro, "La legislación de tierras públicas nacionales y el régime legal vigente en las nuevas provincias (1950–1970)." Buenos Aires: EUDBA, 1972 [1917].

Cárcano, Ramón J. *Guerra del Paraguay: orígenes y causas.* Buenos Aires: Domingo Viau, 1939.

———. *Juan Facundo Quiroga: simulación, infidencia, tragedia.* Buenos Aires: López, 1933.

———. *Urquiza y Alberdi: intimidades de una política.* Buenos Aires: La Facultad, 1938.

Cháneton, Abel. *Retorno de Echeverría.* Buenos Aires: Ayacucho, 1944.

Chávez, Fermín. *El revisionismo y las montoneras. La "Unión Americana." Felipe Varela. Juan Saá y López Jordán.* Buenos Aires: Theoría, 1966.

———. *Vida y muerte de López Jordan.* Buenos Aires: Theoría, 1957.

D'Amico, Carlos. *Buenos Aires: sus hombres, su política (1860–1890).* 1890; Buenos Aires: Americana, 1952.

del Correo, Gaspar P. *Facundo y Fierro: la proscripción de los héroes.* Buenos Aires: Castañeda, 1977.

Díaz, César. *Memorias.* Prologue by Juan E. Pivel Devoto. Montevideo: Departamento de Investigaciones del Museo Histórico Nacional, 1968.

Duarte, María Amalia. "Sarmiento frente a la revolución jordanista de 1870." *Humanidades* (Universidad Nacional de la Plata) 37, no. 2 (1961): 279–90.

Echeverría, Esteban. *Dogma socialista.* Prologue and notes by Alberto Palcos. La Plata: Universidad Nacional de la Plata, 1940.

———. *Obras completas de Esteban Echeverría.* Edited and prologue by Juan María Gutiérrez. Buenos Aires: Zamora, 1972.

———. *Páginas autobiográficas.* Buenos Aires: EUBA, 1962.

Estrategia. Serie documentos 2: *Protección a la industria nacional. Debate de 1876, Cámara de Diputados de la Nación.* Buenos Aires: Instituto Argentino de Estudios Estratégicos y de las Relaciones Internacionales, n.d.

Etchepareborda, Roberto. "La estructura socio-política argentina y la generación del ochenta." *Latin American Research Review* 13 (1978): 127–34.

———. *Rosas: controvertida historiografía.* Buenos Aires: Pleamar, 1972.

Ferrer, Aldo. *The Argentine Economy.* Translated by Marjory M. Urquidi. Berkeley and Los Angeles: University of California Press, 1967.

Franco, Luis. *De Rosas a Mitre: medio siglo de historia argentina 1830/1880.* Buenos Aires: Astral, 1977.

———. *Sarmiento entre dos fuegos.* Buenos Aires: Paídos, 1968.

Frías, Félix. *Escritos y discursos.* 2 vols. Buenos Aires: Librería de Mayo, 1884.

———. *La gloria del tirano Rosas y otros escritos políticos y polémicos.* Prologue by Domingo F. Sarmiento. Buenos Aires: El Ateneo, 1928.

Furlong S.J., Guillermo. "Bartolomé Mitre: El hombre, el soldado, el historiador, el político." In *Investigaciones y ensayos.* 2 vols. Buenos Aires: Academia Nacional de Historia, 1971.

Gaignard, Romain. *La pampa argentina: ocupación, población, explotación. De la conquista a la crisis mundial (1550–1930).* Translated by Ricardo Figueira. Buenos Aires: Solar, 1989.

———. *Recuerdos literarios.* Introduction by Ricardo Monner Sans. Buenos Aires: La Cultura Argentina, 1915.

Gálvez, Manuel. *Vida de Sarmiento.* 3d ed. Buenos Aires: Editorial Tor, 1957.

Gandia, Enrique de. *José Hernández: sus ideas políticas.* Buenos Aires: Depalma, 1985.

García Belsunce, César A. "Mitre y la política de Buenos Aires, 1859–1862." In *Pavón y la crisis de la Confederación.* Armando R. Bazán. Buenos Aires: Equipos de Investigación Histórica, 1965.

García Merou, Martín. *Alberdi: ensayo crítico.* Buenos Aires: Rosso, 1939.

———. *Ensayo sobre Echeverría.* 1895, Buenos Aires: W. M. Jackson, 1944.

Garrels, Elizabeth. "El 'espíritu de la familia' en *La novia del hereje* de Vicente Fidel López." *Hispamérica* 16, nos. 46/47 (1987): 3–24.

Gianello, Leoncio. *Florencio Varela.* Buenos Aires: Guillermo Kraft, 1948.

Giannangeli, Liliana. *Construcción a la bibliografía de José Mármol.* Prologue by Juan Carlos Ghiano. La Plata: Universidad Nacional de la Plata, 1972.

González, J. Natalicio. *La guerra al Paraguay: imperialismo y nacionalismo en El Plata.* Buenos Aires: Sudestada, 1968.

———. *Estudios de historia argentina.* Buenos Aires: Jesús Menéndez, 1918.

Groussac, Paul. *Crítica literaria.* Buenos Aires: Jesús Menéndez e hijo, 1924).

———. *Los que pasaban: selección.* Prologue by Luis Alberto Romero. Buenos Aires: CEAL, 1980.

Guido y Spano, Carlos. *Autobiografía.* Prologue by Irma Cuña. Buenos Aires: Kapelusz, 1969.

Guido Spano [*sic*], Carlos. *El gobierno y la alianza: consideraciones políticas..* Prologue by Estanislao Zeballos. 1866; Buenos Aires: Biblioteca de la Revista de los FFAA de la Nación, n. d.

Guizot, Françoise Pierre Guillaume. *The History of Civilization in Europe.* Translated by William Hazlett. New York: A. L. Burt, n. d.

Gutierrez, Juan María. *Archivo del Doctor Juan María Gutiérrrez: Epistolario.* 4 vols. Edited by Raúl J. Moglía and Miguel O. García. Buenos Aires: Biblioteca del Congreso de la Nación, 1979.

———. *Cartas de un porteño: polémica en torno al idioma y a la Real Academia Española, sostenida con Juan Martínez Villergas, seguida de "Sarmienticidio."* Prologue and notes by D. Ernesto Morales. Buenos Aires: Americana, 1942.

------. *Colección Doctor Juan María Gutiérrrez: Archivo-Espistolario*. Vol. 1. Buenos Aires: Biblioteca del Congreso de la Nación, 1979.

------. *Epistolario de Don Juan María Gutiérrrez*. Edited and prologue by Ernesto Morales. Buenos Aires: Instituto Cultural Joaquín V. González, 1942.

------. *La literatura de Mayo y otras páginas críticas*. Edited and prologue by Beatriz Sarlo [Sabajanes]; notes by Hebe Monges. Buenos Aires: Centro Editor de América Latina, 1979.

------. "La vida y la obra de Esteban Echeverría." In Esteban Echeverría, *Obras completas de Esteban Echeverría*, edited and with a prologue by Juan María Gutiérrez (Buenos Aires: Zamora, 1972), 9–52.

Gutiérrez, Juan María, ed. *Pensamientos, máximas, sentencias de escritores, oradores y hombres de estado de la República Argentina*. Buenos Aires: Coni, 1945.

Halperin Donghi, Tulio. *El espejo de la historia: problemas argentinos y perspectivas hispanoamericanas*. Buenos Aires: Sudamericana, 1987.

------. "La expansión ganadera en la campaña de Buenos Aires (1818–1852)." In *Los fragmentos del poder: de la oligarquía a la poliarquía argentina*. Edited by Torcuato S. di Tella and Tulio Halperín Donghi. Buenos Aires: Jorge Alvarez, 1969.

------. "Una nación para el desierto argentino." In Tulio Halperín Donghi, editor, *Projectdo y construcción de una nación (Argentina 1846–1880)*. (Caracas: Biblioteca Ayacucho, 1980).

------. "Un nuevo clima de ideas." *La Argentina del Ochenta al Centenario*, edited by Gustavo Ferrari and Ezequiel Gallo. Buenos Aires: Sudamericana, 1980.

------. *El pensamiento de Echeverría*. Buenos Aires: Sudamericana, 1951.

------. *Politics and Society in Argentina in the Revolutionary Period*. Translated by Richard Southern. Cambridge: Cambridge University Press, 1975.

------. "Sarmiento: su lugar en la sociedad post-revolucionaria." *Sur* 341 (1977): 121–35.

Halperín Donghi, Tulio, ed. *Proyecto y construcción de una nación (Argentina 1846–1880)*. Caracas: Biblioteca Ayacucho, 1980.

Head, Francis B. *Rough Notes Taken during Some Rapid Journies across the Pampas and among the Andes*. Boston: Wells and Lilly, 1827.

Heras, Carlos. "El vicepresidente de Mitre, Coronel Doctor Marcos Paz." *Boletín de la Academia Nacional de Historia* 35, no. 29 (1958): 206–45.

Hernández, José. "La división de la tierra." In *Prosas del Martín Fierro, con una selección de los escritos de José Hernández*, edited by Antonio Pagés Larraya. Buenos Aires: Raigal, 1952.

------. *Prosas de José Hernández, autor de "Martín Fierro."* Prologue by Enrique Herrero. Buenos Aires: Futuro, 1944.

------. *Vida de "El Chacho,"* In Antonio Pagés Larraya, editor, *Prosas del Martín Fierro, con una selección de de la escrites de José Hernández*. Buenos Aires: Raigal, 1952.

Herrera, Luis Alberto de. *La diplomacia oriental en el Paraguay. Correspondencia oficial y privada del Doctor Juan José de Herrera, Ministro de Relaciones Exteriores de los gobiernos de Berro y Aguirre*. Montevideo: Barreiro y Ramos, 1919.

Historia de la literatura argentina. Vol. 1, *Desde la colonia hasta el romanticismo*. Buenos Aires: CEAL, 1986.

Hulet, Claude L. "La segunda generación romántica argentina: ensayo de apreciación histórico-política." *Cuadernos americanos* 108, no. 1 (1960): 232–48.

Ingenieros, José. *La evolución de la ideas argentinas.* Vol. II, *La restauración.* Buenos Aires: L. J. Rosso y Cía., 1920.

————. "La filosofía social de Echeverría y la leyenda de la 'Asociación de Mayo.'" *Revista de filosofía, cultura, ciencias* 4 (1914): 47–68.

Irazusta, Julio. "Alberdi en 1838: un trascendental cambio de opción práctica." In *Ensayos históricos.* Buenos Aires: La voz del Plata, 1952.

Jeffrey, William H[artley]. *Mitre and Argentina.* New York: Library Publishers, 1952.

Jitrik, Noé. "El *Facundo:* la gran riqueza de la pobreza." In *Facundo, o civilización y barbarie,* edited by Domingo F. Sarmiento, Caracas: Ayacucho, 1977.

Katra, William H. "Echeverría según Sarmiento: la personificación de una nación ultrajada por la barbarie." *Cuadernos Americanos* 255 (1984): 165–85.

————. "Reading *Facundo* as Historical Novel," In *The Historical Novel in Latin America: A Symposium,* edited by Daniel Balderston. Gainesville, Md.: Hispamérica, 1986.

————. "Sarmiento frente a la Generación de 1837." *Revista Iberoamericana* 143 (1988): 525–49.

————. *Sarmiento de frente y perfil.* Geneva and New York: Peter Lang Publishers, 1993.

————. "Sarmiento en los Estados Unidos." *Todo es historia* 255 (1988): 6–45.

————. "Sarmiento y el americanismo." In *Identidad cultural de Iberoamérica en su literatura,* edited by Saúl Yurkievich. Madrid: Alhambra, 1986.

————. *Sarmiento: Public Writer (Between 1839 and 1852).* Tempe: Center for Latin American Studies, Arizona State University, 1985.

Lamas, Alberto. *Escritos políticos y literarios durante la guerra contra la tiranía de D. Juan Manuel Rosas.* Introduction by Angel J. Carranza. Buenos Aires: Cangallo, 1877.

Lanuza, José Luis. *Echeverría y sus amigos.* Buenos Aires: Paídos, 1967.

López, Vicente Fidel. *Autobiografía.* Buenos Aires: La Biblioteca 1896.

————. *Evocaciones históricas: Autobiografía, La gran semana de 1810, El conflicto y la entrevista de Guayaquil.* Buenos Aires: El Ateneo, 1929.

————. *Historia de la República argentina. Su origen, su revolución y su desarrollo político hasta el gobierno del general Viamonte. Continuada hasta 1910 por Emilio Vera y González y ampliada desde el descubrimiento hasta nuestros días por Enrique de Gandia. Nueva edición profusamente ilustrada.* 10 vols. Buenos Aires: Sopena Argentina, 1964.

————. *Panoramas y retratos históricos.* Prologue by Joaquín V. González. Buenos Aires: W. M. Jackson, n.d.

[López, V. F.]. *Vindicación de la República Arjentina en su Revolución y sus guerras civiles, por A. y X., emigrados arjentinos.* Santiago, 1841.

Luna, Félix. *Buenos Aires y el país.* Buenos Aires: Sudamericana, 1985.

————. "Los bárbaros y nosotros." In *Los caudillos,* pp. 13–35.

————. *Los caudillos.* Buenos Aires: Peña Lillo, 1984.

Lynch, John. "River Plate Republics." In *Spanish America After Independence, c.1820–c.1870*, edited by Leslie Bethell. Cambridge: Cambridge University Press, 1985.

Macchi, Manuel E. *Urquiza: última etapa*. 3d ed. Santa Fe: Castellvi [*sic*], 1971.

Machado, Carlos. *Historia de los orientales*. Vol. II. Montevideo: Banda Oriental, 1987.

Martínez, Carlos Dámaso. "Nacimiento de la novela. José Mármol." In *Historia de la literatura argentina*. Buenos Aires: Centro Editor de América Latina, 1986.

Martínez Estrada, Ezequiel. *Meditaciones sarmientinas*. Buenos Aires: Ediciones universitarias, 1968.

———. *Radiografía de la pampa*. Buenos Aires: Losada, 1968.

Masramón, Alberto J. *Urquiza: libertador y fundador*. Buenos Aires: Plus Ultra, 1982.

Mayer, Jorge. *Alberdi y su tiempo*. Buenos Aires: Editorial Universitaria de Buenos Aires, 1963.

Mármol, José. *Amalia: novela histórica americana*. Buenos Aires: Sopena, 1944.

———. *Asesinato del Sr. Dr. D. Florencio Varela. Manuela Rosas*. Prologue by Juan Carlos Ghiano. Buenos Aires: Casa Pardo, 1972.

———. *Carta del Ciudadano Arjentino José Mármol a los S. S. D. Salvador María del Carril, D. Mariano Fragueiro y D. Facundo Zubiría, Delegados al Sr. Director Provisiario, en la República Arjentina*. Montevideo: Imprenta del Nacional, 1853.

Méndez Avellaneda, Juan M. "¿Quién mató a Alejandro Heredia." *Todo es Historia* 126 (November 1977): 78–94

Mercado Luna, Ricardo. *Los coroneles de Mitre*. Buenos Aires: Plus Ultra, 1974.

Mitre, Bartolomé and Juan Carlos Gómez. *Cartas polémicas sobre la guerra al Paraguay*. Prologue by J. Natalicio González. Asunción-Buenos Aires: Guaranía, 1940.

Mitre, Bartolomé. *Antecedentes de Pavón*. Vol. VII of *Archivo del General Mitre*. Buenos Aires: Biblioteca de La nación, 1911.

———. *Arengas de Bartolomé Mitre: Colección de discursos paralmentarios, políticos, económicos y literarios . . . desde 1848 hasta 1888*. Buenos Aires: Librería de Mayo, 1889.

———. *Biografía de José Rivera Indarte*. Valparaíso: Mercurio, 1845.

———. *Correspondencia literaria, histórica y política*. Vol. I. Buenos Aires: Coni Hermanos, 1912.

———. *Correspondencia Mitre-Urquiza, 1860–1868*. Buenos Aires: Museo Mitre & Fundación "Banco de la Provincia de Buenos Aires," 1980.

———. *Estudios sobre la vida y escritos de D. José Rivera Indarte*. Buenos Aires: Imprenta de Mayo, 1853.

———. "Literatura americana: *Rimas* de E. Echeverría." In *Apuntes de la juventud de Mitre y Bibliografía de Mitre*, edited by Adolfo Mitre, Manuel Conde Montero, and Juan A. Farini. Buenos Aires: Academia Nacional de la Historia, 1947.

———. *"Profesión de fe" y otros escritos publicados en "Los debates" de 1852*. Introduction by Ricardo Levine. Buenos Aires: Universidad de Buenos Aires, 1956.

Navarro Viola, Miguel. *El despotismo del estado de sitio de la República Argentina en 1866 y 1867*. Buenos Aires: Imprenta de Mayo, 1867.

Newton, Jorge. *Mitre: una vida al servicio de la libertad*. Buenos Aires: Claridad, 1965.

Núñez, M. *Bustos: el caudillo olvidado.* Buenos Aires: Cuadernos de Crisis, 1975.

Oliver, Juan Pablo. *El verdadero Alberdi: génesis del liberalismo económico argentino.* Buenos Aires: Biblioteca Dictio, 1977.

Orgaz, Raúl A. "Echeverría y su doctrina." *Obras Completas.* Vol. II. Córdoba: Assandri, 1950.

Oroño, Nicasio. *Intervención nacional en la Provincia de Santa-Fe. Correspondencia privada entre el general D. Bartolomé Mitre, Presidente de la República, y D. Nicasio Oroño.* Rosario: Imprenta de "El Ferro-carril," 1868.

Oroño, Nicasio, and Miguel Navarro [Viola]. *Intervención nacional en la Provincia de Santa Fe.* Buenos Aires: Comercio del Plata, 1868.

Ortiz, Ricardo M. *Historia económica de la Argentina, 1850–1930.* Vol. 1. Buenos Aires: Raigal, 1955.

Oszlak, Oscar. *La formación del estado argentino.* Buenos Aires: Belgrano, 1982.

Pagés Larraya, Antonio. "La 'recepción' de un texto sarmientino: *Facundo.*" *Boletín de la Academia Argentina de Letras* 49, nos. 193/194 (1984): 233–85.

Palacios, Alfredo L. "Civilización y barbarie: dualismo simplista inaceptable." *Cuadernos Americanos* 105, no. 4 (1959): 162–202.

Palcos, Alberto. *Echeverría y la democracia argentina.* Buenos Aires: Imprenta López, 1941.

———. *Historia de Echeverría.* Buenos Aires: Emecé, 1960.

———. Prologue to Esteban Echeverría, *Dogma socialista,* critical edition, La Plata: Universidad Nacional de la Plata, 1940.

———. *Sarmiento: la vida, la obra, las ideas, el genio.* Buenos Aires: El Ateneo, 1938.

Paoli, Pedro de. *Los motivos del "Martín Fierro" en la vida de José Hernández.* Buenos Aires: Huemul, 1968.

———. *Sarmiento: su gravitación en el desarrollo nacional.* Buenos Aires: Theoría, 1964.

———. *Los caudillos y la organización nacional.* Buenos Aires: Sílaba, 1970.

Paso, Leonardo. *Historia del origen de los partidos políticos en la Argentina (1810–1918).* Buenos Aires: Centro de Estudios, 1972.

———. *Raíces históricas de la dependencia argentina.* Buenos Aires: Cartago, 1975.

Pavoni, Norma L. *El noroeste argentino en la época de Alejandro Heredia.* Vol. 1: *Política.* Tucumán: Fundación Banco Comercial del Norte, 1981.

Peña, David. *Juan Facundo Quiroga.* Buenos Aires: Hyspamérica, 1986.

Peña, Milcíades. *Alberdi, Sarmiento, el 90: límites del nacionalismo argentino en el siglo XIX.* Buenos Aires: Fichas, 1973.

Peña, Roberto I. "Córdoba en el plan político de Pavón (1852–1863)." In *Pavón y la crisis de la Confederación,* edited by Armando R. Bazán, Buenos Aires: Equipos de Investigación Histórica, 1965.

Peña de Matsushita, Marta E. *El romanticismo político hispanoamericano.* Buenos Aires: Docencia, 1985.

Pereyra, Carlos. *Francisco Solano López y la Guerra del Paraguay.* Buenos Aires: San Marcos, 1958.

Pérez Giulhou, Dardo. *El pensamiento conservador de Alberdi y la Constitución de 1853.* Buenos Aires: Depalma, 1984.

———. "Repercusiones de Pavón en Mendoza (1859–1870)." In *Pavón y la crisis de la Confederación,* edited by Armando R. Bazán, (Buenos Aires: Equipos de Investigación Histórica, 1965).

Piccirilli, Ricardo. *Los López: una dinastía intelectual. Ensayo histórico literario, 1810– 1852.* Buenos Aires: EUDBA, 1972.

Pisano, Natalio J. *La política agraria de Sarmiento: la lucha contra el latifundio.* Buenos Aires: Depalma, 1980.

Ponce, Aníbal. "La vejez de Sarmiento." In *La vejez de Sarmiento. Amadeo Jacques, Nicolás Avellaneda, Lucio V. Mansilla, Eduardo Wilde, Lucio V. López, Miguel Cané.* Buenos Aires: J. Héctor Matera, 1951.

Pontieri, Margarite B. "Concepción de la historia nacional: V. F. López y B. Mitre." In *Historia de la literatura argentina.* vol. 1, Desde la Colonia hasta el Romanticismo (Buenos Aires: CEAL, 1986).

Popolizio, Enrique. *Alberdi.* Buenos Aires: Losada, 1946.

Ramos, Jorge Abelardo. *Del patriciado a la oligarquía, 1862–1904.* Vol. II of *Revolución y contrarrevolución en la Argentina.* Buenos Aires: Plus Ultra, 1976.

Rebollo Paz, León. *De octubre 1850 a octubre 1852.* Vol. I of *Historia de la organización nacional: treinta años en la vida de la República, 1850–1880.* Buenos Aires: Librería del Plata, 1951.

Rivera Indarte, José. *Apuntes sobre el asesinato del general Quiroga: su secretario Ortiz y demás comitiva en el parage de Barranca-Yaco, territorio de Córdoba.* Buenos Aires: Comercio, 1835.

———. *La intervención en la guerra actual del Río de la Plata.* Río de Janeiro: Mercantil de Lopes, 1845.

———. *Rosas y sus opositores.* Montevideo: El Nacional, 1843.

Rojas Paz, Pablo. *Alberdi: el cuidadano de la soledad.* Buenos Aires: Losada, 1952.

———. *Echeverría: el pastor de soledades.* Buenos Aires: Losada, 1951.

Rojas, Ricardo. *El profeta de la pampa: vida de Sarmiento.* Buenos Aires: Losada, 1945.

———. "Introducción." In Juan Bautista Alberdi, *Bases y puntos de partida . . . ,* edited by J. Francisco V. Silva. 2d ed. Cordoba: Imprenta de la Universidad, 1928.

Romero Carranza, Ambrosio. *Desde 1816 hasta 1862.* Vol. II of *Historia política de la Argentina.* Buenos Aires: Pannedille, 1971.

Romero Carranza, Ambrosio. "Un precursor: Don Félix Frías." In Ambrosio Romero Carranza, Alberto Rodríguez Varela, and Eduardo Ventura Flores Pirán. *Historia política de la Argentina.* Buenos Aires: Pamedille, 1971. *La política de ochenta,* edited by Ambrosio Romero Carranza. Buenos Aires: Club de Lectores, 1964.

Romero, José Luis. *A History of Argentine Political Thought.* Translated by Thomas F. McGann. Stanford: Stanford University Press, 1963.

———. *Latinoamérica: las ciudades y las ideas.* Buenos Aires: Siglo XXI, 1976.

Rosa, José María. *La guerra del Paraguay y las montoneras argentinas.* Buenos Aires: Peña Lillo, 1985.

Ruiz Moreno, Isidoro J. "El litoral después de Pavón (septiembre-diciembre 1861). In *Pavón y la crisis de la Confederación.* Edited by Armando R. Bazán, Buenos Aires: Equipos de Investigación Histórica, 1965.

Saenz Hayes, Ricardo. *Miguel Cané y su tiempo (1815–1905).* Buenos Aires: Kraft, 1955.

Sagarna, Antonio. "Juan María Gutiérrez y la Organización Nacional." *Boletín de la Academia Nacional de Historia* 11 (1937–38): 169–207.

Saldías, Adolfo. *Historia de la Confederación Argentina*. Buenos Aires: EUBA, 1968.

Salomon, Noël. "El *Facundo* de Domingo Faustino Sarmiento: manifiesto de la preburguesía argentina de las ciudades del interior." *Cuadernos Americanos* 39, no. 5 (1980): 121–76.

Sarlo Sabajanes, Beatriz. *Guido y Spano*. Buenos Aires: Centro Editor de América Latina, 1968.

——. "La segunda generación romántica. Gutiérrez, Andrade." In *Historia de la literatura argentina*. Vol. 1, *Desde La Colonia Hasta el Romanticismo* (Buenos Aires: CEAL, 1968).

Sarmiento, Domingo F[austino]. *Campaña en el Ejército Grande Aliado de Sud América*. Mexico: Fondo de Cultura Económica, 1958.

——. *El último caudillo de la montonera de los llanos: El Chacho*. In *Los caudillos*. Buenos Aires: El Ateneo, 1928.

——. *Obras completas*. Buenos Aires: Mariano Moreno, 1895–1900.

——. *Obras completas*. Buenos Aires: Luz del Día, 1948–1956.

——. *Sarmiento: cartas y discursos políticos*. Vol. III. Buenos Aires: Ediciones Culturales Argentinas, 1965.

——. *Viajes en Europa, Africa i América*. Vol. II. Santiago: Julio Belin y Co., 1849.

Sastre, Marcos, Juan Bautista Alberdi, Juan María Gutiérrez, and Esteban Echeverría. *El Salón Literario*. Prologue and edited by Félix Weinberg. Buenos Aires: Hachette, 1958.

Sastre, Marcos. *El tempe argentino: impresiones y cuadros del Paraná*. Buenos Aires: Mayo, 1858.

Sábato, Hilda. "La revolución del 90: ¿prólogo o epílogo?" *Punto de vista* 39 (December 1990): 27–31.

Sánchez Zinny, E. F. "El General Juan Lavalle bajo la cruz de la adversidad." In *Los ciento diez jinetes de la gloria*. Buenos Aires: Linari y Cía., 1944.

——. "1874: Mitre contra Avellaneda." *Todo es historia* 167 (April 1981): 8–41.

Scenna, Miguel Angel. "Argentina-Brasil: cuatro siglos de rivalidad." Cuarta parte: "El equilibrio." *Todo es historia* 79 (December 1973): 62–76.

Scobie, James R. *Argentina: A City and a Nation*, 2d ed. New York and London: Oxford University Press, 1971.

——. *La lucha por la consolidación de la nacionalidad argentina, 1852–1862*. Translated by Gabriela de Civiny. Buenos Aires: Hachette, 1964.

——. *Revolutión en las pampas: historia social del trigo argentino, 1860–1910*. Buenos Aires: Hachette, 1968.

Segovia Guerrero, Eduardo. "La historiografía argentina del romanticismo." Ph.D. Diss., Universidad Complutense de Madrid, 1980.

Shumway, Nicolas. *The Invention of Argentina*. Berkeley, Los Angeles, Oxford: University of California Press, 1991.

Sommariva, Luis H. *Historia de las intervenciones federales en las provincias*. Vol. I. Buenos Aires: El Ateneo, 1929.

Söhle, Jorge. *Chavela (novela histórica argentina)*. Rosario: La Velocidad, 1903.

Terán, Oscar. "Alberdi póstumo." In Juan Bautista Alberdi. *Alberdi póstumo*. Buenos Aires: Puntosur, 1988.

————. Prólogo. to *Reflejos autobiográficos, 1813–1841*, by Marco M. de Avellaneda. Buenos Aires: Coni, 1922.

Tonda, Américo A. *Don Félix Frías: el secretario del General Lavalle. Su época boliviana (1841–1843)*. Córdoba: Ediciones Argentina Cristiana, 1956.

Un Voyageur. "Les Deux Rives de la Plata: Montevideo, Buenos-Ayres, Rivera, Rosas." *Revue des Deux Mondes* 50, no. 2 (1843): 5–49.

Varela, Florencio. *Escritos políticos, económicos y literarios*. Edited by Luis L. Domínguez. Buenos Aires: El Orden, 1859.

[Varela, Florencio]. *Observations on Occurrences in the River Plate as connected with ther Foreign Agents and the Anglo-French Intervention*. Montevideo: n.p., 1843.

Varela, Héctor F. *La situación de la República Argentina: su gobierno, su comercio y su política. Carta dirigida al Sr. D. Eduardo Asquerino*. Paris: Walder, 1863.

Varese, Carmen P. de, and Héctor D. Arias. *Historia de San Juan*. Mendoza: Spadoni, 1966.

Ves Losada, Alfredo E. "Campo y ciudad en *Facundo*." *Cuadernos americanos* 15, no. 6 (1956): 185–200.

Vicente Osvaldo Cutilo. *Nuevo diccionario biográfico argentino, 1730-1930*. Buenos Aires: Elche, 1975.

Victorica, Julio. *Urquiza y Mitre: contribución al estudio histórico de la organización nacional*. 1906, Buenos Aires: Hyspamérica, 1986.

Viñas, David. *Literatura argentina y realidad política*. Vol. 1: *De Sarmiento a Cortázar*. Buenos Aires: Siglo Veinte, 1971.

————. *De los montoneros a los anarquistas*. Vol. I of [*Rebeliones populares argentinas*]. Buenos Aires: Carlos Pérez, 1971.

————. *Florencio Varela y el "Comercio del Plata."* Bahía Blanca: Universidad Nacional del Sur, Instituto de Humanidades, 1970.

————. *Las ideas sociales de Sarmiento*. Buenos Aires: EUDBA, 1988.

Zalazar, Roberto. *Pedro Ferré y el federalismo*. Corrientes: Facultad de Derecho, 1963.

————. "Juicio preliminar." In Carlos Guido Spano, [*sic*] *El gobierno y la alianza consideraciones políticas*. Buenos Aires; Biblioteca de la Revista de los FFAA de la Nación, n.d.

Zeballos, Estanislao S. *El tratado de alianza*. Buenos Aires: Cook, 1872.

Zinny, Antonio. *Córdoba, Tucumán, Santiago de Estero, San Luis*. Vol. III of *Historia de los gobernadores de las provincias argentinas*. Buenos Aires: Vaccaro, 1920.

————. *Provincia de Buenos Aires, 1810–1853*. Vol. II of *Historia de los gobernadores de las provincias argentinas*. Notes by Eduardo F. Sánchez Zinny. Buenos Aires: Huemul, 1942.

Zorraquín Becú, Horacio. *Tiempo y vida de José Hernández, 1834–1886*. Buenos Aires: Emecé, 1972.

Index